United States Relations with China and Iran

New Approaches to International History

Series editor: Thomas Zeiler, Professor of American Diplomatic History, University of Colorado Boulder, USA

New Approaches to International History covers international history during the modern period and across the globe. The series incorporates new developments in the field, such as the cultural turn and transnationalism, as well as the classical high politics of state-centric policymaking and diplomatic relations. Written with upper level undergraduate and postgraduate students in mind, texts in the series provide an accessible overview of international, global and transnational issues, events and actors.

Published

Decolonization and the Cold War, Leslie James and Elisabeth Leake (2015)
Cold War Summits, Chris Tudda (2015)
The United Nations in International History, Amy Sayward (2017)
Latin American Nationalism, James F. Siekmeier (2017)
The History of United States Cultural Diplomacy, Michael L. Krenn (2017)
International Cooperation in the Early Twentieth Century, Daniel Gorman (2017)
Women and Gender in International History, Karen Garner (2018)
The Environment and International History, Scott Kaufman (2018)
International Development, Corrina Unger (2018)

Forthcoming

Canada and the World since 1867, Asa McKercher
An International History of Modern Colonial Labour: Debates and Case Studies,
Miguel Bandeira Jerónimo and José Pedro Monteiro
The International LGBT Rights Movement, Laura Belmonte
Reconstructing the Postwar World, Francine McKenzie
Scandinavia and the Great Powers, Michael Jonas

United States Relations with China and Iran

Toward the Asian Century

Edited by
Osamah F. Khalil

BLOOMSBURY ACADEMIC

LONDON • NEW YORK • OXFORD • NEW DELHI • SYDNEY

BLOOMSBURY ACADEMIC
Bloomsbury Publishing Plc
50 Bedford Square, London, WC1B 3DP, UK
1385 Broadway, New York, NY 10018, USA

BLOOMSBURY, BLOOMSBURY ACADEMIC and the Diana logo are trademarks of
Bloomsbury Publishing Plc

First published in Great Britain 2019
This paperback edition published in 2021

Series design by Catherine Wood

Cover image: Five US Presidents pose for picture in front of the Reagan Library,
04 November 1991 in Simi Valley. (© HAL GARB/AFP/Getty Images)

A catalogue record for this book is available from the British Library.

A catalog record for this book is available from the Library of Congress.

ISBN: HB: 978-1-3500-8773-6
PB: 978-1-3501-9608-7
ePDF: 978-1-3500-8774-3
eBook: 978-1-3500-8775-0

Series: New Approaches to International History

Typeset by Newgen KnowledgeWorks Pvt. Ltd., Chennai, India

To find out more about our authors and books visit www.bloomsbury.com
and sign up for our newsletters.

Contents

Acknowledgments

In September 2017, Syracuse University's Maxwell School of Citizenship and Public Affairs launched the United States and the World Workshop series. This regular series examines key issues in US foreign relations. The inaugural workshop was developed in conjunction with the US State Department's Office of the Historian and was inspired by issues covered in the *Foreign Relations of the United States (FRUS)* series. This volume is based on the original presentations and moderated roundtable discussions at the initial workshop.

The Workshop series received generous support from the Maxwell Dean's Office. Special thanks to Dean David Van Slyke, Associate Deans Carol Faulkner and Andrew London, and Senior Associate Dean Michael Wasylenko. It has benefited from additional support from the Daniel Patrick Moynihan Institute of Global Affairs and Director Margaret Hermann, Syracuse's Office of Research and Vice President Zhanjiang (John) Liu, and the Middle Eastern Studies Program. Special thanks are owed to Juanita Horan and Havva Karakas-Keles of the Moynihan Institute for their tireless efforts.

Support from the Department of History and the Piggott Fund has been invaluable to the workshops and this volume. Special thanks to Norman Kutcher for his generous advice and encouragement. Thanks also to Andrew Wender Cohen, David Bennett, Yüksel Sezgin, and Mehrzad Boroujerdi.

Thanks to Tom Zeiler for including this volume in his excellent New Approaches to International History series. I am indebted to Dan Hutchins, Sophie Campbell, Shyam Krishnan Nallur, and Bloomsbury's editorial and production teams for their assistance and hard work.

This volume would not have been possible without the generosity of its contributors. They were gracious with their time and patient with my many requests. They have my thanks and admiration.

My wife, Dalal Yassine, and daughter, Laila, were sources of inspiration and encouragement that helped make this project possible. This volume is dedicated to them.

List of Illustrations

Figures

Table

Contributors

Editor

Osamah F. Khalil is Associate Professor of History at Syracuse University's Maxwell School of Citizenship and Public Affairs. He is the author of *America's Dream Palace: Middle East Expertise and the Rise of the National Security State* (2016).

Contributors

Ervand Abrahamian is Professor Emeritus of History at Baruch College and the Graduate Center at the City University of New York. He is the author of *Iran between Two Revolutions, A History of Modern Iran*, and *The Coup: 1953, The CIA, and the Roots of Modern US-Iran Relations*.

Abolghasem Bayyenat is a Stanton Nuclear Security Postdoctoral Fellow at Harvard University's Belfer Center for Science and International Affairs. He received his Ph.D. in Political Science from Syracuse University. His current research is focused on Iran's nuclear decision-making processes, and Iranian political elites' national security and foreign policy thinking. Prior to pursuing doctoral studies, he worked for several years in Iran researching Iran's foreign trade regime and the multilateral trading system.

Malcolm Byrne is Deputy Director and Director of Research at the nongovernmental National Security Archive. He is also Director of the US-Iran Relations Project. He is the author of *Iran-Contra: Reagan's Scandal and the Unchecked Abuse of Presidential Power* (2014) and coeditor of *Becoming Enemies: U.S.-Iran Relations and the Iran-Iraq War, 1979–1988* (2012) and the award-winning *Mohammad Mosaddeq and the 1953 Coup in Iran* (2004).

David Collier received a PhD in Political Science from Boston University in 2013. He has worked at the Centre for the Study of Islam in Glasgow, the Center for International Relations in Boston, and more recently at The Asia Group, a policy and strategy organization in Washington, DC. Collier is currently serving as an adjunct professor in Boston University's Washington Program. He is the author of *Democracy and the Nature of American Influence in Iran, 1941–1979* (2017).

Erik French is a Visiting Lecturer at the College at Brockport. He received his PhD in Political Science from Syracuse's Maxwell School of Citizenship and Public Affairs. He was a Sasakawa Peace Foundation fellow with Pacific Forum from 2014–16. His research focuses on alliance strategy, deterrence, and US foreign policy.

Dimitar D. Gueorguiev is Assistant Professor of Political Science at Syracuse's Maxwell School. Gueorguiev's co-authored book *China's Governance Puzzle* (2017) deals with reforming authoritarian governance through transparency and public inclusion. In a forthcoming book, *Retrofitting Leninism*, Gueorguiev explores the refinement of authoritarian control through organization and technology.

Adam M. Howard is Director of the US Department of State's Office of the Historian and is an adjunct professor of History and International Affairs at George Washington University. He received his PhD in History from the University of Florida and is the author of *Sewing the Fabric of Statehood: Garment Unions, American Labor, and the Establishment of the State of Israel* (2017).

Richard H. Immerman recently retired from Temple University, where he was Professor of History, Edward Buthusiem Distinguished Faculty Fellow, and Marvin Wachman Director of the Center for the Study of Force and Diplomacy. At Temple he won the Paul Eberman Faculty Research award; previously he had won the University of Hawaii's Board of Regents Excellence in Research award. The recipient of the Stuart Bernath Book and Lecture prizes from the Society for Historians of American Foreign Relations (SHAFR), he served as SHAFR's fortieth president. Immerman's publications include *The CIA in Guatemala* (1982), *Waging Peace* (2000), *John Foster Dulles* (1998), *Empire for Liberty* (2010), *The Hidden Hand: A Brief History of the CIA* (2014), and *Understanding the U.S. Wars in Iraq and Afghanistan* (2015). He was Assistant Deputy Director of National Intelligence for Analytic Integrity from 2007 to 2009, held the Francis W. De Serio Chair in Strategic Intelligence at the United States Army War College from 2013 to 2016, and has chaired the Historical Advisory Committee to the Department of State since 2010.

Terry Lautz is former Vice President of the Luce Foundation and was a Visiting Professor and Moynihan Research Fellow at Syracuse University from 2010 to 2019. He has served as a trustee and chair of the Harvard-Yenching Institute, the Lingnan Foundation, and the Yale-China Association, and was a Director on the Board of the National Committee on U.S.-China Relations. Lautz is the author of *John Birch: A Life* (2016) and *Americans in China: Encounters with the People's Republic* (2021).

Yingyi Ma is Associate Professor of Sociology and Senior Research Associate at the Center for Policy Research at Syracuse's Maxwell School. She is also Director of Asian/ Asian American Studies. Ma received her PhD from Johns Hopkins University. Her book, *Ambitious and Anxious: How Do Chinese College Students Succeed and Struggle in American Higher Education*, will be published by Columbia University Press in fall 2019.

Pedram Magsoud-Nia is a PhD candidate in Political Science at the Maxwell School of Citizenship and Public Affairs. His research focuses on the evolution of the modern state in the Middle East.

David Nickles received a PhD in History from Harvard University and is the author of *Under the Wire: How the Telegraph Changed Diplomacy* (2003). At the Office of the Historian, he is chief of the division that compiles *Foreign Relations of the United States* volumes relating to Asia and the Middle East. He has compiled volumes on US relations with Japan (1969–72), China (1973–6), East and South East Asia (1973–6), and China (1977–80).

Alexander R. Wieland is a historian in the Middle East and Asia division of the Department of State's Office of the Historian, where he has worked as a compiler for the *Foreign Relations of the United States* series since 2006. Currently, he is engaged in researching and editing the series' three-volume history of the George H. W. Bush administration's policy toward the Gulf crisis from 1989 to 1992. Prior to joining the Historian's Office, he received his PhD in International History from the London School of Economics and Political Science.

Introduction: The Waning American Century?

Osamah F. Khalil

Writing in February 1941, Henry Luce heralded the dawning of the "American century." With Nazi rule extending from the gates of Moscow to Paris, the publisher of *Time* and *Life* magazines derided isolationism and called for the United States to embrace its potential. "As America enters dynamically upon the world scene," Luce wrote, "we need most of all to seek and to bring forth a vision of America as a world power which is authentically American and which can inspire us to live and work and fight with enthusiasm." [1] Nearly eight decades later, the United States has surpassed Luce's vision and is the world's predominant military, political, economic, and cultural power. Yet warnings of the end of American primacy and the postwar international order abound. [2]

The perception that the United States is, or soon will be, in decline is inextricably linked to the increased prominence of countries in Asia. These predictions have been inspired in part by forecasts of shifting economic power over the next several decades. By 2050, analysts project that China and India will have the largest economies in the world, followed by the United States.[3] By the mid-century point, the "Emerging 7" (E7) economies of Brazil, China, India, Indonesia, Mexico, Russia, and Turkey are also expected to eclipse those of the Group of Seven (G7—Canada, France, Germany, Italy, Japan, the UK, and the United States). Yet these are only predictions and the E7 countries share a number of economic and political vulnerabilities and structural impediments that could hinder their potential growth.[4] Nor is this limited to emerging economies. From the 2008 global financial crisis to Brexit, American and European political and financial institutions have faced significant challenges of legitimacy that have contributed to uncertainty about the American-led international order. Will that order survive? Or will the American century be supplanted by one centered in and around Asia?[5]

Yet economic prowess is not the only factor that determines great power or superpower status. The United States boasts the most powerful military on the planet and one with global reach. China has increased defense spending over the past decade and it was estimated to be $228 billion in 2017. However, it lags far behind the United States, which spends over $610 billion annually and accounts for at least 35 percent of global expenditures. Meanwhile, Russia and India only account for 5 percent ($66.3 billion) and 3 percent ($63.9 billion) respectively of global defense expenditures. In contrast, analysts estimate that Iran's defense spending is at least $10 billion annually.[6] Nor can any of these countries boast America's global political influence or cultural impact. But the fear of American decline persists and it is unclear how the United States will respond to these shifts in global power.

Moreover, the depiction of Asia in broad and threatening terms is also historically rooted. Not only were the "Orient" and the "East" European inventions, but the arbitrary boundaries between "Europe" and "Asia" and the exclusion of the area now called the "Middle East" from both reflect ideology not geography.[7] After the Chinese Communist Revolution and the Korean War, American policymakers often depicted containment in racialized terms. Indeed, the "yellow peril" was an element of official and popular discourse from the 1955 Asia-Africa Conference in Bandung, Indonesia to the Vietnam War.[8] Richard Nixon's frequently cited 1967 *Foreign Affairs* article offers one insight into the policymaker's imaginary and its influence on constructed geographies. Written in preparation for the 1968 presidential election, Nixon outlined his future foreign policy and a possible rapprochement with China. It was in Asia, Nixon warned, that there was "the greatest danger of a confrontation which could escalate into World War III." As the United States was "one anchor of a vast Pacific community," it was deeply involved in and concerned about Asian affairs. "Our interests and our ideals propel us westward across the Pacific, not as conquerors but as partners, linked by the sea not only with those oriental nations on Asia's Pacific littoral but at the same time with occidental Australia and New Zealand, and with the island nations between," he wrote.[9]

Like the construction of Asia, discussions of the liberal order and its impending decline have also reflected a Euro-American perspective. Although scholars have emphasized that the US-led order is based on consent rather than coercion, this tends to understate the structural benefits to the great powers and the impediments to developing nations. Even after overcoming the legacies of colonialism, including foreign debts often to the former colonizing power, the lack of infrastructural development, weak political institutions, and contentious borders, developing nations must contend with the reality that there is no viable alternative to the US-led order. During and after the Cold War, opposition to Washington carried the risk not only of isolation, but open or covert intervention. While there have been calls to reform the existing order to accommodate rising powers and fledgling alternative institutions are emerging, it is uncertain that the benefits will be distributed in a more just and equitable fashion globally. Indeed, it may be difficult to differentiate between the old order and the new.[10]

This volume explores the changing international landscape by examining America's relationship with two countries: the People's Republic of China and the Islamic Republic of Iran. Since the election of Donald J. Trump, tensions with both countries have increased. In the case of China, the United States withdrew from the Trans-Pacific Partnership and has engaged in a trade war with Beijing.[11] The Trump administration also withdrew from the 2015 Joint Comprehensive Plan of Action (JCPOA) with Iran and has reinstated sanctions against Tehran.[12] Two predominant narrative trends converge in, and are contested by, this volume: First, that the lack of recognition and tense relations between the United States and the People's Republic of China would inevitably be reconciled. Second, that a contentious relationship between the United States and the Islamic Republic of Iran has been unavoidable.

However, this volume is not a comprehensive examination of Sino-American and US-Iranian relations. Nor does it contend that Washington's relationship with other countries in Asia, including Russia, India, and Turkey, are less important. Rather, it posits that the twenty-first century will be shaped by relations between the United States and key countries in Asia. Because of the similarities and differences in their interactions with the United States over the past six decades and their growing bilateral ties, China and Iran offer intriguing comparative case studies. Therefore, this volume is centered on three major themes: interaction, normalization, and confrontation. It provides an insight into how and why Washington has developed and implemented its policies toward Beijing and Tehran. The volume also explores how China and Iran have adopted policies toward the United States and internationally. Furthermore, it benefits from the insights of leading scholars discussing the future of relations between Beijing and Tehran. Finally, this volume is an invitation to other scholars to produce similar comparative and interdisciplinary studies.

Over the past six decades, relations between the United States and the People's Republic of China have evolved from open hostility and confrontation to normalization and cooperation. Although the dramatic break in tensions between Washington and Beijing marked by President Nixon's 1972 visit to China was not inevitable, it was sought by both sides.[13] Nor was the evolution of Sino-American relations predictable, especially in the post–Cold War era. Unlike the competition with the Soviet Union, the United States and China have economic and trade ties that have deepened significantly since the late 1970s. That China is America's largest trading partner and owns a substantial percentage of US treasuries are significant, but incomplete, aspects of a more complex relationship between the two countries.[14] This is reflected in part in Washington's strategy toward Beijing, a combination of containment and engagement that has been referred to as "congagement."[15] As the contributions in the first part of this volume demonstrate, Sino-American relations from diplomats to university students have been and remain dynamic and vibrant.

Like its relations with China, the United States has had extended periods of tension and collaboration with Iran. Indeed, relations with Tehran directly influenced America's policies toward the Persian Gulf and the broader Middle East with global implications. Under Mohammad Reza Shah Pahlavi's regime, Tehran was Washington's key ally in the Persian Gulf. The nearly four decades of hostility between the United States and Iran since the 1979 Iranian Revolution has been marked by brief periods of engagement.[16] After the Cold War, the United States applied a policy of "dual containment" of Iraq and Iran. Although there were hopes that a reconciliation between Washington and a reformist government in Tehran was possible at the end of the 1990s, the September 11, 2001 attacks contributed to a more aggressive US foreign policy that sought regime change in Iran as one of its goals. Fourteen years later, the successful negotiations over Iran's nuclear program with the JCPOA suggested that a different relationship between Washington and Tehran was possible. Part 2 of this volume details why the future of US-Iranian relations could either be cordial or even more antagonistic than in the past.

Meanwhile, Sino-Iranian relations have expanded over the past two decades. In the postwar era, relations between Beijing and Tehran centered around energy resources.[17] China is currently the world's largest net oil importer and is Iran's leading customer of crude oil as well as its largest trading partner. In 2017, Iran supplied roughly 7.5 percent ($11.9 billion) of China's $162.2 billion of crude oil imports, which represented a 27.2 percent increase from the previous year. Furthermore, there was over $37 billion in trade between China and Iran in 2017.[18] The military relationship between Beijing and Tehran has also expanded since the JCPOA was signed. Although Iran produces a significant amount of its own weapons, it also purchases arms from Russia and China.[19]

Washington's withdrawal from the JCPOA was part of the Trump administration's broader "maximum pressure" campaign against Tehran. The campaign was designed to force Iran to renegotiate the nuclear agreement on terms that were more advantageous to the United States. Regional and international tensions increased through 2019. In early January 2020, Iranian Major General Qassem Soleimani and Abu Mahdi al-Muhandis, the Deputy Chairman of Iraq's Popular Mobilization Units, were killed along with several aides in a U.S. airstrike in Baghdad, Iraq. That same day, a separate attack in Yemen failed to kill Soleimani's deputy, Abdul Reza Shahlai. Soleimani led the Quds Force of Iran's Islamic Revolutionary Guard Corps. The Quds Force was primarily focused on external operations, and Soleimani coordinated with Iran's state and non-state allies across the region. This included cooperating with the United States in the multi-nation coalition against the Islamic State. In justifying the assassination, the Trump administration claimed that Soleimani was responsible for a deadly mortar attack on an Iraqi military base used by U.S. forces as well as orchestrating violent protests at the American Embassy in Baghdad. However, it was later revealed that Iraqi security forces blamed Islamic State elements for the attack on the base and shared their findings with the U.S. military. Iran's retaliatory missile strikes against U.S. forces and the accidental downing of Ukraine International Airlines Flight 752 after taking off from Tehran airport appeared to offer an opportunity to deescalate the crisis. That same month, the COVID-19 virus began sweeping the globe and had a dramatic impact on China, Iran, and the United States. While Iran struggled to contain the virus, hawks within the Trump administration believed it offered an opportunity to continue pressuring Tehran to accept a new nuclear agreement on American terms. Instead, China and Iran negotiated an expansive economic and security partnership that challenged the Trump administration's policies.[20]

Although the Trump administration's rhetoric and actions have challenged traditional trade and economic relations, China's Belt and Road Initiative has the potential to transform them altogether. Beijing has reportedly invested roughly $1 trillion in the creation of a "new Silk Road" and plans to spend even more over the next decade. The ambitious initiative currently involves sixty-eight countries in an array of land and sea infrastructure and trade projects that encompass half the globe. With a combined population of over 4 billion people and accounting for nearly 40 percent of global GDP, if the Belt and Road Initiative is successful it could reshape political, economic, and cultural relations in the twenty-first century and beyond. Speaking at the 2017 Belt and Road Forum in Beijing, Chinese president Xi Jinping explained that China hoped to create "a big family of harmonious co-existence."[21]

Yet the initiative has attracted significant skepticism and consternation in the United States.[22] This includes the Department of Defense, which explained to the US Congress in its 2018 annual report that "China's leaders increasingly seek to leverage China's growing economic, diplomatic, and military clout to establish regional preeminence and expand the country's international influence." The Pentagon warned that the Belt and Road Initiative could lead to the economic dependence of participating countries and their alignment with

Chinese interests. It asserted that this could "deter confrontation or criticism of China's approach to sensitive issues."[23]

The criticism is not limited to China's potential rivals. Indeed, some countries participating in the initiative have balked at the uneven trade relations with Beijing and the burden of debt-fueled investments. This has been compounded by the uncertain, and in some cases dubious, short- and long-term potential of the infrastructure projects to succeed. One prominent example is Sri Lanka's Mattala Rajapaksa International Airport. Funded through Chinese loans and completed in 2014, the facility has the capacity for one million passengers annually. Yet slightly more than fifty thousand passengers traveled through the airport in 2017. Other infrastructure projects across southern Asia have been put on hold or may be canceled.[24] While the Belt and Road Initiative may offer a different vision of the future, one that is not based on Euro-American notions of Asian deficiency and dependency, it is not necessarily as altruistic as President Xi has suggested. Instead, it may merely reflect the goals and interests of an aspiring hegemon, whose actions resemble those of other great powers that sought regional and global domination.

These topics are explored in greater detail in the following chapters, which are the product of the inaugural United States and the World Workshop hosted by Syracuse University's Maxwell School of Citizenship and Public Affairs. The chapters in this volume are based on the original presentations and moderated roundtable discussions at the September 2017 workshop.

The first part of this volume examines Sino-American relations following Nixon's visit to China and stalled normalization talks. In Chapter 1, David Nickles explores how President Jimmy Carter evolved from a critic of improved relations with Beijing to an advocate for normalization. Nickles contends that this episode provides an opportunity to assess the influence of individual leaders on foreign policy. Yet he cautions that the transformation of Sino-American relations also constrained Carter's successors.

Terry Lautz expands on the normalization negotiations between Beijing and Washington during the Carter administration in Chapter 2. Drawing on a range of archival sources and interviews, Lautz reveals that normalization was achieved despite a fundamental disagreement over continued US arms sales to Taiwan. Lautz demonstrates that the United States insisted on maintaining a military relationship with Taiwan for domestic political reasons. Meanwhile, Deng Xiaoping reluctantly agreed because China needed Washington's support against Moscow and hoped for American assistance in modernizing China's economy. Yet as recent events have shown, the Taiwan issue remains a source of considerable mistrust and misunderstanding between Washington and Beijing.

Nearly four decades after normalization, integration, and modernization, Dimitar Gueorguiev contends that China is not headed in a democratic direction. In Chapter 3, Gueorguiev reviews the origins and evolution of the democratization angle in US foreign policy toward China. He argues that it has been employed opportunistically and inconsistently by Washington and Beijing.

Chinese students on the campuses of American universities and colleges have been a nearly ubiquitous reminder of improved Sino-American relations since the early 1980s. Drawing on student interviews from a range of academic institutions, Yingyi Ma examines the impact of study in the United States on Chinese youth in Chapter 4. Instead of adopting American values and identity, Ma found that many Chinese students have felt a renewed interest in and awareness of being Chinese while away from China. She argues that Chinese international students are transnational with their increased and more reflexive understanding of both societies.

In Chapter 5 , Erik French explores the trilateral relationship between the United States, Japan, and China. He analyzes how the United States' strategy for addressing Sino-Japanese territorial disputes in the East China Sea has evolved in the post–Cold War era. French argues that Washington has successfully reassured and deterred Beijing when it has coordinated with Tokyo.

Chapter 6 features a moderated roundtable discussion on the present and future of Sino-American relations as well as Sino-Iranian ties. This includes the potential for greater involvement by China in the Middle East and South Asia and the prospects for the Belt and Road Initiative.

In July 2017, the US State Department's Office of the Historian published a retrospective *Foreign Relations of the United States (FRUS)* volume covering the 1953 coup d'état that deposed Iranian prime minister Muhammad Mossadeq.[25] In Part 2, the volume explores over sixty years of US-Iranian relations during and after the 1953 Coup. Ervand Abrahamian analyzes the newly declassified and published documents in Chapter 7 and contends that they reveal greater American involvement in Iranian politics than has previously been acknowledged or understood by scholars. At the center of these efforts, Abrahamian demonstrates, was US ambassador to Iran Loy Henderson and the embassy staff. Henderson was a key proponent of deposing Mossadeq nearly a year before Dwight D. Eisenhower took office.

In Chapter 8, Malcolm Byrne details the efforts by the National Security Archive to declassify the records related to the 1953 Coup. He examines the archive's use of the Freedom of Information Act (FOIA) and the flaws and unnecessary frustrations of the declassification process. Byrne assesses how the leaking and declassification of US diplomatic and national security documents has contributed to the literature on US-Iranian relations and the historiography of the 1953 Coup.

Utilizing archival sources and oral histories, David Collier examines why the United States was caught seemingly unaware by the Iranian Revolution in Chapter 9. Collier assesses how Washington lost cognizance of Mohammad Reza Shah Pahlavi's unstable internal position. By focusing on a framework that highlights the importance of linkage and leverage between Iran and the United States, Collier argues that the Iranian Revolution was a predictable event that only surprised the United States due to the failures of successive administrations over the previous two decades.

In Chapter 10, Adam M. Howard and Alexander R. Wieland analyze how President Jimmy Carter's administration developed its policy toward the Persian Gulf region during and after the Iranian Revolution. Relying on available *FRUS* volumes, Howard and Wieland focus on the "two-camp" divide in the Carter administration between Secretary of State Cyrus Vance and National Security Advisor Zbigniew Brzezinski. They challenge the conventional wisdom that the Iranian Revolution and the Soviet invasion of Afghanistan validated Brzezinski's traditional Cold War approach at the expense of Vance's emphasis on human rights. Instead, Howard and Wieland contend that in the Persian Gulf, continuity in US foreign policy proved more prevalent than change.

Washington's efforts to establish a robust American military presence in the Persian Gulf after the Iranian Revolution had the unintended consequence of strengthening the new regime led by Ayatollah Ruhollah Khomeini. In Chapter 11, Pedram Maghsoud-Nia argues that the revolution was a critical juncture in Iran's modern history. He demonstrates that the animus between Washington and Tehran over the past four decades has contributed to the strengthening and legitimation of Iran's postrevolutionary state institutions.

Abolghasem Bayyenat explores the negotiations between Washington and Tehran over the Iranian nuclear program culminating in the 2015 JCPOA in Chapter 12. Bayyenat demonstrates that the United States had a predominant influence on the negotiations. He details how Washington's maximalist demands contributed to a recalcitrant Iranian position. Bayyenat concludes that the pragmatic approach adopted during President Barack Obama's second term elicited a similar response from Tehran and led to an agreement.

In Chapter 13, the contributors assess the present and future of US-Iranian relations in a moderated roundtable discussion. The participants reflect on the difficulties in researching and studying contentious subjects and politics. In addition, they discuss the possibility of closer ties between China and Iran.

Finally, Richard Immerman draws on his experience in academia and government in the afterword to reflect on the responsibility of historians to engage in contemporary debates. Immerman contends that rather than fear the presentist label, historians must embrace discussions of the past, present, and future. This includes participating in debates on foreign and domestic policies, where their expertise and training can provide context and insights. In short, it is precisely what this volume hopes to accomplish.

Notes

1 Henry R. Luce, "The American Century," *Life* 10, 7 (February 17, 1941): 61–5. On Luce's influence, see Alan Brinkley, *The Publisher: Henry Luce and His American Century* (New York: Vintage, 2011). For a critical assessment of Luce's essay, see Neil Smith, *American Empire: Roosevelt's Geographer and the Prelude to Globalization* (Berkeley: University of California Press, 2003), 17–21.

2 For example, a number of articles and op-eds have been published after Trump's election and inauguration. See Joseph Nye Jr., "Will the Liberal Order Survive? The History of an Idea," *Foreign Affairs* 96, 1 (January/February 2017): 10–16; Stewart Patrick, "The World Order is Starting to Crack," *Foreign Policy* (July 25, 2018). See the special issue of *International Affairs* 94, 1 (January 2018): 1–172, including G. John Ikenberry, "The End of Liberal International Order?" See also Robert Kaplan, *The Return of Marco Polo's World: War, Strategy, and American Interests in the Twenty-First Century* (New York: Random House, 2018), among others.

3 PricewaterhouseCoopers (PwC) Global, "The World in 2050," (https://www.pwc.com/gx/en/issues/economy/the-world-in-2050.html). For a comparative analysis of China and India, see Chris Ogden, *China and India: Asia's Emergent Great Powers* (Cambridge, UK: Polity Press, 2017).

4 As of this writing, analysts are warning that an emerging financial crisis in Turkey could have global implications similar to 2008. See Matt Phillips, "Why the Collapse in Turkish Currency Matters Globally," *New York Times*, August 14, 2018.

5 Kishore Mahbubani, "The Case against the West: America and Europe in the Asian Century," *Foreign Affairs* 87, 3 (May–June 2008): 111–24; Amitav Acharya, *The End of American World Order*, 2nd edition (Cambridge, UK: Polity Press, 2018).

6 See the Stockholm International Peace Research Institute, SIPRI Military Expenditure Database (https://www.sipri.org/databases/milex); Kenneth Katzman, *Iran: Politics, Human Rights, and U.S. Policy* (Washington, DC: Congressional Research Service, May 21, 2018).

7 Martin W. Lewis and Karen Wigen, *The Myth of Continents: A Critique of Metageography* (Berkeley: University of California Press, 1997), 35–41; Philip Bowring, "What is Asia?" *Far East Economic Review* 135, 7 (February 12, 1987): 30–1; On the emergence of "East Asia" as a geographic region, see T. J. Pempel, ed., *Remapping East*

      Asia: The Construction of a Region (Ithaca, NY: Cornell University Press, 2005) and Christopher Dent, *East Asian Regionalism*, 2nd edition (New York: Routledge, 2016); On the Middle East as an ideational construct, see Osamah Khalil, "The Crossroads of the World: U.S. and British Foreign Policy Doctrines and the Construct of the Middle East, 1902–2007," *Diplomatic History* 38, 2 (April 2014): 299–344.

8   Christina Klein, *Cold War Orientalism: Asia in the Middlebrow Imagination, 1945–1961* (Berkeley: University of California Press, 2001); Christopher J. Lee, *Making a World after Empire: The Bandung Moment and Its Political Afterlives* (Athens: Ohio State University Press, 2010); Walter LaFeber, "Zelig in U.S. Foreign Relations: The Roles of China in the American Post-9/11 World," in *Iraq and the Lessons of Vietnam: Or, How Not to Learn from the Past*, ed. Lloyd C. Gardner and Marilyn B. Young (New York: The New Press, 2007), 201–15.

9   Richard Nixon, "Asia after Viet Nam," *Foreign Affairs* 46, 1 (October 1967): 111–25.

10   See G. John Ikenberry, *Liberal Leviathan: The Origins, Crisis, and Transformation of the American World Order* (Princeton, NJ: Princeton University Press, 2011); Ali Burak Güvan, "Defending Supremacy: How the IMF and the World Bank Navigate the Challenge of Rising Powers," *International Affairs* 93, 5 (2017): 1149–66; Inderjeet Parmar, "The US-led Liberal Order: Imperialism by Another Name?" *International Affairs* 94, 1 (2018): 151–72; Cynthia Roberts, Leslie Armijo, and Saori Katada, *The BRICS and Collective Financial Statecraft* (New York: Oxford University Press, 2017).

11   Natasha Bach, "Trump Appears to Have Changed His Mind about TPP—Again," *Fortune* April 18, 2018; Katie LoBosco, "Trade War: The US and China Just Slapped New Tariffs on Each Other," *CNN.com*, August 23, 2018.

12   Mark Landler, "Trump Abandons Iran Nuclear Deal He Long Scorned," *New York Times*, May 8, 2018; Harris Gardiner and Jack Ewing, "U.S. Reinstating Iran Sanctions, Defying Europe," *New York Times*, August 7, 2018.

13   For Beijing's decision-making, see Chen Jian, *Mao's China and the Cold War* (Chapel Hill: University of North Carolina Press, 2001); Gordon H. Chang, *Fateful Ties: A History of America's Preoccupation with China* (Cambridge, MA: Harvard University Press, 2015); Odd Arne Westad, *The Cold War: A World History* (New York: Basic Books, 2017).

14   Brian Chappatta and Liz McCormick, "A Guide to the Giant Foreign Buyers of U.S. Debt," *Bloomberg*, January 11, 2018.

15   The scholarship on China's "rise" and the potential for a conflict with the United States is voluminous. Some of the recent works include Graham Allison, *Destined for War: Can America and China Escape Thucydides's Trap?* (New York: Houghton Mifflin Harcourt, 2017); David C. Kang, *American Grand Strategy and East Asian Security in the Twenty-First Century* (Cambridge, UK: Cambridge University Press, 2017); Richard McGregor, *Asia's Reckoning: China, Japan, and the Fate of U.S. Power in the Pacific Century* (New York: Penguin, 2017); Michael Pillsbury, *The Hundred-Year Marathon: China's Secret Strategy to Replace America as the Global Superpower* (New York: St. Martin's Press, 2016); Gideon Rachman, *Easternization: Asia's Rise and America's Decline From Obama to Trump and Beyond* (New York: Other Press, 2017); On congagement, see Aaron L. Friedberg, *A Contest for Supremacy: China, America, and the Struggle for Mastery in Asia* (New York: W.W. Norton, 2011).

16   On US-Iranian relations during and after the shah's reign, see Ervand Abrahamian, *The Coup: 1953, the CIA, and the Roots of Modern U.S.-Iranian Relations*

(New York: New Press, 2013); Roham Alvandi, *Nixon, Kissinger, and the Shah: The United States and Iran in the Cold War* (New York: Oxford University Press, 2014); Malcolm Byrne, *Iran-Contra: Reagan's Scandal and the Unchecked Abuse of Presidential Power* (Lawrence: University of Kansas Press, 2014); David Collier, *Democracy and the Nature of American Influence in Iran, 1941–1979* (Syracuse, NY: Syracuse University Press, 2017); Andrew Scott Cooper, *Oil Kings: How the U.S., Iran, and Saudi Arabia Changed the Balance of Power in the Middle East* (New York: Simon & Schuster, 2011); Mark Gasiorowski, *U.S. Foreign Policy and the Shah: Building a Client State in Iran* (Ithaca, NY: Cornell University Press, 1991); Trita Parsi, *Treacherous Alliance: The Secret Dealings of Israel, Iran, and the United States* (New Haven, CT: Yale University Press, 2007).

17 For the origins of Sino-Iranian relations, see Mohamed Bin Huwaidin, *China's Relations with Arabia and the Gulf, 1949–1999* (London: Routledge, 2002); Carrie Liu Currier and Manochehr Dorraj, eds., *China's Energy Relations with the Developing World. Continuum Publishers* (New York: Continuum, 2011); Manochehr Dorraj and James English "Iran-China Relations and the Changing Political Map," in *Alone in the World: Iran's Foreign Policy Since 2001*, ed. Thomas Juneau and Sam Razavi (London: Routledge, 2013).

18 See U.S. Energy Information Agency, China Country Report (https://www.eia.gov/ beta/international/analysis.php?iso=CHN) and Iran Country Report (https://www.eia. gov/beta/international/analysis.php?iso=IRN); Ed Crooks, "The Global Importance of China's Oil Imports," *Financial Times*, September 25, 2017; Daniel Kliman and Abigail Grace, "China Smells Opportunity in the Middle East's Crisis," *Foreign Policy*, June 14, 2018.

19 Franz-Stefan Gady, "China, Iran to Deepen Military Ties ," The Diplomat, December 14, 2017; Kuang Keng Kuek Ser, " Where Did Iran Get Its Military Arms over the Last 70 Years?" PRI's The World, June 1, 2016; John Hudson, Missy Ryan, Josh Dawsey, "On the day U.S. forces killed Soleimani, they targeted a senior Iranian official in Yemen," *The Washington Post*, January 10, 2020; Alissa Rubin, "Was U.S. Wrong About Attack That Nearly Started a War With Iran?," *New York Times*, February 6, 2020; Mark Mazzetti, Helene Cooper, Julian E. Barnes, Alissa Rubin, Eric Schmitt, "As Iran Reels, Trump Aides Clash Over Escalating Military Showdown," *New York Times*, March 21, 2020; Farnaz Fassihi, Steven Lee Myers, "Defying U.S., China and Iran Near Trade and Military Partnership," *New York Times*, July 11, 2020.

20 Rachel Adams-Heard and Nick Wadhams, "China Rejects U.S. Request to Cut Iran Oil Imports," *Bloomberg*, August 3, 2018.

21 James Griffiths, "China's New World Order: Xi, Putin and Others Meet for Belt and Road Forum," *CNN*.com May 14, 2017; Tom Miller, *China's Asian Dream: Empire Building along the New Silk Road* (London: Zed Books, 2017).

22 Some examples include, Virginia Postrel, "The Boosterism Behind China's Silk Road Story," *Bloomberg* May 24, 2017; Brenda Goh and John Ruwitch, "Pressure on as Xi's 'Belt and Road' Enshrined in Chinese Party Charter," *Reuters*, October 24, 2017; Philip Bowring, "China's Silk Road Illusions," *New York Review of Books*, October 25, 2017; Richard Fontaine and Daniel Kliman, "On China's New Silk Road, Democracy Pays a Toll," *Foreign Policy*, May 16, 2018; Sadanand Dhume, "I Think I'm Going to Kathmandu, Say the Chinese," *Wall Street Journal*, June 28, 2018; "China's Empire of Money Is Reshaping Global Trade," *Bloomberg*, August 1, 2018.

23 Office of the Secretary of Defense, "Annual Report to Congress: Military and Security Developments Involving the People's Republic of China, 2018," (Washington, DC: Department of Defense, August 2018), i–ii.

24 Michael Safi and Amantha Perera, "'The Biggest Game Changer in 100 Years': Chinese Money Gushes into Sri Lanka," *The Guardian*, March 25, 2018; Hannah Beech, "Second Thoughts on a Chinese Spending Spree," *New York Times*, August 21, 2018; "China's Empire of Money Is Reshaping Global Trade"; Will Doig, *High-Speed Empire: Chinese Expansion and the Future of Southeast Asia* (New York: Columbia Global Reports, 2018).

25 There are a number of transliterations of Muhammad Mossadeq's name. They vary depending on the source and country (i.e., US State Department, the UK's Foreign Office, the *New York Times*, *Times* of London, *Time* Magazine, *International Journal of Middle East Studies*, etc.). After consultation with the contributors, it was decided to use "Muhammad Mossadeq" throughout the volume. The original transliterations in the titles of cited sources and those used by government agencies in declassified documents have been retained.

Part One

Toward Normalization: The United States and the People's Republic of China, 1972–Present

1

Rise of the Institutions: The Normalization of Sino-American Relations

David P. Nickles[1]

The normalization of diplomatic relations between the United States and the People's Republic of China in 1979 provides an opportunity to assess the role of individuals in driving important, historic events. While popular culture tends to promote the notion that political leaders determine the course of history, Western scholars have instead argued that political, economic, and sociocultural structures determine outcomes, and that individual leaders, however much they capture public imagination, are largely interchangeable when considered from a broad perspective.[2] In Communist China, in contrast, professional historians had long focused on the role of socioeconomic forces, but have more recently become interested in the influence of individuals on international politics.[3] The normalization of Sino-American relations provides an intriguing opportunity to explore this issue since a small number of individuals dominated the relationship throughout the 1970s until another small number of individuals replaced them.

The initial rapprochement between the United States and China owed much to two men, Mao Zedong and Richard Nixon, who significantly altered an international system that seemed to be structured partly on the basis of enmity between their two countries. For more than two decades after 1949, when the Chinese Communist Party triumphed over nationalist Chinese forces in the civil war, intense hostility characterized the relationship between the People's Republic of China and the United States. War between the two countries, perhaps even involving nuclear weapons, seemed a possibility at periods of highest tension, such as China's Korean War intervention against US troops and the 1950s crises in the Taiwan Straits. As ideological rivalry between China and the Soviet Union intensified, US officials sometimes perceived Chinese foreign policy, with its support for Communist revolution across the developing world, the greatest immediate challenge to US foreign policy.[4] During this period, Nixon and Mao vilified one another's countries and opportunistically depicted domestic rivals as servants of foreign treachery, famously exemplified by Nixon's exploitation of red-baiting and Mao's manipulation of political purification campaigns.

Yet, in a classic example of *Realpolitik*, during the early 1970s Mao and Nixon overcame the longstanding hatred between their countries to improve relations. They did this partly in response to a rise in Soviet military power that both found threatening, and partly for domestic political reasons. Nixon hoped that better relations with China would facilitate an end to the unpopular Vietnam War, while Mao sought to lessen foreign threats in an effort to reduce the domestic influence of the Chinese military, which had assumed vast responsibilities during the chaos of the Cultural Revolution.[5] Their reputations as hardliners shielded them and provided credibility as they executed one of the most shocking diplomatic maneuvers of the Cold War era, confounding their more ideological supporters.[6]

By 1973, the United States and China had established de facto embassies, called liaison offices, in one another's capitals. It appeared that they might normalize their diplomatic relations and exchange accredited ambassadors before the end of Nixon's second term. However, on the American side, formal recognition was thwarted by the Watergate scandal, Nixon's 1974 resignation, and the Republican right's criticism of the détente policy of Nixon and his top foreign policy aide, Henry Kissinger, for allegedly making too many concessions toward Communist powers. At the end of May 1975, former California governor Ronald Reagan, who was hinting that he might seek to challenge President Ford for the Republican nomination, gave a speech in which he said that the United States must make clear that it intends to meet its treaty obligations to the Republic of China, and that Ford should not visit Communist China without also visiting Taiwan.[7] In July 1975, four of the top China hands in the US government sent Secretary of State Kissinger a memorandum advocating that the United States explore with Chinese leaders "steps toward a fully normalized relationship."[8] Kissinger met with them a few days later, and explained why he rejected their advice: "For political reasons it's just impossible for the U.S. to go for normalization before '76. If there's any one thing that will trigger a conservative reaction to Ford, that's it."[9] Reagan criticized the Ford administration on May 28, 1976 for preparing to yield to China's "demand that we sacrifice Taiwan" in order to normalize relations with Communist China.[10] The next day, Kissinger warned Huang Zhen, the head of the unofficial Chinese diplomatic mission to the United States, that the progress in Sino-American relations could be erased if Reagan won the 1976 Republican presidential nomination instead of Ford and became US president. Kissinger hastened to add that Reagan would not win.[11]

On the Chinese side, Mao's enthusiasm for better relations with the United States cooled as Nixon and Kissinger employed a détente policy to improve relations with the Soviet Union. In meetings with Westerners, Chinese officials criticized détente as a cynical attempt to redirect Soviet aggression toward China and away from the West. They also noted that détente was naive in its cynicism, and referred to it as cowardly appeasement in the tradition of "Munich."[12] Even aside from unhappiness over détente, domestic events in China such as the resurgence of the Cultural Revolution in 1973 and the declining health of Mao and Zhou Enlai (the key implementer for Mao's opening to the United States), might have thwarted normalization even had Nixon remained in office. Mao allowed the "Gang of Four," ultraleftists who were suspicious of improving relations with the capitalist West, to attack Zhou's pragmatic foreign and domestic policies.[13] As Zhou became sicker and Mao became more critical of him, Deng Xiaoping began to assume Zhou's role as a pragmatist and executor of Chinese diplomacy with the United States. Yet Deng, who had only recently been rehabilitated after being removed earlier in the Cultural Revolution, received withering criticism from the Gang of Four. Following Zhou's death in early 1976, Deng was purged a second time, which seemed to end the prospect for better Sino-American relations for the foreseeable future.[14]

In November 1976, when Jimmy Carter was elected president, the future of Sino-American relations was unclear. The four men most associated with the improvement in relations—Mao, Zhou, Nixon, and Kissinger—were dead or out of office. Would their successors move toward normalization? Such a question seemed even more salient as the new leaders on both sides were critical of the policies of their predecessors. Carter had begun his presidential campaign with a declaration of his belief that the United States should "set a standard within the community of nations … [for] dedication to basic human rights and freedoms." He also called for "Minimum secrecy within government."[15] Carter's remarks seemed aimed at the brutal realism and secret agreements associated with Nixon and Kissinger's foreign policy. In addition, Carter, who was always one to drive a hard bargain, asserted that the Nixon and Ford administrations should have been tougher when negotiating with the Soviets and the Chinese.[16]

After Carter entered the Oval Office, he expressed distaste for the methods that Nixon and Kissinger had used when ingratiating themselves with their Chinese counterparts. In May 1977, his National Security Advisor, Zbigniew Brzezinski, sent Carter the record of Nixon's conversations with Mao and Zhou from the 1972 trip to China. Brzezinski noted with admiration that they provide "a good guide to negotiating with the Chinese." Carter thoroughly disagreed, declaring, "Zbig, I read all of it. Very interesting. I don't share your high opinion of Nixon. Obviously he was adept at assuaging the Chinese—at the expense of [Secretary of State] Rogers, American people, India, Soviets, etc. Also we were almost abject in our dealings with them."[17] A month later, Carter told Brzezinski, "We should not ass-kiss [the Chinese] the way Nixon and Kissinger did."[18] When Carter met with his top advisors to discuss the possibility of normalizing diplomatic relations with China, he declared his unwillingness to curry favor with Chinese statesmen by criticizing the Soviet Union in their presence: "there is no reason to knock the Soviets. I don't want to do what Nixon and Kissinger did, which almost nauseated me. They knocked our allies, the Russians, and so on. If the Chinese did the same thing to us, I would despise them."[19] President Carter initiated a tradition followed by most US presidents who followed him (George H. W. Bush being a notable exception) of saying his predecessor had been too soft on China.[20]

In China, the death of Mao was followed by a struggle for power between pragmatists, who might be more open to improved relations with capitalist countries, and ideological hardliners inspired by anti-capitalist Maoist doctrine who seemed more skeptical of the United States. The arrest of the Gang of Four in October 1976 signaled the growing strength of the pragmatists. China's political leadership became increasingly willing to break from Maoist orthodoxy, particularly with regard to education and the economy. Yet, even after Deng Xiaoping reemerged as a leading Chinese political figure following the downfall of the Gang of Four, it still seemed conceivable he might be cautious about seeking bold diplomatic initiatives following his two previous removals from power.[21] The nominal leader, Hua Guofeng, had even more reason to avoid controversy given his lack of authority and political support, which eventually resulted in his removal from office. More broadly, it was not clear that Chinese leaders would be willing to make concessions, particularly on the subject of Taiwan, which would be necessary for the US Congress to support a presidential decision to establish diplomatic relations with China.

Moreover, in the United States, many observers anticipated an improvement in Sino-Soviet relations following the death of Mao that might provide China with an alternative to improving relations with the United States. Before Mao's death, Brzezinski had predicted that post-Maoist China would seek to reconcile with the Soviet Union.[22] On November 10, 1976, the US embassy in Moscow reported, "In the two months since Chairman Mao's death, the Soviets have carefully orchestrated a series of gestures intended to demonstrate their interest in better relations with China." Nonetheless, the embassy doubted this effort would be successful, noting that the Soviets "are very unlikely to make concessions on those issues which matter most to the Chinese: the border and the Soviet troop presence along it."[23]

Ultimately, the new political leaderships in the United States and China, whatever their criticisms of Nixon and Mao, decided to build upon their bold diplomatic initiative. The top American officials believed that improved Sino-American relations would contribute to a more peaceful and less conflictual Asia Pacific region, as well as to better global governance. In the words of Cyrus Vance, Carter's secretary of state, "As I saw it, China was a great country that had an important role to play in the final quarter of the twentieth century, not simply one that might be a useful counterweight to the Soviet Union."[24] In addition, Brzezinski, like Nixon and Kissinger before him, saw the Sino-Soviet antagonism as a mechanism to divide and weaken the Communist world. Moreover, Brzezinski felt certain that it was easier to deal with the Soviets when they were nervous about improved Sino-American relations. In his memoirs, he wrote that he thought "a great deal" about the "Soviet dimension" to relations with China "even though I knew that publicly one had to make pious noises to the effect that U.S.-Chinese normalization had nothing to do with U.S.-Soviet rivalry."[25] Harold Brown, the secretary of defense, noted that much of the Soviet military was oriented against China and would be freed up for other missions if Sino-Soviet relations thawed.[26] The Carter administration was also aware of economic benefits that could be gained if US exporters had access to the China market, which had long excited American businesses. When top US officials met to discuss the possibility of normalizing relations with China, Secretary of the Treasury Michael Blumenthal observed, "The business community ... could be very helpful" in supporting this policy, which would help offset opposition in Congress.[27]

Likewise, the Chinese government expressed concern about the growing power and adventurism of the Soviet Union and Vietnam. Chinese diplomat Huang Zhen told Carter, "Although our two societies have different social systems and operate under different ideologies, under current international conditions, we have many common points. For example, we both must cope with Soviet expansionism and aggression."[28] Deng's efforts to reduce China's diplomatic isolation became more urgent as he observed Vietnam, which was allied to the Soviet Union (they signed a friendship treaty on November 3, 1978), prepare to invade Cambodia, which was a Chinese client.

Meanwhile, the Carter administration was navigating between geostrategic interest (which suggested supporting China over Vietnam), legal opposition to the invasion and occupation of a foreign country (which required opposing Vietnam's occupation of Cambodia), and human rights (which might see merit in Vietnam's toppling of Cambodia's Khmer Rouge regime, which had committed massive atrocities). Deng tried to put the situation into language that Americans could understand, telling Carter, "Vietnam is 100 percent the Cuba of the East."[29] Indeed, following normalization, China launched a limited invasion of Vietnam to teach it a "lesson," and the Carter administration later sided with China in the effort to seat the Khmer Rouge in the Cambodia (Kampuchea) seat at the United Nations.[30] Even aside from geopolitical considerations, Deng sought better economic relations with the United States in order to acquire the technology, knowledge, and capital necessary for his ambitious plans to modernize China.[31] Both Carter and Deng were attuned to the geopolitical advantages to be gained from better Sino-American relations, but they were more attentive than their predecessors had been to possible economic benefits.

What were the effects of normalization? They can be seen in three areas. The first was security, as China and the United States cooperated more closely to combat the Soviet threat. Deng oversaw a reorientation of Chinese foreign policy away from a Maoist emphasis on inspiring revolutions in developing countries (the area Mao termed the "third world"), toward pursuing its own development, and containing the Soviet Union.[32] This shift facilitated Sino-American cooperation during periods of Cold War crisis, such as the Soviet invasion of Afghanistan in December 1979, after which the United States began selling non-lethal military equipment to China. A second area of change after normalization was in economic relations. The two countries settled their relatively modest but legally and emotionally important financial claims against one another, which facilitated future US investment in China.[33] The United States loosened restrictions on exporting high technology goods to China. Carter hoped to treat the Soviet Union and China on an equal basis when it came to trade. However, as relations with the Soviet Union deteriorated, the Carter administration showed partiality to China by granting it most-favored-nation trade status, which was withheld from the Soviets. In the longer run, this contributed to the development of a close trade relationship that expedited Chinese modernization and increased economic interdependence between the two countries.[34] Bilateral trade grew from $1.1 billion in 1978 to $4.9 billion in 1980.[35]

The third effect of normalization related to the methods employed in Sino-American diplomacy. To understand this, one needs to consider how this relationship had operated before the establishment of formal diplomatic relations on January 1, 1979. Until then, there was considerable continuity between the diplomatic approaches to China by the Nixon, Ford, and Carter administrations, despite the latter's effort to portray its foreign policy as being a dramatic departure from that of its predecessors. Like them, Carter used secrecy and a narrow decision-making circle to achieve a diplomatic breakthrough. Michel Oksenberg, a member of Carter's National Security Council (NSC) staff and the chief executor of normalization on the American side, praised the closely held and highly centralized style of diplomacy used by his predecessors in the early 1970s: "The personal involvement [of the Chinese and

American leaders] brought a rigor, a precision, a meticulousness in the management of the relationship that is rarely exhibited in world affairs."[36] For his part, Nixon seems to have felt that Carter's secret negotiations vindicated his own much-criticized penchant for secrecy; he told Carter via Oksenberg that despite criticism from "clowns" in Congress, diplomacy must sometimes be secret, particularly when dealing with the Chinese government.[37]

In addition, Carter, like Nixon and Kissinger before him, gave little weight to the issue of human rights when dealing with China.[38] On May 20, 1977, Brzezinski informed the US foreign policy bureaucracy that Carter had directed that a special coordination committee "undertake a review of U.S. policy with respect to human rights," including "areas of strategic concern such as the PRC."[39] In response to Carter's request, an interagency group produced an August 1977 study that explicitly noted the difficulty of applying the human rights agenda to China: "The potential normalization of relations with China and Cuba will place some strain on the credibility of our human rights policy, for in both cases other considerations are likely to govern in the short term. As relations are established, we will be expected to take human rights initiatives." The study further noted, "We should recognize that with respect to human rights we will have little, if any, leverage or influence with the PRC at this stage."[40]

Over the course of the Carter administration, Brzezinski, Oksenberg, and (Assistant Secretary of State for East Asian and Pacific Affairs) Richard Holbrooke tended to triumph in bureaucratic battles against opponents who argued for a more significant role for human rights in US-China policy, such as Jessica Tuchman Mathews of the NSC staff and Patricia Derian, the Assistant Secretary of State for Democracy, Human Rights, and Labor. During late 1978 and early 1979, Chinese participants in the "Democracy Wall" movement articulated their grievances and political aspirations through public posters, speeches, and unofficial journals. In 1979, the Chinese government suppressed this movement with little reaction from the US government.[41] The decision to break relations with the Republic of China and instead recognize the People's Republic of China would have been difficult to justify from a human rights perspective since, as Brzezinski noted, "In my opinion, there is a good deal of truth" to the claim that "Taiwan is responsive to the President's human rights stand, while the PRC is a gross violator of human rights as we understand it."[42]

Not surprisingly, Soviet officials perceived a double standard according to which the United States championed Soviet dissidents while downplaying Chinese human rights abuses. Some of this uneven application of standards resulted from US notions of geopolitical interest, the very factors that led the United States and China to improve their relations in the first place. Some also resulted from perceived trends: whereas the human rights situation in the Soviet Union was not dramatically better than it had been a decade earlier, in China there had been significant improvement since the Cultural Revolution, which had ended only a few years previously. Furthermore, some of the Carter foreign policy team, while supporting the advancement of human rights, also thought of themselves as hard-headed realists who eschewed naive efforts to take on problems, however horrible, that were beyond US capacities to solve. Oksenberg at one point criticized the CIA for injecting "the human rights issue into our China policy considerations" by producing a classified report on abuses in Chinese labor camps. Oksenberg argued that the United States lacked the leverage to accomplish anything meaningful by raising such concerns: "Let us look forward to the day when our diplomatic relations with China are such that we can begin to raise this issue, and the Chinese will have a sufficient stake in their relationship with us that they will simply have to respond."[43]

What accounts for continuities in diplomatic tactics given the different personalities and views of Nixon, Kissinger, and Carter? Secrecy, the de-emphasis of human rights concerns, and the centralization of policy formulation and execution all made sense when attempting to improve relations with the representatives of a proud nation with grievances against the outside world and a relatively poor human rights record. Although Vance advised in June 1978 that top members of Congress be kept informed in order to lessen opposition, Carter was more hesitant, responding, "as late as possible—*very* small group—in my office."[44] The desire to avoid public scrutiny seemed a useful precaution when major agreements between the United States and China (e.g., the Shanghai Communique and the normalization agreement) only seemed possible if the two sides papered over their differences and agreed to disagree. Greater public scrutiny during the negotiating process might have made such agreements more challenging if it forced diplomats to be more explicit about their disagreements, such as whether the United States would continue to sell weapons to Taiwan. As Terry Lautz discusses in Chapter 2, the issue of US arms sales to Taiwan was a major impediment to the normalization talks, and nearly prevented achieving an agreement.

Furthermore, US officials faced a strenuous domestic political environment in which the "Taiwan Lobby" desperately opposed their efforts to improve relations with the People's Republic of China. Even though the Taiwan lobby was far less formidable than it had been during the 1950s and 1960s, when McCarthyism was stronger, it still possessed loyal allies including powerful senators such as Barry Goldwater, Bob Dole, and John Tower. Nixon, who had worked both sides of the issue, warned Carter of Taiwan's "almost fanatical core of support in the nation and in the Congress."[45] The Republic of China audaciously attempted to cultivate the citizens of Georgia, lavishing attention on Carter's hometown of Plains. US policymakers also saw evidence that the Taiwan lobby sought to leverage its influence through an alliance with the "Israeli lobby."[46] Near the end of 1977, Oksenberg observed that "Israel has been drifting toward closer relations with Taiwan, with arms sales forming the link." In a memorandum, he warned that "Israel should not have major military-security links with the outcast nations of the world: South Africa, Rhodesia, the ROC [Republic of China]," suggesting instead that the United States encourage Israel to "broaden its connections with Third World countries." He also noted, "An Israeli-Taiwan connection has an impact on U.S. domestic politics, for it provides the basis for cooperation between the Taiwan and Israeli Lobbies."[47] The influence of the Taiwan lobby helps account for the perception, which Nixon and Carter shared, that secret negotiations, followed by a surprise public announcement, were the best approach when pursuing a breakthrough in US relations with the People's Republic of China.

In the longer run, however, normalization made it possible for the United States and China to develop a different sort of relationship with extensive contact between the two bureaucracies and growing society-to-society interactions. During the last two years of the Carter administration, the two countries signed "35 treaties, agreements, and protocols."[48] By the end of the Carter years, they had reached agreements on postal intercourse, textile trade, grain sales, civil aviation, trade exhibitions, exchanges of student and visiting scholars, scientific cooperation, consular relations, and many other subjects. During the decade following the establishment of relations, about 80,000 Chinese students and academics came to the United States.[49] In June 1979, Oksenberg stated that the administration had a goal that "most government agencies with the legislative mandate and with the budget to do so will have initiated programs with the Chinese counterpart agencies."[50] While Deng saw these interactions as a means to modernize China, the Carter administration (in the words of a scholarly observer) sought "to institutionalize and stabilize Sino-American relations by expanding the points of contact between the two countries to create a relationship as multifaceted and broadly based as possible."[51] The Carter administration hoped that by greatly increasing the political, economic, social, and cultural contact between the two countries, they would make it more likely that Chinese modernization would not be inimical to US interests.[52] Later in this volume, Yingyi Ma examines the experience of Chinese students in the United States as transnational actors.

Since 1949, the United States and China have not lacked grounds for dispute, given the two countries' sometimes bitter disagreements over political ideology, socioeconomic systems, their own military, diplomatic, and intelligence rivalries, and the question of who will be the dominant power in East Asia. Unfortunately, by making the Sino-American relationship more interdependent, China and the United States created more grounds for conflict in areas such as trade, human rights, intellectual property, and media depictions. Nonetheless, due to normalization, channels for handling these conflicts became more robust and regularized. By the time of the next important Sino-American agreement, in August 1982, which addressed the contentious subject of US arms sales to Taiwan, negotiations on the US side were handled where one might expect them to be in a well-functioning bureaucracy: the head of the China desk at the Department of State, overseen by the Assistant Secretary of State for East Asian and Pacific Affairs, sent instructions to and received recommendations from the US ambassador to China.[53] This was an enormous change from the subterfuges that had previously been essential to the relationship, such as Kissinger's secret trip to China and his commandeering of Department of State employees to do China-related work that they hid from their bosses, or the Carter White House's request that Roger Sullivan, a Department of State China expert, call in sick for three consecutive days to help the NSC staff complete preparations for normalization.[54] Of course, at exceptional moments, when normal diplomatic procedures broke down or seemed insufficient, such as occurred after relations deteriorated following the Chinese government's June 1989 killing of protesters at Tiananmen Square, leaders on both sides have retained the option to employ secret diplomacy to manage Sino-American relations.[55]

The success of the effort to institutionalize the relationship is evidenced by the contrast between the 1976 and 1980 elections. The change from Ford to Carter as a result of the 1976 election was not determinative of Sino-American relations, since a second Ford administration, with Kissinger as the dominant figure in US foreign policy, planned to pursue the establishment of diplomatic relations with China that the Carter administration ultimately did pursue. In contrast, the 1980 election could have had enormous ramifications for relations had Carter not succeeded in formalizing the relationship. This is because it is difficult to imagine Ronald Reagan breaking diplomatic relations with the Republic of China. In 1976, Reagan wrote in the *New York Times*, "We must neither jeopardize the safety of our long-time ally on Taiwan, nor sever our ties with it."[56] Such a commitment to the Republic of China, if enacted, would have made the normalization of relations with Communist China impossible. With such opinions in mind, Oksenberg told a diplomat from the People's Republic of China that normalization could become more difficult if it did not happen before the 1980 election because Republican support appeared to be declining.[57] Without formal diplomatic relations, it is doubtful that China would have agreed to the greatly intensified Sino-American strategic cooperation, trade, and society-to-society relations that occurred after normalization, and it is easy to imagine that China and world politics might have developed quite differently. In a famous essay about the German statesmen Otto von Bismarck, Kissinger wrote, "A society that must produce a great man in each generation to maintain its domestic or international position will doom itself," but Kissinger never put the relationship between the United States and China on a stable basis that made diplomatic virtuosity less essential.[58] In the end, perhaps the most significant influences of the Carter administration on Sino-American relations were that it institutionalized the relationship so that outsized personalities or ideologues had considerably less impact than they would previously have had, laying the foundation for a relationship of such complexity, and with so many grounds for conflict, that considerable diplomatic skill in its management was still necessary.

Notes

1 The opinions expressed in this chapter are my own personal views and do not necessarily represent the official position of the Department of State or the US government.

2 Many trends in Western historical scholarship contributed to a de-emphasis of the role of individuals, among them Marxism, social history, the *Annales* school in France, the influence of the social sciences, and an interest in "history from below."

3 Yafeng Xia and Zhi Liang, "China's Diplomacy toward the United States in the Twentieth Century: A Survey of the Literature," *Diplomatic History* 41, 2 (April 2017): 242.

4 For evidence that some US officials perceived China, rather than the Soviet Union, as the more dangerous influence on Indonesia, see the memorandum prepared for the 303 Committee (and the third footnote to this document), February 23, 1965, Document 110 in *Foreign Relations of the United States* [hereafter *FRUS*], 1964–8, Volume XXVI, Indonesia; Malaysia-Singapore; Philippines, ed. Edward C. Keefer (Washington: US GPO, 2000); Bernd Schaefer, "Introduction: Indonesia and the World in 1965," in *1965: Indonesia and the World*, ed. Bernd Schaefer and Baskara T. Wardaya (Jakarta: Goethe-Institut Indonesien & Gramedia Pustaka Utama, 2013), 5–6.

5 On Mao's motivations when playing the American card, see Roderick MacFarquhar and Michael Schoenhals, *Mao's Last Revolution* (Cambridge, MA: Belknap Press, 2006), 320.

6 For a description of the doctrinal somersaults required from supporters of Chinese foreign policy during the early 1970s, see John W. Garver, *Foreign Relations of the People's Republic of China* (Englewood Cliffs, NJ: Prentice Hall, 1993), 166–9; Chen Jian, *Mao's China and the Cold War* (Chapel Hill: University of North Carolina Press, 2001), 269–70; Yafeng Xia, *Negotiating with the Enemy: U.S.-China Talks during the Cold War, 1949–1972* (Bloomington: Indiana University Press, 2006), 176.

7 Lou Cannon, "Reagan Says U.S. Must Act to Halt Communist Gains," *Washington Post*, June 1, 1975, 11.

8 Memorandum from Habib, Gleysteen, Lord, and Solomon to Secretary of State Kissinger, July 3, 1975, Document 112 in *FRUS*, 1973–6, Volume XVIII, China, ed. David P. Nickles (Washington: US GPO, 2007).

9 Memorandum of Conversation, July 6, 1975, Document 113 in *FRUS*, 1973–6, Volume XVIII, China.

10 Lou Cannon, "Reagan See 'Sacrifice' of Taiwan by President," *Washington Post*, May 29, 1976, A4.

11 Memorandum of Conversation, May 29, 1976, Document 146 in *FRUS*, Volume XVIII, China, 1973–6.

12 Kazushi Minami, "Re-Examining the End of Mao's Revolution: China's Changing Statecraft and Sino-American Relations, 1973–1978," *Cold War History* 16, 4 (2016): 361–5; Memorandum of Conversation, October 20, 1975, Document 122 in *FRUS*, 1973–6, Volume XVIII, China; Memorandum of Conversation, July 8, 1976, Document 157 in *FRUS*, 1973–6, Volume XVIII, China.

13 Li Jie, "China's Domestic Politics and the Normalization of Sino-U.S. Relations, 1969–1979," in *Normalization of U.S.-China Relations: An International History*, ed. William Kirby, Robert Ross, and Gong Li (Cambridge, MA: Harvard University Press, 2005), 66–72. The "Gang of Four" was led by Jiang Qing, Mao's last wife. The other members were prominent figures during the Cultural Revolution and Mao loyalists: Wang Hongwen, Yao Wenyuan, and Zhang Chunqiao.

14 Jie, "China's Domestic Politics and the Normalization of Sino-U.S. Relations," 72–8.

15 Jimmy Carter, "Address Announcing Candidacy for the Democratic Presidential Nomination at the National Press Club in Washington, DC," December 12, 1974, The American Presidency Project (http://www.presidency.ucsb.edu/ws/index. php?pid=77821).

16 John Dillin, "Jimmy Carter—Where He Stands," *Christian Science Monitor*, March 11, 1976, 9.

17 Memorandum from Brzezinski to Carter, May 24, 1977, Document 28, *FRUS*, 1977–80, Volume XIII, China, ed. David P. Nickles (Washington: US GPO, 2013).

18 Zbigniew Brzezinski, *Power and Principle: Memoirs of the National Security Adviser, 1977–1981* (New York: Farrar, Straus, Giroux, 1983), 200.

19 Memorandum of Conversation, July 30, 1977, Document 41 in *FRUS*, 1977–80, Volume XIII, China.

20 James Mann, *About Face: A History of America's Curious Relationship with China, from Nixon to Clinton* (New York: Alfred A. Knopf, 1999), 79. In addition to having been a prominent member of the previous administration, Bush may have been influenced by having served as chief of the US Liaison Office in Beijing during the Ford administration.

21 On Deng's initially accommodating behavior upon his return to power in 1977, see Ezra F. Vogel, *Deng Xiaoping and the Transformation of China* (Cambridge, MA: Belknap Press, 2011), 200.

22	Justin Vaisse, *Zbigniew Brzezinski: America's Grand Strategist* (Cambridge, MA: Harvard University Press, 2018), 314.

23	Telegram 17617 from Moscow Embassy to the Department of State, Access to Archival Databases https://aad.archives.gov/aad/, the US National Archives, College Park, Maryland.

24	Cyrus Vance, *Hard Choices: Critical Years in America's Foreign Policy* (New York: Simon and Schuster, 1983), 78–9. See also Breck Walker, "'Friends, But Not Allies'— Cyrus Vance and the Normalization of Relations with China," *Diplomatic History* 33, 4 (September 2009): 593–4.

25	Brzezinski, *Power and Principle*, 196.

26	Edward C. Keefer, *Harold Brown: Offsetting the Soviet Military Challenge, 1977–1981* (Washington: Historical Office of the Office of the Secretary of Defense, 2017), 395–6.

27	Summary of Conclusions of a Policy Review Committee Meeting, June 27, 1977, Document 34 in *FRUS*, 1977–80, Volume XIII, China.

28	Memorandum of Conversation, February 8, 1977, Document 5 in *FRUS*, 1977–80, Volume XIII, China.

29	Memorandum of Conversation, January 29, 1979, Document 202 in *FRUS*, 1977–80, Volume XIII, China.

30	Memorandum of Conversation, January 29, 1979, Document 205 in *FRUS*, 1977–80, Volume XIII, China; Betty Glad, *An Outsider in the White House: Jimmy Carter, His Advisors, and the Making of American Foreign Policy* (Ithaca: Cornell University Press, 2009), 238–9.

31	Vogel, *Deng Xiaoping*, 311–12, 321–3, 332; Li, "China's Domestic Politics and the Normalization of Sino-U.S. Relations," 82–3.

32	Minami, "Re-examining the End of Mao's Revolution," 369–75.

33	Many of the claims grew out of the mutual confiscation of property that occurred during the Chinese revolution. On the US side, there were nearly seven hundred claimants, among which were organizations and individuals, to $196.6 million (settled at 41 cents on the dollar or $80.5 million), but the biggest claims were made by a number of large corporations (Boise Cascade, Exxon, General Electric, Caltex, and International Telephone and Telegraph). In turn, the United States agreed to release Chinese assets estimated at $80.5 million. (Judith Miller, "China-Claims Agreement Pleases U.S. Companies," *New York Times*, March 3, 1979, 29.) In addition, Blumenthal told Carter that the People's Republic of China, as the successor government to the Republic of China, owed $26 million to the Export/Import bank, although the Chinese government argued that Taiwan should pay this sum. Blumenthal stated that private bond holders had claims against China, but that "bond holders take risks and this is not a matter of concern to us." Memorandum of Conversation, March 6, 1979, Document 225 in *FRUS*, 1977–1980, Volume XIII, China.

34	Regarding Carter's desire to grant most favored nation status to both China and the Soviet Union, see Jimmy Carter, *Keeping Faith: Memoirs of a President* (Toronto: Bantam Books, 1982), 201–2. For an overview of Carter's China policy after mid-1978, see memorandum from Oksenberg to Brzezinski, December 19, 1980, Document 327 in *FRUS*, 1977–80, Volume XIII, China.

35	Harry Harding, *A Fragile Relationship: The United States and China since 1972* (Washington: The Brookings Institution, 1992), 99.

36	Michel Oksenberg, "A Decade of Sino-American Relations," *Foreign Affairs* 61, 1 (Fall 1982): 178.

37 Memorandum from Oksenberg to Brzezinski, December 19, 1978, Document 175
in *FRUS*, 1977–1980, Volume XIII, China; Letter From Former President Nixon to
President Carter, December 20, 1978, Document 178 in *FRUS*, 1977–80, Volume XIII,
China. Of course Carter, unlike Nixon, did not exclude his own secretary of state from
involvement in China diplomacy.

38 Carter's China policy, as James Walker Smith has noted regarding his Panama policy,
challenges "the claim of some historians that Carter intended his human rights policy
as a replacement for Cold War containment." See Smith's H-Diplo FRUS Review of
Laura R. Kolar, ed., *FRUS*, 1977–80, Vol. XXIX, Panama (No. 31, July 11, 2017).

39 Presidential Review Memorandum/NSC-28, May 20, 1977, Document 46 in *FRUS*,
1977–80, Volume II, Human Rights and Humanitarian Affairs, ed. Kristin Ahlberg
(Washington: US GPO, 2013).

40 Study Prepared by the Ad Hoc Inter-Agency Group on Human Rights and Foreign
Assistance, August 15, 1977, Document 73 in *FRUS*, 1977–80, Volume II, Human
Rights and Humanitarian Affairs.

41 See memorandum from Mathews to Brzezinski, May 17, 1978, Document 107 in
FRUS, 1977–80, Volume XIII, China; Mann, *About Face*, 100–3; Glad, *An Outsider
in the White House*, 237. A Department of State official criticized the severity of
the prison sentence (but not the conviction itself) imposed on Wei Jinsheng, a
prominent dissident who participated in the Democracy Wall movement. See also the
memorandum from Oksenberg to Brzezinski, October 17, 1979, Document 279 in
FRUS, 1977–80, Volume XIII, China.

42 Memorandum from Brzezinski to Carter, July 29, 1977, Document 40 in *FRUS*,
1977–80, China.

43 Memorandum from Oksenberg to Brzezinski, June 20, 1977, Document 33 in *FRUS*,
1977–80, Volume XIII, China. In a later memo, Oksenberg made a similar statement
about anticipating "the day when we can speak more forthrightly about the [human
rights] situation" in China, and also argued that the United States should not criticize
Khmer Rouge atrocities in Cambodia because doing so would be hypocritical moral
posturing given recent history: "the defense of human rights is a privilege which
irresponsible nations should not seek to exercise." Memorandum from Oksenberg to
Brzezinski, April 18, 1978, Document 22 in *FRUS*, 1977–80, Volume XXII, Southeast
Asia and the Pacific.

44 Memorandum from Vance to Carter, June 13, 1978, Document 119 in *FRUS*, 1977–80,
Volume XIII, China; Vance, *Hard Choices*, 118.

45 Letter from Nixon to Carter, December 20, 1978, Document 178 in *FRUS*, 1977–80,
Volume XIII, China.

46 Memorandum from Brzezinski to Carter, July 29, 1977, Document 40 in *FRUS*, 1977–
80, Volume XIII, China.

47 Robert Gates, who was a special assistant to Brzezinski on the NSC staff, returned the
memo to Oksenberg with Aaron's request that it be rewritten: "With some emphasis,
David asked me to tell you to avoid sending memos to him that contain such phrases
as 'deter Israel's drift toward Taiwan,' 'links with the outcast nations of the world,' and
'cooperation between the Taiwan and Israeli lobbies.'" Memorandum from Oksenberg
to the president's deputy assistant for National Security Affairs (David Aaron),
December 16, 1977, Document 70 in *FRUS*, 1977–80, Volume XIII, China.

48 Oksenberg, "A Decade of Sino-American Relations," 191.

49 Harding, *A Fragile Relationship*, 96–9; Mann, *About Face*, 105; Memorandum from Brzezinski to Carter, October 10, 1980, Document 322 in *FRUS*, 1977–80, Volume XIII, China.

50 Harding, *A Fragile Relationship*, 96–9, 408 n88.

51 Harding, *A Fragile Relationship*, 98.

52 Robert S. Ross, *Negotiating Cooperation: The United States and China, 1969–1989* (Stanford: Stanford University Press, 1995), 157. Many scholars have argued that the rise of countries to great power status is frequently associated with major wars. For example, see Robert Gilpin, *War and Change in World Politics* (Cambridge, UK: Cambridge University Press, 1981); Graham T. Allison, *Destined for War: Can America and China Escape Thucydides's Trap?* (Boston, MA: Houghton Mifflin Harcourt, 2017).

53 John H. Holdridge, *Crossing the Divide: An Insider's Account of Normalization of U.S.-China Relations* (Lanham, MD: Rowman & Littlefield, 1997), 230–1.

54 James Lilley with Jeffrey Lilley, *China Hands: Nine Decades of Adventure, Espionage, and Diplomacy in Asia* (New York: Public Affairs, 2004), 153–4, 156–8; Nicholas Platt, *China Boys: How U.S. Relations with the PRC Began and Grew* (Washington: New Academia/Vellum Books, 2009), 68–9; Vogel, *Deng Xiaoping*, 329.

55 Maureen Dowd, "2 U.S. Officials Went to Beijing Secretly in July," *New York Times*, December 19, 1989, A1; Vogel, *Deng Xiaoping*, 650–1, 653–4.

56 Ronald Reagan, "Expanding Our Ties with China," *New York Times*, July 28, 1976, 24.

57 Memorandum of Conversation, August 26, 1977, Document 322 in *FRUS, 1977–1980*, Volume XIII, China.

58 Henry A. Kissinger, "The White Revolutionary: Reflections on Bismarck," *Daedalus* 97, 3 (Summer, 1968): 889.

2

Unstoppable Force Meets Immovable Object: Normalizing US–China Relations, 1977–9

Terry Lautz[1]

Introduction

President Richard Nixon's historic trip to China in February 1972 opened a door that had been locked shut for more than two decades. Yet it would take nearly seven more years to establish full diplomatic relations between the People's Republic of China (PRC) and the United States of America. It was as though Beijing and Washington were engaged to be married, but could not agree on the terms for the wedding. The sticking point was that Washington would have to divorce Taipei—the Republic of China (ROC) on Taiwan—in order to consummate its relationship with mainland China. From an American perspective, China seemed to be an unstoppable force and Taiwan an immovable object on the road to normalization.

The United States acknowledged a one-China principle in the 1972 Shanghai Communique, but official relations with the PRC existed in a diplomatic limbo so long as the United States maintained an embassy in Taipei and Taiwan had an ambassador in Washington. Beijing and Washington opened liaison offices with a small number of staff in each other's capitals in 1973, but the scope of their operations was limited. It was not possible to exchange ambassadors, set up embassies and consulates, arrange aviation and shipping agreements, or set up long-term cultural and educational exchanges. The two governments could not negotiate trade deals, businesses could not set up offices, and journalists could not be in residence. The prolonged process of untying the Taiwan knot was called normalization, implying that the absence of relations with China was abnormal.

The US commitment to Taiwan, which was not fixed until the outbreak of the Korean War in 1950, was the legacy of a Cold War policy to isolate Communist China. Derecognizing Taiwan in order to accept the reality of Mao Zedong's new China posed a serious domestic political problem for any American president. There would be hell to pay with the conservative Republican wing of Congress, whose members had accused the Truman administration of the "loss of China." Even in the 1970s, nothing less than US dependability and credibility, already questioned by the failing war in Vietnam, was at stake. Taiwan's supporters believed the United States should not under any circumstances betray a close and loyal friend that was an anti-Communist ally.

Nixon wanted to achieve normalization during his second term, but his resignation from office in 1974 prevented him from doing so. Gerald Ford, an unelected president, hoped to proceed, but the Communist victory in Vietnam in April 1975 made further progress impossible. Jimmy Carter was determined to get the job done after his election in 1976, but was delayed by the need to get Senate ratification of treaties returning the Panama Canal zone to Panama.

From the PRC's perspective, the "liberation" of Taiwan and "reunification" with the mainland was unfinished business of the civil war between Mao Zedong and Chiang Kai-shek, who had retreated to Taiwan (then known in English as Formosa) with the remnants of the Nationalist army. Mao and Zhou Enlai made it clear to Nixon and Henry Kissinger that anything short of a complete break in US diplomatic relations with Taiwan was unacceptable if Washington wanted relations with Beijing. There was little room for compromise, and power struggles during the final throes of the Cultural Revolution meant that no Chinese leader had enough authority to negotiate an agreement with the United States. It was only after Deng Xiaoping rose to power, after the deaths of Mao and Zhou, that a path to normalization seemed possible.

Policy analysts, scholars, and various participants, including President Carter, have published accounts of the normalization process. Some of these draw on documents that became available through the Jimmy Carter Library circa 1999. It was not until 2013, however, that the State Department's Office of the Historian published the most comprehensive and authoritative record, edited by David P. Nickles and Adam M. Howard, in the *Foreign Relations of the United States (FRUS)* series.[2]

The *FRUS* documents show that a successful outcome of the negotiations between the United States and China was not guaranteed. While the United States did agree to sever diplomatic relations with Taiwan—in addition to removing American troops and terminating its mutual defense treaty—normalization was achieved in January 1979 in spite of a fundamental disagreement over continued US arms sales to Taiwan. The problem was not resolved and remains a thorn in the side of Sino-American relations to this day.

Why did the United States insist on maintaining a military relationship with Taiwan? Why wasn't this issue settled when diplomatic relations were established between Beijing and Washington? And why was China willing to go ahead with normalization if continued US arms sales to Taiwan were unacceptable?

The Uncertain Road to Normalization

Concerned about congressional resistance, the Carter administration threw a blanket of secrecy over the negotiations, which started in earnest in the summer of 1978. Breaking the stalemate with Beijing might prove impossible if opponents in Congress believed that Taiwan was being "sold down the river." For this reason, only a handful of people in the US government were involved and the most important negotiations were held in Beijing where it was easier to avoid publicity. Communications between the White House and the US Liaison Office (USLO) in Beijing were handled through the highly classified "Voyager" channel controlled by the CIA. Secretary of State Cyrus Vance and a few others at the State Department were kept informed, but the White House controlled the process from start to finish.

Only two Americans managed the final stages of negotiations in Beijing: Leonard Woodcock and J. Stapleton Roy. Woodcock, in his late sixties, arrived as head of the USLO in July 1977. The tough and taciturn former leader of the United Auto Workers in Detroit had no China background or previous experience as a diplomat, but was a seasoned negotiator with a reputation for integrity and strong political connections with members of Congress. Carter wrote in his memoirs that he "admired Leonard personally, and knew him to be quiet but forceful, a man whose age, experience, and demeanor would be an advantage in dealing with the Chinese leaders. Further, my choice of a person of his stature in the American community was a clear signal to the Chinese that we wanted closer relations." Carter assured Woodcock that he would "take on the political responsibility" for selling normal relations to the American people. "The only remaining obstacle, of course, is our commitment not to abandon the peaceful existence of the Chinese who live on Taiwan."[3]

J. Stapleton ("Stape") Roy was a career US foreign service officer in his early forties, chosen by Woodcock to be his deputy in Beijing. Fluent in Chinese, Roy was born to missionary parents who taught at Nanjing University, served in Taiwan early in his career, and was stationed in Moscow when Nixon met with Mao in 1972. He was relatively junior for the Liaison Office position, but having worked for three years as deputy director of the State Department's China desk in Washington, he was extremely well-informed about the history of Nixon and Kissinger's secret discussions with the Chinese. (The conditions proposed in those talks provided the template for normalization.)

Woodcock, by his own admission, tended to be an optimist, while Roy played the role of careful and cautious pessimist. As a professional diplomat, he believed his job was to anticipate problems and "try to look for things that could go wrong.... I would always point out what I saw as potential stumbling blocks that still lay ahead." Roy would present his view, Woodcock would give his assessment, and Roy would draft memos within those parameters. "We never had a disagreement in terms of where we ended up," Roy told me.

Despite their completely different backgrounds and personalities, the two men proved to be an ideal team for the job. Woodcock knew how to listen and when to push an issue, while Roy had a nuanced understanding of political and cultural differences between Americans and Chinese. Woodcock later recalled, "One of the best things that I did was choosing Stape to be the Deputy, because he was worth his weight in gold through the whole period." Roy, who has strong misgivings about amateurs doing diplomacy, returned the compliment: "What I liked about Woodcock was he was truly a professional negotiator. He had an uncanny ability to sense where you were in a negotiation" and to say the right thing at the right time.[4] Roy drafted detailed reports, now available in the *Foreign Relations of the United States*, on their meetings in Beijing for Woodcock's review and approval before sending them directly to the White House through the secret back channel. During periodic trips to Washington, Woodcock coordinated with Zbigniew Brzezinski, the National Security Council director, and Roy worked with Michel Oksenberg, the NSC's China specialist.

After several months of preliminary discussions in Washington, New York, and Beijing, an agreement for normalization finally started to take shape in early December 1978. The initial breakthrough came when Woodcock and Roy met with Vice Foreign Minister Han Nianlong on December 4 in the Liaoning Room of the Great Hall of the People. (Foreign Minister Huang Hua was in the hospital with flu and pneumonia.) The Americans had no official interpreter of their own, but Roy, who took close to verbatim notes, was able to vouch for the accuracy of the translations.

Han informed Woodcock and Roy that the PRC was prepared to announce a joint communique on January 1, 1979, now that the United States had agreed to China's three conditions: to sever diplomatic relations with Taiwan (which the United States recognized as the Republic of China); to withdraw its military forces from Taiwan; and to abrogate its mutual defense treaty with Taiwan that dated from 1954. Vice Foreign Minister Han agreed that the United States could continue people-to-people contacts with Taiwan and maintain nongovernmental agencies there. This compromise was the same formula used by Japan when it broke relations with Taiwan and recognized the PRC in 1973. A major difference was that Japan had no formal security ties with Taiwan.

Han then raised a potential roadblock, saying, "We have clearly stated our emphatic objection to the U.S. expressed intention of continuing its arms sales to Taiwan after normalization. Such sales would only convince the Chinese people that the U.S. government is still using armed force to support the Chiang [Ching-kuo] clique's actions against them and is still interfering in China's internal affairs."[5] He also made it clear that China would not make a commitment to a peaceful resolution of the Taiwan problem, as requested by the United States. How and when the PRC would "liberate" Taiwan would be China's decision, declared Han.

The two sides had opposing views on arms sales. The United States believed continued sales were essential, not only to reassure domestic opponents in Congress that an ally was not being ditched, but also to discourage China from invading Taiwan. The Carter administration reasoned that US military support would give Taipei the confidence to consider some form of reunification with the mainland at a future date. The Chinese, on the other hand, were convinced that arms sales would only make reunification more difficult and would increase the likelihood of their having to use force. Despite the impasse, Han told Woodcock and Roy at the end of their discussion that Vice Premier Deng Xiaoping would like to meet them at an early date. Deng, who was in the process of consolidating his position as China's paramount leader, was ready to move forward and finalize the terms for normalization.[6]

"A New and Potentially Decisive Phase"

Nine days later, on the morning of Wednesday, December 13, Deng Xiaoping received Leonard Woodcock and Stapleton Roy in the Jiangsu Room of the Great

Hall of the People. Deng happily accepted President Carter's invitation for a senior Chinese leader to visit the United States after diplomatic relations had been established. He then raised two substantive issues during the one-hour and twenty-five-minute meeting. First, he strongly urged the United States to include an anti-hegemony statement—China's code word for the opposition to the Soviet Union—in the communique announcing normalization. The same language appeared in the 1972 Shanghai Communique and should be included again, said Deng. Second, he asked that no new weapons be sold to Taiwan during the one-year period while the US–Taiwan security treaty was terminated. Nothing was said by either side about arms sales after the one-year hiatus.

Woodcock cabled Brzezinski and Vance that the meeting "has launched us into a new and potentially decisive phase of the normalization process—a phase fraught with both opportunities and pitfalls for both sides.... It quickly became evident from Teng's [Deng's] approach that he was determined to pin down a normalization agreement at an early date. In the process, many seemingly troublesome issues were brushed aside.... In short, on a wide range of issues, many of considerable substantive importance, Teng opted for movement rather than legalistic quibbling over details."

But Woodcock's report, authored by Roy, went on to caution that Deng "did not explicitly confirm that we could resume arms sales once the Treaty [with Taiwan] had formally lost effect [at the end of 1979].... [W]e cannot blithely assume that the Chinese have given us a green light for arms sales from 1980 on. Nevertheless, this was the distinct implication of Teng's comments." Deng had been decisive and it seemed as though the pieces of the normalization puzzle finally were falling into place.[7]

After receiving further instructions from the White House, Woodcock and Roy met with Deng for a second time at 9:00 p.m. on Thursday, December 14. (Two other Chinese officials as well as an interpreter and a notetaker were present. Woodcock's secretary also attended this meeting.) Deng agreed to Carter's request to advance the normalization announcement to December 16—which would be the 15th in Washington—because Carter was concerned that any leaks could torpedo the entire process. Deng reviewed the text of the joint communique and agreed to the draft with only minor changes. Woodcock confirmed that the United States would not sell any weapons or military equipment to Taiwan during 1979 while the Mutual Defense Treaty was being terminated, as Deng had requested, but stated that any arms or equipment already in the pipeline would be delivered. Deng agreed to this and to a proposed US unilateral statement. He then read China's unilateral statement that Woodcock accepted without any changes. These ancillary documents, highly unusual in the annals of diplomacy, allowed each side to express caveats or differences, just as they had in the 1972 Shanghai Communique.[8]

Both parties left the meeting thinking that the deal was done. Woodcock cabled Washington that Deng was "clearly elated by the outcome of our session, called this a most important matter, and asked that his personal thanks be conveyed to the President, Secretary Vance and Dr. Brzezinski." Woodcock added, "There is no doubt in my mind that we have clearly put on the record our position with respect to arms sales."[9] But this would not prove to be the case.

Almost a Deal Breaker

After sifting through the record of negotiations with the Chinese, the White House was concerned that Deng still did not understand that the United States intended to resume arms sales to Taiwan after a one-year hiatus. Woodcock was therefore instructed to arrange yet another meeting with Deng. He and Roy dreaded doing so, but had to agree there was room for a possible misunderstanding. Roy recalls, "We were trying to be ruthlessly honest in terms of assessing where the Chinese were. That's when the message came in [from the White House] saying we have to go back to Deng and be very explicit on the subject.... We knew that Deng would not be happy."[10]

Woodcock and Roy met with Deng for a third time at the Great Hall at 4:00 p.m. on Friday, December 15. In an interview with Michel Oksenberg a few years later, Woodcock remembers Deng's outraged response when he was informed about the US position on providing military supplies to Taiwan: "Why are you raising this arms sales question again? His look as much as said: You stupid son of a bitch, we know what you're going to do and you know what we're going to do. Then he thumps the arm of his chair and says, 'We absolutely will never agree. We can never agree.' [He was] absolutely opposed."[11]

Looking back on this crucial encounter, Roy is convinced that Deng believed the United States would end arms sales to Taiwan after 1979. Deng was genuinely angry, says Roy. "He didn't just sit there. He actually stood up and stormed around for about ten minutes. He was truly upset. Here we were and we thought we'd come to the conclusion of these difficult negotiations and all of a sudden we had reopened an issue which was a deal breaker from his standpoint. It was only after he had calmed down when he turned to Woodcock and said to him, 'What should we do?' That's when Woodcock said he thought it would be easier to deal with this problem from within a diplomatic relationship than without a diplomatic relationship. His judgment was that we should go ahead. That's when Deng said, 'Okay.'" As the two Americans walked down the wide stairs of the Great Hall to their car, Woodcock told Roy that he thought for a moment "everything was going down the drain."[12]

Woodcock and Roy reported to Washington on the confrontation with Deng, which took place less than a day before normalization was scheduled to be announced. "When I confirmed our intention to continue selling arms to Taiwan after 1979," wrote Woodcock, "Teng stated emphatically that he could not agree and said that 'such sales would block efforts to find a rational means of settling the Taiwan issue peacefully'.... I pointed out that American political realities were such that no administration could be in the position of denying arms to Taiwan, and that we did not expect the Chinese to agree to such sales. He repeatedly stressed the importance of having the President avoid direct answers on arms sales that would force the Chinese into responding.... In short, Teng will not give us a free ride. I continue to believe we should move ahead."[13]

After the nearly fatal meeting with Deng on December 15, there were still some loose ends to tie up before the public announcement scheduled for the following morning. On that cold, dark night Roy rode his bicycle—which was easier than getting a car and driver at a late hour—through Beijing's deserted streets to the Chinese Foreign Ministry. Contrary to Deng's wishes, Carter had decided that arms sales could not be ignored in explaining the decision to normalize relations to the American public. Roy therefore provided the text of what the president would say about arms sales in response to a planted question from the press, and the Chinese gave Roy what they would say in response. Roy informed the National Security Council that Carter's text had been delivered and confirmed that the Chinese response had been received before returning to his apartment. "When I got back into bed around 3:30 a.m. and my wife woke up, that was the first time that I revealed to her what was going on."[14]

In Taipei, President Chiang Ching-kuo was awakened around 2:20 a.m. to meet with US Ambassador Leonard Unger who told him that a joint communique recognizing Beijing and breaking relations with the ROC would be issued later that morning. Informing him in the middle of the night, only hours before the announcement in Washington and Beijing, was a terrible loss of face for Chiang, who reacted in shock and anger. He said that for the United States to acknowledge the Chinese position that there is only one China and Taiwan is part of China "in effect turns Taiwan over to the PRC." Unger tried to reassure him that the United States would work with Taiwan "to preserve and expand our constructive relationship" and mentioned continued access to American weapons to underscore his point.[15] This did little to mollify Chiang or assuage the way he had been treated. Like Chiang, key members of the US Congress learned about the agreement to switch diplomatic relations only a short time before Carter's public announcement.

President Carter announced the normalization of diplomatic relations between the United States and China on television and radio at 9:00 p.m. on Friday, December 15 in Washington, which was 10:00 a.m. on Saturday, December 16 in Beijing. Hua Guofeng, chairman of the Communist Party, held a press conference to announce the news to the Chinese people. The joint communique stated that the United States of America and the PRC would recognize each other and establish diplomatic relations two weeks later on January 1, 1979.

Carter said the decision to recognize the PRC as "the sole legal Government of China" marked the acceptance of a "simple reality" that would contribute to "the cause of peace in Asia and the world." In its unilateral document accompanying the communique, the United States stated that it would break relations with Taiwan, withdraw its military forces, and end the 1954 Mutual Defense Treaty. "The American people and the people of Taiwan will maintain commercial, cultural, and other relations without official representation and without government diplomatic relations." The United States expressed its interest in a peaceful resolution of the Taiwan issue—which China had refused to do—and did not specifically mention arms sales. Hua Guofeng, however, made an oral statement that China "absolutely would not agree" to the sale of weapons to Taiwan.[16]

Deng's Decision to Normalize

The driving force for the United States and China to normalize was their shared concern about the Soviet Union's global ambitions. But what explains the confusion and misunderstanding over arms sales to Taiwan that almost derailed the process?

The Americans were well aware that continuing to supply weapons to the ROC might put normalization out of reach. President Carter spoke about "the restrained sale of some very carefully selected defensive arms" when he met with Ambassador Chai Zemin, head of China's Liaison Office, in Washington on September 19, 1978. Carter also told Chai, "the people of Taiwan have the scientific capability for the development of atomic weapons, and we feel some relations with us are important to prevent this dangerous development." The Chinese ambassador gave an unambiguous reply: "[F]or the U.S. to continue to sell weapons to the Chiang Clique would not be in conformity with the spirit of the Shanghai Communique."[17]

Foreign Minister Huang Hua was even more adamant when he met with Cyrus Vance and Leonard Woodcock in New York on October 3, telling them that Washington's insistence on providing military support to Taiwan "only shows that you have not yet made up your mind to normalize Sino-U.S. Relations." He allowed for no flexibility on this issue. "The U.S. should clearly understand that this is a question concerning China's sovereignty and territorial integrity and that it is an important matter of principle.... We are firmly opposed to any form of 'two Chinas,' 'one China—one Taiwan,' 'one China—two governments,' and so on."[18]

It seems, however, that Deng Xiaoping was willing to ignore this unresolved issue during the countdown to normalization. In his first two meetings with Woodcock and Roy, he focused on the suspension of arms sales during 1979 while the US security treaty with Taiwan was being terminated and was concerned with getting the United States to agree to an "anti-hegemony" statement directed against the Soviet Union. Neither side tackled the question of weapons sales to Taiwan after 1979.

Other factors may have come into play. First, Carter's decision to announce the communique in mid-December, rather than January 1 as originally planned, added more pressure to close the deal. Second, the American negotiators would have been exhausted by the nonstop, back-and-forth communications with Washington, which was thirteen hours different from Beijing. And third, working in two languages added an additional layer of complexity and increased the likelihood of miscommunication, despite Roy's fluency in Chinese and the skill of the Chinese interpreter, Ms. Shi Yenhua. Under a tight deadline to reach the finish line, it seems that both sides heard what they wanted to hear on arms sales.

"Looking back on it," says Roy, "you can assume that everything was going to fall into place. But that wasn't necessarily the case. Some people in retrospect say the Chinese were always prepared to let us continue arms sales, [that] they knew it had to happen. That's not true at all. I think Deng had sold the deal to his colleagues by saying that we would be stopping arms sales."[19]

Yet if the Chinese were so strongly opposed to arms sales to Taiwan, why was Deng willing to go ahead with normalization? Roy points to two factors that the US side was not aware of and was unable to assess at the time. The first was the Third Plenum of the Chinese Communist Party's 11th Central Committee, convened from December 18 to 22, where Deng consolidated his power and embarked on a plan of "reform and opening up" to modernize China's economy. To achieve his goal, he believed it was essential to have access to American science, technology, education, trade, and investment. The second factor was Deng's determination to use military force to "teach

Vietnam a lesson," a decision triggered by a Treaty of Friendship and Cooperation signed by the Soviet Union and Vietnam in Moscow on November 4, 1978. According to Roy, "there was a real risk that the Soviet Union might create problems on China's [northern] border if China attacked Vietnam. Having diplomatic relations with the U.S. would be a deterrent to the USSR."[20]

Roy's explanation is borne out by the *FRUS* record of Deng's discussions with President Carter when he came to Washington in late January 1979.[21]The declassified memos of their discussions show that Deng was preoccupied with growing Soviet influence. Vietnam's December 25, 1978 invasion of Cambodia [Kampuchea] to overthrow the Khmer Rouge made Deng more determined to punish Vietnam. Carter told Deng that a military strike against Vietnam would be a "serious mistake" but voiced no public criticism. Deng said his decision was firm and on February 17, not long after his return to Beijing, China attacked Vietnam.

Deng also asked for US economic and technical assistance with China's Four Modernizations: agriculture, industry, national defense, and science and technology. All four are "inter-related," he told Carter, but "to solve the agricultural problem is one of the most fundamental of our four modernizations.... We hope you can help us."[22]

When the Taiwan question finally came up in their third meeting, Carter told Deng that "any reference to patience or peaceful resolution on your part to the Congress or to the [American] public would be very helpful." Deng said in response, "We Chinese cannot hide that Taiwan is part of China" and asked that both the American and Japanese governments "urge Taiwan authorities to engage in negotiations with our government.... Please do not create a condition under which Chiang Ching-kuo could thrust his tail to the skies and think he has nothing to fear and thereby prevent negotiations. Because if Chiang Ching-kuo simply refuses to conduct negotiations with us, what else can we do [but use military force]?" Deng warned there were two circumstances under which China would not use peaceful means to resolve the issue. "One situation is when the Taiwan authorities just absolutely refuse to talk with us.... Another situation would be for the Soviet Union to go into Taiwan. I think if that were to take place then maybe both our countries will work together to solve the problem."

Knowing he could not reverse the US decision to sell arms to Taiwan, Deng asked the American government to be "very prudent." He dismissed any distinction between defensive and offensive weapons. "Regardless of what defensive weapon it might be, it would not be difficult for them to cross Taiwan Strait." He reassured Carter that China would adopt "a fair and reasonable policy and will try our very best to use peaceful means to solve the Taiwan problem. On this question," said Deng, "we have patience, but this patience cannot be unlimited."[23]

Conclusion

Carter and Deng shared two major goals in agreeing to establish full diplomatic relations between the United States and China in 1979. One was to contain the USSR's ambitions and encourage Moscow to agree to limit its nuclear arms. The other was to promote China's economic development in order for the Asia Pacific to be a more stable, peaceful, and prosperous region. Deng's determination to make China wealthy and powerful dovetailed with America's interest in the potentially vast China market as well as a long-held ambition to remake China in its own image.

The Taiwan question delayed the normalization process for seven years, and because of the US position on arms sales, a full resolution proved to be impossible. To this day, as historian Steven Goldstein writes, "the fundamental issues that created confrontation and deadlock in the Taiwan Strait remain unsettled." Normalization "neither eliminated the Taiwan issue as a divisive element nor permitted the disentanglement of the United States from the legacy of the Chinese Civil War embodied in cross-strait relations."[24]

Since normalization, American presidents have regularly stumbled over Taiwan. Soon after diplomatic relations were established, Republican presidential candidate Ronald Reagan caused an uproar when he advocated the restoration of official relations with Taiwan. After becoming president, he backed down and agreed to a communique in August 1982 stating that the United States "intends to reduce gradually the sales of arms to Taiwan, leading over a period of time to a final resolution." This has not happened. In 1995, President Clinton, pressured by the US Congress, allowed Taiwan president Lee Teng-hui to visit Cornell University, his alma mater. Beijing accused the United States of supporting two Chinas and attempting to sabotage cross-strait relations. President George W. Bush declared in April 1999 that the United States "would do whatever it took to help Taiwan defend itself." But in December 2003, he admonished Taiwan president Chen Shui-bian—who advocated for independence—not to make unilateral decisions that would change the status quo between Taiwan and China.

In December 2016, president-elect Donald Trump's phone call with Taiwan's president Tsai Ying-wen, suggested that the Trump administration might seek to upgrade US relations with Taipei. Trump seemed to believe that Taiwan could be used to leverage better deals with Beijing on trade and North Korea. After his inauguration, Trump reversed course, affirming with China's president Xi Jinping the US commitment to a "one China" policy. In 2018, the US Senate and House unanimously passed the Taiwan Travel Act which encourages visits between US and Taiwanese officials "at all levels." President Trump quietly signed the bill into law in March, reversing a policy observed since 1979.

Taiwan remains a source of basic mistrust and misunderstanding between China and the United States. Some Chinese believe the United States only pays lip service to "one China." As evidence of American hypocrisy, they point to the Taiwan Relations Act (TRA), passed by Congress in April 1979, which authorizes the United States to sell arms and provide training, conduct trade, lend money, recognize the passports of Taiwanese citizens, and grant its diplomats immunity from US law. Critics in China believe Washington's support for Taiwan is evidence of a larger conspiracy to block China's reunification and oppose its rise as a regional and global power.

If anything, the Taiwan conundrum has grown more complicated since the island became a democracy in the 1990s. Most of its population now consider themselves to be Taiwanese, not Chinese, which suggests they no longer accept the claim that Taiwan is a province of China. This means that US policy—which acknowledges the position that "all Chinese on either side of the Taiwan Strait maintain there is but one China and that Taiwan is a part of China"—is effectively meaningless.

The United States is caught in a bind. It does not want the island to move in the direction of declaring independence, which would provoke Beijing's retaliation and threaten peace in the entire region. Nor does it want China to absorb Taiwan so long as its population of 23 million is opposed to unification with the PRC.

The nettlesome arms sales problem was highlighted once again in June 2017 when the Trump administration approved the sale of $1.42 billion in radar, missiles, torpedoes, and other weapons to upgrade Taiwan's defense capabilities. As in the past, Beijing lodged formal diplomatic protests in response.[25] This ritualistic pattern of periodic deals followed by stern protests has gone on for nearly forty years. Because China could easily overwhelm Taiwan militarily, some argue that US arms sales are increasingly symbolic. Others believe that continued military support is essential to discourage the PRC from seizing Taiwan.

For the United States, Taiwan is both an albatross and a beacon of freedom and democracy. Washington wants to avoid being entrapped by Taiwan through a military conflict with China, but cannot afford to walk away and disown the issue. As a small, prosperous democratic society threatened by a massive authoritarian state, Taiwan, which depends on the United States for its survival, is an emblem of America's commitments and values. For China, however, Taiwan is an obstacle to a unified nation, a threat to the legitimacy of the Chinese Communist Party, and a potential danger to the nation's security. For the Taiwanese, an overwhelming majority of its people favor continued autonomy fearing their lifestyle and freedoms would be curtailed by the PRC, while realizing actual independence is not a viable option.

Is continued US support for Taiwan an outdated policy and a dangerous liability that could spark a war between the United States and China? Or is Taiwan a strategic asset for the United States that stands in the way of China's potential domination of the Asia-Pacific region? China's leaders clearly will not relinquish their claim and will do whatever it takes to prevent the establishment of Taiwan as a separate nation. Washington's policy is to maintain an ambiguous status quo for as long as possible, hoping for a peaceful resolution that would be acceptable to people on both sides of the Taiwan strait. This uneasy arrangement has lasted for nearly four decades. Yet as Deng Xiaoping told Jimmy Carter in 1979, "we have patience, but this patience cannot be unlimited."

Notes

1 I am grateful to Richard Bush and Douglas Spelman for their helpful comments.
2 David P. Nickles and Adam M. Howard, eds., *Foreign Relations of the United States, 1977–1980*, Vol. 13: *China* (Washington, DC: US Government Printing Office, 2013). Hereafter cited as *FRUS*, Vol. 13. Steven Goldstein's excellent book *China and Taiwan* (Cambridge, UK: Polity Press, 2015) draws extensively on the *FRUS* documents.
3 Jimmy Carter, *Keeping Faith: Memoirs of a President* (New York: Bantam Books, 1982), 190.

4 Leonard Woodcock Oral History, Tape 14, February 9, 1982, Michel Oksenberg Papers, Bentley Library, University of Michigan. Telephone interview with Stapleton Roy, September 14, 2016.

5 After Chiang Kai-shek's death in 1975, his son Chiang Ching-kuo succeeded him as Taiwan's president.

6 *FRUS*, Vol. 13, Document 159.

7 *FRUS*, Vol. 13, Documents 166 and 167. Until the *pin-yin* system was adopted in the United States, Deng's name was spelled Teng, based on the Wade-Giles Romanization system.

8 *FRUS*, Vol. 13, Document 168. Richard Bush provides first-rate analysis of the ancillary documents in his book *At Cross Purposes: U.S.-Taiwan Relations Since 1942 (M.E. Sharpe: Armonk, NY, 2004)*.

9 *FRUS*, Vol. 13, Document 168.

10 Telephone interview with Stapleton Roy, September 14, 2016.

11 Leonard Woodcock Oral History, Tape 18, March 3, 1982, Michel Oksenberg Papers, Bentley Library, University of Michigan.

12 Telephone interview with Stapleton Roy, September 14, 2016; Leonard Woodcock Oral History, Michel Oksenberg Papers, Tape 18, March 3, 1982.

13 *FRUS*, Vol. 13, Document 170.

14 Telephone interview with Stapleton Roy, September 14, 2016.

15 *FRUS*, Vol. 13, Document 173.

16 See Richard Bush, *At Cross Purposes*, 138–41. The US government continues to represent its interests through the American Institute in Taiwan (AIT), which is nominally unofficial.

17 *FRUS*, Vol. 13, Document 135.

18 *FRUS*, Vol. 13, Document 138.

19 Telephone interview with Stapleton Roy, September 14, 2016.

20 Ibid.

21 Roy remained in Beijing to manage the USLO while Leonard Woodcock accompanied Deng on his tour of America. Woodcock became the US ambassador to China as of March 1, 1979 and Roy was appointed deputy chief of mission.

22 *FRUS*, Vol. 13, Documents 206 and 209.

23 *FRUS*, Vol. 13, Document 208.

24 Steven Goldstein, *China and Taiwan*, 66–7.

25 The George W. Bush and Obama administrations each sold more than $12 billion in arms to Taiwan.

3

Beyond Peaceful Evolution: Chinese Domestic Politics and US Foreign Policy

Dimitar D. Gueorguiev

Economically, politically, and ideologically, relations between the United States and the People's Republic of China (PRC) represent one of the defining fixtures of the twenty-first century. Broad recognition of this fact has nourished a cottage industry of scholarship aimed at forecasting what might come of this relationship, with scholars and policymakers divided as to whether the two great powers are moving toward inevitable conflict[1] or, potentially, a new phase of constructive competition and cooperation.[2]

Part of this debate boils down to whether China will maintain the basic features of the international status quo, established by the United States after the Second World War, or attempt to revise the system to better suit its own interests and ambitions.[3] Recent developments in China's foreign policy offer a mixed picture.[4] China's increasing assertiveness, concerning territorial claims and economic policy, combined with a growing sense of insecurity within the United States, seems to put the two along a predictable path toward war.[5] Still, others point to China's strategic investment in the existing institutional architecture and the importance of maintaining constructive engagement with Beijing.[6]

A constant across all perspectives is that an important, if not principal, determinant of China's foreign policy posture resides within its domestic politics. China's internal dynamics have bearing on foreign policy and US–China relations in at least two ways. First, some see China's nondemocratic regime as an obstacle between Beijing and Washington that will make it harder for the two countries to find common ground and resolve differences peacefully.[7] A somewhat different interpretation is that Chinese foreign policy reflects domestic political insecurity. As Shirk stresses in *Fragile Superpower*, whenever China's leaders feel their domestic legitimacy is in question, they tend to back themselves up into a corner, play the nationalist card, and escalate aggressively.[8]

The intersection of both arguments reveals a precarious dilemma. Under the democratization perspective, erosion of the Chinese Communist Party's (CCP) grip on power—in favor of a more democratic alternative—is conducive toward better relations. By contrast, the stability perspective cautions that political insecurity at home could spark contest abroad. This apparent tension between domestic authoritarian instability and international democratic peace is well known in the international relations literature,[9] and has tempered the US foreign policy posture toward China's Communist regime throughout much of the PRC's existence.

It was John Foster Dulles, secretary of state under the Eisenhower administration, who first proposed the notion of "peaceful evolution" as a strategic mind-set for engaging hostile Socialist states. The basic premise underpinning peaceful evolution is twofold. First, that promoting regime change in such settings is costly and risky. Second, that engagement undermines socialism through political, economic, and cultural penetration. The argument applies generally, to all Communist states, but it was tailored specifically with regard to the PRC, a hugely important player with rocky relations toward both Washington and Moscow. While the principles of peaceful evolution were never fully adopted, the underlying logic has played an instrumental role in guiding key milestones in the US–China relationship, including diplomatic normalization under the Nixon administration and China's entry into the World Trade Organization (WTO) under Clinton.

Yet, despite decades of integration and modernization, there is little indication that China is headed in a democratic direction. In this chapter, I review the history of democratization-oriented US foreign policy toward China, as recorded in US government statements and communications as well as perceptions in Chinese academic and political circles. Furthermore, I assess the degree to which forces associated with peaceful evolution are changing China. Contrary to the peaceful evolution argument, I conclude that a more open, sophisticated, and better-connected Chinese society is contributing to authoritarian resilience, not its erosion. Moreover, I find that the notion of peaceful evolution has instead been employed opportunistically and inconsistently, by both sides, and is in need of a replacement.

Two Perspectives on Peaceful Evolution

Peaceful evolution finds its inspiration in liberal views of the international system, dating as far back as Immanuel Kant.[10] More recently, these views have been elaborated on by scholars who provide empirical support for the idea that democracies are less likely to go to war with one another.[11] While the mechanisms underpinning the relationship have yet to be demonstrated, likely contributing factors include: the belief that when citizens, who bear the brunt of conflict, are enfranchised they opt for peaceful alternatives; that institutions that coexist alongside democracy, like participation in multilateral organizations, help mediate conflicts; and that liberal ideology itself biases against war.

These arguments are subject to intense criticism, both empirically and theoretically.[12] Indeed, it is not hard to imagine how popular passions under a democratic China might push volatile issues like the forced reunification of Taiwan, territorial claims in the East and South China Seas, or past grievances with Japan to the forefront of political discourse, jeopardizing what has thus far been an arguably modest Chinese foreign policy posture. Regardless, policymakers in both Washington and Beijing routinely reference the notion of democracy promotion and peaceful evolution in their foreign policy rhetoric. As such, it is arguably just as important to understand how both sides have to come to understand and communicate the concept of peaceful evolution, as whether or not it actually works.

Perspective from Washington

Democracy promotion has played a part in American foreign policy dating back to at least the eighteenth century with the moral support offered to the French revolutionaries.[13] With regard to China, these efforts are easily traced back to the work of nineteenth century American missionaries.[14] Although Americans in the nineteenth century saw China as fertile ground for "propagating the democratic gospel," as Rubinstein puts it, contemporary approaches, specifically those associated with peaceful evolution, are more closely associated with the anti-communism of the 1950s.

A more precise point of origin, however, rests with the angst that prevailed over the US foreign policy establishment during the summer of 1949.[15] Despite over two billion dollars' worth of American grants and credits—alongside large quantities of military and civilian war surplus property—Chiang Kai-shek and his nationalist government failed to hold off Mao Zedong and the People's Liberation Army. In April of that year, the Nationalists had evacuated from Nanjing to Taiwan and only time stood in the way of a formal proclamation for a new PRC.[16]

While waiting for the dust to settle, Secretary of State Dean Acheson, released a thorough white paper on recent Sino-American relationship, titled "United States Relations with China with Special Reference to the Period 1944–1949."[17] The 1,054-page report, issued in August of 1949, had two objectives, or rather two audiences. The first was an attempt to head off impending domestic criticism targeting Acheson and Truman over their apparent "loss" of China,[18] by placing full blame on Chiang Kai-shek. The second, aimed at Beijing, was an attempt to paper over tensions and mistrust between the Unites States and the proto-PRC, stressing the long-standing friendship with the Chinese people and respect for China's territorial integrity. The white paper thus argues that American intervention had not only been contrary to traditional American policy but also "doomed" to fail. Presumably, this was intended to signal that such further attempts would not be pursued going forward.

Acheson's preemptive overture arguably failed, in both respects. But it set a tone for American democracy promotion that was particularly sensitive to China and the dangers of explicit intervention. The concept of peaceful evolution, coined in a series of speeches by Acheson's successor, John Foster Dulles, was in no doubt influenced by what happened in China a decade earlier. Despite being an avid anti-Communist and proponent of containment policy, Dulles argued that the United States should nudge, not coerce, Communist countries like China into line with Western democracies. This was to be accomplished through peaceful means, including moral support for nascent opposition movements, cultural exchange, cultivation of markets, and the spread of information, all of which would eventually lead to the erosion of Marxist–Leninism.

According to most scholars, Dulles's peaceful liberation theory was never fully enacted.[19] My own review of declassified documents compiled by the US Department of State's Office of the Historian, confirm that no explicit references to peaceful evolution have been made with regard to China.[20] Nevertheless, the notion of peaceful evolution was seized on by Mao Zedong and his colleagues in the 1950s as a call to arms against American subversion—an issue I will turn to in the next section. At the time, the rhetorical nuance of peaceful evolution was in many ways eclipsed by the political urgency of the "domino theory," which argued that combating communism was an immediate priority wherever communists were making gains. Although the domino theory did not apply to China, where Mao and the CCP were firmly in control, it set the stage for full-scale US intervention in Indochina, where Communist forces seemed vulnerable. It was at this point that the more benign principles of peaceful evolution became confounded with the far more aggressive character of regime change.

The confluence of peaceful and nonpeaceful means of democracy promotion accelerated during the 1980s. The Reagan administration advocated dismantling communism through a "war without gun smoke," on the one hand, while funding and facilitating regime change operations on the other. The most consequential drama, of course, was in the Soviet Union, where a new party secretary was moving forward with social and economic reforms that aligned almost perfectly with the chain of events predicted under peaceful evolution. Then in the spring of 1989, public demonstrations began popping up across China. By May of that year, the streets of Beijing were under siege by protesters demanding political liberalization. Shortly thereafter, the stunning collapse of the Soviet Union unleashed a new element of hubris within the United States. Francis Fukuyama penned his boldly titled essay "The End of History," and American leaders stepped up funding for democracy promotion while openly advocating regime change. In his State of the Union address in 1994, President Bill Clinton asserted, "Ultimately, the best strategy to ensure our security and to build a durable peace is to support the advance of democracy elsewhere." Alas, by way of a brutal crackdown, the CCP survived 1989. But the events in Tiananmen, followed by the back-to-back revolutions in Eastern Europe were a deeply sobering experience for the Chinese leadership, almost as if a giant clock was winding down on them.[21] Yet, as I discuss in the next section, the CCP did not bunker itself off from the world. Instead, it stepped on the gas and met the forces of peaceful evolution head on.

Over the last three decades, the world has become far less sanguine about the prospects for democratization and peaceful evolution. A number of countries that adopted democratic institutions in the 1990s have since abandoned them[22] and those that underwent American-induced regime change have yet to recover, economically or politically.[23] Fukuyama has since revisited and amended his original thesis, especially with regard to China, explaining that "Americans have long hoped China might undergo a democratic transition as it got wealthier, and before it became powerful enough to become a strategic and political threat. This seems unlikely, however."[24] Interestingly, so has the White House. The National Security Strategy (NSS) of 2006 concludes that "China's 'transition remains incomplete'; China is urged to 'continue down the road of reform and openness', thereby 'adding political freedom to economic freedom.'"[25] By contrast, the 2017 NSS reflects, "For decades, U.S. policy was rooted in the belief that support for China's rise and for its integration into the post-war international order would liberalize China. Contrary to our hopes, China expanded its power at the expense of the sovereignty of others."[26]

It is still too early to tell just how far the Trump administration is willing to depart from established policy for democracy promotion. While there has been no mention of human rights or democracy during President Trump's recent meetings with leaders from China, North Korea, or Russia, the White House still references a lack of democracy in explaining hostile relations with Iran, going so far as setting up a Farsi-language broadcast to encourage local citizens to protest in the streets.[27] Moreover, the architecture for democracy promotion is still very much in place. Over the past decade, more than $2 billion in foreign assistance has been allocated annually for democracy promotion activities, including support for good governance, rule of law, and the promotion of human rights.[28]

Only a fraction of this amount goes to China, mainly because there are few organizations in China that are willing to accept money from the US State Department and practically none who will do so openly. Likewise, American diplomats have become far more careful in referencing democracy in relation to the China policy. Most recently, US secretary of state Rex Tillerson[29] went a step further and endorsed China's call for "A New Model of Great Power Relations," claiming that this should not only be the approach going forward but had in fact been the defining idea of US–China relations over the past 40 years.[30] Regardless, the view from Beijing has changed little since the early days of the PRC.

Perspective from Beijing

China's leaders take "peaceful evolution" (heping yanbian) literally. It is, in the eyes of Beijing, a deliberate attempt at undermining socialism through the political, economic, and cultural penetration of Communist states. From this light, foreign assistance is regarded as bait, cultural exchange as ensnarement, and moral appeal as venom. Despite the sharp vitriol, the invocation of peaceful evolution in Chinese political discourse is vague and nebulous. For Chinese politicians, the notion of peaceful evolution has proven instrumental for discrediting anything from large-scale protests to academic studies. All are easily rebranded as pawns and plants in deep conspiracies masterminded by foreign agitators.[31]

China's animus toward peaceful evolution is also deeply rooted and has remained remarkably consistent for over five generations of leadership.[32] On the eve of establishing the PRC, Mao wrote "for a very long period, U.S. imperialism laid greater stress than other imperialist countries on activities in the sphere of spiritual aggression, extending from religious to 'philanthropic' and cultural undertakings." According to Mao, the Truman administration and its emissaries were "organizing a U.S. fifth column" to "overthrow the people's government led by the CCP."[33]

More than animus, Mao's thought on the subject, and that of his lieutenants, reveals a profound sense of insecurity. The threat of peaceful evolution was so palpable that, in a sense, the CCP's mere survival was interpreted as an unlikely feat of defiance. Consider Zhou Enlai's National Day reception speech in 1966, just as the Cultural Revolution was beginning to ramp up. Zhou proclaimed: "imperialists, modern revisionists and reactionaries in various countries are hurling vicious abuse at us precisely because our great cultural revolution has dug out the roots of their subversive activities and their attempts at 'peaceful evolution' in China and has thus hit them where it hurts most."[34] By this time, however, Washington was far more preoccupied with a brewing war in Vietnam and escalating tensions with the Russians.[35] Moreover, the world had yet to realize the full magnitude of Communist China's tragic industrialization failure during the Great Leap Forward (1958–62).[36] Even China's first nuclear test, in October 1964, evoked more confusion than response from Washington.[37] To the extent that the Johnson administration had a coherent policy on China, it was via the escalating war in Indochina.[38]

Mao passed away in 1976. As discussed by David Nickles and Terry Lautz in this volume, the United States and China had by then engineered one of the most dramatic examples of international reconciliation and strategic reorientations known to man. Over the next decade, Mao's sober-minded successors would have to pry open the shutters that had for decades protected China from peaceful evolution. By 1978, Chinese farmers and manufacturers were actively seeking out Western technology. Remarkably, protesters were even allowed to gather in Beijing's streets, calling for better jobs, freedom, and even human rights, in what came to be known as the "Beijing Spring."[39] In 1979, images of Deng Xiaoping, donning a cowboy hat in Texas were broadcast throughout the world—even in China—signaling, without any qualification, a willing embrace of Western culture, a fact that would be etched in stone when George Michael and Andrew Ridgeley, a British pop duo collectively known as Wham! rocked the Great Wall in 1985.[40]

Much of this was, however, borne by expedience. CCP leaders were well aware of China's untapped economic potential, and courting the West was a means to an end. But they were neither ignorant nor complacent about the prospects of liberalization inertia. They needed only to look north, to Gorbachev's reforms in the Soviet Union, to see how quickly authority could unravel. Indeed, it would not be long before the CCP approached its own critical juncture.

By spring of 1989, with popular demonstrations spreading across multiple cities, China's leaders would soon have to decide whether to yield and allow for the gradual political opening that seemed so inextricably linked to economic progress or risk it all by heeding their survival instincts and violently crushing any and all calls for democracy. In the late hours of June 3, 1989, CCP leaders made their choice in the heart of Beijing. By morning the next day, thousands had lost their lives.[41] Many more lost their hope and humanity and, China seemed bent on returning to its dark totalitarian roots. Even Deng Xiaoping, the principal architect behind the PRC's economic opening, was resolutely handing down death sentences.

Blame for the Tiananmen protests, not to mention the violent military response, was laid squarely on the dark magic of democracy promotion. "There is a proposal in the United States now," Deng explains, "to fight a world war without gun smoke." "Capitalism hopes to declare a final victory over socialism. In the past, it used weapons, including atomic bombs, hydrogen bombs, which was opposed by people of the world. But now it is engaged in the peaceful evolution."[42] Li Zhun, an official in the Propaganda

Department, elaborated: "With the dramatic changes in the international situation, Western hostile forces have not only accelerated the pace of peaceful evolution against socialist states, but have increasingly regarded China as the main stumbling block to their pursuit of power politics and defeat of socialism."[43]

Deng's successor, Jiang Zemin, who would go on to oversee broad-based economic and social liberalization, was equally vocal about the menace of clandestine peaceful evolution. "U.S. policy toward China has always had two sides. A peaceful evolution against China is the long-term strategic goal of some people in the United States," Jiang explains. "Essentially, they do not want to see China's reunification or development. They will keep the pressure on China on the issues of human rights, trade, arms sales, Taiwan, the Dalai Lama, and so on."[44]

The "Color Revolutions" in Eastern Europe and Central Asia, followed by the Arab Spring movement in North Africa and the Middle East, only crystallized fears of democratic contagion. By the end of Hu Jintao's tenure (2002–12), these anxieties had moved from rhetoric to official theory. In March 2011, the Chinese Academy of Social Sciences (CASS) released a book penned by its vice president Li Shenming, titled *Preparing for Danger in Times of Safety: Recollections on the 20-Year Anniversary of the Collapse of the Russian Communist Party* (Ju An Si Wei: Sulian Wang Dang Ershi Nian de Sikao), which concludes that the root cause for Soviet collapse was not the Socialist system, but rather the ideological corruption of then-president Mikhail Gorbachev.

Soon thereafter, an online documentary titled *Silent Contest* (Jiaoliang Wusheng) offered a similar thesis: the CCP was in a battle for the hearts and minds of the Chinese people against a conspiratorial American policy of engagement.[45]The overtly nationalist and incendiary documentary was quickly scrubbed from the Chinese internet by censors, though it is still accessible on YouTube. In the documentary, Hu Jintao is quoted: "If problems appear in this [ideological] battle front, it may well lead to social unrest or even the end of our political system. To create chaos in a society, and overthrow our government, our enemies start by piercing a hole in our ideological system, and confusing the people's minds."[46] Also quoted in the documentary, current president Xi Jinping, who also happened to write a PhD dissertation on scientific socialism, explains: "The strategy of Western countries to contain our development will never change. They will never allow a socialist country to carry out a smooth peaceful development. For this, we must remain vigilant and not allow ourselves to be fooled."[47]

Assessing Peaceful Evolution

While the threat of peaceful evolution remains a hallmark of Chinese political thought, it is unclear whether the social and economic forces underpinning the theory are exerting much pressure on the CCP's sustained political monopoly. Over the last four decades, China has grown faster and farther than any non-democracy in history. If the subtle forces of modernization were not enough to upend the reign of the party-state,[48] then the CCP's inability to keep up with the pace of social and economic development surely would be?[49]

Such an upending has not occurred. If anything, the CCP appears to be peeling back many of the democratic institutional reforms experimented with in the 1980s and 1990s, like placing a moratorium on the expansion of local elections and adopting ever more draconian tactics for repressing political dissidents. These trends are clearly visible in international measures of democracy. In Figure 3.1, for example, data from Freedom House and the Economist Intelligence Unit suggest that China is as good as or better than the average autocracy at boosting civil liberties and participation. At the same time, China has sharply regressed from the rest when it comes to political liberalization and press freedoms.

Today, peaceful evolution serves merely as pretense for Chinese authorities to impose a host of draconian policies, from blocking foreign media to obstructing academic and institutional cooperation. The state-run press and Chinese politicians opportunistically resurrect peaceful evolution during periods of heightened political vulnerability. In response to Hong Kong's pro-democracy protests in 2014, the *Global Times*, a well-known nationalist mouthpiece of the Chinese state, ran an editorial titled "To guard against color revolution, first oppose peaceful evolution," (*Yao fang yanse geming, xian fan heping yanbian*).[50]

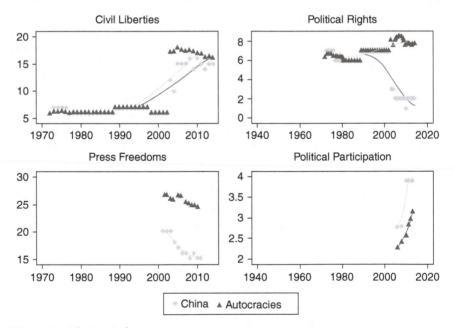

Figure 3.1 Selective Reform

Notes: Data on Civil Liberties and Political Rights comes from the raw Freedom House additive scales that range from 0 to 40 and 0 to 60, respectively. Data on Political Participation comes from the Economist Intelligence Unit's Democracy Index, which ranges from 0 to 10, with 10 being the most democratic. Data on Press Freedoms comes from the country rankings of Reporters without Borders and ranges from 0 to 92, with rank 92 representing the most free press environment.

Authoritarian Resilience

To harp on about the fact that China is not moving in a democratic direction in spite of decades of engagement and modernization is unnecessary. As the 2017 NSS document, referenced earlier, concludes, wishful thinking has proven wrong, and there is little sign that US policymakers are banking on any political opening in Beijing anytime soon. Yet, while the failure of peaceful evolution in China may be self-evident, thinking about the reasons for why it failed is instructive.

Again, we can take 1989 as critical juncture. As discussed in the previous section, the Tiananmen protests presented the CCP leadership with an existential threat, much in line with the predictions of peaceful evolution. Indeed, most China scholars at the time were convinced that the regime would soon collapse.[51] That the leadership responded with as much force and rhetoric as it did is perhaps unsurprising.

What is remarkable, however, is that 1989 did not thrust China back into isolation. Despite sweeping international criticism and a package of economic and security sanctions from the United States, Deng Xiaoping, ever the pragmatist, took it upon himself to keep China's economic opportunity in sight. With the help of the pen name "Huang Fuping," Deng proceeded by speaking from both sides of his mouth, appeasing conservatives by promising a political status quo while at the same time rekindling the prospect for economic liberalization by signaling to investors that China was still open for business.[52]

The mood, and Deng's unique approach, is perhaps best illustrated by a popular joke circulating around the period: Bill Clinton, Boris Yeltsin, and Jiang Zemin are each driving down a road and approach an intersection. Clinton turns right without signaling; so does Yeltsin. Jiang hesitates and asks his passenger, Deng Xiaoping, which way to go. "Signal left and turn right," Deng replies.[53]

More than simply pushing forward with market reforms, like applying for status within the WTO and privatizing a substantial portion of the state-run economy, in recognizing the link between markets and information, China's leaders also invested heavily in communications technology and infrastructure. It was at this time that China's internet backbone, positioned along three international hubs, in Beijing, Shanghai, and Guangzhou, and along five domestic exchange points, in Shenyang, Xi'an, Chengdu, Wuhan, and Nanjing, were brought together to form what would soon become the largest Internet network on the planet.[54] Today, China boasts over 700 million internet users, nearly a quarter of the global population.

China's embrace of information, arguably the most potent harbinger of democracy, was not just about hardware. As Zhao Yuezhi and others have documented, the CCP allowed, even cultivated, a renaissance in information software, ranging from online journalism to a budding market in e-commerce.[55] These developments were paralleled by huge investments in censorship and information control.[56] Yet, it would be wrong to conclude that China's media or the Chinese internet is sterile. While censors actively try to suppress and distract people from organizing in the streets, they appear remarkably tolerant of individual criticism against the regime.[57] Likewise, we have seen widespread demonstrations across China, with groups coming together to protest working conditions, environmental quality, and poor social services,[58] often with apparent endorsement from central leaders.[59] Most recently, millions of Chinese have started posting complaints and grievances directly and publicly to their local governments. Experimental studies suggest response rates to public inquiries may be higher than in many democracies.[60]

If we are to believe in the liberalizing forces of peaceful evolution, then these moves must be putting pressure on China's one-party system. As Larry Diamond argues, in his critique of Fareed Zakaria's notion of liberal autocracy, it is "just not possible in our world of mass participation and democratic consciousness to give people the right to think, speak, publish, demonstrate, and associate peacefully, and not have them use those freedoms to demand as well the right to choose and replace their leaders in free and fair elections."[61] Diamond is probably right, but he does not consider the ways mass participation can help nondemocratic regimes learn about, respond to, and incorporate public opinion into their governance strategies and policies, without resorting to elections. Indeed, if successful, selective and regime-managed forms of public inclusion could undermine the desire for electoral participation.

Put differently, there are growing signs that adoption of advanced communications technology has aided rather than compromised Leninist one-party rule in China. Mao's mass-mobilization tactics, for instance, were crude tools that tended to spiral furiously out of control because they were delegated to local agents who themselves had incentives to misrepresent the flow of information from the leaders to the masses.[62] Technology, has however, made mass mobilization far more viable. Today, Chinese citizens can submit complaints or tip-offs about corruption online, email their local leaders if they have questions, and comment on policy proposals at both the local and the national level.[63] In short, the digital revolution has, in a sense, brought Mao's mass-line revolution back to life.

The prospects for institutional democracy, those organized around democratic procedures and political competition, are dire. Whereas traditional democratic institutions—elections and legislatures—engender political discourse and cultivate constituencies, technology has facilitated a closed-circuit information channel that allows the CCP leadership to gather information while distorting and preventing horizontal civil society.[64] More importantly, as nondemocratic versions for public engagement become more viable, democratic models will increasingly fall out of favor. Put simply, when citizens can report corruption directly to oversight bodies the utility of sanctioning through elections diminishes. Likewise, when citizens can directly express support for specific items of policy the instrumental value of competing party platforms and candidates also declines. Indeed, successive rounds of rigorous studies confirm that China's unelected leaders are extremely popular, and that this popularity appears genuine.[65]

If true, scholars and policymakers may want to reconsider the assumptions underpinning theories of democratic evolution as well as the implications for the future of US–China relations. While it may be the case that a democratic China would be easier to deal with than a Communist China, there is simply no indication that the PRC, its leaders, or its people are headed in such a direction.

Steps Forward

What are the implications for US-Sino relations if China does not democratize? This question is not new. Indeed, it was the subject of an entire volume in 2000, edited by Friedman and McCormick, titled *What if China Doesn't Democratize? Implications for War and Peace*. The contributors' overall conclusion is that a democratic China would be no more peaceful or cooperative with its neighbors, or the United States, than a China dominated by the CCP. Instead, entrenched nationalism and irredentism would continue to propel Chinese foreign policy, perhaps even more passionately, towards a confrontational posture.

We can group this perspective with other well-informed, pessimistic views on US–China relations. Such views, however, share more than a common conclusion. All are premised on the notion of a democratic China as an eventual end state. Indeed, the Friedman and McCormick volume does not in fact answer the question posed in its own title, perhaps because all the contributors, as the coeditor notes on page 339, believe that eventual democracy in China is likely, or in Pei Minxin's case already taking place. To the extent that a nondemocratic China is considered, it exists as a dysfunctional state, plagued by "domestic governance challenges" that would destine the country an unreliable and noncompliant international actor.

But what if we allow for the possibility that China can meet its governance challenges, without adopting democratic institutions? That the CCP can incorporate the Chinese people by means other than election and through practice contrary to traditional civil society? That China can, in a genuine sense, modernize but not democratize? As argued in the previous section, this scenario is not a hypothetical one but the pursuant strategy of China's current leaders. Whether they succeed remains an open question, but this should not discourage us from seriously entertaining the prospect that contemporary China simply is not heading in any shape or form toward democracy.

Letting go of an overly hopeful democratization narrative may seem like a capitulation to a more cynical *realpolitik* view of the world. Alternatively, perhaps US-Sino relations should be reduced to a purely transactional state of affair, whereby balance of payments and security concerns dictate policy. Both of these would be the wrong lesson to walk away with. As alluded to in the introduction, the most critical determinant of future peace or conflict is whether China intends to upend the international status quo or grow within it. For decades, the issue of democratization has been superimposed on this much more general insight, and, in some respects, has served as a distraction. The factors that would discourage a revisionist China are not contingent on democratization. On the contrary, setting aside the issue of regime type may offer some clarity on managing the transpacific relationship.

Engagement Is Still the Best Policy

First, resigning the democratization narrative, whether it is aggressive or peaceful, does not mean abandoning engagement. On the contrary, doing away with the hopeful narrative of democratization reveals just how important engagement—social, political, but especially economic—really is. As argued earlier, proponents of the democratic peace theory do not always agree on which features of democracy are actually preventing conflict. The most convincing dimension, however, is arguably economic. Put simply, when two states are economically engaged, via trade and investment, there is simply no way of inflicting pain without feeling it too. In other words, the economic costs of contest between economically interdependent adversaries is precisely what facilitates peaceful alternatives, or as James Fearon puts it, economic costs expand the "bargaining range."[66] Seen from this light, the currently brewing trade war with China is, if anything, increasing the likelihood of military conflict by undercutting mutual incentives to avoid it.

More than simply interdependence, engaging China is arguably the most powerful tool America has for shaping China's national interests and foreign policy posture.[67] To be clear, China's interests, as a developing country and direct competitor to the United States, are bound to clash with that of the existing international order. Indeed, we are already witnessing as much with regard to territorial disputes in the South China Sea. However, we should also acknowledge that for nearly three decades now, China has been adapting to the existing international structure, inheriting many of its core principles and preferences. Indeed, many of the "alternative" institutions China has backed over the last couple of years bear a strong resemblance to existing platforms. The Asian Infrastructure Investment Bank has much in common with the Asian Development Bank. Proposed FTAs like the Regional Cooperation Economic Partnership or the Free Trade Area of the Pacific are hollowed-out versions of the Trans-Pacific Partnership,[68] and China's One Road, One Belt system has been described as a China-sized Marshall Plan.[69]

Finally, we should be weary of drawing too bold a contrast between liberal and realist views of foreign policy. After all, it was realpolitik, in the form of anti-Soviet balancing, not democracy promotion that inspired the thaw between the United States and China under Nixon. American policymakers today may benefit from taking a similar view of China relations.

Assuming that preemptive containment or even war, à la Allison's trap hypothesis, are not in the immediate offing, what then are the long-term American national interests vis-à-vis China?[70] Take, for instance, economic interests. The Trump administration's punitive tariffs are couched primarily on the basis of unfair terms of trade, an unabashedly mercantilism view of economic relations. Yet, given China's vast and largely untapped domestic market of consumers, it might be in America's interest to forgo immediate concessions so as to profit from future access. As the current trade imbroglio festers, Chinese businesses and consumers will increasingly turn to other players for goods and contracts.

Lead by Example

One of the important but all too often marginalized features of democracy promotion, and indeed an integral feature of peaceful evolution, is that leading democracies influence through example rather than rhetoric. During the 2016 presidential campaign, then candidate Donald Trump made the argument that "when the world looks at how bad the United States is, and then we go and talk about civil liberties, I don't think we're a very good messenger."[71] With poverty rates hovering around 13 percent,[72] alongside increasingly visible racial tensions, candidate Trump arguably had a point. Unfortunately, President Trump's unceasing attacks on journalists, political critics, and even average citizens, set a devastating example to strongmen leaders around the world. Ironically, however, sustained media scrutiny over Trump's campaign and his presidency may be doing more to spread the free press gospel than formal endorsements and admonishments.[73]

Even if America cannot lead China into political democracy by example, it can set norms and precedents for many correlates of democracy, including foreign policy. One way American leaders do this is by holding themselves to higher standards, such that any behavior below them immediately stands out in contrast. This logic extends to honoring commitments even if they are costly and avoiding bellicose statements even if they may be politically expedient, areas in which the current administration has taken unprecedented liberties. The bottom line is that, as China's economic and strategic capacity advances, it too will face internal pressures to assert sovereignty and protect domestic interests. The Trump administration's opportunism in these same arenas today make it that much easier and unsurprising for China to act in similar fashion tomorrow.

Redirecting Criticism

Although a strict understanding of the peaceful evolution doctrine reads that democracy is best served by example, a hallmark in American practice has been criticism. In particular, the United States routinely chastises China for its human rights abuses. The apparent goal of such pressure is perhaps twofold. First, it demonstrates American commitment to values of liberty and morality. Second, it is a means by which to put pressure, internationally and domestically, on China's leaders by raising awareness over its repressive tactics. As discussed in the previous section, however, these criticisms have arguably been counterproductive—especially for those on the receiving end of abuse. By publicly criticizing China for jailing and repressing dissidents, America only reinforces the CCP's narrative that domestic critics are foreign agents. Given China's tight restrictions on information and debate, the official narrative is unfortunately hard to challenge.

A more general problem with the human rights critique is that China's Communist leaders have never based their legitimacy on respect for the rights of individuals. Moreover, Chinese public opinion toward the regime does not appear to take human rights into much account. As mentioned earlier, surveys consistently show that the central leadership enjoys stratospheric levels of trust and satisfaction, despite widespread acknowledgment of state repression. Instead, China's leaders couch their legitimacy on delivering economic growth and competent governance.[74] It is therefore on these same dimensions where public scrutiny is highest. For example, a modest air quality monitor installed in the US embassy in Beijing has arguably done more to push the Chinese leadership toward reform on environmental policy than decades of human rights admonishments have with respect to social policy.

The point here is not to compromise American values, but rather to better understand and more effectively target the Chinese domestic audience. Unfortunately, Americans still do not have a good grasp of Chinese public opinion, and certainly lag behind their China peers' understanding of American public opinion. This is understandable. In the United States, an open media, numerous think tanks, and incessant polling offers a granular and almost instantaneous reading of the American public's pulse on issues ranging from foreign intervention to immigration. This is simply not the case with regard to China, where scholars and casual observers alike often draw inference from statements in the tightly controlled state-run press. Unfortunately, without a deeper understanding of Chinese public opinion, it is unlikely that American pressure will serve its intended purpose. For example, when the US Congressional Executive Commission on China put out its annual report in 2014, stating that the United States "should increase support for Hong Kong's [ongoing "Umbrella"] democracy movement," it simply played into Beijing's narrative that the movement was orchestrated from abroad.[75]

Similar examples of US pressure missing its target include contemporary rhetoric concerning Russian election tampering and Iran's nuclear weapons program. Russian leaders and average citizens alike are clearly proud of the possibility that they may have influenced thr US election. Stressing the argument to that audience seems misguided. Indeed, even Putin's strongest opponents see the issue as deeply counterproductive.[76] Similarly, criticizing Iran's nuclear program may be helping, rather than hurting, what is otherwise an unpopular government in Tehran by activating nationalist sentiments.[77] In both cases, a more nuanced appreciation of domestic public opinion, rather than confidence in liberal principles, could go a long way in helping sharpen America's message.

In the case of China, at least, the challenge is not a lack of information. The Chinese government has access to vast amounts of information from social media platforms that openly hand over data to authorities, as well as private polling firms asked with providing unvarnished files directly to officials.[78] The Chinese government is also supporting Chinese social scientists with funding and data access.[79]

With regard to foreign policy, studies from China show that the Chinese public is quite ambivalent about challenging the United States in global leadership.[80] Furthermore, a new generation of US-based Chinese researchers is taking advantage of open Chinese data to reveal a nuanced image of Chinese ideology, one that does not fit neatly into democracy–autocracy or capitalist–Communist dichotomies.[81] As of now, there is still room for more international collaboration in public opinion research, similar to that occurring in some of the natural sciences.[82] Taking advantage and investing further into this area would be good for both sides, insofar as it can help avoid misunderstandings and misperceptions. But such relationships are hard to forge under the cloud of democratization rhetoric, real or perceived.

Notes

1   Richard Bernstein and Ross H. Munro, *The Coming Conflict with China* (New York: A.A. Knopf, 1997).

2 Henry Kissinger, *On China* (New York: Penguin Press, 2011).

3 Alastair I. Johnston, "Is China a Status Quo Power?" *International Security* 27, 4 (2003): 5–56; Scott L. Kastner and Phillip C. Saunders, "Is China a Status Quo or Revisionist State? Leadership Travel as an Empirical Indicator of Foreign Policy Priorities," *International Studies Quarterly* 56, 1 (2012): 163–77.

4 Alastair I. Johnston, "How New and Assertive is China's New Assertiveness?" *International Security* 37, 4 (April 2013): 7–48.

5 Graham T. Allison, *Destined for War: Can America and China Escape Thucydides's Trap?* (Boston, MA: Houghton Mifflin Harcourt, 2017).

6 Thomas J. Christensen, *The China Challenge: Shaping the Choices of a Rising Power* (W. W. Norton, 2015); James Steinberg and Michael E. O'Hanlon, *Strategic Reassurance and Resolve: U.S.-China Relations in the Twenty-First Century* (Princeton, NJ: Princeton University Press, 2014).

7 John R. Oneal and Bruce M. Russet, "The Classical Liberals Were Right: Democracy, Interdependence, and Conflict, 1950–1985," *International Studies Quarterly* 41, 2 (June 1997): 267–94; Aaron L. Friedberg, "The Future of U.S.-China Relations: Is Conflict Inevitable?" *International Security* 30, 2 (October 2005): 7–45.

8 Susan L. Shirk, *China: Fragile Superpower* (Oxford: Oxford University Press, 2008).

9 Edward D. Mansfield and Jack L. Snyder, *Electing to Fight: Why Emerging Democracies Go to War* (Cambridge, MA: MIT Press, 2005).

10 See "Eternal Peace" in Immanuel Kant, *The Philosophy of Immanuel Kant* (New York: Modem Library, 1949), 430–76.

11 Oneal and Russet, "The Classical Liberals Were Right: Democracy, Interdependence, and Conflict, 1950–1985."

12 Michael E. Brown, Sean M. Lynn-Jones, and Steven E. Miller, eds., *Debating the Democratic Peace* (Cambridge, MA: MIT Press, 1997).

13 Michael W. Fowler, "A Brief Survey of Democracy Promotion in US Foreign Policy," *Democracy and Security* 11, 3 (July 2015): 227–47.

14 Murray A. Rubinstein, *Propagating the Democratic Gospel: Western Missionaries and the Diffusion of Western Thought in China, 1830–1848* (Taipei, Taiwan: Academica Sinica, 1981).

15 Some date peaceful evolution (PE) even further back to US ambassador to Moscow, George Kennan, who in 1946 advocated "peaceful coexistence" with the Soviet Union, arguing that future generations of socialists would bring about "peaceful evolution," although China had not yet entered this discussion. See the Long Telegram of 1946, available here: https://goo.gl/7TxExf.

16 The PRC was formally established on October 1, 1949.

17 A copy of the report can be accessed here: https://goo.gl/NzQPhU.

18 Noam Chomsky points out that the terminology "loss of China" is revealing of US foreign policy attitudes, as it is only possible to lose something that one owns. See: Noam Chomsky, " 'Losing' the world: American decline in perspective, part 1," *The Guardian*, February 14, 2012, https://goo. gl/vXjmXg.

19 Russell Ong, "'Peaceful Evolution,' 'Regime Change' and China's Political Security," *Journal of Contemporary China* 16, 53 (November 2007): 717–27.

20 The terminology does appear in some references toward Vietnam.

21 Jialin Zhang, *China's Response to the Downfall of Communism in Eastern Europe and the Soviet Union* (Hoover Institution on War, Revolution, and Peace, Stanford University: Hoover Press, 1994).

22   Larry Diamond, "Facing Up to the Democratic Recession," *Journal of Democracy* 26, 1 (2015): 141–55.

23   Fowler, "A Brief Survey of Democracy Promotion in US Foreign Policy."

24   See Francis Fukuyama, "US Democracy Has Little to Teach China," *Financial Times*, January 17, 2011, https://goo.gl/xDMf1y.

25   The National Security Strategy of the United States of America (March 2006), 41.

26   The National Security Strategy of the United States of America (December 2017), 25.

27   See Michele Kelemen and Alex Leff, "Trump Administration's Support for Iran Protests May Backfire, Experts Warn," *NPR* July 23, 2018, https://goo.gl/wYEHEA.

28   Marian L. Lawson and Susan B. Epstein, *Democracy Promotion: An Objective of U.S. Foreign Assistance*, technical report (Congressional Research Service, 2017).

29   Tillerson resigned abruptly on March 31, 2018; apparently over disagreements with President Trump, rhetoric on China not included.

30   For discussion, see Robert Daly, "What Just Happened in Beijing?" *Foreign Policy*, March 21, 2017, https://goo.gl/NMkv6P.

31   Ong, "'Peaceful Evolution,' 'Regime Change' and China's Political Security."

32   Maochun Yu, "Marxist ideology, Revolutionary Legacy and Their Impact on China's Security Policy," Chap. 2 in *Routledge Handbook of Chinese Security*, ed. Lowell Dittmer and Maochun Yu (Routledge Hand-books Online, 2015), 34–48.

33   Mao Zedong, "Farewell, John Leighton Stuart!" in *Selected Works of Mao Zedong*, Vol. IV (Selected Works of Mao Zedong, Beijing: Foreign Languages Press, 1969), 439.

34   Translation available at: https://www.marxists.org/reference/archive/zhou-enlai/1966/09/30.htm.

35   Although US involvement in Vietnam dates back to at least 1950, it was not until 1965 that the first US marines officially arrived in Vietnam.

36   For a discussion of different estimates see: (National Research Council, *Rapid Population Change in China, 1952-1982* [Washington, DC: National Academies Press, January 1984]).

37   See William Burr and Jeffrey T. Richelson, "Whether to 'Strangle the Baby in the Cradle': The United States and the Chinese Nuclear Program, 1960–64," *International Security* 25, 3 (January 2001): 54–99, based on documents published by the National Security Archives, available here: https://goo.gl/vMDTmb.

38   Robert Garson, "Lyndon B. Johnson and the China Enigma," *Journal of Contemporary History* 32, 1 (January 1997): 63–80.

39   Kjeld Erik Brodsgaard, "The Democracy Movement in China, 1978–1979: Opposition Movements, Wall Poster Campaigns, and Underground Journals," *Asian Survey* 21, 7 (July 1981): 747–74.

40   See Celia Hatton, "When China woke up to Wham!," *BBC News* (Beijing) April 9, 2015, https://goo.gl/YXzNdS

41   Liang Zhang, *The Tiananmen Papers*, ed. Andrew J. Nathan and Perry Link (New York: Public Affairs, 2001).

42   Deng Xiaoping, "We Are Confident that We Can Do Things Better in China," in *Selected Works of Deng Xiaoping*, Volume 3 (September 16, 1989): 102, available at: https://goo.gl/wijzB3.

43   See Nicholas Kristof, "Changes in China Stir Fear of U.S.," *New York Times*, September 19, 1991, https://goo.gl/vBLzwe.

44   Jiang Zemin, "We Must Never Deviate from Maintaining Our Nation and State's Utmost Interest in Foreign Affairs," in *Selected Works of Jiang Zemin*, Volume 1 (July 12, 1993), 325.

45 Jiaoliang Wushen 较量无声 (Silent Contest), National Defense University, The
    PLA General Political Department, the People's Liberation Army General Staff, and
    Chinese Academy of Social Sciences, June 2013. The 90-minute documentary can still
    be viewed on YouTube at: https://www.youtube.com/watch? v=M_8lSjcoSW8.
46 Translated from: "如果这个阵地出了问题，就可能导致社会
    动乱甚至丧失政权。敌对势力要搞乱一个社会、颠覆一个
    政权，往往总是先从意识形态领域打开突破口，先从搞乱人们的思想下手。"
47 Translated from: "西方国家遏制我国发展的战略图谋是不会
    改变的。他们决不希望我们这样一个社会主义大国顺利实现
    和平发展。在这个问题上，我们们要保持高度警觉，不能抱任何幻想。"
48 Seymour Martin Lipset, "Some Social Requisites of Democracy: Economic
    Development and Political Legitimacy" [in English], *American Political Science
    Review* 53, 1 (September 1959): 69–105.
49 Samuel Huntington, *Political Order in Changing Societies* (New Haven, CT: Yale
    University Press, 1968), 215–16.
50 Available at: https://goo.gl/LwHCCq.
51 See: Multiauthor special issue on Chinese democracy "Documents on Democracy,"
    Journal of Democracy 9, 1 (1998): 183–6.
52 Haifeng Huang, "Signal Left, Turn Right: Central Rhetoric and Local Reform in
    China," *Political Research Quarterly* 66, 2 (June 2013): 292–305.
53 Jiang Zemin was CCP General Party secretary at the time although Deng was still
    calling the shots from an unofficial advisory position. For background on the joke,
    see: http://www.webcitation.org/6npVsas1n.
54 Zixiang Tan, William Foster, and Seymour Goodman, "China's State-Coordinated
    Internet Infrastructure," *Communications of the ACM* 42, 6 (June 1999): 44–52.
55 Yuezhi Zhao, Communication in China: Political Economy, Power, and Conflict
    (Lanham, MD: Rowman & Littlefield, 2008); Susan L Shirk, *Changing Media,
    Changing China* (Oxford: Oxford University Press, 2010).
56 Daniela Stockmann, *Media Commercialization and Authoritarian Rule in China*
    (Cambridge, UK: Cambridge University Press, 2013).
57 Gary King, Jennifer Pan, and Margaret E. Roberts, "How Censorship in China Allows
    Government Criticism but Silences Collective Expression," *American Political Science
    Review* 107, 2 (May 2013): 326–43.
58 Kevin J. O'Brien, "Rightful Resistance," *World Politics* 49, 1 (October 1996): 31–55.
59 Peter Lorentzen, "Designing Contentious Politics in Post-1989 China," *Modern China*
    43, 5 (September 2017): 459–93.
60 Tianguang Meng, Jennifer Pan, and Ping Yang, "Conditional Receptivity to Citizen
    Participation: Evidence from a Survey Experiment in China," *Comparative Political
    Studies* 50, 4 (December 2014): 1–35.
61 Larry Jay Diamond, "The Illusion of Liberal Autocracy," *Journal of Democracy* 14, 4
    (2003): 169.
62 This point is convincingly demonstrated in Kung and Chen, who connect promotion
    incentives to local famine deaths during the Great Leap Forward.
63 Jonathan R. Stromseth, Edmund J. Malesky, and Dimitar D. Gueorguiev, *China's
    Governance Puzzle: Enabling Transparency and Participation in a Single-Party State*
    (Cambridge, UK: Cambridge University Press, 2017).
64 Gary King, Jennifer Pan, and Margaret E. Roberts, "How the Chinese Government
    Fabricates Social Media Posts for Strategic Distraction, Not Engaged Argument,"
    American Political Science Review 111, 3 (August 2017): 484–501; Jidong Chen and

Yiqing Xu, "Why Do Authoritarian Regimes Allow Citizens to Voice Opinions Publicly?" *The Journal of Politics* 79, 3 (July 2017): 792–803.

65 Bruce J. Dickson, *The Dictator's Dilemma: The Chinese Communist Party's Strategy for Survival* (Oxford: Oxford University Press, 2016); Wenfang Tang, *Populist Authoritarianism: Chinese Political Culture and Regime Sustainability* (Oxford: Oxford University Press, 2016).

66 James D. Fearon, "Bargaining, Enforcement, and International Cooperation," *International Organization* 52, 2 (March 1998): 269–305.

67 Christensen, *The China Challenge: Shaping the Choices of a Rising Power*.

68 Dimitar D. Gueorguiev and Mary E. Lovely, "The Trans-Pacific Partnership: Perspectives from China," in *The World Trade System: Trends and Challenges*, ed. Jagdish Bagwatti, Pravin Krishna, and Arvind Panagariya (Cambridge, MA: MIT Press, 2016), 231–65.

69 Michael D. Swaine, "Chinese Views and Commentary on the 'One Belt, One Road' Initiative," *Chinese Leadership Monitor* 47, 2 (2015): 1–24.

70 In short, Allison points out that in twelve of sixteen past cases, where a rising power has confronted a ruling power, the result has been war. See Allison, *Destined for War: Can America and China Escape Thucydides's Trap?*.

71 For transcript, see: https://goo.gl/n9dh2g.

72 The comparative statistic in China is about 7 percent, as measured by the percentage of people living on less than $1.90 a day. Source: World Bank.

73 A recent experimental study of Chinese college students shows a marked increase in democracy evaluation tied to reading uncensored news from the *New York Times* concerning post–2016 election American politics. See Chen, Yuyu, and David Y. Yang. "The Impact of Media Censorship: 1984 or Brave New World?" American Economic Review, forthcoming (2018).

74 Dingxin Zhao, "The Mandate of Heaven and Performance Legitimation in Historical and Contemporary China," *American Behavioral Scientist* 53, 3 (October 2009): 416–33.

75 See Congressional-Executive Commission on China, 2014 Annual Report, p. 9, available at: https://goo.gl/1HtvWQ. Today, China is betting on its understanding of American public opinion and electoral politics to push back on US tariffs, by targeting vulnerable districts that voted for Trump in 2016.

76 See Andrew Higgins, "Why Putin's Foes Deplore U.S. Fixation on Election Meddling," *New York Times* November 23, 2017, https://goo.gl/sgRQMr.

77 See Shervin Malekzadeh, "What Trump Doesn't Get about Ideology in Iran. It's about Nationalism, Not Theocracy," *Washington Post*, June 25, 2018, https://wapo.st/2SI4w5s.

78 Recent estimates suggest that there are over eight hundred public opinion monitoring companies in China (public and private), employing over two-million analysts, charged with dissecting and reporting public sentiment data to government departments. See Michelle Fong, "China Monitors the Internet and the Public Pays the Bill," *Global Voices* July 29, 2014, https://goo.gl/N8zZNU.

79 For examples of Chinese researchers working with social media data, see Xueqi Cheng et al., Social Media Processing, 6th National Conference, Proceedings (2017), 356.

80 In one study, less than 20 percent of Chinese respondents expressed ambition for China to become a global superpower; 25 percent felt China should avoid a global leadership role altogether. See Zheng Su et al., "A World Leader-To-Be? Popular Attitudes Toward China's Global Role," in *Perception and Misperception in American*

and Chinese Views of the Other, ed. Alastair I. Johnston and Mingming Shen (Washington, DC: Carnegie Endowment for International Peace, 2015), 23–39.

81 Jennifer Pan and Yiqing Xu, "China's Ideological Spectrum," *Journal of Politics* 80, 1 (2018): 254–73.

82 Such as in areas of biomedical and environmental health research.

4

Transnational Agents: Chinese International Students in America

Yingyi Ma

Former US secretary of state Henry Kissinger endorsed Tsinghua University's newly established Schwarzman Scholars, a master's program in global affairs. He stated, "We need to forge deeper understanding between the U.S. and China, and diminish cultural biases to mitigate possible tensions and create opportunities for both countries."[1] The program admits students from all over the world, but mainly from China and the United States. Kissinger is right that graduates from this kind of program have the potential to help forge a deeper understanding between the United States and China. This chapter shifts attention to Chinese international students studying in the United States, and argues that they too are promising agents to bridge the divide between both countries.

Ever since China implemented its reform and opening-up policy in the late 1970s, there has been a "fever" to study abroad. Andrew Kipnis[2] has described this fever as education desire, which refers to the broadly shared aspiration among various segments of Chinese society to go to college. The reform era has opened up the minds and hearts of ordinary Chinese and connected them with the outside world; therefore, higher education in the West has become the object of desire for many aspiring Chinese who travel to the United States with scholarships funded by the Chinese government or with American university assistantships. What is different in recent years is the new trend of self-funded Chinese students studying as undergraduates in the United States. Figure 4.1 shows that since 2014, Chinese undergraduates have overtaken graduate student enrollment in American higher education institutions. Furthermore, the growth curve of Chinese student enrollment is far steeper than that of all the other countries. Even after the Trump administration moved against China on multiple grounds, from a trade war to visa restrictions,[3] international student enrollment from China in the academic year 2016–17 grew by 6.7 percent, compared to an overall decline in enrollment from other countries.[4]

However, the Chinese government has become leery of Western values and Western influences on their youth. In 2015, the then education minister Yuan Guiren vowed to ban university textbooks that promoted Western values. "Never let textbooks promoting western values enter into our classes," according to an official account of his

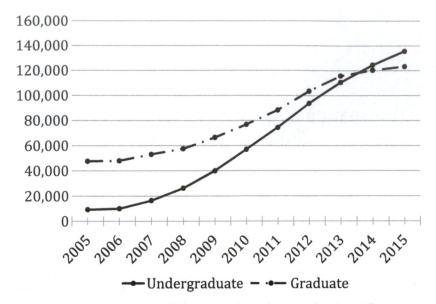

Figure 4.1 Dramatic increase of Chinese undergraduate students' enrollment versus graduate students

remarks.[5] This backdrop of official Chinese rhetoric highly critical of Western values stands in contrast to the fever of Chinese students flocking to American schools. This is remarkable as well as ironic. What is the impact on Chinese youth of studying in the United States, in terms of their attitudes toward the United States and China? I argue here that Chinese international students straddle both China and the United States during their formative years in the education systems and other societal domains of the two countries, and, given this, they hold the promise of becoming transnational agents. Understanding their experiences and thoughts is not only key to providing sufficient support for them, but also a potential opportunity to cultivate future transnational agents who can understand both China and the United States better than those who have no such experiences. I argue that this generation of Chinese international undergraduates are especially well-positioned to be transnational agents due to their liberal arts core training and extended exposure to American campus life than their predecessors who are often graduate students. This is especially significant, because the US–China relationship is the most important bilateral relationship in the world today.[6]

Using primary data collected by means of a sequential, mixed-method design involving both online surveys and in-depth interviews, I am able to provide a systematic and in-depth examination of Chinese international undergraduates at diverse types of American postsecondary institutions. I am also able to provide the quantitative survey results of 507 Chinese international students who completed the whole survey ranging from demographic information, their academic backgrounds, their campus experiences, and their stay versus return intentions. From this sample, I have conducted sixty-five in-depth interviews, each ranging from one to two hours.

This chapter draws on data from both survey and in-depth interviews to address the following research questions:

1. How does the international (and often Western) education Chinese youth receive influence their views about America?
2. How does their overseas education influence their views about China? (For instance, how can we make sense of Chinese international students' protests against the Dalai Lama on American college campuses?)

The findings fall along two lines. First, that Chinese students renew their interest in China after studying in the United States, and they become more reflexive about their own culture and society than before. Second, Chinese students increase their understanding of the United States. As transnational agents, they can be viewed through the following lenses: (1) in terms of their renewed interest in China and (2) in terms of their ability to navigate the bias and discrimination they have experienced in the United States.

An Interest in China: Renewed and Reflexive

To be sure, a large majority of Chinese international students came to study in the United States due to their interest in America, and especially in the American educational system. Indeed, Figure 4.2 shows that the perception that American education can benefit their future tops the reasons for their study in the United States, and a remarkable 68 percent of the survey respondents opted out of the Chinese College Entrance Examination. Yet after they study in the United States, their interest

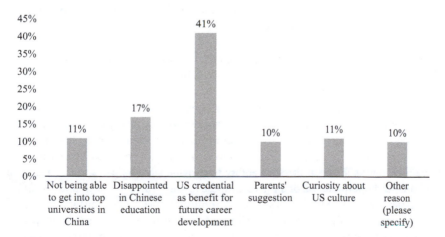

Figure 4.2 Distribution of the most important reasons for studying in the United States (N=507)

in China is renewed, and what is more important, they are becoming more reflective and reflexive about their lives and their country. This reflection and reflexivity at times manifests in their defense of their country and their government.

Interest in Chinese Culture and Society

These students often cherish their freedom after they arrive in the United States—the freedom of being away from parents, to explore a new place, to manage their spare time, to take courses, and participate in extracurricular activities on campus, and so on. However, after a while, they find a renewed interest in their own culture—Chinese culture and society—something they thought they were eager to abandon. This, to some extent, resonated with Eric Liu's profound statement in *Accidental Asian*: "Freedom well nurtured can grow fondness."[7]

Yue, from Yangzhou, a city in Jiangsu province, is an example. Before she left China, she had little interest in Chinese history and culture; all she desired to know was about American culture. Her parents were business entrepreneurs and did not know English. They hired an American tutor for her before she arrived in the United States, trying to improve her English and provide some early cultural exposure. She declared economics as her major at Syracuse University, just as planned. According to Yue, "My parents always said, economics is what is needed in a market economy. It is useful knowledge in either China or the U.S." During her second semester, she encountered her American advisor, who happened to be a China specialist. He encouraged her to take a course with him on Chinese Buddhism. She enjoyed the course so much that she made religion her second major, in addition to economics. She described the change:

> I had not appreciated until now how rich and fascinating Chinese culture was. Before I came to the U.S., I thought religion was superstition, and Buddhism, although it originated in Asia, was nothing but belonging to the old world and backward. However, my American professor made me realize that Buddhism is full of wisdom and depth. I am very proud of it.

Yue regained a sense of knowledge and appreciation about what she used to dismiss as "backward" and "old world." She was influenced by her studies in religion and found pride in her culture as a foreign student.

Joey, a Shanghai native, came to Johns Hopkins University to study computer engineering. He took a Chinese history course and was totally absorbed by it. He was especially fascinated by the analysis of modern Chinese history by his American professor—a middle-aged, white male who could speak very good Mandarin. Joey gave high marks for his professor's ability to provide what he perceived as a neutral and nuanced interpretation of modern Chinese history. This positive impression of his American professor, and this class overall, motivated Joey to read history books. He said: "I was not really into reading in China. As a student, you are too busy preparing for and taking tests to read. But now I am very interested in reading, especially about my own culture and history." During the interview process, I probed for his reflections on such a change:

Interviewer: How do you think this kind of reading about your own culture and
history in America affects you?
Joey: It made me feel more Chinese.
Interviewer: So the feeling is more intense when you are away from China?
Joey: Yes, indeed.

This kind of exposure to Chinese culture and history away from home made Joey more Chinese; he felt he had come to truly know China while he was away from it.

Other students cared more about mundane aspects of life, such as eating and entertainment. Chinese restaurants have mushroomed around the college towns where an increasing number of Chinese international students are arriving. They reminisce about their hometown flavors, and when they are homesick, they miss authentic Chinese food the most. For example, Wing studied at the University of Wisconsin at Madison. As a Guangzhou native, she described her change of attitude about food:

Before I studied in America, I considered pizza, steak, and spaghetti as fancy food, and they are indeed more expensive than the local food in China. Eating them is like a fashionable and high-status thing to do. However, now American food is part of my daily life, and I realize that Chinese food is much more tasty and has more variety than western food.

This realization, that Chinese food is the best, is broadly shared among Chinese international students in America. Chinese restaurants and various kinds of Asian eateries are but one of the visible impacts of the growing number of Chinese international students on American universities and in their communities. A salient example is that, in the neighborhood surrounding the University of Iowa campus, there are more bubble tea stores than Starbucks. In addition to their sentiments about Chinese food and drinks, the students engage in Chinese modes of entertainment, such as karaoke and mahjong, while they are away from their home country.

In short, these students' fondness for the Chinese way of life was renewed and reinforced after they arrived in the United States. This was not just nostalgia, although certainly there is some element of it. What is more significant, it was an affirmation of self-identity and an affinity for one's homeland. At times, this affinity touched on some sensitive political issues, among which the protests against the Dalai Lama stands out as one of the most high-profile acts of engagement by Chinese international students in recent years.

Making Sense of Their Protest against the Dalai Lama

It is an understatement that the Dalai Lama has won the support of the American government and its people. Indeed, he has become a celebrity in America. From top Washington political leaders to shining Hollywood stars, supporters take pride in meeting with the Dalai Lama, who has been heralded as a hero for pursuing peace and freedom in the Western world. The culmination of his recognition in the West was the Nobel Peace Prize awarded to him in 1989, recognized that "his struggle for the liberation of Tibet consistently has opposed the use of violence. He has instead advocated peaceful solutions based upon tolerance and mutual respect in order to preserve the historical and cultural heritage of his people." Unsurprisingly, he has been one of the most sought-after speakers on college campuses in the United States. However, Chinese international students have engaged in multiple open protests against his visits.[8]

In 2012, at Syracuse University, Chinese students stood outside the auditorium where the Dalai Lama was participating in a university-sponsored event called "Common Ground for Peace." The students held various signs, some of which read "Stop media distortion," "Da-Liar: Your smiles charm but your actions harm," and "Violence is not Peace," in both English and Chinese.[9]

On a different occasion, Chinese students from the University of California at San Diego (UCSD) expressed outrage toward their school's choice of the Dalai Lama as a commencement speaker in 2017. In an era when the United States and China represent the first- and second-largest economies in the world, there are increasing grounds of mutual interest between the two, but few issues are as divisive as the issue of Tibet. UCSD's chancellor, Pradeep K. Khosla, called the Dalai Lama "a man of peace" who "promotes global responsibility and service to humanity." However, in the eyes of Chinese students, the Dalai Lama is a separatist, dividing their home country.

The perspectives of these students are often perceived by Americans to be the same as their government's perspective. However, it is overly simplistic to interpret their views in terms of direct guidance or intervention from the Chinese government. Unfortunately, that is often how they are interpreted, even by eminent academics in the United States. For example, consider this report from *Inside Higher Ed*, published on February 16, 2017:

> Robert Barnett, the director of the modern Tibetan studies program at Columbia University, said there are major principles at stake. "Does the university accept to be bullied by the foreign government in terms of who it selects as a speaker, especially when that subject of that foreign government's bullying is almost certainly, without any serious question of all, not deserving of that bullying and is certainly being misrepresented and indeed demonized by the Chinese government?" he asked. "Do we allow the Chinese government's propaganda to dictate major cultural decisions in other countries?"[10]

The above interpretation makes the voices of Chinese students invisible, replaced by the Chinese government, in an effort to "dictate major cultural decisions in other countries." This is a rather strong, unfounded assumption. I argue that we should consider the Chinese students' own voices, and the question of how these are formed merits discussion and debate. To the extent that Chinese students do have their own voices in their protests against the Dalai Lama on American college campuses, we need to acknowledge and respect those voices rather than dismiss them as the outcome of brainwashing by the Chinese government.

While Americans are concerned that Chinese students are being indoctrinated by the Chinese government to adopt anti–Dalai Lama politics, Chinese students argue that it is the Americans who need to hear a different message. As Guo from Syracuse University said,

> Many Americans have never been to China, and they are influenced by their media and other second-hand information. Tibet has been better off under China's rule, Huang said. Both the Tibetan's life expectancy and economy have improved since 1950. I would want to ask those Americans to go to Tibet and talk to ordinary Tibetans.

Guo had direct interactions on this thorny issue with Americans when he was in high school. He attended a private high school in New Hampshire. In history class, he and the two other Chinese students faced off with eight or nine American students in a debate over whether the Chinese government exercised violence in its crackdown on Tibet. While his American friends used the terms *violence* and *crackdown*, he and his team tried to explain that the Dalai Lama's position is not the only, or even the major, position of the Tibetan people. He specifically noted that the Dalai Lama embodies a traditional hierarchical power structure that entails huge inequality among its people, which directly goes against the principles and creed of equality that their American friends endorse.

Despite the loud protests on campuses and even more rancorous mobilizations against the visit on social media, the Dalai Lama still gave the commencement address at UCSD. Interestingly, the Dalai Lama was a commencement speaker in 1998 at Emory University, but there were no visible protests or major protests reported. Apparently, overseas Chinese voices against the Dalai Lama are getting stronger than before.

Jolina, a native from Nanjing, is an applied math and statistics major at Emory University. According to her, Emory has a very close relationship with the Dalai Lama, and members of the Dalai Lama's entourage visit the university on a regular basis. The Dalai Lama is an honorary guest professor at Emory. Jolina expressed her position on this: "There are two perspectives to view the visit of the Dalia Lama. One is from the perspective of religion, which I have no problem with; the other is from the perspective of politics, advocating an independent Tibet, which I do disagree with."

However, not all Chinese students take this stance. In the same school, Coco deviates from her Chinese friends. She was pressured by her Chinese friends to protest with them. She refused and said that she can understand both positions, and she is not willing to advocate for either. But she acknowledged that the American public, including the university's position on this is not taking into account the full complexity of the issue. She explained, "History is complicated, so is the relationship of Tibet and China. I think Americans only buy into one version of this history, and that is communist China bullying Tibet." Coco's comment about the incomplete understanding of Americans on the complicated historical evolution of Tibet is right on target. As opposed to the heroic image of the Dalai Lama, what lies in the shadow is an unfavorable view of the Chinese government, which is often portrayed by American media in unflattering terms and touted as "communist China" in headline news. Meanwhile, issues of gross human rights violations dominate Americans' understandings of China.[11]

A Realistic Understanding and Empathetic Engagement in the United States

Understanding and Engagement in the United States

Vanessa Fong argues in *Paradise Redefined*[12] that Chinese youth envision Western developed societies as a paradise, and that it is the motivation to be part of this paradise that drives them to study abroad. They desire to be part of this "imagined developed world community composed of mobile, wealthy, well-educated and well-connected people worldwide." Drawing on Benedict Anderson's concept of an imagined community,[13] Fong examined the gap between imagination and reality for Chinese youth. The study participants in *Paradise Redefined* were born in the 1970s and 1980s, whereas the participants in my study were born at least a decade later. In other words, the China my participants grew up in is richer, more powerful, and more connected to the West. No wonder that during the time of Fong's study, few students came to the United States for college and only 8 percent studied in the United States.

Now the situation is different. An increasing number of Chinese youth choose to study as undergraduates in the United States. Their dream has quickly materialized into reality, and as a result, after studying in the United States, they have a much deeper, more realistic, and more nuanced understanding of American society.

I argue that this generation of undergraduates from China has a much more profound understanding than their predecessors, who came here primarily as graduate students, who live independently and focus intensely on established research areas. They were often concentrated in science, technology, engineering, and mathematics fields and spent most of their time in the United States in research labs. The new wave of Chinese undergraduates will have more opportunities to interact with Americans through shared dorms and the required undergraduate core courses they take together. They will also have more engagement through campus organizations, off-campus volunteer work, and internships.

Nicole came from a key high school in Nanjing and enrolled in Emory University. She joined a service fraternity. She enjoyed her community service work, including tutoring black youth in Atlanta and community gardening. She complained about her service work in China. She was once assigned by her school to stand in the subway in Nanjing to give people directions. She felt her service work in the United States was more meaningful. She described the change in her impression of the United States:

> I initially thought American society is very rich and most people are wealthy. My work with black kids in the city of Atlanta was eye-opening: they were poorer than even poor people in Nanjing that I know. Poor kids in China have families that can take care of them, but poor black kids in the U.S. have no good caretakers. But they are so good and eager to learn. The inequality in the U.S is something that I never realized until now.

Nicole's understanding of America became much more realistic than before, and she was impressed by both the glaring inequality in the United States and the eagerness of the black kids in Atlanta, whom she tutored.

Wei, a social science and education major at St. Olaf College in Minnesota, was so transformed by her experiences in American colleges that changing biases and cultivating empathy became her purpose in life; as she says,

> I want to work at jobs that can help people develop their empathy. I want to help people let go of their previous biases and their prior thinking, which has been influenced by their government, their country's history, and their own personal experiences. We tend to have biases against certain nations, races, or occupations. How can we get rid of those biases and live together peacefully? How can we communicate effectively across differences in our backgrounds? I hope that I can help people realize that we are all equal and we all have strengths and weaknesses. I want to help people change their biases.

She did pursue this ideal, against the relentless opposition of her mother, who wanted her to go to a prestigious graduate school and enter a secure and lucrative profession such as finance or accounting. She is now in Cambodia, working for a humanitarian organization to help with local women's literacy and life skills.

Other Chinese students may not have articulated their thoughts in this sophisticated manner. But they have talked about their experiences such as attending talks by figures like former US secretary of state Hillary Clinton and celebrated talk show host Oprah Winfrey, and how those events broadened their horizons and led them to give more thought to issues that they took for granted. Lei came to the University of Portland after one year in a local college in China. She was very unsatisfied with the quality of Chinese higher education and applied to restart her college life in the United States. She described her overseas study experience as if she was "reborn." She explained: "I have acquired so many new attributes during my study here, that I literally have been reborn into a different person. I am more open, more motivated to learn, and more sociable."

When I asked what were the new attributes she has acquired, her response was: empathy. She described why she thinks so:

> I will give you one example. Recently I paid a visit to the museum of Martin Luther King, Jr. in Atlanta, and I was crying over the struggles and fights that Dr. King and others endured during the Civil Rights era. I was really shocked when I was crying, because I used to cry only over my own business, or about my family. It was hard to imagine that I could cry over others' lives that are from a different country and that happened even before I was born.

Lei recalled the incident quite emotionally, and she attributed the cultivation of empathy to her studies here in the United States. Lei was a campus connector and was active in various campus organizations. She cherished this opportunity of engagement, as she used to focus almost exclusively on testing in China.

This sense of empathy and a more profound understanding about America is helpful not only for their personal development, but also is healing when they navigate biases and discrimination in the United States.

Navigating Biases and Discrimination

Chinese international students interact with their American classmates, American professors, and university staff members, such as those in administrative support units, counseling centers, and career services. How do they feel about these interactions? The survey questions asked Chinese students to think about the following statements: "I have been treated as equal to American students by classmates," "I have been treated as equal to American students by professors," and "I have been treated as equal to American students by service professionals." The survey respondents were asked to indicate their attitudes about the above statements on a Likert scale ranging from one (strongly disagree) to five (strongly agree). Comparisons of the statements were concerned with which of the three registered the most positive experience for the Chinese students (the least amount of unequal treatment) and which registered the least positive experience (the most amount of unequal treatment)?

About 60 percent of students agreed or strongly agreed that they had been treated equally by American professors, and a similar number of students agreed or strongly agreed that they had been treated equally by university staff, whereas less than 45 percent agreed or strongly agreed that they had been treated equally by American classmates. In other words, the Chinese international students were the least positive about their interactions with their American peers: more than half felt that they had been treated unequally. This is significant not only for their social integration on American campuses, but also for their perceptions of America as a nation preaching equality and liberty for everyone.

What kinds of students were more likely to perceive unequal treatments from Americans? First-generation college students, compared to their peers whose parents were college-educated, were more likely to report that they disagreed or strongly disagreed with the statement "you are treated equally by your American classmates." Students who started as college students in the United States, as opposed to those who started in high school, were more likely to report that they disagreed or strongly disagreed with the statement. Students who perceived their English to be "poor" or "fair" were more likely to report that they disagreed or strongly disagreed. It is important to note that these are all only correlations, not causal relationships.

Beyond the numbers, Chinese students experienced real instances of discrimination, and at times, ugly xenophobia. In February 2017, a number of students with Chinese names reported having their name tags ripped off their doors in several residence halls at Columbia University. This act of vandalism happened in the week following an executive order signed by President Trump that heavily restricted immigration to the United States. In response, Chinese students produced a video together called *Say My Name*, in which students talked about the stories behind their names. This video went viral on Facebook, with over a quarter million views. The Chinese students were widely applauded for their heroic efforts to turn "an episode of ugly xenophobia into an opportunity for better understanding."[14]

Conclusion

American immigration scholars argue for the immigrant advantage theory,[15] which means that immigrant parents straddle their host country and home country and are able to reap the best of two worlds in educating their children, which helps explain the rapid upward mobility of their children. Likewise, Chinese international students, straddling two worlds and reaping the benefits of both the American and Chinese educational systems, have the potential to serve as a bridge between the two societies and promote better understanding between the United States and China. In this sense, they can be the transnational agents to accomplish the worthy goal that Kissinger advocated of "diminishing cultural biases to mitigate possible tensions and create opportunities for both countries."[16]

As international students are away from China and become part of the overseas Chinese population, they may develop a new consciousness toward their home country. Their interest in China is renewed, from food to history. They are also reflexive about their previous understanding on China. This may arise in part from American education, which offers curricula and activities that cultivate their critical thinking skills and exposes them to domains of knowledge that they rarely had the chance to experience previously.[17] Through community engagement and volunteer activities, they have also gained empathy. This helps them navigate bias and discrimination that is prevalent in a race-conscious society such as the United States. Few issues are as divisive as the popularity of the Dalai Lama in the United States and Chinese students' strong opposition to his message. For Chinese students to really become transnational agents, their voices and positions cannot be taken as synonymous with or indoctrinated by the Chinese government. American universities need to respect their voices and in given circumstances, create opportunities for Chinese students to play an active role in open discussions and debates over this controversial issue.

In sum, adaptation, like communication, is a two-way street. When we expect international students to adapt to American colleges, we do not want to neglect the active role on the part of American colleges to adapt as well. This entails understanding, patience, and sometimes perhaps, inconvenience on the part of American universities. If done well, this new wave of Chinese international students will serve as transnational agents that can help diminish the biases and tensions and boost healthy interactions between the United States and China.

Notes

1   Henry Kissinger, "Support for Schwarzman Scholars," (https://www.schwarzma nscholars.org/support-for-schwarzman-scholars).

2   Andrew B. Kipnis, *Governing Educational Desire: Culture, Politics, and Schooling in China* (Chicago, IL: University of Chicago Press, 2011).

3 Swanson, Ana, "Trump's Trade War With China Is Officially Underway," 2018, https://www.nytimes.com/2018/07/05/business/china-us-trade-war-trump-tariffs.html.

4 Institute of International Education. Open Door Report 2017.

5 Jamil Anderlini, "'Western values' forbidden in Chinese universities," 2015, https://www.ft.com/content/95f3f866-a87e-11e4-bd17-00144feab7de.

6 Henry Kissinger and Nicholas Hormann, *On China* (New York: Penguin Press, 2011); Marc Lanteigne, *Chinese Foreign Policy: An Introduction* (London: Routledge, 2015).

7 Eric Liu, *The Accidental Asian: Notes of a Native Speaker* (New York: Vintage, 1999).

8 "The Nobel Peace Prize for 1989, The 14th Dalai Lama," October 5, 1989, https://www.nobelprize.org/prizes/peace/1989/press-release/.

9 Jessica Iannetta, "Students Protest Dalai Lama's Visit Outside of SU Student Center," *The Daily Orange*, 2012, http://dailyorange.com/2012/10/students-protest-dalai-lamas-visit-outside-of-su-student-center/.

10 Elizabeth Redden, "Chinese Students vs. Dalai Lama" *Inside Higher Ed*, 2017, https://www.insidehighered.com/news/2017/02/16/some-chinese-students-uc-san-diego-condemn-choice-dalai-lama-commencement-speaker.

11 Nancy Abelmann and Jiyeon Kang, "A Fraught Exchange? US Media on Chinese International Undergraduates and the American University," *Journal of Studies in International Education* 18, 4 (2014): 382–97.

12 Vanessa Fong, *Paradise Redefined: Transnational Chinese Students and the Quest for Flexible Citizenship in the Developed World* (Palo Alto, CA: Stanford University Press, 2011).

13 Benedict Anderson, *Imagined Communities: Reflections on the Origin and Spread of Nationalism* (New York: Verso Books, 2006).

14 Kenneth Tan, "Chinese Students at Columbia University Fight Racism by Explaining the Meaning behind Their Names," 2017, https://shanghaiist.com/2017/02/15/say-my-name/.

15 Philip Kasinitz, John H. Mollenkopf, Mary C. Waters, and Jennifer Holdaway, *Inheriting the City: The Children of Immigrants Come of Age* (New York: Russell Sage Foundation, 2009).

16 Kissinger, "Support for Schwarzman Scholars."

17 Yingyi Ma, "Is the Grass Greener on the Other Side of the Pacific?" *Contexts* 14, 2 (2015): 34–9.

5

Between Deterrence and Reassurance: The US–Japan Alliance and the East China Sea, 1991–2016

Erik French

Introduction

This chapter considers the consequences of changes in the US strategy for addressing Sino-Japanese territorial disputes in the East China Sea (ECS) since the end of the Cold War. First, it examines how Washington's commitment to and consultation with Japan with respect to the ECS disputes has shifted over time. Second, it assesses whether these developments have been accompanied by changes in Japan's support for US policy. Third, it considers whether changes in US strategy and Japanese support have been associated with shifts in the extent of US success in deterring and reassuring China with respect to the ECS disputes. In doing so, this chapter addresses a recurring debate over US strategy in the Asia-Pacific: should the United States coordinate closely with or distance itself from Japan in order to better manage relations with China? This chapter finds that the United States has had the most success in deterring and reassuring China when it has coordinated carefully with Japan in managing the ECS disputes. When the United States has distanced itself from Japan, however, it has undermined its ability to deter China and prevent escalation.

Background: The East China Sea Disputes

The Sino-Japanese dispute over the Senkaku Islands has its roots in divergent interpretations of history. China claims that its ownership of the islands dates to at least the sixteenth century and that Japan seized the Senkakus as part of Taiwan after the First Sino-Japanese War in 1895.[1] China insists that Japan has no right to the islands given the Allied Cairo Declaration in 1943 requiring that Japan return the territory it took from China by force. The Japanese government, however, argues that the Senkakus were *terra nullius* in 1895 when Japan first established a presence on the islands.[2] On these grounds, Japan claims the islands are an indisputable part of its territory.

A broader dispute over the exclusive economic zones (EEZs) in the ECS emerged in the 1990s as the United Nations Convention on the Law of the Sea (UNCLOS) came into effect. Japan and China each claim overlapping EEZs.[3] China's EEZ claim is based on its continental shelf. Japan's EEZ claim, in contrast, is based on a median line division between the Chinese and Japanese territorial waters.

Japan and China each have significant interests at stake in these disputes. Both states see a strategic advantage in controlling the Senkakus given that the islands are a part of the "first island chain."[4] Japan and China also have an interest in accessing the potential untapped (albeit limited) seabed resources in the ECS, including modest oil and gas fields.[5] There are also potentially lucrative fishing grounds in the ECS that both states would prefer to control.[6]

Most importantly, however, the Senkaku Islands have political significance. Japanese and Chinese citizens, particularly nationalists, care intensely about control over this territory. For Japan, the Senkakus have become a symbol of national pride. For China, the Senkakus are part of the territory that was stripped from China by Japan and other imperial powers during its "Century of Humiliation."[7] Its continued separation from the People's Republic of China is seen as a constant reminder of past humiliation and China's need to strive for national reunification.

Washington has not taken a side in the dispute over the sovereignty of the Senkakus or the validity of each state's EEZ claims. The United States does, however, have a reputational interest at stake given Japan's current administrative control over the Senkakus. If the United States were to tolerate Chinese militarized challenges to Japan's control of the islands, it would damage American credibility as an ally more generally. The Senkakus also form part of the "first island chain," a series of islands running from Japan to the Malay archipelago that curtail the Chinese navy's ability to access the West Pacific, and therefore have strategic significance for US efforts to keep Chinese maritime power in check.[8]

The Debate: Alliance Strategies, Reassurance, and Deterrence

In the context of the ECS dispute, the United States has attempted to balance reassurance and deterrence toward China. On the one hand, Washington seeks to reassure China that the United States (and its Japanese ally) will not fundamentally alter the status quo in the ECS by developing or militarizing the Senkaku Islands. In doing so, it seeks to prevent an unnecessary escalatory spiral triggered by misplaced fears about American and Japanese revisionism in China. On the other hand, the United States seeks to deter China from challenging Japan's administrative control of the Senkaku Islands through military coercion. In particular, it aims to convince China that the allies have the resolve and capabilities necessary to make such coercion fruitless and costly for Beijing.

Policymakers and scholars alike debate the relative efficacy of different alliance strategies for managing relations with China.[9] US alliance strategy varies between two ideal types: distancing and coordination. These strategies are distinguished by the extent of Washington's commitment to and consultation with its ally. A coordination strategy features strong and well-specified commitments to and extensive consultation with Japan. A distancing strategy, in contrast, features weak and vague commitments and limited consultation.

Advocates of distancing argue that US coordination risks encouraging an overconfident Japan to adopt a hard-line stance toward China in the ECS (and elsewhere), undercutting Washington's reassurance toward Beijing and entrapping the United States in an unnecessary escalatory spiral.[10] They also contend that an overconfident Japan may seek to "free-ride" off of the United States' commitment to the alliance and, in doing so, will fail to support Washington's deterrence efforts toward China.[11] Distancing strategies, alternatively, restrain Japan and incentivize it to support US policy in an effort to better secure its partnership with the United States. As such, distancing strategy will serve to better manage relations with Japan and China in the ECS.

Conversely, advocates of coordination argue that distancing strategies cause Japan to fear that the United States will abandon it in the face of pressure from China, leaving Japan to fend for itself. If Tokyo fears abandonment too intensely, it may hedge by either adopting a confrontational or accommodative stance toward China in the ECS. This behavior will, in turn, undercut US reassurance and/or deterrence toward China. US coordination with Japan, in contrast, will encourage Tokyo to reciprocate, working more closely with Washington in managing the ECS dispute. Consequently, the allies will be more successful in efforts to deter and reassure China. Similarly, when the United States works closely with Japan, it should serve as a credible signal of American resolve, reinforcing US efforts to deter Chinese challenges to the status quo in the ECS.

This chapter engages this debate by considering the impact of shifts in US alliance strategy between these two ideal type strategies in the ECS since the end of the Cold War. It demonstrates that the United States has had the most success in managing the ECS disputes when it has strengthened its coordination with Japan. Conversely, the weaker the US coordination with Japan, the less successful it has been in deterring and reassuring China in the ECS.

Strategic Ambiguity: 1991–6

Background

The end of the Cold War and the implementation of the UNCLOS drove maritime disputes in the ECS back to the front of Chinese and Japanese policy agendas.[12] In 1992, China abandoned its past policy of shelving the dispute by passing its Law on the Territorial Sea and the Contiguous Zone. This law provided a legal basis for the Chinese government to both access resources in the Senkakus and use force to protect the islands.[13] As Chinese vessels began encroaching on the Senkakus and surrounding water with increasing frequency, tensions mounted with Japan.

In 1996, the Japan Youth League (JYL)—a private group of right-wing activists—escalated the simmering dispute by repeatedly landing on the Senkakus. The JYL traveled to and from the privately held islands, established a small lighthouse in July, built a war memorial in August, and repaired the lighthouse in September.[14] The Japanese government chose to neither support nor oppose (or impede) the JYL's activities. With each trip, Beijing grew increasingly irate. Activists in Taiwan and Hong Kong took up the Chinese cause, sending boats and flotillas in an attempt to land on the islands.[15] By the peak of the crisis in September, the Chinese military had threatened military action and was conducting major military exercises on its northeast coast.[16]

US Alliance Strategy

Washington's strategy toward Japan during this period prioritized distancing over strategic coordination. Trade disputes, Japanese political turnover, and the lack of Japanese participation in the Gulf War predisposed American policymakers to prioritize strategies that did not lean too heavily on Japan. The alliance underwent a period of drift with strategists in the Clinton administration questioning the utility of the alliance relationship for American interests. More narrowly, the administration sought to keep its distance from the Senkaku Island dispute. American policymakers saw the dispute as overblown and a distraction from more pressing regional matters.[17] Most importantly, American officials were aware of the resurgence of the nationalist far right in Japanese politics and were keen to avoid emboldening this faction within Japan.

By the 1990s, with tensions rising over the islands for the first time since the 1970s, the United States was hesitant to commit to the defense of the Senkakus.[18] Ambassador Walter Mondale controversially stated in a public interview in 1995 that "American forces would not be compelled by the treaty to intervene in a dispute" that involved the Senkakus.[19] Assistant Secretary of State Winston Lord refused to comment on a hypothetical Senkaku contingency.[20] State Department deputy spokesman Glyn Davies later announced that "We're simply going to confine ourselves to calling on both sides to resist the temptation to provoke each other."[21] State Department spokesperson Nick Burns similarly refused to clarify the US commitment in a press briefing on October 3.[22]

Similarly, US consultation with Japan on the Senkakus was relatively limited. Prior to 1996, there is little evidence that the allies discussed the security of the Senkakus or how to manage the issue with China. By 1996, alliance dialogue was largely focused on updating the US–Japan defense guidelines and containing regional contingencies in places like the Korean peninsula; Washington did not prioritize the Senkakus in their consultations with Tokyo.[23]

Japan's Perceptions and Policy

From 1991 to 1996, Japan feared abandonment and engaged in limited hedging behavior. Washington's decision to limit its commitments to the Senkakus contributed directly to Japanese fears of abandonment. One Japanese diplomat reportedly fretted: "This is so different from their former statements. It's terrible."[24] A high-ranking Japanese defense official would later argue that this distance "created incredibly strong distrust towards America."[25]

Japan acted upon its concerns by adopting a more confrontational position on the Senkakus than it had in the past. While Japan had prevented activists from traveling to the Senkakus only five years earlier, exercising restraint, its response to developments in 1996 was far less accommodative toward Beijing.[26] The government refused to restrain the JYL in response to Beijing's protests. Instead, it justified their conduct. Chief Cabinet Secretary Seiroku argued publicly "I personally don't think we should say this and that about something being constructed legitimately with permission from the Japanese landlord."[27] An unidentified government official similarly stated that the "We neither support nor oppose the [JYL's] activities."[28]

Reassurance and Deterrence toward China

Distancing by the United States and Japanese hedging were accompanied by significant Chinese escalation. Early on, during the initial drift in allied relations during the late George H. W. Bush and early Clinton administrations, China passed new legislation authorizing it to use force to secure the Senkakus and other Chinese territorial claims, a clear departure from the tacit consensus to shelve the dispute from the 1970s. Around the same time, Chinese ships began firing warning shots at Japanese vessels near the Senkakus—as many as twelve incidents were reported in 1991.[29] In 1995, China escalated further, sending fighters near the islands for the first time, prompting Japan to scramble interceptors.[30] Chinese research vessels also began regularly plying waters claimed by Japan.[31]

In 1996, Japan's confrontational approach seems to have convinced Chinese leaders that they needed to escalate still more forcefully. The Chinese Ministry of Foreign Affairs (MOFA) spokesman announced that "the building of facilities on the islands by some Japanese without authorization constitutes a serious encroachment on China's territorial sovereignty. We are greatly concerned about this."[32] *The People's Daily* framed Japan's tolerance of the JYL as a "challenge to China"—a deliberate provocation to test Beijing's resolve.[33] China acted on these perceptions, escalating in response to the JYL landings in 1996. The Chinese navy dispatched two submarines to the Senkaku Islands in July, conducted major war games simulating blockades and amphibious assaults on island targets, and threatened to use force to defend its claims to the islands.[34]

The Armitage Doctrine: 1996–2009

Background

The 1996 crisis petered out at the end of the year, ushering in a long period of stability in the ECS. The following year saw China and Japan develop a joint fisheries agreement to help facilitate the use of resources in the ECS.[35] Although the Senkaku dispute occasionally reemerged—most notably in 2004 when activists attempted to take matters into their own hands—Beijing and Tokyo did their best to constrain these groups from disrupting their bilateral relations. Indeed, by 2007, Japan and China seemed on the brink of even closer cooperation in the ECS, having concluded a new arrangement for energy exploration.

US Alliance Strategy

From 1996 to 2009, US alliance strategy toward Japan emphasized greater coordination both in general and with respect to the Senkakus and the ECS. Most significantly, Washington offered an amplified commitment to the Senkakus and engaged in greater policy consultation and information sharing. The United States articulated what would come to be known as "the Armitage Doctrine," named after Richard Armitage who would become deputy secretary of state under Bush. The United States would now explicitly commit to the defense of the Senkakus under Article 5 of the Security Treaty but remain neutral on all other issues including sovereignty. Deputy assistant secretary of defense for Asia and the Pacific Kurt Campbell first privately affirmed to the Japanese government that the United States was committed to the defense of the islands in late October.[36] This private commitment was followed up by repeated public and private affirmations by US officials throughout the Clinton and George W. Bush administrations that staked US reputation to the defense of this territory.[37] Under the George W. Bush administration, the United States backed up this verbal commitment with increased military coordination with Japan. In 2005 and 2006, the United States began training with Japanese forces to practice the defense of islands against hostile forces.[38] These measures served as both a signal of Washington's commitment toward Tokyo and its resolve toward Beijing.

The United States similarly began to consult more extensively with Japan on relations with China both in general and in the ECS in particular. Broadly speaking, the allies developed and reinforced existing mechanisms for dialogue and information sharing with the conclusion of the defense guideline revisions in 1997. The 1997 Defense Guidelines committed the United States to "conduct bilateral work, including bilateral defense planning in case of an armed attack against Japan, and mutual cooperation planning in situations in areas surrounding Japan."[39] This included planning to address seaborne invasions, guerilla incursions, and threats to sea lanes and nearby waters— all directly relevant to the security of the Senkakus and the ECS. The United States pledged to work with Japan to "make every effort, including diplomatic efforts, to prevent further deterioration" of tensions in these areas that could result in an armed attack on Japan.[40]

Washington also took advantage of the new defense guidelines to share key information with Japan on developments in and near the Senkakus and the ECS. In November 2004, the allies reportedly helped share intelligence to monitor a Chinese Han-class nuclear submarine as it moved by the Senkakus and Okinawa and into Japanese territorial waters; the United States shared data from P3-C surveillance craft that allowed Japan to monitor the Chinese boat's progress.[41]

Japanese Perceptions and Policy

After the expanded American commitment—both to the Senkakus and to the alliance more generally—Japan's fears of abandonment declined significantly. The anxiety over the dependability of the United States in the event of a crisis with China over the Senkakus that was so noticeably present throughout 1996 was noticeably absent after deputy assistant secretary of defense for Asia and the Pacific Campbell's commitment. In an address before the Japanese Diet in November after Campbell's private assurances, the Japanese deputy minister of foreign affairs Hitoshi Tanaka expressed confidence in its ally: "The United States is aware of the obligation" to defend the Senkakus.[42]

After Campbell's assurances, Tokyo took a far more restrained stance toward the Senkakus. First, it curtailed its own nationalist activists. While Japan had felt pressured to refrain from opposing the JYL actions in the Senkakus in 1996, it was able to curtail nationalist groups more successfully from 1997 to 2009 without worrying about signaling irresolution or incurring undue political costs. Japanese Ministry of Foreign Affairs Spokesman Nobuaki Tanaka called a 1997 landing by Japanese nationalists "quite regretful." He emphasized that the Japanese government would work to discourage such landings.[43] In 2002, Japan leased the islands from their private owners to allow them to deny Japanese activists the ability to land and provoke China.[44] When the JYL sought to land again in 2004, the government blocked them.[45] Japan proceeded to nationalize the JYL lighthouse in 2005, removing the JYL's excuse to travel to the islands.[46]

Second, Japan took a firm but reasonable approach to dealing with Chinese nationalist activists attempting to land on the islands. Most notably, in 2004 the Japanese government intervened to prevent Japanese police from pressing charges against Chinese nationalist activists that had landed on the Senkakus. Instead, it returned the nationalists to China in a deft display of restraint. After this incident, the Japanese Diet attempted to pass a security resolution to retaliate for the landings. Instead of bowing to pressure in the Diet, Japanese prime minister Junichiro Koizumi's "office heavily advised the Diet on the issue of the Senkaku security resolution ... to keep it as unprovocative as possible."[47]

Deterrence and Reassurance toward China

Beijing was somewhat more reassured by Japan's efforts to restrain its nationalists during this period. Following the 1997 incident, for instance, the spokesperson for the MOFA noted appreciatively that the Japanese government had expressed the view that the landings contravened Japan's policy.[48] China similarly seems to have recognized the growing American commitment to its ally's control over the Senkakus. The "United States and Japan [have] joined hand [sic] in establishing a firm military alliance in East Asia" the state-run *Global Times* noted in response to Washington's recommitment to the defense of the Senkakus.[49] A top Chinese scholar remarked that the 2006 exercises demonstrated "the Clinton administration indicated that it will firmly stand by the side of its Japanese ally, and this policy is continued by the Bush administration."[50]

China's behavior reflected these perceptions. Beijing refrained from any significant escalation during this period; although it issued diplomatic protests and engaged in periodic intrusions into airspace and waters claimed by Japan, it managed the dispute in a restrained fashion. During the 2004 incident, China issued diplomatic protests but refrained from significant militarized threats. A Chinese source cited in the Japanese press claimed that "the Chinese government wanted to avoid complicating the issue or getting mired in it."[51] After the conclusion of the 2004 incident and the return of the Chinese activists, Tokyo asked Beijing to ensure that protesters did not engage in similar activity in the future. Shortly afterward, a Chinese nationalist group planning to travel to the Senkakus announced that they would be postponing their trip.[52] Some analysts have reported that Tokyo and Beijing each issued private assurances after the crisis: Tokyo stated that they would promptly return any Chinese activists trying to access the islands, while Beijing pledged to keep Chinese activists from leaving the mainland.[53]

During this period, China also engaged in some limited cooperation in the ECS. In 2001, China agreed to a "notification system" obliging it to inform Tokyo when Chinese vessels moved into Japan's EEZ.[54] In 2007, China agreed to discuss economic cooperation in the ECS with Japan; this led to a Sino-Japanese agreement in 2008 to explore the potential natural gas reserves in the contested ECS.

Fallout from the Financial Crisis: 2009–13

Background

From 2009 to 2013, a combination of factors led to major setbacks in Sino-Japanese relations over the Senkaku Islands that rendered the existing US strategy outdated. In particular, domestic dysfunction in Japan and rising assertiveness in China triggered a series of crises with lasting implications for the US–Japan–China relations. While improvements in American coordination with Japan had served it well in the past, the intensification of the dispute required stronger coordination between the allies; deterrence and reassurance both faltered in part due to the existing limits to the extent of US coordination toward the Senkakus with Japan.

After several years of increasing Chinese assertiveness in maritime territorial disputes in both the East and South China Seas, tensions boiled over when an inebriated Chinese captain rammed his fishing trawler into a Japanese Coast Guard vessel near the Senkakus. The new, inexperienced Democratic Party of Japan (DPJ) government under Kan Naoto in Japan mishandled the trawler incident; it detained and indicted the captain, inciting a massive backlash from Beijing.[55] Under intense economic and diplomatic pressure, Tokyo was coerced into accommodating Beijing by returning the captain.[56]

This standoff ushered in a period of heightened tension; China began aggressively increasing the frequency and severity of its challenges to Japanese control of the Senkakus. This cumulated in a backlash from the Japanese right: Ishihara Shintaro, the governor of Tokyo and a fervent nationalist, pledged to purchase the Senkakus from their private owners in 2012. The Japanese government, now under a new DPJ government led by Noda Yoshihiko, preemptively purchased the islands to prevent Ishihara from damaging both Sino-Japanese relations and the DPJ's already tarnished nationalist credentials. Beijing saw the move as bold-faced revisionism, however, and responded with massive escalation. It would take a new US strategy, beginning in early 2013, to help ease the rapidly mounting tensions.

US Alliance Strategy

From 2009 to 2013, the Obama administration largely continued the strategy of its predecessors of limited coordination with Japan over the Senkaku Islands. The administration adhered to the Armitage Doctrine of committing to the defense of the Senkakus under Article 5 but remaining decidedly neutral on all other issues pertaining to the islands. In 2009, assistant secretary of state for Public Affairs Philip Crowley clarified that "if you ask today would the treaty apply to the Senkaku Islands, the answer is yes."[57] During both the 2010 incident and the 2012 crisis, Secretary of State Hillary Clinton reemphasized this commitment, stating repeatedly in private and in public that the Senkakus were covered by Article 5 and that the United States remained otherwise neutral. Gates, Mullen, and others similarly made it clear that the United States was committed to Japan's defense.

Consultation suffered somewhat under the Hatoyama administration in 2009 and 2010. A Brookings Institution report concluded that "high-level communication between Washington and Tokyo became so strained that the Obama administration effectively barred any significant celebrations in 2010 to commemorate the 50th anniversary of the US-Japan Security Treaty."[58] Relations improved somewhat after Hatoyama's departure in 2010; still, Washington was initially reluctant to get involved in the details of the trawler dispute later that year. National Security Council (NSC) official Jeffrey Bader would similarly contend that the United States would not manage the dispute: it "was not playing nor going to play a mediating role."[59] As the dispute escalated, however, the Obama administration moved to consult more closely with both parties.[60]

Japan's Perceptions and Policies

Alliance management became challenging during this period. Growing tensions with China and shifting relative power drove Japan to hedge in 2010 and 2012, undercutting both allied deterrence and reassurance in the ECS. Although the US commitment to defend the Senkakus if they were under Japan's administrative control and were attacked was clear, ambiguities remained about the scale and scope of the commitment. As Japanese policy scholar Sato Yoichiro opined, "there is a perception in Japan that the U.S. commitment is ambiguous."[61]

This contributed to a growing fear of Chinese revisionism and strong belief that Japan needed to do something dramatic to demonstrate its resolve, or risk deterrence failure. Kan's decision to back down in the face of Chinese pressure in 2010 only intensified Japanese concerns. Even moderate Japanese parliamentarians and policy elites were critical of the release of the Chinese captain after the trawler incident.[62] Many worried that the move had damaged Japan's ability to assert its claims over the Senkakus.[63] When the nationalization crisis loomed, "the leaders of both major parties believed that Japan had to send a signal of resolve to Beijing in order to ward off any potential attempt to seize the disputed islands."[64] The Noda administration (2011–12) had to find a way to signal strength; as such, Japan pursued a hedging strategy, ignoring US advice to avoid nationalizing the islands. A report by the Center for Strategic and International Studies (CSIS) claims, "it was well known within [Noda's] inner circle that the underlying motivation was countering a perceived Chinese revanchist threat."[65]

Deterrence and Reassurance toward China

From 2009 to 2013, Chinese perceptions shifted. First, China increasingly saw Japanese intentions as revisionist. These perceptions contributed directly to China's decision to escalate the crisis. Choong reports that interviews with Chinese officials indicated that "to the Chinese, Japan's rationale for nationalization ... was a ruse. To them, the purchase was a Japanese plot to present Beijing with a fait accompli."[66] Ren Xiao, director of a Chinese think tank in Fudan University, argues that "for China this was an unacceptable change to the status quo."[67] Chinese leaders also blamed the Obama administration's Asian "rebalance" or "pivot" strategy: a policy announced in 2011 committing the United States to renewing and reinforcing its diplomatic, economic, and military engagement in the Asia Pacific. Despite Washington's disapproval of Japan's policy, China feared that the Obama administration's strategy had—either unwittingly or intentionally—emboldened Tokyo to take these steps.[68] Japan's purchase of the island undercut allied reassurances toward China that the alliance would pursue stability rather than revisionism in the region.

At the same time, China saw an opportunity to revise the status quo itself, degrading Japan's control over the islands and challenging the gaps in the existing American commitment. Glaser writes that "it is also likely that at least some in China saw Japan's action as presenting an opportunity to challenge the status quo of the islands dispute. China could assert its sovereignty claim and ratcheted up tensions over the islands without appearing as the provocateur."[69] Fudan University's Ren Xiao claims, "The objective is to bring about de facto joint jurisdiction and joint patrolling in the relevant waters to deny Japan's unilateral 'control' of the islands. Beijing wants to force Japan to change its 'no territorial dispute' position."[70]

China acted on these perceptions, escalating the dispute quickly and aggressively. In particular, China dramatically increased the number of Chinese ships intruding on the waters surrounding the Senkakus.[71] Vice-chair of CMC Xu Caihou "urged the army not to be slack and be prepared for any possible military combat."[72] Several Chinese government planes flew over or near the disputed territory.[73] At one point, this triggered Japan to scramble F-15 fighters to intercept, prompting China to scramble its own J-10 fighters.[74] In January 2013, Chinese ships twice locked their fire-control radar onto Japanese assets—a helicopter and a frigate—prompting widespread regional alarm.[75]

New Commitments: 2013–16

Background

Throughout 2013, Japan and China sparred over the ECS. The year 2013 saw the return of the Liberal Democratic Party to power in Japan under Shinzo Abe on a platform that included a robust assertion of Japanese sovereignty claims. It also saw China declare an Air Defense Identification Zone (ADIZ) encompassing much of the ECS, including the Senkakus. By 2014, however, relations had begun to stabilize. Both Japan and China made efforts at rapprochement, cumulating in a meeting between Chinese president Xi Jinping and Abe at that year's Asia Pacific Economic Cooperation Leaders Summit.

US Alliance Strategy

The Obama administration noticeably strengthened its strategic coordination with Japan toward the ECS and Senkakus throughout this period of time. Secretary of State Clinton made the first move to do so on January 18, 2013, stating that the United States was not only committed to defending the islands but that "we oppose any unilateral actions that would seek to undermine Japanese administration."[76] For the first time, the United States had explicitly stated it was committed not only to defend the Senkakus from direct attack but also to preserve Japan's administrative control against any unilateral challenges. A year later, President Obama himself confirmed this obligation several times publicly. While the president's statements were reiterations of existing policy, they still represented a dramatic increase in commitment: the president put his reputation directly on the line, rendering the commitment significantly costlier and consequently more credible. Throughout 2014 and 2015, the United States further solidified its commitment to Japan through the new defense guidelines revisions.

Washington backed up these verbal commitments with strengthened military cooperation. The US Air Force began surveillance flights using advanced Airborne Warning and Control System aircraft over the Senkakus and deployed P-8A Poseidon maritime patrol craft in 2013.[77] At the same time, the United States moved to modernize United States Marine Corps () transportation in Okinawa, introducing the MV-22 Osprey to replace its aging CH-46 helicopters.[78] These new assets reinforced the credibility of the United States' expanded commitments.

Washington also strengthened its consultation with Tokyo. US secretary of defense Chuck Hagel and Secretary of State John Kerry consulted closely with their Japanese counterparts after China's ADIZ announcement.[79] The new defense guidelines in 2015 further strengthened and institutionalized consultation on "gray zone" threats to issues like the ECS.[80] The guidelines developed a "whole-of-government Alliance Coordination Mechanism" to "assess the situation" and "share information" when contingencies arise.[81] They agreed to achieve "shared maritime domain awareness including by coordinating with relevant agencies, as necessary."[82] This amplified coordination was on display in 2016 when a Chinese warship intruded in Japanese waters in the ECS. In response, an American defense official reported that "Japan has informed the U.S. and is in close communication with Washington."[83]

Japan's Perceptions and Policies

The strengthened alliance commitment and consultation helped assure Japan of the United States' trustworthiness as an ally. Japanese officials were relieved by the new American commitment, describing Clinton's initial articulation of the points as "extremely major and significant."[84] After Obama's recommitment to the defense of the Senkakus, Prime Minister Abe stated that US–Japan ties were "rock solid" and that "I have total utmost faith in Obama."[85]

A more confident Japan felt less pressure to send aggressive signals of resolve, instead adopting a resolute but restrained approach to the dispute. Abe articulated this new approach best: "While Japan will not concede and will uphold our fundamental position that the Senkaku islands are an inherent territory of Japan, we intend to respond calmly so as not to provoke China."[86] In a speech at the Center for Strategic and International Studies in 2013, Abe laid out this vision for restraint coupled by resolve still more clearly: "We simply cannot tolerate any challenge now, or in the future. No nation should underestimate the firmness of our resolve. No one should ever doubt the robustness of the Japan-U.S. Alliance. At the same time, I have absolutely no intention of climbing up the escalation ladder. In fact, my government is investing more into people to people exchanges between Japan and China."[87] Perhaps most significantly, Tokyo took steps to mend ties with Beijing, refusing to compromise on sovereignty but presenting proposals for mutual deescalation and crisis management.[88]

At the same time, the United States and Japan were able to issue stronger joint deterrence signals to help counteract China's growing assertiveness. In 2013, Japan participated in the United States' "Dawn Blitz" exercise designed to prepare for an amphibious assault on remote islands.[89] The allies also joined with Australia to issue a particularly strong reaction to China's ADIZ later that year, stating that they opposed "any coercive and unilateral actions that could change the status quo or increase tensions in the ECS."[90] They also jointly defied the ADIZ later that month, sending a combined twelve reconnaissance and fighter craft through the ECS.[91] In 2014, Japan also participated in the "Iron Fist 2014" military exercise with US forces, again practicing operations on offshore islands.[92]

Deterrence and Reassurance toward China

By the end of 2013, according to top Sinologist Taylor Fravel, "the dispute appears to have stabilized."[93] Fravel and Johnson both argue that China intentionally reduced its operations in the ECS to signal its willingness to de-escalate the crisis in 2013 and 2014.[94] By 2014, Beijing appeared to be deliberately reducing the tempo and scale of its operations around the Senkakus.[95] Japan's defense minister Akira Sato went so far as to argue that "China is starting to show signs of softening," which created an opportunity for detente.[96] In September 2014, Japan and China resumed military contact and began discussing a crisis-management mechanism to reduce the chances of escalation in the

ECS.[97] Both Japan and China also managed to reach an agreement on four points to facilitate the resumption of dialogue over the ECS before an Asia-Pacific Economic Cooperation Leaders Summit meeting between Abe and Xi.[98]

Conclusion

Closer coordination appears to have had a positive effect on Washington's ability to reassure and deter China in the ECS. Across the cases, increases in US coordination are associated with greater confidence in Japan, greater Japanese support for US policy, and more successful deterrence and reassurance toward China. Limited coordination appears to be linked to Japanese fears of abandonment, which are in turn closely connected to choices to either adopt a more confrontational or accommodative stance toward China. These hedging strategies often made reassurance or deterrence more difficult for the United States.

These findings suggest that the United States should reinforce its commitment to and consultation with Japan in the ECS. In particular, Washington should consider (1) strengthening coast guard cooperation with Japan, (2) assisting Japan in the development of its amphibious capabilities, (3) developing tailored gray zone joint response plans for a range of scenarios in the ECS, and (4) encouraging Japan to continue to exercise restraint and develop crisis-stability measures to manage the ECS dispute. These steps should help shore up Washington's commitment to Tokyo and synchronize allied policy toward the dispute, which in turn should improve the United States' ability to both deter and reassure China in the ECS.

These findings also suggest that the United States should maintain and strengthen its coordination with Japan on other issues. Areas of mutual concern include the Taiwan Strait, the Korean Peninsula, and the South China Sea. In each domain, the United States relies on continued Japanese assistance. In the Taiwan Strait, US access to Japanese air bases in Okinawa is critical to the United States' ability to deter Chinese military coercion against Taipei.[99] On the Korean Peninsula, Japan's support for US diplomatic initiatives, economic sanctions, and military contingency planning is vital to American efforts to secure Chinese support for pressure directed against North Korea.[100] In the South China Sea, Japan's growing naval cooperation with the United States helps to reinforce Washington's attempts to deter China from continuing its militarization of this critical waterway.[101] Moving forward, the United States would be well-advised to continue strengthening its commitment and consultation with Japan in each of these domains to encourage Tokyo to broaden and deepen its collaboration with Washington.

Notes

1   For one of the more comprehensive Chinese accounts, see: "Diaoyu Dao, an Inherent Territory of China," PRC State Council Information Office, accessed September 20, 2017, http://www.china-embassy.org/eng/zt/bps/t974694.htm.

2 For Japan's account, see: "The Senkaku Islands: Seeking Maritime Peace Based on the Rule of Law, Not Force or Coercion," *Japanese Ministry of Foreign Affairs*, accessed September 1, 2017, http://www.mofa.go.jp/region/asia-paci/senkaku/pdfs/senkaku_pamphlet.pdf.

3 Ronald O'Rourke, *Maritime Territorial and Exclusive Economic Zone (EEZ) Disputes Involving China: Issues for Congress* (Washington, DC: Congressional Research Service, 2017).

4 Kazumine Akimoto, "The Strategic Value of Territorial Islands from the Perspective of National Security," *Review of Island Studies* (October 9, 2013), https://www.spf.org/islandstudies/research/a00008.html.

5 "East China Sea," EIA, accessed September 1, 2017, https://www.eia.gov/beta/international/regions-topics.cfm?RegionTopicID=ECS.

6 "Tensions in the East China Sea," CFR Conflict Tracker, accessed September 20, 2017, https://www.cfr.org/global/global-conflict-tracker/p32137#!/conflict/tensions-in-the-east-china-sea.

7 Merriden Varrall, "Chinese Worldviews and China's Foreign Policy," Lowy Institute for International Policy, accessed September 24, 2017, https://www.lowyinstitute.org/publications/chinese-worldviews-and-china-s-foreign-policy.

8 James Holmes, "Defend the First Island Chain," *Proceedings Magazine* 140 (2014).

9 See Aaron L Friedberg, "The Debate over US China Strategy," *Survival* 57 (2015).

10 See Wu Xinbo, "America Should Step Back from the East China Sea," *The New York Times*, April 23, 2014; Christopher Layne, "China's Challenge to US Hegemony," *Current History* 705 (2008).

11 Ted Galen Carpenter and Eric Gomez, "East Asia and a Strategy of Restraint," *War on the Rocks* (August 10, 2016).

12 Reinhard Drifte, "The Japan-China Confrontation over the Senkaku/Diaoyu Islands—Between 'shelving' and 'dispute escalation,'" *The Asia Pacific Journal* 12 (2014).

13 "Law on the Territorial Sea and Contiguous Zone," United Nations, accessed September 12, 2017, http://www.un.org/depts/los/LEGISLATIONANDTREATIES/PDFFILES/CHN_1992_Law.pdf.

14 Michael Green, *Reluctant Realism: Foreign Policy Challenges in an Era of Uncertain Power* (New York: Palgrave Macmillan: 2001).

15 Vivian Lee, "Mainland Group May Swell Numbers," *South China Morning Post*, October 5, 1996.

16 Stephen Hutcheon, "China Faces Military Muscle to Warn Japan on Claim to Islands," *The Age*, September 25, 1996.

17 Youichi Funabashi, *Alliance Adrift* (New York: CFR Press, 1999); Green, *Reluctant Realism*.

18 "Treaty of Mutual Cooperation and Security between the United States of America and Japan," Asia for Educators, accessed September 21, 2017, http://afe.easia.columbia.edu/ps/japan/mutual_cooperation_treaty.pdf.

19 Nicholas Kristof, "An Asian Mini-Tempest over Mini-Island Group," *The New York Times*, September 16, 1996; Nicholas Kristof, "Treaty Commitments: Would You Fight For These Islands?" *The New York Times*, November 20, 1996.

20 Funabashi, *Alliance Adrift*, 402.

21 "Daily Press Briefing – September 23, 1996," The US Department of State.

22 Funabashi, *Alliance Adrift*, 401.

23 Ezra Vogel and Paul Giarra, "Renegotiating the Security Relationship," in *Case Studies in Japanese Negotiating Behavior*, ed. Michael Blaker, Paul Giarra, and Ezra Vogel (Washington, DC: USIP Press, 2002).

24 Funabashi, *Alliance Adrift*, 403.

25 Ibid., 411.

26 Green, *Reluctant Realism*, 85–6.

27 Ibid., 86.

28 Kevin Sullivan and Mary Jordan, "Asian Nations Squabble over Small Islands," *The Washington Post*, July 31, 1996.

29 "China's Neighbors Anxious over Islands," *Baltimore Sun*, July 26, 1992.

30 Peter Hartcher, "Air Conflict over Disputed Islands; China–Japan," *Australian Financial Review*, August 25, 1995.

31 James Manicom, *Bridging Troubled Waters: China, Japan, and Maritime Order in the East China Sea* (Washington, DC: Georgetown University Press, 2014), 93.

32 Tan Tarn How, "Beijing Tells Tokyo to 'Take Effective Action,'" *The Straits Times*, July 19, 1996.

33 Tan Tarn How, "Beijing accuses Tokyo of trying to flex its muscles," *The Straits Times*, August 31, 1996.

34 Felix Soh, "China 'Sent 2 Submarines to Disputed Diaoyu Isles,'" *The Straits Times*, August 24, 1996; Kristof, "An Asian Mini-Tempest"; Green, *Reluctant Realism*.

35 Manicom, *Bridging Troubled Waters*, 81.

36 Funabashi, *Alliance Adrift*, 409.

37 "US Confirms Security Treaty Covers Senkakus," *Yomiuri Shimbun*, November 28, 1996; Funabashi, *Alliance Adrift*, 407.

38 Richard Samuels, *Securing Japan: Tokyo's Grand Strategy and the Future of East Asia* (Ithaca, NY: Cornell University Press, 2008). "Japan, US Hold Joint Drill over Diaoyu Islands Contingency," *BBC Monitoring Asia Pacific*, December 30, 2006.

39 "The Guidelines for Japan–US Defense Cooperation (September 23, 1997)," The Ministry of Defense of Japan, accessed September 3, 2017, http://www.mod.go.jp/e/d_act/anpo/19970923.html.

40 Ibid.

41 "China Sub Tracked by US Off Guam Before Japan Intrusion," *The Japan Times*, November 17, 2004.

42 "Security Treaty Likely Covers Senkakus," *Yomiuri Shimbun*, November 16, 1996.

43 "Press Conference by the Press Secretary May 30, 1997," Ministry of Foreign Affairs of Japan, accessed March 1, 2019, https://www.mofa.go.jp/announce/press/1997/5/530.html#5.

44 Taylor Fravel, "Explaining Stability in the Senkaku (Diaoyu) Islands Dispute," in *Getting the Triangle Straight: Managing China-Japan-US Relations*, ed. Gerald Curtis, Ryosei Kokubun, and Wang Jisi (Washington: Brookings Institution Press, 2010), 25–6.

45 Manicom, *Bridging Troubled Waters*, 58.

46 Fravel, "Explaining Stability in the Senkaku (Diaoyu) Islands Dispute," 25–6.

47 "Joint Statement of the US-Japan Security Consultative Committee," The Ministry of Foreign Affairs of Japan, accessed August 20, 2017, https://www.mofa.go.jp/region/n-america/us/security/scc/joint0502.html.

48 Manicom, *Bridging Troubled Waters*, 52.

49 "Global Times Article Notes PRC Attitude on U-Japan Military Alliance," *Renmin Ribao* April 13, 2004.

50 The Chinese scholar, Zhu Feng, also worries that the moves will undermine regional stability and damage relations with China—although these concerns do not seem to have been borne out. "Chinese Scholars View Implications of US-Japan Joint Drill over Diaoyu Islands," *BBC Monitoring Asia Pacific*, January 3, 2007.

51 "Anti-Japanese Protests Push Beijing to Take Hard Line," *Yomiuri Shimbun*, March 28, 2004.

52 Irene Wang and Alice Yan, "Capital Fetes Seven Diaoyu 'Heroes'; the Landing is Called a Patriotic Triumph but a Second Mission Has Been Delayed," *South China Morning Post* March 29, 2004.

53 William Choong, *The Ties That Divide: History, Honour, and Territory in Sino-Japanese Relations* (London: Institute for International and Strategic Studies, 2014).

54 Drifte Reinhard, *Japanese-Chinese Territorial Disputes in the East China Sea—Between Military Confrontation and Economic Cooperation*. Working Paper, Asia Research Centre, London School of Economics and Political Science (2008).

55 Michael Green, Kathleen Hicks, Zack Cooper, John Schaus, and Jake Douglas, *Countering Coercion in Maritime Asia: The Theory and Practice of Gray Zone Deterrence* (Washington, DC: CSIS, 2017).

56 Green et al., *Countering Coercion in Maritime Asia*, 91–4.

57 "Daily Press Briefing – August 16, 2010," The US Department of State, accessed September 21, 2017, https://2009-2017.state.gov/r/pa/prs/dpb/2010/08/146001.htm.

58 Peter Ennis, "Why Japan Still Matters," Brookings Institute, accessed September 20, 2017, https://www.brookings.edu/research/why-japan-still-matters/.

59 "Press Briefing by Press Secretary Robert Gibbs, Special Assistant to the President and Senior Director for Asian Affairs, Jeff Bader, and Deputy National Security Advisor for Strategic Communications Ben Rhodes," The White House Office of the Press Secretary, accessed August 20, 2017, https://obamawhitehouse.archives.gov/the-press-office/2010/09/23/press-briefing-press-secretary-robert-gibbs-special-assistant-president-.

60 Jeffrey Bader, *Obama and China's Rise: An Insider's Account of America's Asia Strategy* (Washington, DC: Brookings Institution Press, 2013).

61 Scott Neuman, "Chinese Patrol Boats Stand Down in Islands Row with Japan," *NPR*, September 14, 2012.

62 Green et al., *Countering Coercion in Maritime Asia*, 92–4.

63 Ibid., 92–4.

64 Ibid., 147.

65 Ibid., 135.

66 Ren Xiao, "Diaoyu/Senkaku Disputes—A View from China," East Asia Forum, accessed November 1, 2017, http://www.eastasiaforum.org/2013/11/04/diaoyusenkaku-disputes-a-view-from-china/.

67 Xiao, "A View from China."

68 Quoted in Michael Swaine, "Chinese Views Regarding the Senkaku/Diaoyu Islands Dispute," *China Leadership Monitor* 41 (2013).

69 Bonnie Glaser and Leon Bai, "Chinese Perspectives on the Senkaku/Diaoyu Islands Dispute," in *Japan's Territorial Disputes*, ed. Michael McDevitt and Catherine Lea (Washington, DC: Center for Naval Analyses, 2013).

70 Xiao, "A View from China."

71 Green et al., *Countering Coercion in Maritime Asia*, 137–45.

72 "Senior Official Urges No Slackness in Military Preparation," *China Daily*, September 14, 2012.

73 Swaine, "Chinese Views," 15–17.

74 Ibid.

75 Ibid.

76 Andrew Quinn, "Clinton Assures Japan on Islands, Invites Abe to US in February," *Reuters*, January 18, 2013.

77 David Cenciotti, "US Navy Deploys Newest Patrol Aircraft to Japan Amid China Air ID Zone Crisis," *The Aviationist*, December 1, 2013.

78 Cenciotti, "US Navy Deploys Newest Patrol Aircraft to Japan."

79 "Japan Confirms US Cooperation after China's Senkaku Foray," *Nikkei Asian Review*, June 10, 2016; Chelsea Carter and Kevin Wang, "US: China Claim of Air Rights over Disputed Islands 'Creates Risk of Incident,'" *CNN*, November 24, 2013.

80 The Ministry of Defense of Japan, "The Guidelines for Japan–US Defense Cooperation, 2015," accessed September 24, 2017, http://www.mod.go.jp/e/d_act/anpo/shishin_20150427e.html.

81 "The Guidelines for Japan–US Defense Cooperation, 2015."

82 Ibid.

83 "Japan Confirms US Cooperation," *Nikkei Asian Review*.

84 Mizuho Aoki, "Obama Assures Abe on Senkakus," *The Japan Times*, April 24, 2014.

85 Aoki, "Obama Assures Abe."

86 Andrew Quinn, "Clinton Assures Japan on Islands, Invites Abe to US in February," *Reuters* January 18, 2013.

87 The Ministry of Defense of Japan, "Japan is Back," accessed August 20, 2017, http://www.mofa.go.jp/announce/pm/abe/us_20130222en.html.

88 Barney Henderson, "Japan and China Agree to Reduce Tensions over Senkaku Islands," *The Telegraph*, November 7, 2014.

89 Justin McCurry, "War Games Near California," *Christian Science Monitor*, June 27, 2013.

90 "Joint Statement of the Japan–United States–Australia Trilateral Strategic Dialogue," US Department of State, accessed September 5, 2017, https://2009-2017.state.gov/r/pa/prs/ps/2016/07/260442.htm.

91 Tania Branigan and Ed Pilkington, "China Scrambles Fighter Jets towards US and Japan Planes in Disputed Air Zone," *The Guardian*, November 30, 2013.

92 Helene Cooper, "In Japan's Drill with the US, a Message for Beijing," *The New York Times*, February 22, 2014.

93 Taylor Fravel, "China's Assertiveness in the Senkaku (Diaoyu) Islands Dispute," MIT Political Science Department Research Paper No. 016–19 (2016).

94 Taylor Fravel and Alastair Iain Johnson, "Chinese Signaling in the East China Sea?" *The Washington Post*, April 12, 2014.

95 Stephen Harnern, "China De-Escalating the Senkaku/Diaoyu Crisis, but Will Abe Respond," *Forbes*, August 21, 2014.

96 Henderson, "Japan and China Agree."

97 Ibid.

98 Kristine Kwok, "China, Japan Agree to Resume High-Level Talks in Bid to Ease Maritime Tensions," *South China Morning Post*, November 7, 2014.

99 Richard Bush and Michael O'Hanlon, *A War Like No Other: The Truth about China's Challenge to America* (Hoboken, NJ: John Wiley & Sons, 2007); Kerry Gershaneck, "Taiwan's Future Depends on the Japan–America Security Alliance," *The National Interest*, June 7, 2018; Eric Heginbotham, Michael Nixon, Forrest Morgan, Jacob Heim, Jeff Hagen, Sheng Tao Li, Jeffrey Engstrom, Martin Libicki, Paul DeLuca, David Shaplak, David Frelinger, Burgess Laird, Kyle Brady, Lyle Morris, *The US–China*

Military Scorecard: Forces, Geography, and the Evolving Balance of Power, 1996–2017 (Santa Monica, CA: RAND, 2015).

100 Victor Cha, *The Impossible State: North Korea, Past and Future* (New York: HarperCollins, 2012).

101 Richard Drifte, *Japan's Policy towards the South China Sea—Applying "Proactive Peace Diplomacy?"* (Frankfurt: Peace Research Institute Frankfurt, 2016).

6

Beyond Normalization: A Roundtable Discussion on the Present and Future of Sino-American Relations

This roundtable discussion with Nickles, Lautz, Gueorguiev, Ma, and French explores relations between Beijing and Washington during the Barack Obama and Donald Trump administrations.[1] The participants examine the implications of Sino-American relations for the East Asian region, including with North and South Korea as well as Japan. Finally, the contributors discuss China's efforts to build relations with other Asian countries, including Iran, and the Belt and Road Initiative.

Osamah F. Khalil

David, your chapter discussed how the international conditions that existed in the early 1970s encouraged the rapprochement between the United States and the People's Republic of China. Do you think that the factors that contributed to improved relations between Washington and Beijing are still relevant today? Is there something similar or consistent that you can discern?

David Nickles

Unfortunately, I think to a large extent the answer is no. Having a common enemy can help countries transcend their disagreements. The Soviet Union, in the eyes of both Washington and Beijing, provided that enemy during the 1970s, and this was the main reason they were able to overcome a previously intense hostility. Neither the United States nor China has great relations with Russia now, but their relations with Moscow are nowhere near as bad as during some periods of the 1960s, 1970s, and 1980s. This lack of a common enemy, combined with many areas of competition between China and the United States, is arguably pushing the two powers further apart.

---

[1] This chapter is based on a moderated roundtable discussion hosted at Syracuse University's Maxwell School of Citizenship and Public Affairs in September 2017. The discussion drew on papers presented by the participants, which were early versions of the chapters in this volume.

However, the United States and China have many common concerns. They could form a more cooperative relationship by pursuing mutual interests regarding issues such as the world economy and the environment. Likewise, both countries would benefit from promoting peace and prosperity, particularly in areas of joint concern such as the Korean Peninsula. One of the most hopeful legacies of the 1970s is the belief held by Jimmy Carter and Deng Xiaoping that their own country could benefit from interacting with the other. But of course, despite some common interests, these issues of global governance can also produce disagreements. China and the United States don't always see eye to eye on climate change, trade policy, or Korea. I'd like to think that these issues can bring the two countries together, and maybe they will. But improved Sino-American relations are not inevitable. There are, unfortunately, some very serious challenges in the relationship.

Yingyi Ma

I'm wondering to what extent the rise of China is a threat to these issues such as security?

Nickles

In recent decades, the United States has tended to focus on security challenges from the Middle East, but there are some parts of the US government that believe that the rise of China may ultimately be more decisive. Historically, the international system has not done well at integrating rising powers. The United States, Russia, Germany, and Japan rapidly increased their power during the late nineteenth century. Russia, Germany, and Japan all played a role in initiating major systemic wars during the first half of the twentieth century. In contrast, the United States was more easily assimilated into the international system than the others, but to a large extent this was because it wasn't very close to other major powers, so it was more easily appeased and there was less reason for conflict.

It's going to be very challenging for the world to incorporate a dynamic and militarily powerful China, especially since China lives in a difficult neighborhood. It has conflicts with Vietnam, Russia, Japan, and India. So the rise of China could be associated with some real problems. And then, of course, there is the US–China rivalry as well.

Dimitar Gueorguiev

When it comes to US–China relations and rivalry, it is important to put things into context. One of the themes touched on by both David and Terry in their chapters was just how difficult normalization was for the Chinese, especially for Deng Xiaoping. Thirty years of anti-American rhetoric and proxy wars in East and Southeast Asia meant there was a great deal of mistrust and apprehension brought into the negotiations. Moreover, unlike his predecessor Mao Zedong, Deng was in charge, but he did not have total control over the Chinese Communist Party. Instead, Deng was considered the first among equals, and his policy ambitions had to receive at least tacit support from more conservative members in the Politburo, who remained deeply suspicious of the United States. Arguably, what made normalization possible was a shared conviction that China had a great deal of unrealized potential—in terms of favorable demographics and a huge labor endowment. The potential access to markets and capital resulting from normalization thus amounted to an immense window of opportunity to tap and realize that potential. In other words, the prospects for returns in the future made it possible to overcome differences in the present.

Today, the tables have turned in some respects. Incomes and wages in China have risen sharply, and, while China remains a dominant exporter, domestic consumption is rising as well. As such, we can imagine that in maybe ten, twenty, thirty years down the line, China's domestic market could become an immensely valuable destination for American exports. However, increasing import flows may and most likely will tempt protectionist sentiments within China, just as trade deficits are doing in the United States today. Keeping the future in mind suggests that maintaining a friendly and cooperative relationship with China today will deliver dividends for the US economy in the long run.

Erik French

Graham Allison's *Destined for War* argues that a rising China is going to potentially create a conflict with the United States.[2] This idea has been at the center of the scholarly debate on US–China relations since the 1990s. It is important to note that while there are parallels, as Allison suggests, between past power transitions and the current case, there are also substantial differences. The US–China relationship is characterized both by significant economic interdependence and the way both of these countries see their respective roles in the world.

The presence of a mutual nuclear deterrent is also a stabilizing factor, reducing the chances of war between the two countries. While I agree with Allison that the rise of China presents significant challenges for the United States, I also think it would be dangerous to conclude that a war between them is inevitable.

Khalil

Erik, even though there's the caution about not fearing a rising China, there are unintended consequences that you touched on. Can you discuss how the actions may end up leading to an escalation between Washington and Beijing?

French

Both countries will need to keep in mind the potential for this dynamic as they make policy. The core task for both countries is to find a stable, peaceful equilibrium where they are both satisfied. This requires both states to acknowledge that they can't get what they want through force. That requires mutual security and mutual deterrence.

But it also requires reassurance, which means that even while the United States seeks to strengthen its regional military capability to ensure access to the Western

---

2 Graham Allison, *Destined for War: Can America and China Escape Thucydides's Trap?* (New York: Houghton Mifflin Harcourt, 2017).

Pacific and to the South and East China Seas, it has to make it clear through confidence-building measures, through dialogue, through military-to-military contacts, that it doesn't see China primarily an adversary. It has to highlight that the United States' interest in having military access to this region is to reassure its allies, not to undermine China's security.

Furthermore, the United States has to emphasize to China that were it to cease reassuring its allies, if the United States were to pull back from the region, it would potentially undermine China's security. If the United States pulls back, what you would likely see is a significant military buildup by Japan that would likely result in a still more tense relationship between Tokyo and Beijing. You might see Japan reaching out even more aggressively than it has in the past to Taiwan, to India, and other countries to partner with in order to contain China's rise. This might result in an unstable power-balancing dynamic.

Right now, the US presence has a dampening effect. The key is to try to find a way to convince China that is the case, while also accommodating legitimate Chinese concerns about its role in the region. Washington has to make it clear that it is not going to simply exclude China from the regional order.

Terry Lautz

I think China's leaders know very well that the United States provides stability in the region. And there's more ambiguity in Chinese thinking about the US presence than we often realize. In fact, I would say that sometimes the Chinese position is not ambiguous at all because Beijing has understood for a long time that the US security relationship with Japan prevents Japan from becoming a nuclear power. For an older generation of Chinese, and even in the younger generation, there are vivid memories of Japan's war with China and its occupation during the Second World War.

There is a visceral sense of nationalism among many Chinese that goes back to that period when China was at the mercy of foreign powers. But for China to say to the United States, "Please, just go away, and recognize that this is our sphere of influence" would be very shortsighted on the part of Beijing. And if anything, Chinese policymakers are very good at looking at the longer term. And this is especially true because of the way Chinese politics is constructed. They have much more continuity than we do in American politics, which is dictated by our relatively short election cycles.

The status quo on regional security issues is being disrupted by China's rise as a military power as we can see from tensions in the South China Sea. And yet when Beijing states that Taiwan is a core issue, they also say that it's not an urgent issue. Yes, they want to resolve it and are willing to apply pressure, as we have seen recently, but they are not going to go to war over Taiwan right away because there are too many other reasons for us and for them to maintain stability in the region. In the final analysis, China's foreign policy is still driven mainly by concerns about economic growth and trade. And while this equation is shifting as China becomes more assertive, deep economic ties with the United States suggest that China's rise is less likely to lead to conflict with the United States.

Ma

I want to emphasize that the rise of China has been an ongoing trend, especially given that this is a very special historical moment that China has a strong political leader, President Xi Jinping, who probably has a much more coherent narrative of leadership and ambition to really assert China on the global stage.

President Xi has advanced the concept of the Chinese dream, which is an apparent parallel to the American dream. However, the Chinese dream is not only about individual hard work and the good life, but also about the revival of China as a nation. Around the world, from "one belt, one road," to the expansion of Confucius Institutes, these are all efforts by Chinese leaders to assert themselves on the world stage by spreading Chinese language and culture and making an impact on other countries. At the same time in the United States, we have a highly unpredictable American president who often behaves unpresidentially. And you have seen the policy changes of the American government, including backing out of the Paris Climate Accord and the Trans-Pacific Partnership (TPP), thereby leaving a void in the global leadership that China could potentially fill.

So I would argue that the rise of China has come at a very special historical moment, especially having these unusual political leaders from China and the United States. This could potentially generate dramatic shocks to the international system.

Khalil

Dimitar, you mentioned Chinese nationalism. What is the role of Chinese nationalism and what are the implications for US foreign policy, not just toward China but more broadly in the Asia-Pacific region?

Gueorguiev

Nationalism is a tricky concept. What we know is that public discourse in China appears to be becoming increasingly nationalistic, in part thanks to some of the same kind of social media echo chambers that are present here in the United States. What nationalism does, I think, irrespective of how a regime is constituted, is to push politicians into a more hawkish direction, or at least constrain the range of peaceful foreign policy options available to them.

With regard to China, political leaders seem very sensitive to nationalism, so much so that they tend to preempt criticism by backing themselves into a corner and adopting the most nationalistic rhetoric they can whenever issues of Chinese sovereignty or territorial integrity come into question.

The most likely explanation for why they behave this way is that if they don't, they leave open the opportunity that somebody within the regime's fragile collective leadership might take advantage of the nationalist mantle. The bottom line is that we should anticipate China to overreact on issues where nationalism is at stake.

At the same time, the Chinese are incredibly pragmatic and flexible in the way they use rhetoric and diplomacy. Consistent with Eric's point about China not necessarily wanting to challenge the United States or the existing order more broadly, consider what happened in the South China Sea with the disputed islands in the territory claimed by China, Vietnam, the Philippines, and a number of other countries. The UN Convention on the Law of the Seas (UNCLOS) was tested in a trial initiated by the Philippines and Vietnam a few years ago. The consequence of that trial was that China's claim was to some extent dismissed. In China, the state-run press immediately launched a tirade, dismissing the ruling as nonsense and biased. Yet, while the Chinese unequivocally rejected the ruling they didn't abrogate the convention, which, according to the agreement, is the only way a signatory can formally disagree with a ruling. As such, we can interpret China's behavior as simultaneously placating nationalism while legally accepting international law.

French

I think the problem is that even while there may be a tacit acceptance of the UNCLOS ruling, China has continued the activity that was determined to be a violation of Philippine territorial sovereignty. This includes reclamation activities and the militarization of some of these reefs. This is going to be difficult to change, because to some extent, there are rational strategic purposes for China to be doing this. The challenge in finding a resolution to the dispute is that the source of the dispute—sovereignty over territory—is in some ways indivisible. Either the nine-dash line in the South China Sea is recognized as Chinese territory since time immemorial or it is not. That makes it much more difficult to find a compromise that satisfies all parties. The United States and China need to find a way to separate the sovereignty question from the questions of freedom of navigation, economic exploration, and militarization, because there is much more room for compromise on the latter issues.

Nickles

Nationalism ties into the legitimation challenges that China, like all countries, faces. During the Mao era, the regime gained prestige for having driven out foreign imperialists and from the ideological fervor of the people. But as China became more militarily secure and the appeal of Communist ideology declined, the regime legitimated its rule by fostering economic growth, which has been remarkable for decades. There are limits to this strategy since the economy is growing at a slower pace as China becomes more developed. Another source of legitimation is good governance, and I think governance in China is sometimes better than Americans perceive it to be. But over time, citizens take the achievements of their government for granted, and focus instead on the problems and injustices they see about them. So good governance, like national security, ideology, and economic growth, may not be enough to provide legitimation indefinitely.

One temptation, which is potentially very dangerous, occurs when leaders believe they can increase their popularity and placate angry citizens by directing their anger outward against other countries. This could be over territorial disputes or other issues of national prestige.

Khalil

Yingyi, in your student interviews you observed not just the latent sense of nationalism, but an overt sense on the issue of Tibet. I'm wondering if you noticed a trend in some of those interviews, particularly how it relates to political changes or political issues?

Ma

The students are incredibly diverse. The diversity also pertains to their attitudes toward Tibet, I've also had students saying that they don't really join protests by their Chinese peers against the Dalai Lama's visits to their campuses. They're actually pressured by their peers. And they would say, no, I'm not interested in this. What I found is, along with this rising nationalism, is also a palpable sense of political apathy and indifference.

And that is probably very consistent, not just among the students overseas but also among the youth in China. I think that students here are actually more exposed to these kinds of free debates and critical dialogue than students in China, where critical discussions of politically sensitive issues are heavily censored. So, it's very hard to identify a pattern among a younger generation of Chinese students on the nationalism issue. If anything, Chinese students overseas are more aware of being Chinese than their peers in China.

Among the students who exhibited nationalistic tendencies, I think that is related to the legitimacy of Chinese governance that David just mentioned. The legitimacy is still heavily tied to economic opportunities. Overseas Chinese students, especially this new wave of international students who often self-fund their American college education, are beneficiaries of China's economic growth. To them, their China is a land of opportunities, wealth, and promise.

Other than nationalism, these students also have a growing sense of identification with their home country. The theme emerges that students feel a renewed interest in China and a growing sense of being Chinese from afar.

Lautz

I think it's useful to make a distinction between nationalism and patriotism. Patriotism reflects pride in your country, a sense of confidence and love of country. Too often, we confuse patriotism with nationalism, which, as Dimitar says, is very complex. But we tend to view nationalism as an expression of power and a one-sided view of the world that "either you're with us or you're against us." It's us versus everybody else and we are superior.

So there's a fundamental difference between pride and patriotism and the kind of a virulent, more negative form of nationalism. We can see both in China, and both are logical responses to China's rapid rise. The other thing that Yingyi has mentioned, which is also not new at all, is culturalism—not nationalism or patriotism but culturalism—the sense of Chinese identity which is so strong that no matter where you are in the world you are always Chinese. And so these might be useful categories to keep in mind in trying to understand China's rise.

Khalil

Terry, you discussed tensions over Taiwan in the late 1970s and how much of an obstacle it was in in the negotiations between Beijing and Washington. Even though it is a less important issue today, the United States continues selling arms to Taiwan. In keeping with the theme of this workshop series, how do these historical events shape the world we live in now? How important are those arms sales now? And whose interests do they really serve?

Lautz

There are those who argue that this is a policy that's outlived its usefulness, that given the importance of US–China relations, Taiwan is not a major issue anymore and it's a Chinese problem. This camp believes that the United States should back off and let China and Taiwan resolve the issue themselves. On the other hand, there are those who want to move in the opposite direction, as Trump did initially, saying that the United States should reinforce its relationship with Taiwan in order to defend Taiwan as a domocracy and to gain leverage over China. The consensus is that the United States should continue to provide arms to Taiwan in order to maintain stability in the region.

Some believe that Washington should link North Korea with Taiwan because that would put more pressure on North Korea. In other words, if the United States softens its position and stops selling arms to Taiwan, it might be an incentive for Beijing to put more pressure on North Korea to denuclearize. I think this would be an ineffective and even dangerous form of linkage for at least two reasons. First, it would not be acceptable to Beijing because they have consistently held the position that the status of Taiwan—and their claim that Taiwan belongs to China—is not negotiable. They are willing to live with the status quo for now, but are not willing to bargain over Taiwan. It is a basic question of sovereignty for them. Second, in terms of maintaining US credibility and its alliances with South Korea and Japan, it would be dangerous to signal that the United States no longer is concerned about Taiwan's security. In terms of American credibility, legitimacy, and defense of South Korea, Japan, and other allies, this would be a very dangerous road to go down. So I don't see it happening.

French

Every time the United States delivers one of these arms packages to Taiwan, it provokes a minor crisis. It is worth considering, however, what would happen if the United States stopped selling arms to Taiwan. One of two things could happen. There would likely be shockwaves around the region. This move could damage American credibility, particularly relationships with South Korea and Japan. Many regional allies might take this as a signal that the United States is no longer dependable. They would worry that China is now so powerful that the United States is unwilling to contest it, even when the security of its regional partners is at stake.

But I think just as problematically, Taiwan might start seeking to purchase weapons from other partners. Japan has just started selling weapons abroad again for the first time in a long time. And Japan has very significant interests at stake in Taiwan. Imagine how provocative it might seem to China if Japan were to begin selling arms to Taiwan? Remember, Japan seized Taiwan from China in the first Sino-Japanese war via the humiliating Treaty of Shimonoseki in 1895. This would be much more destabilizing than US arms sales.

I think the United States pulling back from arms sales to Taiwan would be very problematic. They provide an important symbol of American credibility and help stabilize the dispute by allowing Taiwan to feel secure enough to conduct negotiations with the mainland. But the weapons are also operationally significant. The missile defense systems that Washington has sought to deliver to Taiwan will be critical to the survivability of Taiwan's air force in the event of some type of conflict with China. As such, these weapons sales are also militarily significant for Taiwanese deterrence. And if the United States' goal is cross-strait stability, then it needs to maintain the sales.

Lautz

There are those who say arms sales to Taiwan are just symbolic at this point because China is so strong militarily. But the thing to keep in mind is what has been described as the "poisoned shrimp" strategy. This is what Singapore did. Tiny little Singapore is surrounded by large, potentially threatening neighbors in Indonesia and Malaysia. So the idea is to make it as costly as possible if Singapore is going to be swallowed.

For Taiwan, the US strategy is very similar. China could easily overwhelm Taiwan with a naval blockade, but the goal is to make that option as costly and as poisonous as possible. So it is still in Washington's interest to continue selling arms to Taiwan for the sake of regional stability, which was a fundamental reason for the normalization of US–China relations in the first place.

Gueorguiev

The United States and China have so many "big" problems to address, from trade to maritime security disputes, that it can at times be difficult to start conversations. Sometimes smaller issues are easier to have give-and-take on. The arms sales are good examples of that. Washington and Beijing can argue and bargain about how many fighter planes or missile sites would be too much. At the end of the day, such details are unlikely to have a fundamental impact on the underlying security balance, so the negotiations process offers both sides an opportunity to take some concessions back home. So, ironically, it's not obvious that resolving the arm sales issue would be that great for diplomacy.

Khalil

Yingyi, when we think about these political tensions, whether it's political tensions over North Korea or diplomatic tensions between Washington and Beijing, how does that influence Chinese students who want to come to the United States? Does it deter them? Do you find it playing a role at all?

Ma

I think that this new administration has definitely deterred some students, not just in China but across the globe. The most recent enrollment data released by the Open Doors Report shows that in 2017, universities reported on average a 7 percent decline in new international students. However, international students from China still increased over the previous year, albeit at a slower rate. And that slower rate of increase of Chinese students coming to the United States began well before the Trump presidency started. I was in China over the summer, and the international education sector is still booming. So the interest there has not really faded much.

But there is a concern among students about social acceptance because of the inflammatory remarks made by this president and his administration, potentially not making the United States as welcoming a country to international students. And also, students are concerned about potential visa policy changes, the H-1B visa crisis and the threat by the Trump administration of raising the minimum wage for an H-1B visa, and that really has alarmed a lot of Chinese students who want to get a job and stay here.

This could potentially create a more challenging pathway to jobs and permanent residence and citizenship than before, and those may be areas of concern for Chinese students. However, in my study of Chinese undergraduates, less than half of the students want to stay in the United States. More than half of the students decided to return to China after finishing their studies. For those people who want to stay in the United States, some of the reasons being that this younger generation, they don't just want to repeat their parents' lifestyle—basically overwork and no family time.

And other students who want to stay are worried about other social ills such as pollution and corruption and even their next generation's education. But still, a rising number of people we call "returnees" go back. American education is still very attractive to millions of Chinese parents who are not only thinking about their children's educational future, but they're actually thinking about their children's well-roundedness that goes beyond mere credentials.

Although there continues to be an emphasis on educational credentials, upper-middle-class Chinese parents have a rising need for their children to have the quality education that is not test-oriented, with a critical thinking component, emphasizing communication, and a global outlook. These parents view American society as the ideal place to have it.

Gueorguiev

I would like to challenge a little bit this narrative that Trump is undermining the legitimacy of the United States abroad. I heard a talk recently about a research project in Beijing University where researchers, with cooperation from the university, randomly handed out VPN access to students. Then they monitored what students were reading on the web. Finally, they asked students questions about democracy in the United States and China's own system of government.

And what they found is that once Trump was elected, impressions of the United States declined. But over time, the participants got more enamored with the United States. The reason behind this change, the researchers argued, was that students were so surprised and kind of encouraged by the fact that the US media can attack and scrutinize the executive-in-chief. I think that example—and I think the United States should always be the example—in and of itself was much more effective in turning the students toward democracy and liberal values than any statements or postures from the past.

Khalil

Dimitar in your chapter you discussed what could be described as the opposite of Francis Fukuyama's "End of History" argument, where authoritarianism not liberal democracy appears to predominate. In the examples that we have discussed, TPP and the Paris Accords, Beijing has decided that they're going to hold on to international institutions, the same institutions that the United States help build. And yet the Chinese Communist Party seems to fear peaceful evolution. Would you describe it that way? And does that in some way validate the theory of peaceful evolution?

Gueorguiev

I think China's leaders are perhaps overly sensitive to the threat of a democratic opening within the party or from the public. More importantly, I think it is instrumental for the regime to highlight foreign plots for democratization and regime change as lurking constantly in the background. For one, it offers the regime a compelling pretense to censor the internet. Within the political establishment, hard-liners also need a pretense to discredit their reformist peers. Again, peaceful evolution provides a useful, vague type of category that they can use to describe ideas and policies they don't like.

Khalil

Yingyi made the point about soft power and China adopting this notion of American soft power for their own ends. One thing that has also been discussed is China's economic power and this has been on display with its Belt and Road Initiative. With this initiative, China is not looking toward its major trading partner, the United States; instead, it is attempting to establish a new "Silk Road" that would extend westward toward Iran and beyond. What are the implications of this initiative?

Gueorguiev

Earlier, Yingyi invoked the work of Henry Kissinger, who in his most recent book on China contends that Chinese chess and Western chess, and by extension their foreign policy mind-sets, are fundamentally different. Western chess is combative and focused on the theater at hand, whereas, *wei qi* is more passive, taking into consideration the whole board. If you have some sort of tension in one spot, what *wei qi* tells you is to look at calmer arenas. That is, move into the periphery.

Given the tension that you have in the East China Sea, the South China Sea, and Taiwan right smack in the middle, what better strategy than to look west and move toward Central Asia? From that perspective at least, I think one can definitely observe a strategic geopolitical push westward on the part of China.

At the same time, geopolitical concerns are only part of the story. Another part invariably has to do with money and investment. What China realized in the 2000s was that their investment strategy wasn't very smart. Put simply, parking trade surplus in US Treasury bonds is not going to deliver that much. You've got to put it somewhere with higher prospects on return. So the Belt and Road Initiative is as much an investment as it is a geopolitical strategy.

Unlike the United States, however, China does not have a sophisticated foreign policy establishment. The Chinese Communist Party has always been a domestically oriented political system, and they never really focused as much on foreign relations and political engagement. Unsurprisingly, some of these investments are backfiring. There is a lot of animosity toward China's "gratitude," which is very surprising.

I think China is having to learn fast on its feet. As such, even though the Belt and Road Initiative sounds dramatic, it may not to prove to have a significant influence on the regional or global balance of power.

French

The Belt and Road Initiative may have serious ramifications for Sino-Iranian relations. The initiative involves investment in some of Iran's natural gas reserves. China is obviously very interested in Iranian energy resources, which is why Beijing has a history of some economic and political cooperation with Tehran. Will China develop still closer ties with Iran as its economic involvement increases via the Belt and Road Initiative?

It will also be interesting to see whether, as relations between Iran and the United States continue to deteriorate, China uses it somewhat cynically as an opportunity to back Iran as a way of stymieing US policy in the Middle East and thereby distracting the United States from Sino-American disputes in the Pacific.

The other interesting question is the extent to which the Belt and Road Initiative will divide the Middle East. A number of Arab Gulf States have expressed significant interest in the investment and opportunities coming from China. But there's also been some reticence and some concern that it will empower and benefit Iran more than the Arab Gulf States. This will be an interesting dynamic to watch.

Lautz

One question is whether worsening US–China relations would lead China to be closer to Iran. As Erik suggests, probably more important is whether increased US sanctions on Iran would push Tehran in the direction of Beijing. And that seems to be already happening. The Chinese are selling arms to Iran, and Iran provides oil to China.

But historically, China has been loath to get mired in complicated foreign policy issues. As Dimitar explained, Beijing hasn't developed that capability because the mantra, the guiding principle for the Chinese all along has been "non-interference in domestic affairs." Partly this is absolutely self-serving because the Chinese don't want the United States or others to be involved in Tibet or Taiwan. That's our business, they say. And so this dates from the earliest period of the PRC.

For many years, even though China is a big power and a member of the Permanent Five in the UN, it was extremely reluctant to exercise its veto power. It is only more recently that China has realized they have global interests and have to be more involved. Nevertheless, there is still a reluctance on China's part to get enmeshed with Middle East politics.

French

Some of China's outreach is seen as in the economic interest of China and as looking for outlets for capital, not only the Belt and Road Initiative and the new Silk Road project but also the other investments along the Indian Ocean littorals. There is also a geostrategic perspective, that maybe some of these projects are designed to pave the way for a stronger Chinese presence in the Indian Ocean and in Central Asia and potentially even in the Middle East.

And there is the new Chinese base in Djibouti. It is very difficult to disentangle the geostrategic theory of why this is happening from the economic theory of why this is happening. I think if we begin to see more Chinese navy port calls in some of these places that they are investing and greater military cooperation between China and these host states, then maybe you would start to see the geostrategic theory as more persuasive. But right now, I think the economic motives are dominating.

Gueorguiev

China's leaders and their foreign policy tactics are highly opportunistic, and they have the capital and willingness to take on risk that is needed for taking advantage of these opportunities. But I think they are easily getting in over their heads in some areas. One of my favorite examples is Sri Lanka.

When former Sri Lankan president Mahinda Rajapaksa moved to end the countries long-standing civil war, he did so using extreme force. The war effort in turn made Rajapaksa a bit of a pariah in the international community and made it very difficult to attract Western donors and redevelopment money, even after the war had ended. It was in this vacuum that the Chinese stepped in with financial and technical assistance. The initial relationship proved quite fruitful and paved the way for Sri Lanka to become a pearl in China's Indo-Pacific "string of pearls."

Then, in 2015, Rajapaksa decided to hold an early election and lost to one of his lieutenants. Part of his opponent's winning argument was that Rajapaksa had sold Sri Lanka out to the Chinese. Then suddenly, billions of dollars in Chinese investments were put on hold, some canceled. And it's because the Chinese never really invested in anything in Sri Lanka other than Rajapaksa. And that type of narrow opportunism, I think, is backfiring in places like Sri Lanka as well as countries in Africa.

Part Two

Toward Confrontation: The United States and Iran, 1953–Present

7

Revisiting the Coup: Assessing the New US Documents on Iran, 1951–4

Ervand Abrahamian

Introduction

After many delays, the US State Department published a volume of documents in June 2017 for the Muhammad Mossadeq period in Iran. The volume begins with the nationalization of oil in April 1951 and ends with the CIA-MI6 coup of August 1953 and the subsequent signing of the Oil Consortium Agreement in October 1954. It had already published a volume in 1989 covering the same period in its regular series entitled *Foreign Relations of the United States*—better known as the *FRUS*.[1] This appeared five years beyond the then standard thirty-year rule. Despite its length, it was so skimpy, especially for periods of heightened crises, that it stirred up a "scandal" in the American Historical Association. It was hard to believe that during such periods no dispatches were being exchanged between the embassy in Tehran and the State Department in Washington. Moreover, it contained little on the 1953 Coup. The State Department's Historical Advisory Committee as well as Bruce Kuniholm, the prominent historian and former member of the State Department, dismissed the whole volume as a total "fraud."[2]

As a result of the "outcry" in the academic community, the US Congress in 1991 passed a statute requiring the State Department as well as other agencies, such as the CIA and the National Security Council (NSC), to declassify documents relevant to US foreign policy. The department announced it would bring out a new *FRUS* volume on Iran for these same years.[3] This volume was ready by 2004, but its release was delayed first by the UK—publication rules require additional permission if a third a party is explicitly mentioned.[4] It was further delayed by the Obama administration fearful of jeopardizing its ongoing nuclear negotiations with Iran.[5] Once these hurdles were overcome, the new volume saw light of day in 2017.[6]

The new volume, containing 375 documents and totaling 950 pages, includes not only State Department communications, but also documents from the CIA, the NSC, especially frequent National Intelligence Estimates (NIEs), and from the cabinet meetings under both the Truman and Eisenhower administrations.[7] The editor bills the new volume as a "retrospective supplement" to the earlier one. The 1989 volume supposedly provided "a thorough accurate, and reliable account of the role the US played in mediating the dispute" between Iran and the UK. The 2017 volume supposedly places the whole crisis solidly within the "broader context of the Cold War." The editor admits the new volume still withholds ten full documents, excises a paragraph or more from thirty-eight, and makes minor cuts in another eighty-two. He also admits that many CIA cables for the 1953 "covert action" had apparently been "destroyed" in 1961–2 during routine "office relocations."

The reception for the new volume has been cool. Mark Gasiorowki, a leading expert on the 1953 Coup, declared that the documents "don't really add very much" and "don't contain any major new revelations.... They fail to address a number of key unanswered questions about how the coup was carried out."[8] Andrew Bacevich, the eminent historian of US foreign policy, wrote that the volume, despite its length, "fell short of being genuinely comprehensive."[9] Malcolm Byrne, the main advocate for declassification in the National Security Archive, remarked that the volume contained little in way of sensational information. "The big news," he declared, "is that there may be no news in the volume."[10]

These authorities were disappointed mainly because they were looking for new information on the actual coup of August 15–19. In fact, not much new remains to be revealed about these fateful days because the famous Wilber report, leaked in 2000, provided an astoundingly definitive, detailed, and reliable account of the whole venture.[11] Donald Wilber, who had administered the "psychological warfare" side of the entire enterprise, compiled his report immediately after the coup for internal consumption alone and as a practical handbook for future such ventures. The report can truly be categorized as a primary "eyes only" source based on direct information and without any propagandistic intentions. The only part of the document not leaked in 2000 was an annex promising to list all the officers, journalists, senators, deputies, and clerics on the CIA payroll.[12] This annex does not appear in the new volume. In fact, the new *FRUS* volume has absolutely no mention of the Wilber report.[13]

The 2017 *FRUS* may have disappointed those seeking brand new information on the coup, but it does provide a wealth of information for historians interested in Iran— especially the role of the United States in internal Iranian politics. In fact, the State Department's reluctance to release these old documents can be linked to its eagerness not to reveal how deeply US ambassador Loy Henderson and his embassy staff were immersed in the nitty-gritty of internal politics. After all, the CIA is expected to get its hands dirty in covert operations. But diplomats and embassy staff are supposed to stay above the fray and preserve the pretense they do not mess around in domestic matters. Explicit mention of such involvement is deemed to be taboo.

Proof of this taboo can be found in two documents that appear in both versions of the *FRUS*. In fact, these two are the only documents that appear in both versions. The 1989 *FRUS* contains a long NSC memorandum spelling out the importance of Iran. Only Section 5, Part b—totaling a short sentence—was originally redacted.[14] The 2017 *FRUS* provides the brief deduction: "The conduct of special political operations by the US-UK, and the coordination of US-UK support for pro-Western elements."[15] Similarly, the older version contains the minutes of the NSC meeting immediately after the coup where Secretary John Foster Dulles "felt obliged to say that a number of people in Iran had kept their heads and maintained their courage when the situation looked tough...."[16] The new version fills the dots: "He felt that the CIA in particular was entitled to great praise. He also expressed himself as pleased with the cooperation between the CIA, State, and FOA."[17] The latter stood for Foreign Operations Administration and included agricultural aid programs such as Point IV.

These two brief deductions merely reveal the very tip of the iceberg. The 2017 volume, however, throws glaring light on the deep involvement of US diplomats in internal Iranian politics. This is further illuminated by reams of cables released recently both by WikiLeaks and by the CIA's Electronic Library.[18] The deepest involvements came in three key crises: in the July Uprising—known as *Siyeh-e Tir* (July 21); in the open confrontation between the shah and Mossadeq in February 1953—known as the 9 Esfand (February 28) Crisis; and ultimately on August 18—on the very eve of the climactic coup.

The July Uprising

The conventional account of the Anglo-Iranian crisis tends to exaggerate the differences between Britain and America. Almost all who have written on the subject claim that the UK from the very start insisted Mossadeq would never come to a satisfactory settlement, but that the United States entered the dispute as an "honest broker" hoping to persuade Iran to reach a "fair compromise." According to this account, the UK began thinking of a coup early on, but the United States did not reach this conclusion until late in the day—in January 1953 when Eisenhower replaced Truman in the White House. The UK had to "talk" the United States into participating in the coup. In other words, the UK was the driving force behind Mossadeq's overthrow whereas the United States was merely a reluctant participant that had to be sweet talked into the venture.

The documents—especially the new ones—reveal that the UK–US differences were much more nuanced. As soon as the *majles* passed the nationalization bill in April 1951, George McGhee, the US assistant secretary of state and himself an oilman, rushed to Tehran to dissuade the shah from finalizing the bill into law.[19] He found the shah uncooperative. The shah spelled out his reasons to Loy Henderson, the newly arrived American ambassador with long experience of negotiating oil concessions in neighboring Iraq:[20]

> Brits tell me I should be strong man and take resolute action, but these so-called strong men like my father, Hitler, Stalin, etc. took resolute and bold action when they knew national sentiment was behind them. They never moved against basic feelings [of] their peoples. In this case national feelings are against Brits in oil matters; these feelings have been inflamed by demagogues; no matter how strong and resolute I may wish to be, I cannot take unconstitutional move against strong current national feelings. What slogans have I to change this time?..... I am convinced that attempt on my part to remove Mossadeq just now would give his friends and my enemies opportunity to convince Iran public that Crown has degenerated into mere Brit tool and such prestige as Crown has would disappear.

Only hope as I see it is for Mossadeq either to become more sober and reasonable or for him to make so many mistakes that responsible leaders of Iran will overthrow him in Majles.

McGhee, who continued as Truman's point man throughout the oil crisis, soon formulated a strategy for the administration. He was even named by the Eisenhower administration as a suitable emissary to go to Iran in June 1953 to persuade the shah to participate in the coup.[21] According to the strategy formulated by McGhee as early as May 1951, the United States as well as the UK would publicly accept the "principle of nationalization" and "Iran's sovereignty" over its natural resources, but the actual "control"—management and running—of the oil industry would be kept firmly in the hands of Western companies.

The British ambassador in Washington reported the US position was very close to the UK since the two "had a joint interest in the matter"—that is, the concern that nationalization would spread to other countries including ones in which American companies operated. "Mr. McGhee," he reported, "suggested acceptance of the pretence and the 'façade' of nationalization while maintaining control."[22] In other dispatches, the term "cloak" replaced "pretence" and "façade." He added that McGhee agreed "whatever decisions were made control should not be relinquished, and that the essence of the problem was how to concede something to this emotional concept of 'nationalization' but still retain control of oil operations." McGhee also assured representatives of the American majors, led by Aramco, Gulf, and Standard Oil of New Jersey, that any final agreement reached would in no way jeopardize their investments elsewhere.[23] The Gulf Oil representative argued that it would be better to lose Iran to communism than have Mossadeq succeed with oil nationalization.[24]

McGhee explained in his memoirs that the obvious solution was to accept nationalization "as the expressed desire of the Iranian people," but, at the same time, "retain control" over the actual oil industry.[25] He speculated: "It may be possible to establish Iranian partial ownership without in fact diminishing effective British control." The CIA and the NSC outwardly supported this strategy. The former stressed: "It is tactically important to give unequivocal lip service to nationalization."[26] The latter urged "further efforts to be made to find a formula that would square with the principle of nationalization without serious detriment to effective British control."[27]

Mossadeq saw this formula for what it was—an attempt to mislead and hoodwink him. A letter written by Prime Minister Clement Attlee to Truman sums up the essence of this convoluted language: "We have to agree on the principle of nationalization ...... like dominion status. It might well be that in negotiating an agreement in such a context a number of modifications would be introduced and that the resulting agreement would confer some thing that was, in act, a good deal less than dominion status." He added: "A breach of contract of this nature might well jeopardise other overseas contracts, not merely those held by British and United States."[28] Professor Elwell-Sutton, who had long experience in both the Foreign Office and in the Anglo-Iranian Oil Company, hit the nail on the head: "Put very succinctly, the British attitude was that, in return for their recognising the principle of nationalisation, the Persian government should forgo its insistence on that principle."[29]

Throughout the crisis, the United States and UK adamantly proclaimed that they fully accepted the principle of nationalization. In private, however, they were equally adamant that the sacred principle of contracts should not be undermined. At the very start of the crisis, the NSC concluded:[30]

> We could not afford to be neutral with respect to the continuing dispute between Britain and Iran. We should indeed give vigorous support to Britain. The Iranian P.M, and Government have unilaterally broken a contact and such a breach of contract was not only wrong in itself, but was likely to set an example and precedent which could induce Iraq and other countries to suppose that they could undertake similar actions. This was a highly contagious situation which we should do all we can to check.

Similarly toward the end of the crisis, President Eisenhower told his NSC that "the example of Iran may have grave effects on US oil concession in other parts of the world" and that "we must respect the enormous investments the British have in Iran.... We don't want to break with the British."[31] His defense secretary weighed with "we should not help destroy what was left of the idea of sanctity of contracts."[32] Henderson was equally adamant: "We must preserve sanctity of international contracts, in particular in the position of the oil firms which have contracts with various countries for the exploitation of oil products and other raw materials."[33] He further elaborated: "We desired to have good relations with Mossadeq but not at the price of our approving the cancellation of the British oil concession. We did not believe that such an expropriation was in the basic interest of Iran, GB, or the US. Acts of this kind tend to undermine the mutual trust that was necessary if international trade was to flourish."[34] After the coup, when it came to drawing up the Consortium agreement, the NSC ruled: "Settlement must not establish precedent adversely affecting the presently established international oil industry in a way inimical to US interests."[35] Significantly, this ruling appears almost at the very end of the 2017 *FRUS* volume.

It did not take long for the United States to come round to the UK position that Mossadeq could not be talked into accepting a hollow form of nationalization. Allen Dulles, the then CIA deputy director, had reluctantly gone along with McGhee, but his initial reaction had been that the "only way to save Iran was for the Shah to throw out Mossadeq, close the majles, and rule by decree."[36] Dulles, later as CIA director, was instrumental in organizing the eventual coup. In fact, the main organizers of the coup—Kermit Roosevelt, Richard Helms, Frank Wisner, John Waller, and Donald Wilber—had manned the CIA Iran desk even under Truman. Their views had been more in tune with the British MI6 than with their own government. In other words, they constituted a "deep state," "colluded" with an outside power, and disseminated much "fake news" about the oil crisis.

The United States and the UK convened a high level meeting in May 1952 to discuss a possible replacement for Mossadeq. The session was prompted by Henderson stressing that the "oil problem cannot be resolved so long as Mossadeq remains Prime Minister."[37] They scrutinized credentials of eighteen candidates headed by Ahmad Qavam and General Fazlallah Zahedi.[38] Qavam was a described as "old," "sick," and "corrupt," but, more importantly, willing to settle the oil dispute. Henderson, who had recently "inadvertently" met him, deemed him "the best successor to Mossadeq."[39] The shah, however, "feared and distrusted him." Zahedi was described also as "corrupt," "unscrupulous," and "ambitious," but "willing to seek a settlement on oil controversy on a realistic basis." Moreover, he was not tarnished with the British brush having been imprisoned by them in 1942–5 because of his Nazi connections. The American press later billed him as a "gentleman farmer" to give him a more favorable image in rural Virginia.[40]

The short-list included Allahyar Saleh—a leading figure in Mossadeq's National Front. Saleh was a diplomat's diplomat, soft-spoken, American educated, a respected ambassador in Washington, and acceptable to the shah since he, unlike Mossadeq, did not insist that the "monarchy should reign not rule." Henderson, however, adamantly opposed his candidacy arguing he was as "stubborn as Mossadeq in matter of oil dispute."[41] The CIA volunteered to "take covert action to 'neutralize' Saleh."[42]

Henderson—helped by the British—engineered the appointment of Qavam as prime minister on July 18. He did so in part by forcefully telling the shah that now was "the time for positive action,"[43] and in part by exerting considerable influence within the majles. The new documents reveal for the first time that the CIA had played a significant role in the elections for the 17th Majles. In fact, the CIA had congratulated itself for its "remarkable success."[44] Mossadeq, reluctant to implicate the United States, stopped the voting as soon as a quorum of seventy deputies had been elected. He accused the military of rigging provincial results. Although the CIA document on the elections remains heavily redacted and embassy communications continue to be scanty for June–July 1952, it became clear to Mossadeq by mid-July that the opposition could possibly muster enough votes for Qavam.[45] The NSC had speculated that once the majles convened "Mossadeq's chances of remaining in power would be diminished."[46] The British embassy soon discovered that Dr. Muzaffar Baqai—leader of the self-styled Titoist organization known as the Toiler's Party—had secretly offered to vote for Qavam while claiming to be a staunch supporter of Mossadeq.[47] Baqai had probably benefited from CIA largess.

Mossadeq, however, cognizant of majles intrigues pulled a fast one. On July 17, he went to the majles with a new cabinet. He asked for special powers to deal with the financial difficulties brought about by the British embargo on oil exports; and, most surprising of all, requested the portfolio of the war ministry arguing that the military should be under civilian supervision and the constitution entrusted the monarch with merely symbolic authority over the armed forces.

This prompted a constitutional crisis: the fundamental laws clearly placed the military under civilian supervision, but both Pahlavi monarchs had always insisted that they as commanders-in-chief had ultimate, full, and direct control over the armed forces. When the shah refused to back down, Mossadeq promptly resigned and declared: "I cannot bring to a successful conclusion the struggle the nation has embarked on unless I personally take charge of the War Ministry. As your Majesty has not approved this, it is better that the future government should be formed of someone who fully enjoys your confidence and will be able to carry out your Majesty's orders."[48] In closed session, the deputies appear to have given Qavam a slim "vote of inclination." The shah asked him to form a new government.

This sparked the July Uprising. Large crowds—bolstered by a nationwide general strike—converged on the parliament building in Tehran and on the main squares in the provincial capitals. The military at first tried to disperse the crowds, killing nearly twenty people and injuring two hundred in Tehran alone. Qavam—backed fully by both Henderson and George Middleton, the British charge d'affaires—sought special powers to declare martial law, disband the majles, and arrest leading opponents. The shah refused and instead ordered the military back into their barracks. Henderson later put the whole blame of the fiasco on the shah for failing to support Qavam against the "mob."[49] Mossadeq had triumphed hands down. He had not only retained the premiership but had also obtained the cabinet he sought, the special powers, and the war ministry. This was the first time since 1925 that the shah had lost control of the armed forces.

Middleton reported: "the Shah and indeed the whole Court had been paralyzed with fear. Ala (Court Minister) whom I saw this morning said that the danger to public security was so great that only the resignation of Qavam would satisfy public opinion. He said we had underestimated the power of Mossadeq and only with his return would the internal situation improve."[50] Middleton later elaborated:[51]

> The Shah was in the grip of fear: fear of taking a decision, and of taking a decision that might expose him to the fury of the populace should Qavam remain in power. This attitude of the Shah's is one of the central features of the crisis: we had long known that he was indecisive and timid, but we had not thought that his fear would so overcome his reason as to make him blind to the consequences of not supporting Qavam. The rioting destroyed the last shred of the Shah's courage. Both Henderson and I sought to stiffen him and spoke in strongest terms possible ... I can only repeat what I have previously written about the Shah's character: he hates taking decisions, and cannot be relied upon to stick to them when taken; he has no moral courage and easily succumbs to fear.... Mossadeq has so flattered the mob as the source of his power that he has, I fear, made it impossible for a successor to oust him by normal constitutional methods.

He added: "Henderson and I are convinced that 'only a coup d'état' could save the situation."[52] The War Office wrote it was time to look for an Iranian Neguib—alluding to the Egyptian general who had recently overthrown King Farouk.[53] The Foreign Office sent a top-secret message to Washington reporting that a senior US diplomat "wished for a Neguib."[54] Henderson added some qualifications to his talk of a coup. He argued a coup would not succeed without the nominal support of the shah. Young officers were more likely to follow him than someone like Zahedi. He also argued the reluctant shah needed to be drawn into the venture by a direct threat. "Ambassador Henderson," reported the CIA, "added that the time had arrived when we should give serious consideration for his replacement ... perhaps Prince Abdul Reza."[55]

Without conceding the shah may have had a more realistic assessment of the uprising, the US embassy soon described the uprising as a virtual "civil war."[56] Similarly, Middleton admitted the "disorders in the provinces were more severe than we suspected," and some cities, such as Isfahan, had been taken over by the insurgents.[57]

He described the uprising as a historic "turning point" ending the rule of the old landed class.[58] In later years, he reminisced that Qavam had been "quite mad" in thinking that he could take charge. He also speculated that the July Uprising could have easily turned into "another 1917."[59]

Immediately after the crisis, Henderson had an "exhausting and depressing" meeting with Mossadeq. He claimed he had nothing to do with the election of Qavam, that he had met the gentleman only twice—and that by accident, and that he always adhered to his government's strict policy of never interfering in the internal affairs of another country. "I told Mossadeq," he reported, "that US was in many ways trying to help Iran. He laughed and said if we were really trying assist by other than words, we were certainly succeeding in hiding our helpful activities."[60] Meanwhile Dean Acheson, Truman's secretary of state, immediately after the July Uprising, proposed a US–UK plan: "a. possible joint action. b. possible alternative to Mossadeq. c. method to bring about such alternative to power. d. form and encourage support which would be necessary."[61] Coup preparations were being made long before the election of President Eisenhower.

The February 28 Crisis

In early February an army column was ambushed in Bakhtiyari territory by local tribesmen. About thirty soldiers were killed. US communications for the run-up to the February crisis remain sketchy, but a CIA dispatch admits that MI6 had been arming the Bakhtiyaris. The CIA itself had been busy stockpiling weapons among the neighboring Qashqais on the pretext of creating a guerrilla force to fight a future Soviet invasion.[62] On February 20, Mossadeq sent a "brisk message" to the shah threatening not only to resign but also to expose to the nation the links existing between members of the royal court and the British-instigated Bakhtiyari revolt. Ala, in "utmost secrecy," rushed to inform Henderson that the shah, having "lost his nerve," had immediately offered to leave the country for an extended vacation. He was making preparation to depart on February 28 with his queen, master of ceremonies, two servants, and several guards. Ala confessed he had failed to dissuade the shah since the latter was "hysterical" and on the verge of a "nervous breakdown."[63] Henderson reported: "I agreed with Ala that departure would be first step in the dissolution of the monarchy." He added:[64]

> I dislike remaining inactive at time when monarchical institution which we have in past regarded as stabilizing influence in the country is in grave danger.... Members of Embassy and other American agencies here endeavoring to ascertain whether any political or other forces exist which might at least in name of Shah oppose this latest Mossadeq move. Story of Shah's imminent departure may leak prior his departure.

The information was conveniently "leaked" on the very eve of the scheduled departure. Henderson reported that in the early morning of February 28, news of the planned departure spread like wildfire. Some three hundred angry royalists gathered outside the palace just as Mossadeq arrived to see the shah off. They had been trucked in by army officers and Sh'aban Bemorkh (Brainless Sh'aban)—a thug hired by both Ayatollah Behbahani and Ayatollah Kashani. The former was a prominent court cleric. The latter had been a vocal Mossadeq supporter, but in recent months had had a series of long, closed meetings with Henderson, Zahedi, the director of Point IV, and Professor George Lenczowski—an academic working for the CIA.

Henderson reported: "I decided that I was free to try to effect cancellation of the departure." He forcefully conveyed this to the shah first indirectly through a military attaché and Ala, and then directly through a secure phone. "I told Ala," he reported, "that even though I might later be charged with interference in Iranian affairs, I would welcome the offer to speak directly to the Shah ... I assured the Shah that the US government would consider him leaving not in the best interest of his country. I added that a very important personage for whom he had most friendly feeling has also expressed sincere hope he would not leave."[65] Henderson conveyed a similar message personally to Mossadeq. On leaving the latter's residence, he noted that a "surly mob" blocked the entryway. An embassy dispatch later remarked in passing that this "mob" had moved from the palace to the prime minister's residence nearby and had tried to crash an army jeep through the gates into the building.[66] Mossadeq later claimed the mob had been hired to kill him.[67]

At the end of the day, the shah announced he would not be leaving the country. Three months later the shah profusely thanked Henderson for dissuading him from leaving: "He wished the Ambassador to know that he believed if it had not been for the actions of the Ambassador at that time the institution of monarchy would have been overthrown."[68] In describing the whole event to the NSC, Henderson repeated his long-standing belief that "there is no hope of settling the oil problem so long as Mossadeq is in power."[69]

The 1953 Coup

Henderson played an equally decisive role in the actual coup. The original plan spelled out by Wilbur contained two component parts. The first—labeled the "quasi-constitutional coup"—required Colonel Naseri, the Imperial Guard commander, to lead a military convoy on the midnight of August 15 to Mossadeq's residence, and deliver a royal *farman* (decree) naming General Zahedi as prime minister. Zahedi, in turn, would appoint General Batmanqalech as his chief of staff. Batmanqalech, meanwhile, with his convoy would occupy the headquarters of the chief of staff in central Tehran. The second part—the pure military side of the coup—consisted of Batmanqalech ordering tank commanders loyal to the shah to move into the city and occupy the strategic points. This was necessary because the top commanders of the five military bases in the capital were all deemed to be staunch supporters of Mossadeq. They had full authority over troop movements in and out of the five bases—including the delivery of fuel and ammunition. To short-circuit them, the coup required a chief of staff who could override them and give orders directly to tank officers.

The first part of the coup proved a fiasco. When Naseri and Batmanqalech approached their targets they found themselves facing half-a-dozen tanks. Mossadeq, tipped off indirectly by a guard officer, had placed them there. Naseri was arrested. Batmanqalech went into hiding. And the shah fled the country. Some in Washington and London concluded all was lost. But Roosevelt and colleagues on the ground knew that only the first part of the plan had failed. They promptly improvised to implement the second part. This improvisation brought in Henderson.

Henderson, who had taken a "prolonged vacation" so as to be absent during the coup, was in Beirut when he heard of the fiasco. He rushed back to Tehran on a military plane and was received at the airport by Mossadeq's son. On his way from the airport he saw jubilant crowds toppling royal statues, denouncing the shah, and shouting anti-British and anti-American slogans. Straightaway he met Roosevelt in the embassy compound. Roosevelt later informed Washington that he, Henderson, Zahedi, the head of the American military mission, and unnamed others had a "big council of war" meeting inside the embassy compound.[70] Henderson then requested an urgent meeting with Mossadeq. Roosevelt, in his memoirs, remembers that Henderson was worried that Mossadeq would ask him if the United States supported the shah. He was prepared to reply that the "US had no intention of interfering in the affairs of a friendly country." Roosevelt remarked: "To this noble sentiment I made no comment. Diplomats are expected, if not required to say such things."[71]

Henderson was granted a meeting with Mossadeq for the following afternoon—August 18. Without any sense of irony, the CIA sent him the following advice: "Mossadeq's innate suspiciousness, which has probably been reinforced by the events of the weekend, may lead him to link the attempt to unseat him with recent hardening of US policy towards him and to represent the attempt of an 'imperialist' plot engineered by the US and UK."[72]

This fateful meeting has been described in significantly different ways. The 1989 *FRUS* contains a long "British Memorandum"—probably written for Churchill by Roosevelt—giving blow-by-blow account from July 11 until August 21. It included the following: "Mr. Henderson called on the Prime Minister during the afternoon.... Their meeting ended abruptly. According to well-placed sources, it was soon after this that the plans of events of the 19th August were put into operation."[73] The very same document declassified but not published in the 2017 *FRUS* volume fills the dotted gap: "and, according to a reliable source, warned him that his continued persistence in remaining in office was not in the best interests of Persia. It was learned that Dr. Mossadeq strongly resented this warning, and told Mr. Henderson that he had no right to interfere in the internal affairs of the country."[74]

Henderson's own report for the State Department is fuller but still self-censored. He writes the meeting lasted a full hour and began on a polite note. Mossadeq was his "courteous self" but revealed a "certain amount of smoldering resentment."[75]

He blamed the British for the coup attempt although he must have known from his own police reports that the CIA had been involved. Henderson expressed "sorrow" for the chain of events while he had been away. Mossadeq gave a "sarcastic smile." The tone, however, drastically shifted when Henderson turned to the "extreme serious" matter at hand—the failure of law authorities to protect American lives. He issued the not-so-subtle ultimatum that if the authorities did not immediately establish law and order in the streets, he would have no choice but to evacuate all Americans. He stressed the United States could not continue to recognize a government that was unable to control its own streets. He mentioned in passing that he had heard rumors the shah had dismissed him. This raised the question whether he was still the legal prime minister. He also held out the possibility of American assistance if US "missions were assured of maximum cooperation from Iranian authorities." Before leaving, Henderson assured Mossadeq that his embassy would never contemplate providing sanctuary to members of the opposition.

Henderson later provided a less sanitized account to the Columbia University History Project.[76] He reminisced that when he raised the issue of "mobs" threatening Americans, Mossadeq picked up the phone "in my presence," called the chief of police, and instructed him to "restore order by breaking up the roving gangs." "Apparently Mossadeq's orders," Henderson said, "were carried out with alacrity. When I was returning to the Embassy an hour later, I saw the police breaking up the gangs."

What is more, the government asked all supporters to obey the martial law authorities and to stay off the streets. This fitted neatly into the original CIA plan requiring streets to be empty of government supporters so as to permit the tanks to move unhindered into the city. The CIA did not want a repeat of the July Uprising. A similar account of the meeting appeared immediately after the coup in *Time*.[77] The magazine stressed that "things began to happen as soon as the meeting ended." It explained that when Henderson threatened to evacuate all Americans and withhold government recognition, Mossadeq had fallen for the bait and ordered the police to crack down. This had been his "fatal mistake." Since only Henderson, Mossadeq, and the latter's interpreter had been present at the meeting, this account was most probably leaked by Henderson himself. *Time*, like most magazines at the time, billed the overthrow of Mossadeq "as a spontaneous uprising of the people" against the "wily old dictator" and for "their beloved young and popular monarch." Terms such as coup, CIA, MI6, and even oil nationalization were scrupulously avoided. As Michel Foucault liked to stress, what is not mentioned is invariably more significant than what is.

Notes

1 *Foreign Relations of the United States, 1952–54* (hereafter *FRUS*) (Washington, DC: 1989), Vol. X, Iran, 1951–4, 1–1092.
2 National Security Archive, "Have the British Been Meddling with the FRUS ...," http://www2.gwu.edu/~nsarchiv/NSAEBB/NASAEBB435/. See also Warren Kimball, "Classified," *Perspectives*, February 1997, 9–10; Roham Alvandi, "Open the Files on the Iran Coup," *New York Times*, July 9, 2014.
3 Warren Kimball, "Classified!," *Perspectives*, February 1997, 9–10, 22–4; Stephen Weissman, "Censoring American Diplomatic History," *Perspectives* September 2011: 48–9; Weissman, "Why is US withholding documents ...?," *Christian Science Monitor* March 25, 2011.
4 R. Gorham, "Iran: The Ghotbi Pamphlet and the Mussadiq Period," Foreign and Commonwealth Office (FCO) 8/3187; R. Muir, "Iran: Release of Confidential

Records," FCO 8/3216. The head of the Middle East Department in the FCO wrote to the British embassy in Washington: "The State Department has given us firm enough assurance in the past that they can and will protect against disclosure of information which HMG has given them in confidence. Before files are released under the Freedom of Information Act, there should be no difficulty for the Americans in first removing from them copies of any telegrams etc. from us and US documents which record our views, even in the case of papers which are not strictly 'official information furnished by a foreign government.' What is not clear is whether they could withhold American documents which referred to joint Anglo/US view about say the removal of Mussadiq in 1953. In the current situation, there is good chance that public opinion will once again focus on that chapter of Iranian history. We hope therefore that the US administration would agree on a joint approach to minimize the damage which could be done to our interests by the release of the US records." FCO 8/3216.

5   Anonymous, "US hold up '53 coup documents," *Iran Times*, December 26, 2014.

6   For a general survey of the delays see Azadeh Moaveni's interview with Malcolm Byrne, "History Should be Messy and Complicated," http://iranwire.com/en/ projects/2164.

7   *FRUS, 1952–54* (Washington, DC: 2017), Iran 1951–4, 1–970.

8   Mark Gasiorowski, "New Details on the 1953 Coup in Iran," www.lobelog.com.; Arash Azizi, "Many Actors Should Get the Blame for the 1953 Coup," https://iranwire.com/ en/features/4779.

9   Andrew Bacevich, "A Prize from Fairyland," *London Review of Books*, November 2, 2017.

10   Roland Brown, "The 1953 Coup: What Secrets Remain," https://iranwire.com/en/ features/4672.

11   Donald Wilber, "Overthrow of Premier Mossadeq of Iran, November 1952–August 1953" (Washington, DC: CIA Historical Division, 1954), 1–172, http://cryptome.org/ cia-iran-all.htm. This document—with some names redacted—was later published as a book: Donald Wilber, *Regime Change in Iran* (London: Russell Press, 2006), 1–111.

12   Wilber, "Overthrow of Premier Mossadeq," 29.

13   The CIA later tried to minimize the Wilber report by releasing two documents: *Zendebad Shah!: The Central Intelligence Agency and the Fall of Iranian Prime Minister Mohammed Mossadeq* (Washington, DC: CIA History Staff, 1998); and *The Battle for Iran, 1953* (Washington, DC: CIA History Staff, n.d.), They were made available through http://www2.gwu.edu/~nsarchiv/NSAEBB/NSAEBB476/ and http://www2.gwu.edu/~nsarchiv/NSAEBB/NSAEBB435/. These two, however, are not as reliable as the Wilber report. The Wilber report was written right at the time of the coup based on primary sources. The latter was written decades later based on secondary and even tertiary sources. The former focused on the actual coup. The latter tried to compress the coup into the context of long history. The former addresses the question why the military officers succeeded. The latter focuses on the "crowd" that provided merely acoustical distractions. The former answers the question how the coup succeeded. The latter aimed to delink the coup from latter events—especially the Islamic Revolution. The latter two, moreover, remain heavily redacted. In the initial release of Zendebad Shah, 71 pages of 102 remained blank. In the second release in 2017, 59 still remained so. The CIA even insinuated that Wilber had a "personal axe to grind." He may have had one by the time he died and left the document to be leaked at an appropriate time, but he definitely had no cause for complaint in 1954—immediately after the coup's success. Despite strengths of

the Wilber report and weaknesses of the later ones, royalists from Iran have latched on the latter minimizing the role of the military and passing the blame (or success) of the coup onto court clerics. See Darioush Bayandor, *Iran and the CIA: The Fall of Mosaddeq Revisited* (New York: Palgrave, 2010).

14 NSC, Statement of Policy Proposed by the National Security Council (June 27, 1951), *FRUS* (1989), 71–6.

15 NSC, Statement of Policy Proposed by the National Security Council (undated), *FRUS* (2017), 107.

16 S. Gleason, Memorandum on the Meeting of the NSC (August 27, 1953), *FRUS* (1989), 773.

17 S. Gleason, Memorandum on the Meeting of the NSC (August 27, 1953), *FRUS* (2017), 720.

18 WikiLeaks, Public Library of US Diplomacy, https://search.wikileaks.org/; CIA, Electronic Library, https://www.cia.gov/library/readingroom/search/site/Iran%2C%20 1951-79.

19 George McGhee, *Envoy to the Middle East* (New York: Harper & Row, 1983), 327.

20 Loy Henderson, Telegram to the State Department (September 30, 1951), *FRUS* (1989), 187.

21 CIA, Preliminary Operation Plan for TPAJAX (June 6, 1953), *FRUS* (2017), 587.

22 British Ambassador (in Washington), Telegram to F.O, FO 371/Persia 1951/34-91470; British Ambassador, Anglo-US Talks in Washington, British Petroleum Archive/00043859. See also Memo on Conversations with the British Ambassador, *FRUS* (1989), 37–42.

23 State Department, Meeting on AIOC Problem with US Oil Companies, *FRUS*, *1951–54* (Washington, DC: 1982), Vol. V, 309; State Department, Memorandum on Conversations (April 17, 1951), *FRUS* (1989), 34. For an excellent study of the role of the American majors in the crisis see: David Painter, *Oil and the American Century* (London: John Hopkins University Press, 1986); and Instructor's Notes, "The United States, Great Britain, and Mossadegh," George Washington University, http://data. georgetown.edu/sfs/programs/isd/.

24 James Goode, *The United States and Iran: In the Shadow of Mussadiq* (New York: St. Marin's Press, 1997), 29–30.

25 McGhee, *Envoy to the Middle East*, 335.

26 CIA, "Intelligence Bulletin (May 8, 1951), CIA Electronic Library.

27 National Estimate Board, Memo on Iranian Developments (May 1, 1951), *FRUS* (2017), 76.

28 Clement Attlee, "Letter..," FO371/Persia 1951/34–9154; and FO 248/Persia 1951/34–1527.

29 L.P. Elwell-Sutton, *Persian Oil: A Study in Power Politics* (London: Lawrence and Wishart, 1955), 252.

30 NSC, Memorandum of Meeting (May 16, 1951), *FRUS* (2017), 90.

31 NSC, Memorandum of Meeting (March 4, 1953), *FRUS* (2017), 477, 492.

32 NSC, Memorandum of Meeting (March 11, 1953), *FRUS* (2017), 489.

33 Henderson, Memorandum (August 30, 1953), this document is unclassified, but not in the 2017 *FRUS* volume.

34 Don North, "Interview with Ambassador Loy Henderson (December 1970), Oral History Project (New York: Columbia University, 1972).

35 NSC, Certain Problems Relating to Iran, 1954, *FRUS* (2017), 875–80.

36 CIA, Meeting of the Director (May 9, 1951), *FRUS* (2017), 87.

37 Henderson, Telegram to Department of State (May 9, 1952), *FRUS* (2017), 267.
38 William Rountree, Memorandum of Conversation (May 16, 1952), *FRUS* (2017), 232–8.
39 Robin Zaehner, Telegram to Foreign Office (June 11, 1952), FO/248/Persia 1952/1531.
40 Anonymous, "New Iran Premier: General Zahedi a Nationalist, a Farmer, and a Boulevardier—Mossadegh a Contrast," *New York Times* August 20, 1953.
41 Henderson, Telegram to State Department (May 24, 1952), *FRUS* (2017), 240; Henderson, Telegram to State Department (June 6, 1952), *FRUS* (2017), 245; Henderson, Telegram to the State Department (June 13, 1952), *FRUS* (2017), 254. In one dispatch, Henderson described Saleh as even "more dangerous, irreconcilable, and demagogic" on the oil issue than Mossadeq. Henderson, Telegram to the State Department (June 13, 1952), *FRUS* (2017), 252.
42 Acting Chief of Near East Division, Memorandum (September 2, 1953), *FRUS* (2017), 742.
43 Henderson, Telegram on Conversation with Ala (June 6, 1952), *FRUS* (2017), 243.
44 Acting Chief of Near East Division, Memorandum (February 20, 1952), *FRUS* (2017), 214–16.
45 *FRUS* (1989) and *FRUS* (2017) do not contain dispatches from Tehran from June 20 until July 18.
46 John Leavitt, Memorandum for National Estimates (March 28, 1953), *FRUS* (2017), 722.
47 R.J., Confidential Report (August 21, 1952), FO 248/Persia 1052/1531.
48 British Embassy, Telegram to the Foreign Office (July 18, 1952), FO 248/1539.
49 NSC, Henderson Remarks in the NSC (June 25, 1953), *FRUS* (2017), 599.
50 British Embassy, Telegram to the Foreign Office (July 21, 1953), FO 371/Persia 1952/98601; A long version of this telegram in FO 284/Persia 1952/1531.
51 British Embassy, Review of Recent Crisis (July 28, 1952), FO 371/Persia 1952/98602.
52 British Embassy, Telegram to the Foreign Office (July 28, 1952), FO 371/Persia 1952/98602.
53 War Office, Notes to the Military Attache (July 19, 1952), FO 371/Persia 1952/98602.
54 Foreign Office, Telegram to the Embassy (July 19, 1952), FO 371/Persia 1952/98602.
55 Henderson, Telegram to State Department (July 31, 1952), *FRUS* (2017), 305; CIA, Preliminary Operation Plan, *FRUS* (2017), 587.
56 NSC, Iranian Situation (July 22, 1952), *FRUS* (2017), 289.
57 British Embassy, Telegram to the Foreign Office (July 28, 1952), FO 371/Persia 1952/98602.
58 British Embassy, Telegram to the Foreign Office, FO 248/Persia 1952/1531.
59 Habib Ladjevardi, "Interview with Sir George Middleton," The Iranian Oral History Project (Cambridge, MA: Harvard University, 1993).
60 Henderson, Telegram to the State Department (July 28, 1953), *FRUS* (1989), 421.
61 Dean Acheson, Memorandum to the Tehran Embassy (July 29, 1952), *FRUS* (2017), 301.
62 CIA, Memorandum from Directorate of Plans (February 25), *FRUS* (2017), 453.
63 Henderson, Telegram to the State Department (February 25, 1953), *FRUS* (2017), 456.
64 Henderson, Telegram to State Department (February 26, 1953), *FRUS* (2017), 458.
65 Henderson, Telegram to State Department (February 28, 1953). *FRUS* (2017), 462–6.
66 Henderson, Report to the NSC (June 25, 1953), *FRUS* (2017), 601.
67 Muhammad Mossadeq, "Report on the 28 February Conspiracy," in *Musaddiq's Memoirs*, ed. Homa Katouzian (London: Jebhe, 1988), 296–305.

68 NSC, Memorandum of Conversation (May 14, 1953), *FRUS* (2017), 556–67.

69 NSC, Remarks to the NSC (June 25, 1953), *FRUS* (2017), 599.

70 CIA. Meeting on TPAJAX (August 28, 2017), *FRUS* (2017), 727–40.

71 Kermit Roosevelt, *Countercoup: The Struggle for the Control of Iran* (New York: McGraw-Hill, 1979), 184.

72 CIA, Memorandum to Ambassador Henderson (August 17, 1953), *FRUS* (2017), 679.

73 British Memorandum, Political Review of the Recent Crisis (September 2, 1953), *FRUS* (1989), 784.

74 British Memorandum, Political Review of the Recent Crisis (September 2, 1953), Declassified in 2018.

75 Henderson, Meeting with Mossadeq (August 18, 1953), *FRUS* (1989), 748–52.

76 Don North, "Interview with Ambassador Loy Henderson" (December 1970), Oral History Project (New York: Columbia University, 1972).

77 Anonymous, "The People Take Over," *Time*, August 31, 1953.

8

When History Meets Politics: The Challenging Case of the 1953 Coup in Iran

Malcolm Byrne

Introduction

Historical investigations of covert operations inevitably face obstacles growing out of national security restrictions. When one of the countries involved is Iran, its strategic location, hostile relations with Washington, and pariah status in the West introduce additional diplomatic, political, and other considerations. In the case of the 1953 Coup in Iran, a further complication has been the decades old demand of the British government that the United States keep its files closed regarding London's participation. Taken together, these circumstances have led to the dramatic overclassification of the American record. For years this has left large gaps in the public's understanding of events and, worse, contributed to a distortion of the history.

This chapter will discuss US government policies regarding public access to this important episode. More specifically, it will focus on the CIA and describe the experiences of three groups—ex-spies publishing memoirs, State Department historians compiling the official record of American foreign policy, and private citizens using the Freedom of Information Act (FOIA)—as each confronted the barrier of excessive classification. The discussion will detail the official and unofficial reasons behind the CIA's refusal to declassify facts that have been publicly known for years, and argue that those rationales were almost entirely unwarranted. Conditions of access have ameliorated to some degree in recent years, but because similar justifications continue to be invoked in other sensitive areas of US foreign policy, the Iran 1953 case has broader applications.

Early Years

For the first two decades after the coup, public awareness of TPAJAX came from press accounts, a handful of memoirs, biographies, and academic treatments. One of the great ironies when discussing overclassification is that the first published description of the operation originated with a high-level official CIA leak. In October–November

1954, the popular weekly the *Saturday Evening Post* ran a three-part encomium of the CIA. The segment on Iran gave granular detail about the agency's role in ousting Muhammad Mossadeq, hailing it as "another CIA-influenced triumph" by which "the strategic little nation of Iran was rescued from the clutch of Moscow."[1] This version of events went directly against the official US narrative, which was that the overthrow was a spontaneous act by the Iranian people without the benefit of outside help. This was how President Dwight D. Eisenhower and Shah Mohammad Reza Pahlavi depicted it in their respective memoirs. Biographer Stephen Ambrose and historian Richard Immerman undertook an early, serious inquiry with the evidence at hand, as did Richard Cottam, an ex-CIA operative-turned-academic. But even Cottam, who had first-hand knowledge of many details, felt obliged to abide by secrecy restrictions and stick to quoting at length from the *Saturday Evening Post*.[2]

In the 1950s, the CIA benefited from the public's fuzzy understanding of its mission and activities. According to future director of Central Intelligence (DCI) William Colby, it "enjoyed a reputation … not a whit less than golden." The cloak of secrecy surrounding it "added the appropriate touch of mystery to its romantic reputation."[3] Allen W. Dulles, the agency's media-savvy director under Eisenhower, was intent on boosting that image. When the possibility presented itself for a sympathetic profile in the *Saturday Evening Post*, he was enthusiastic. The authors promised to highlight "Red gains through subversion" and make the bureaucratic case "that CIA is the agency to combat those tactics."[4] They even allowed Dulles to review a draft before publication. According to one scholar, the series was "part of a conscious effort" by Dulles "to generate political capital for the agency to secure its place in the Washington bureaucracy."[5]

The practice did not go unnoticed, or uncriticized. Early in the Kennedy administration, presidential advisor Arthur M. Schlesinger Jr., the noted historian who had served in the Office of Strategic Services in the Second World War and thereafter been a periodic consultant to the CIA, complained to the president that "a gross and repeated CIA failing has been its occasional readiness to succumb to the temptation of favorable publicity." He specifically mentioned the 1953 Coup, commenting that the operation was "almost nullified by the flood of self-congratulatory publicity which followed … (e.g. the articles by Richard and Gladys Harkness)."[6] Nevertheless, the *Saturday Evening Post* leak undercut later claims that TPAJAX required absolute secrecy for the sake of national security.

The CIA's fortunes changed after the Bay of Pigs invasion in 1961. Colby and his colleagues blamed that fiasco for "suddenly" making the agency "a perfect scapegoat" for US blunders overseas. "As the agency's public reputation declined," he wrote, "the press, perhaps not coincidentally, moved into the attack."[7] By 1966, senior CIA officials like Lyman Kirkpatrick were "astounded" and "dismayed" that the organization was presumed to be "behind every coup and plot throughout the world," and that CIA was now "practically a dirty word."[8] An agency historian writing about TPAJAX during the mid-1970s reprinted excerpts from the popular literature about the operation specifically to highlight for his classified audience the many "distortions and guesses" that disparaged the organization.[9] Agency officials complained that the public simply did not appreciate its contributions.

Ex-Agents in Their Own Words

The mid-1970s were even tougher on the CIA. Colby, who bore the brunt of this more than anyone, recalled that "[a]ll the tensions and suspicions and hostilities that had been building about the CIA since the Bay of Pigs and had risen to a combustible level during the Vietnam and Watergate years, now exploded." During 1975, known as the Year of Intelligence, "the CIA came under the closest and harshest public scrutiny that any such service has ever experienced not only in this country but anywhere in the world."[10]

The public's antagonism was fed by revelations about illicit intelligence activities. Journalist Seymour Hersh led a wave of reporting about domestic surveillance and antidemocratic operations abroad. Former agents Victor Marchetti, Philip Agee, and Frank Snepp published exposés of other disturbing but authorized covert conduct. Congress created the Church and Pike committees that brought more damaging disclosures about assassination attempts and abuses of power. Wide-ranging legislation followed, designed to constrain the executive branch, especially in the sphere of intelligence. The CIA was put on the defensive and scrambled for years to restore its reputation.

In the midst of this turmoil, a handful of American and British former intelligence officers who had been part of the 1953 Coup decided to memorialize their roles. Kermit Roosevelt, who had coordinated the operation for the CIA from Tehran, was the best known of them. Unfortunately for these would-be authors, the agency's embarrassment over the Marchetti and Agee revelations[11] led to a new requirement that ex-employees submit their manuscripts for clearance prior to publication. Roosevelt's foray through the process has been partially documented thanks to the FOIA and is revealing about agency approaches to so-called nonofficial releases.

In early June 1976, Roosevelt contacted DCI George H. W. Bush—later vice president and president of the United States—to seek permission for his book. At the time, the agency was just finalizing its new regulations for manuscript reviews. Bush evidently approved but still referred Roosevelt to the agency's inspector general, John Waller—another coup veteran—to initiate the review.[12] Waller would forward the matter to the newly formed Publications Review Board (PRB). Roosevelt assumed the exercise would be largely pro forma since he had already "done what was proper to have informed Mr. Bush of his intentions early on." Nevertheless, he promised to cooperate and began to meet with agency lawyers whose first step was to remind him of the secrecy agreement he had signed in 1949.[13]

The CIA's Information Management Staff (C/IMS) quickly concluded there would be "considerable difficulty with the draft of Mr. Roosevelt's book as it presently exists." The specifics are not known—they are still classified—but they struck one reviewer as serious enough to suggest that Roosevelt be advised to forgo a mass market book and write an article for the agency's in-house *Studies in Intelligence* instead.[14] Otherwise, he foresaw a "flat PRB denial." The idea was a nonstarter because CIA lawyers believed the Roosevelt family was counting on book and movie rights for a "substantial amount of income."[15]

Eventually, the reviewers sent Roosevelt a list of 156 items in the manuscript they said were unacceptable. Although most of the substance of their memo has been excised, it included "objections" to revealing the "identities of sources and other assets, all of which are protected by statute" and in a "lesser category, conceivably, … details related to locations of stations, the identities of Agency personnel, cryptonyms, pseudonyms, and relations of an intelligence nature with specific countries." "None of these assertions is vitiated by the passage of time," they added.[16] As will be seen, these topics have long been standard concerns for the CIA.

The reviewers' memo drew its rationales from an executive order (EO) on classification from the early 1970s.[17] That EO exempts the following categories of material from declassification:

1. Classified information or material furnished by foreign governments or international organizations and held by the United States on the understanding that it be kept in confidence.
2. Classified information or material specifically covered by statute, or pertaining to cryptography, or disclosing intelligence sources or methods.
3. Classified information or material disclosing a system, plan, installation, project or specific foreign relations matter the continuing protection of which is essential to the national security.
4. Classified information or material the disclosure of which would place a person in immediate jeopardy.

Roosevelt's manuscript soon came to the attention of agency upper management. In late July 1978, the Directorate of Operations (DO) representative on the PRB informed John McMahon, the deputy director for operations, that the general counsel's office planned to advise Roosevelt of "major problems" with the text. McMahon agreed with their objections and went even further, scrawling on a routing sheet: "I will not approve any publication which in any way refers to CIA activities abroad."[18] Roosevelt was "shocked" at the ruling. "The book has cost me two years of my life," he complained, repeating that the DCI and the shah himself had already given the go-ahead. Agency lawyers retorted that the CIA "had different management today"—and new rules. (Jimmy Carter was now president and George Bush had been replaced as DCI by Admiral Stansfield Turner.[19])

Most of the rationales provided to Roosevelt related to national security. But officers meeting with him at his vacation home on Nantucket (at Roosevelt's insistence) in July 1978 also floated an institutional motivation. They hoped he would agree to their changes because when ex-operative Frank Snepp decided to forgo agency review it "diminished the world-wide confidence in our ability to protect secrets." This is another standard CIA concern. The agency also cited a federal judge's ruling that the true test for determining classification was not how old the information was but its "present impact." Roosevelt agreed with both points.[20]

McMahon's decree reflected DO views, but even in those days it was recognized as an overreach of authority. The general counsel's office advised that the agency "will not be able to defend in court a blanket prohibition as set forth by Mr. McMahon." He would have to be ready to provide a "detailed identification and justification" for any proposed deletions. An agency attorney spelled out what this meant:

> [T]he only information which the Agency can request to be deleted from a manuscript is information which is classified, information which was learned during the course of Agency employment by the author and information which has not [been] placed in the public domain by the United States Government.

"Merely describing information as relating to sources and methods will not suffice," the attorney wrote.[21] Unfortunately, McMahon's way of thinking would endure. A very similar DO attempt to apply a "blanket prohibition" to releasing information would surface in a lawsuit twenty years later, as described later in this chapter.

Meanwhile, Roosevelt pushed back. By December 1978, just as the Iranian Revolution was about to crest, he declared that he had had enough. He told agency lawyers he had substantially complied with all requests, even though "I believe many of your objections are unreasonable." Because of a "commitment to McGraw-Hill, I must proceed with the submission of a final manuscript, which is already overdue."[22] The agency acceded. They accepted his offer to take one more look and came up with two final excisions, both relating to the existence of a CIA "station" within the embassy in Tehran.[23]

Twenty-seven months after Roosevelt first submitted his manuscript, CIA reviewers deemed the book ready for publication.[24] But it was not the same manuscript. "Basically, Roosevelt has reflected quite faithfully the changes that we suggested to him," the final reviewer reported to his superiors, then added: "This has become, therefore, essentially a work of fiction."[25] It was a significant insight into the DO's thinking.

The story does not end there. McGraw-Hill published *Countercoup* in August 1979, but almost immediately pulled it from bookstores, citing "defective production and errata." One of the CIA's main concerns had been to disguise the role of the Secret Intelligence Service (SIS), Britain's overseas intelligence arm, which had helped to plan the coup. Roosevelt's solution, apparently with CIA acceptance, was to substitute Anglo-Iranian Oil Company (AIOC) for SIS. (This was presumably one of the changes that reduced the book to "fiction.") The AIOC had been at the center of the oil nationalization crisis in the early 1950s. The problem was that the AIOC's successor, British Petroleum, threatened to sue over the "wrong, inaccurate," and possibly "libelous" assertion. McGraw-Hill promised to make it right, but in the end simply inserted "British Intelligence" for AIOC—precisely what the CIA and presumably the SIS had wanted to avoid.[26]

Still another twist was to come. Before McGraw-Hill could bring out the revised edition, the US embassy in Tehran was overrun on November 4, 1979, marking the start of the 444-day hostage crisis. In mid-December, CIA director Turner wrote to Secretary of State Cyrus Vance: "It has been our belief that publication of the Roosevelt book at this time could adversely affect our position in the Iran crisis, including increasing the possibility of blowback on the hostages." "Happily," though, Turner could report that deputy CIA director Frank Carlucci had reached out to Roosevelt, who agreed to hold off on publication "until six weeks after the hostages have been released."[27] It would not be the only time policy concerns came into play involving 1953. But in this instance, things did not work out as hoped. Roosevelt and McGraw-Hill eventually grew impatient and published the revised volume in August 1980, while the hostages were still in captivity.

Roosevelt came out far better with the PRB than his fellow coup participant, Donald Wilber. Wilber, who spearheaded the initial planning for the Americans, submitted portions of his memoir, *Adventures in the Middle East*, for review in spring 1983. The resulting "sanitization" was "so thorough and so frustrating" that he decided to describe it in his book, along with reprinting correspondence and other documentation from his former agency. A letter from the Office of General Counsel in late May informed him that "the items of classified information" in his manuscript were "so numerous and interwoven with the story that if they were to be deleted, the remaining material would be nonsensical." As with Roosevelt, the agency hoped he would settle for writing for an internal CIA audience instead.[28]

Wilber's experience illustrated another problem with CIA clearances. Compared to Roosevelt, not to mention William Colby, Harry Rositzke, and other senior spies-turned-authors, Wilber wrote, "I felt that I, as an Indian, was treated less leniently than were the Chiefs."[29] The PRB refused even to itemize its concerns, as it had done for Roosevelt. The most the board would do was to describe five (familiar) categories of concern:

> Acknowledgment of agency presence in specific countries overseas; description of details of particular operations; acknowledgment of the existence of specific liaison relationships and a description of the details of operations conducted with liaison services; description and/or identification of intelligence sources and methods; and description of information which, if revealed, would damage the United States relationships with foreign governments.[30]

Wilber remained "rankled" for years.[31]

The CIA's treatment of writings by former employees raises concerns that go beyond TPAJAX. The agency puts great weight on distinguishing between official and unofficial disclosures. Outsiders including foreign governments, opposition figures, and the proverbial person on the street are presumed to be far more attuned to formal declassifications by the US government (particularly the CIA) than, for instance, leaks of major stories in the media. From the CIA's perspective, autobiographical accounts are considered "nonofficial" releases even after they have gotten PRB clearance.[32]

The problem is that indiscriminate changes of the sort introduced into *Countercoup* are a potential assault on historical accuracy. The "sole purpose" of prepublication review, according to a former PRB chairman, is "to assist authors in avoiding inadvertent disclosure of classified information … just that and nothing more."[33] But if the DO's real goal is to protect sources and methods above all else, Roosevelt's review shows that the result can be flat-out distortion. This may help explain why *Countercoup* is so unreliable. The bulk of its flaws undoubtedly stem from the author's subjectivity and self-interest, but the number of changes required by the PRB and the reviewer's telling characterization of the book as fiction suggest that a contributing cause was the DO's deliberate intent to skew history.

This is an ongoing issue. As recently as 2012, charges of partiality lodged by ex-employees led to a formal investigation into whether the review process unfairly targeted CIA critics. Complaints have since been made against other agencies, including the Defense Department, Justice Department, and National Security Agency, for inappropriate redactions having nothing to do with national security.[34]

Historical *FRUStrations*

Getting access to intelligence records on the 1953 Coup has been a struggle even for other departments of the US government. The most notable case involved the State Department office that produces the official history of US foreign policy. Begun under Abraham Lincoln, *Foreign Relations of the United States* (*FRUS*) has long been the model for government historical series worldwide. But covering Iran policy in the early 1950s became a recurring dilemma for the Office of the Historian (HO), which oversees *FRUS*. In that case, a combination of factors involving foreign policy, spycraft, and bureaucracy generated a full-blown crisis for *FRUS* and delayed full publication on 1953 for almost thirty years.

Plans for a *FRUS* volume on the coup period first came to policymakers' attention in late 1978, on the eve of the revolution. At a meeting with a delegation from the British Foreign and Commonwealth Office, the State Department's Iran desk chief, Henry Precht, raised eyebrows with grim predictions for the future of Iran's monarch, who most observers trusted would survive the upheaval. At the end of his talk, Precht mentioned the upcoming volume almost as an aside, warning that, "if released, there would be some very embarrassing things about the British"—and the shah. Whitehall quickly launched a campaign to block release of the materials. Senior State Department officials were sympathetic; Precht himself promised to sit on the records for as long as possible.[35]

The British effort worked. By 1980, Washington had assured London there would be extensive consultation before any troublesome materials were published. The larger struggle to save the shah was of course doomed. It was the first of a string of policy shocks for the United States in 1979 that led to a push to stanch the further erosion of America's global standing, including by clamping down on the circulation of potentially sensitive documentation. At the same time, new State Department policies on declassification unintentionally emboldened some regional bureaus to weigh in on *FRUS* clearance questions. The bureaus demanded the exclusion of whole categories of information such as clandestine political or propaganda operations, including "any mention of CIA," or disclosures that might "give offense to another government." An additional unfortunate coincidence was that the HO was just beginning to compile volumes on the darkest period of the Cold War, when covert action became a preferred tool of US foreign policy. Fears about awkward secrets coming to light quickly brought *FRUS* to the attention of security-minded gatekeepers at both the State Department and the CIA.[36]

As a result, the Iran volume was delayed for almost a decade. When it finally emerged in 1989, readers discovered that it left out the role of American and British intelligence in the coup. The public uproar has been described elsewhere.[37] When the storm cleared, a series of developments seemed to portend a new era for *FRUS*. The starting point was significant new legislation in 1991 strengthening the HO's mandate to produce a "thorough, accurate, and reliable documentary record." For its part, the Clinton administration responded to the collapse of the Soviet Union that year by adopting a far more aggressive stance toward declassification. Later in the 1990s, no fewer than three DCIs vowed that their agency would embrace a new mind-set on opening up past CIA activities, including reviewing for public release almost a dozen widely familiar but officially unacknowledged Cold War covert actions. Among these was the Iran coup. Toward the end of the decade, the HO pledged to address the gaps in the 1989 volume with an upcoming "retrospective" collection.

Unfortunately, putting these high-flying promises into practice was problematic. For much of the 1990s and early 2000s, a rolling dispute took place behind the scenes between the HO and its affiliated Historical Advisory Committee (HAC) on the one hand and officials from the CIA, particularly the DO, on the other hand. Minutes of quarterly HAC meetings recount the wrangling over several questions: whether the outside academics who sat on the HAC should be allowed to review classified materials; whether State Department historians (even with clearances) should have direct access to CIA operational files; and how to resolve major disagreements between agencies. On top of these were mundane but chronic delays over multiagency coordination, staff turnovers requiring retraining and acculturation, and so on. Not surprisingly, the term "*FRUStrated*" regularly found its way into the HAC's notes.

Even more exasperated than the HAC were members of the CIA's advisory Historical Review Panel (HRP), created in 1984. Historian George Herring served on the HRP for six years in the 1990s (although there was almost a four-year gap between meetings from 1990 to 1994). As he put it later, "it didn't take too long even for me to realize that I was being used to cover the agency's ass."[38] The CIA, as others have pointed out, was steeped in a "culture of secrecy,"[39] especially the DO, which by most accounts was the locus of greatest resistance to opening the record on CIA activities. Herring, for example, recalled "an especially chilling moment" in 1996 when a "troglodyte" from the DO dismissed a recent EO on classification as that "silly old law."[40]

The HO's promised retrospective finally got underway in the first half of 2002. Department historian James Van Hook finished compiling the contents no later than October of the following year, according to the minutes of the HAC, then obtained clearance from his division chief and submitted the collection for declassification by July 2004. Two years later, in 2006, the volume had entered the manuscript review process, drawing in all agencies and departments with "equities" on the topic, including the National Security Council (NSC), which participated on a special panel for resolving declassification disputes. The volume was not mentioned again in official notes until 2011, when it came up at three separate meetings, then vanished once more until September 2014.

Here policy factors came back into play. According to the HAC minutes, when the discussion at the September 2014 session turned to the Iran volume, Chief Historian

Stephen Randolph "stated that the Department had decided to delay publication because of ongoing negotiations with Iran." The talks, over Iran's nuclear program, had begun to gain traction after the 2013 election of President Hassan Rouhani. The volume's postponement for more than two additional years, though, generated deeper frustration within the HAC.[41] The specific circumstances might have differed from the past—the Islamic Republic was for once working in tandem with Washington rather than in opposition—but the upshot was the same: State Department decision-makers feared that hard-line reactions in Iran would undermine US foreign policy objectives. The only other difference was that instead of Republicans it was now Democrats— who historically tend to advocate more for transparency—who were keeping the files closed.

For the rest of the Obama administration, the State Department held firm. Even the successful conclusion of the Joint Comprehensive Plan of Action (JCPOA) in July 2015 was not enough to relax their concerns. Repeated calls to publish the volume from the HO, the HAC, and outside advocates went unheeded. Kerry refused even to meet with representatives of the HAC. Overall, the advisory panel pronounced itself "severely disappointed."[42]

Circumstances finally changed in 2017. During Donald Trump's presidential campaign, the JCPOA had been a regular target of condemnation. This carried over into his presidency as Secretary of State Rex Tillerson and CIA director Mike Pompeo joined in the criticism. Because of a widely remarked upon tendency of the new administration to roll back initiatives of its predecessors, some observers wondered whether the department might revisit the injunction on the *FRUS* retrospective. In April 2017, the HO took the initiative to draft a memorandum to the Bureau of Public Affairs at the State Department, which oversees the HO, proposing a reassessment of the volume's status.

What exactly happened next is unclear since most of those involved are reluctant to discuss it. But a mere two months later, on June 15, the State Department announced that the volume was out. The question was how high up the political ladder the decision had gone. According to scattered reports, the process was as straightforward as resubmitting the matter to the relevant desks at the State Department and the NSC. Afterward, the HAC's Richard Immerman would say only that "the change in State's perspective from the Obama to Trump administration" was "dramatic." Another official familiar with events, interviewed later, agreed that with the new administration there "automatically came a top-level sense of out-with-the-old." This official insisted that the situation did not require going to the senior ranks: "some sensitivities had waned" and "people became more comfortable" with the idea of release. "It was a good time to go back" to the relevant desks because "they were all new people."[43]

Policy considerations formed part of the basis for withholding the volume for decades—from 1978 to 2017. But improbable as it may seem, policy partially accounts for it finally going forward. The documentation in the volume turned out to be light on cloak-and-dagger details of the coup but rich in terms of the context for US policy. The worst omission—no fault of the HO or the HAC—was Britain's shared responsibility for the coup. A few dotted mentions of consultations with London survived culling, but otherwise all traces of the UK role were scrubbed. Over repeated objections, the Intelligence Community deferred to British demands to white out references to their intelligence liaison relationship, notwithstanding that it had long been common knowledge. Worse, that ruling meant excluding not only British records, for which London might have a more legitimate case, but American files, a bonus not even the Foreign and Commonwealth Office entirely expected.[44] As for the rest of the materials, as often happens when documents are declassified, the lack of sensitive content left readers to wonder what it was that had ever required such extraordinary "protection." (Since publication, barely a word has been heard from hard-liners in Tehran.)

The Limits of the Freedom of Information Act

The third case study of seeking access to the records on Iran 1953 involves private citizens and organizations using the FOIA. The National Security Archive has been pursuing the topic since its founding in 1985 and its experiences offer a window into how the process has succeeded and failed. The leading nonprofit user of the FOIA, the archive has filed hundreds of requests on Iran over the years with an eye to breaking loose historically significant materials that can safely be declassified. Areas of interest have run the gamut from the Azerbaijan crisis of 1945–6 to the P5+1 nuclear deal with Iran of 2015. Our experiences bring to mind Winston Churchill's quip about democracy, but with a twist: the FOIA process is broken; the only thing worse would be no FOIA at all.

The 1953 Coup is the most requested topic on Iran at the archive. It is also one of the most frustrating to pursue through FOIA. A fundamental reason is that CIA operatives destroyed an unknown number of relevant cables in the early 1960s, as part of a "routine" office purge, according to official accounts.[45] So, there is no hope of recovering anything remotely approaching the "full" record. Nevertheless, important materials were known to exist. In 1998, the archive filed a series of requests with the CIA that specifically sought two internal histories of Mossadeq's overthrow, one of them a well-known but still-classified report written by one of the operation's chief architects, Donald Wilber.[46]

In May 1999, after the CIA rejected the requests, the archive sued. The CIA responded in part with an affidavit by the chief information officer of the DO justifying the blanket denial of 339 pages in all.[47] That declaration is of interest here for two reasons. The first is that the agency insisted that only one sentence, consisting of nine words, from the roughly 200-page Wilber history could be released, and none of the 139-page second history, "*Zendebad, Shah!*,"[48] could be made public. That single line is: "Headquarters spent a day featured by depression and despair." In his statement to the court, the CIA review officer, William McNair, declared "under penalty of perjury" that releasing more could "reasonably be expected to damage the national security" of the United States.[49] The archive's *pro bono* attorneys replied in a motion that the assertion was "facially incredible, given the vast quantity of information the CIA has already declassified or cleared for release about the events addressed by the requested histories."[50]

The second, broader point of interest about the affidavit is its list of rationales for withholding the rest of the documents. Covering twenty pages, they were an authoritative presentation of CIA—particularly DO—views on what categories of information require classification and are therefore worth understanding. But each is also highly problematic as a justification in this specific case. At the top of the list of concerns was "intelligence sources" including "individual human sources" and "foreign liaison and foreign government information." The CIA's contention was that sources will only cooperate "when confident that they are protected from retribution or embarrassment," or worse. Identification would also "most likely have a serious effect" on recruitment in the future, resulting in a "loss in critical intelligence." Disclosing foreign liaison relationships—that is, those involving other intelligence services—would purportedly expose those governments to "internal and external political pressure" that might curtail the sharing of intelligence with the United States. Even acknowledging a past relationship, the declaration states, would cause problems in the present.

According to the affidavit, several broad "methods" required protection. "Field installations" (such as CIA stations) needed to be kept secret; otherwise local governments would "likely" be pressured to "eliminate the CIA presence ... or retaliate against the U.S. Government." "Unacknowledged domestic facilities" might become targets of a foreign intelligence service. A related worry was that discovery of a given technique from "a precise time period" could compromise its "past and future value." The fact that events occurred long ago, therefore, was said to be irrelevant: simply because a method *might* come into play in the future means it must *always* be protected, according to the intelligence community.

Another method, "cryptonyms"—which consist of "words and letter codes"—are used to mask a person or entity's actual name and ostensibly possess "a great deal of meaning for someone able to fit [them] into the proper cognitive framework." Just knowing that the CIA has chosen to use a cryptonym "instead of plain text" was presented as an "important piece of information" that could be used to work out details about a person or a project. A third methodology is "foreign intelligence relationships." The mere existence of such a relationship is sensitive and exposure could limit its usefulness in future, the affidavit reads.

Finally, the CIA's position was that only the initiated can judge questions of classification and declassification. "What may seem trivial to the uninformed," McNair quotes from the Marchetti case, "may appear of great moment" to someone with a "broad view of the scene" who can put the data "in its proper context."

These justifications for withholding information about the 1953 Coup are open to serious challenge on a number of grounds. The overarching problem with the agency's declaration in the archive's lawsuit was that it framed the issues in the most general terms with no attempt to link them to the realities of the Iran case. But the FOIA requires that agencies enumerate every assertion of classification with a specific description of how each instance of declassification would impair the national security. (Agency lawyers explained this to chief of the DO John McMahon twenty years earlier, but the impulse by some to apply the broadest possible brush persists.)

More broadly, the agency's defense for withholding so much about sources and methods implied that releasing such information about virtually any operation would almost inevitably result in harm to the national security and pose such a threat indefinitely. The problem here is that such all-encompassing claims can easily veer toward the absurd. In a classic example, it took almost a century for the CIA to declassify a selection of documents on the use of invisible ink in the First World War. CIA director Leon Panetta claimed as late as 2011 that declassification had been forced to wait "until recent advancements in technology made it possible to release them." Yet he assured his audience: "When historical information is no longer sensitive, we take seriously our responsibility to share it with the American people."[51] A similar example that came to light a few years earlier involved concerns about revealing agency plans to use balloons to drop propaganda over Eastern Europe in 1948.[52] It is not at all far-fetched to imagine that the same kind of thinking led to the refusal to release a single operational detail from the 200-page Wilber history, such as the fact that the CIA Tehran station used a mimeograph machine to copy the shah's *firmans* against Mossadeq.

A far more responsible approach to declassification by the CIA that occurred just before the archive went to court in 1999 involved another major covert operation from the 1950s, the overthrow of Jacobo Arbenz in Guatemala. In that case, the agency released the vast majority of an internal history, *Operation PBSUCCESS*, making relatively limited excisions throughout in order to protect material that could more justifiably be withheld. Left unredacted was a wealth of detailed information under every category that, when it came to the Iran coup, the CIA chose to deny in its entirety on the grounds of national security. The Guatemala releases covered intelligence sources and methods (air operations, propaganda, and psychological programs); field installations (the CIA station); names of senior officials including a Guatemala station chief, and various organizational data; and at least twenty-eight cryptonyms. Agency declassifiers managed to treat most of the CIA inspector general's multivolume Bay of Pigs report much the same way (although the final volume came out only after court action and changes to the FOIA), showing that the blanket rationalizations used in the Iran 1953 case were unjustified.[53]

The CIA undercut its case by warning reflexively that "serious damage" to US interests would result from virtually any imaginable release of information. It is an open question, for instance, whether the British (the ally being protected in the Iran case) would truly be prepared to cut back meaningfully on cooperation with their most important intelligence partner if any aspect of their role in 1953 were to be declassified—as in fact happened in 2017 (see note 43). The CIA's claims were further undermined by the sheer quantity of documentation that had already been declassified about the Mossadeq period—without any of the predicted harm to US security—by the time of McNair's affidavit. Since then, and particularly since 2011, the CIA has eased off on its earlier resistance and declassified portions of *Zendebad, Shah!* (along with a third internal history from the mid-1970s, *The Battle for Iran*) in response to requests and appeals from the National Security Archive.

Those were welcome developments, but three problems remain. One is that those releases have put the lie to earlier contentions that not a single word of *Zendebad, Shah!*

could safely be made public. In fact, when that document was eventually re-reviewed and partially provided to the archive it turned out that every paragraph approved for initial release had originally been marked "(U)" for unclassified. (Equally inexplicably, one version of the document obtained under appeal redacted all mentions of the word "Shah"—except, of course, for in the title.) A second issue is that large portions of all three of these CIA internal histories on 1953 are still classified. Ironically, the refusal to make public any significant part of the Wilber history led an anonymous source, presumably an exasperated intelligence professional, to leak it to the *New York Times*, which posted it on their website in April 2000 while the archive's lawsuit was still being adjudicated.[54] A third problem is that however baseless the CIA's claims may seem, the intelligence community's often alarmist demands for wholesale secrecy have made many judges unwilling to challenge them out of an overabundance of caution; this means the public often faces an outsized burden in trying to balance genuine security concerns with legitimate countervailing considerations, such as the public's right to know about controversial policy choices by the government.

An additional weakness in the DO's argument was the notion that foreign actors invariably distinguish between "official" and "nonofficial" publications. Like several of the preceding assertions, this seemed to be based on pure supposition and ignored established facts. Iranian media and regime statements have made it clear for years that officials of the Islamic Republic treat not just memoirs like *Countercoup* but even Western scholarly studies as tantamount to official confessions. The fact is that Iran's hard-liners will find any excuse to go after their enemies, whether it is true, false, approved or otherwise. The argument that a PRB-approved publication is materially different from a standard declassification is undoubtedly lost on many others as well.

Conclusion

The US government's denials of access to TPAJAX for so many years came at a significant cost. First of all, the withholding of basic records deprived the public of a significant piece of history about America's role in a critically important part of the world. This had several consequences. One was to limit our ability to understand the full impact of the coup, including how it was perceived—and used—by the Islamic Republic. (The most senior American hostage in Tehran from 1979 to 1981, Bruce Laingen, conceded he never grasped the significance of 1953 for Iranians until one of his captors explained it to him.[55])

Another effect was to make it harder to draw policy lessons from the experience. Former Directorate of Intelligence head Ray Cline once remarked that the "misconceptions" growing out of that "seemingly brilliant success" were in fact "disastrous"—a far cry from how the coup was once portrayed by the likes of Allen Dulles who, according to Cline, "basked in the glory of the exploit."[56] Should the public not have been allowed to know the facts underlying this conclusion? Without all the available evidence, can there be a proper assessment of the policy process that led to the coup, or of the decision-makers who approved it? Take, for example, Appendix E from *Zendebad, Shah!* that assesses the CIA's difficulties balancing operational security and analysis during the coup. The study's author concludes that lack of coordination affected the quality of intelligence that went to policymakers. That is exactly the kind of insight that should and could have been made public long ago yet it was only declassified on appeal in 2017.[57]

On a foreign policy level, it is regrettable that the instinct to protect liaison relationships with foreign governments, especially when those ties were so widely known, allowed even a close ally such as Britain effectively to decide what could or could not go into the official US historical record. Furthermore, the mere act of withholding the full story weakened America's position abroad. Among other things, it encouraged the suspicion that the United States had something embarrassing to hide and it empowered hard-liners in Tehran to use that as a club against the United States and Britain for far too long.

The CIA, too, has paid a price. Years of refusal to declassify the most anodyne particulars about TPAJAX, along with exaggerated warnings of harm to the nation's security, have eroded its credibility. Furthermore, the authorized leaks by Dulles and strikingly inconsistent agency claims of secrecy make clear that more parochial interests are sometimes at work. That in turn has made the job of protecting legitimate secrets more difficult. In the extreme, it has encouraged the very outcome the agency fears most—the uncontrolled exposure of classified information, as occurred with Donald Wilber's history.

Despite the uptick in CIA releases on 1953 since roughly 2011, there are few signs that the agency (or at least the DO) intends to lessen its demands with respect to the classification of US covert activities. For instance, the CIA was unyielding in its insistence that the Wilber document—the most important single record that exists on the coup operation—could not be reprinted in the retrospective *FRUS* volume, even though it had been posted on the Internet for years, on the grounds that declassifying a leaked record would only encourage future leakers. This is another assertion that many observers are likely to struggle to understand. Some recent declassifications have been substantial—such as the Bay of Pigs Clandestine Services History and other retrospective *FRUS* volumes—but the reality is that those decisions were often made in large part because of pressure, from former officials or blue-ribbon panels or legal challenges. There are many professionals inside the intelligence community (and elsewhere in government) who favor more reasonable openness standards but they continue to face resistance from traditional quarters.[58] Because of that, some of the same unjustified barriers to fuller public awareness about the 1953 Coup will continue to stymie our ability to understand other controversial episodes in our recent history.

Notes

1 Richard and Gladys Harkness, "The Mysterious Doings of CIA," Parts 1–3, *The Saturday Evening Post*, October 30, November 6, and November 13, 1954. (The Iran coup article appeared in Part 2 of the Harkness' trilogy, 66–8.)
2 Stephen E. Ambrose and Richard H. Immerman, *Ike's Spies: Eisenhower and the Espionage Establishment* (New York: Doubleday, 1980); Richard W. Cottam,

Nationalism in Iran (Pittsburgh, PA: University of Pittsburgh, 1964). Ambrose and Immerman mostly relied on memoirs but did include an interview with US ambassador to Iran Loy Henderson. The BBC series *End of Empire* by Brian Lapping was also revealing, but did not air until 1985. It was accompanied by Lapping's book of the same title, published by Granada in 1985.

3 William Colby and Peter Forbath, *Honorable Men: My Life in the CIA* (New York: Simon and Schuster, 1978), 181.

4 Harkness to Dulles, undated, marked "read 13 August 1954," quoted in David P. Hadley, "A Constructive Quality: The Press, the CIA, and Covert Intervention in the 1950s," *Intelligence and National Security* 31, 2 (2016): 252.

5 David P. Hadley, "A Constructive Quality: The Press, the CIA, and Covert Intervention in the 1950s," *Intelligence and National Security* 31, 2 (2016): 246–65. An extract of the *Saturday Evening Post* article appears in an internal CIA history—see, generally, Claud H. Corrigan, *The Battle for Iran*, CIA History Staff, undated (circa mid-1970s).

6 Memorandum for the President, "CIA Reorganization," June 30, 1961. John F. Kennedy Presidential Library, John F. Kennedy Papers, National Security File, Departments and Agencies, Box 271, Folder, "CIA 5/1961–8/1961." (Document provided to the author by John Prados.)

7 Colby and Forbath, *Honorable Men*, 184. The press was not alone. Arthur Schlesinger Jr. warned President Kennedy that with the Bay of Pigs the CIA had "about used up its quota" of "visible errors." "One more CIA debacle will shake faith considerably in US policy, at home as well as abroad." Memorandum for the President, June 30, 1961.

8 Kirkpatrick quoted in Christopher Moran, *Company Confessions: Secrets, Memoirs, and the CIA* (New York: St. Martin's Press, 2015), 19–20.

9 Corrigan, *The Battle for Iran*, Appendix C, c-1.

10 Colby and Forbath, *Honorable Men*, 391.

11 Victor Marchetti and John D. Marks, *The CIA and the Cult of Intelligence* (New York: Alfred A. Knopf, 1974); Philip Agee, *Inside the Company: CIA Diary* (New York: Farrar Straus & Giroux, 1975).

12 Memorandum for General Counsel, from John H. Waller, "Agency Review of Proposed Unofficial Publications by Former Employees," January 11, 1977, Confidential. CIA Headquarters Notice 178, dated June 10, 1976, cited in John Hollister Hedley, "Reviewing the Work of CIA Authors: Secrets, Free Speech, and Fig Leaves," *Studies in Intelligence*, Spring 1988.

13 Memorandum for General Counsel from John H. Waller, "Publication by Former CIA Official," January 19, 1977, Nonclassified; Memorandum for Director of Security (Attn: Chief, EAB/OS), from [Name Excised], Associate General Counsel, "Kermit Roosevelt Book on Iran," February 2, 1977, Nonclassified.

14 CIA Routing and Record Sheet for Chairman, Publications Review Board, from Chief, DO/IMS (no subject), July 10, 1978, Confidential; with attached Speed Letter to C/IMS, from [Name Excised], "Second Draft of '28 Mordad: The Countercoup' by Kermit Roosevelt," July 7, 1978, Internal Use Only.

15 CIA Routing and Record Sheet for Deputy Director of Central Intelligence, Director of Central Intelligence, et al, from Director of Public Affairs [Name Excised], "Expected Problem on Book by Former Agency Employee," circa August 14, 1978, Confidential; with attached Memorandum for Director of Central Intelligence, from Herbert E. Hetu, Director of Public Affairs, "Expected Problem on Book by Former Agency Employee," August 14, 1978, Secret; and Memorandum for Chairman of

Publications Review Board, from [Name Excised], Associate General Counsel, "Kermit Roosevelt's Book on Iran," August 4, 1978, Secret.

16 Memorandum for Chairman, Publications Review Board, from William F. Donnelly, "Mr. Kermit Roosevelt's Draft: 28 Mordad: The Countercoup," October 12, 1978, Secret.

17 Executive Order 11652, "Classification and Declassification of National Security Information and Material," dated March 8, 1972 (later amended).

18 CIA Routing and Record Sheet, Author and Addressee Excised, "Directorate Candidate to Discuss Kermit Roosevelt Manuscript," July 26, 1978, Nonclassified; with attached Speed Letter to John McMahon, Deputy Director for Operations, from [Name Excised] DO Alternate, Publications Review Board, July 26, 1978, Internal Use Only.

19 CIA, "Expected Problem on Book by Former Agency Employee," circa August 14, 1978, with attachment; and Memorandum, "Kermit Roosevelt's Book on Iran," August 4, 1978.

20 Memorandum, "Kermit Roosevelt's Book on Iran," August 4, 1978.

21 Memorandum for Chairman, Publications Review Board, from [Name Excised], Associate General Counsel, "Kermit Roosevelt's Draft: 28 Mordad: The Countercoup," September 28, 1978, Nonclassified.

22 Letter to [Name Excised], Associate General Counsel, from Kermit Roosevelt, December 18, 1978, Nonclassified.

23 Memorandum for [Name Excised], Office of General Counsel, from William F. Donnelly, "Manuscript 'Countercoup'," May 1, 1979, Secret, with attached Speed Letter for C/IMS from [Name Excised], "Galley Proofs of 'Countercoup'," April 30, 1979, Nonclassified.

24 See "Chronology of Kermit Roosevelt Case," Nonclassified, attached to Memorandum for the Record, [Name Excised], Associate General Counsel, "Kermit Roosevelt's Book," May 9, 1979, Nonclassified.

25 Memorandum for [Name Excised], Office of General Counsel, from William F. Donnelly, "Manuscript 'Countercoup'," May 1, 1979, Secret, with attached Speed Letter for C/IMS from [Name Excised], "Galley Proofs of 'Countercoup'," April 30, 1979, Nonclassified.

26 David Ignatius, "The Coup Against 'Countercoup': How A Book Disappeared," *The Wall Street Journal*, November 6, 1979, 1, 36. See also, Nancy E. Gallagher and Dunning S. Wilson, "Suppression of Information or Publisher's Error?: Kermit Roosevelt's Memoir of the 1953 Countercoup," with Addendum, "Countercoup II," by Nikki R. Keddie, *Middle East Studies Association Bulletin* 15, 1 (July 1981): 14–17. Another account is Thomas Powers, "A Book Held Hostage," *The Nation*, April 12, 1980, 437–40; Powers cites a McGraw-Hill source as saying Roosevelt checked with the CIA about inserting "British intelligence" and that the CIA got approval from the SIS. For more on the differences between the versions of *Countercoup*, see Malcolm Byrne, "Iran 1953: The Strange Odyssey of Kermit Roosevelt's Countercoup," National Security Archive Electronic Briefing Book No. 468, May 12, 2014.

27 Memorandum for The Honorable Cyrus R. Vance, from Stansfield Turner, "Impact of the Publication of Kermit Roosevelt's Book 'Counter Coup'," December 13, 1979, Secret.

28 CIA Office of General Counsel Letter to Donald Wilber, May 26, 1983, reprinted in Donald N. Wilber, *Adventures in the Middle East: Excursions and Incursions* (Princeton, NJ: Darwin, 1986), 163.

29 Donald Wilber letter to [Name excised], June 1, 1983, reprinted in Wilber, *Adventures in the Middle East*, 167. The "Indians" quote is on p. 157 of the same book. Wilber's sense of unfair treatment is shared by more than a few others; see Moran, *Company Confessions*, 202–3, 269, for example.

30 CIA Publications Review Board letter to Donald Wilber, July 5, 1983, reprinted in Wilber, *Adventures in the Middle East*, 167–8. Also worth noting are two memoirs that touch on 1953 by British ex-officials: C.M. Woodhouse, *Something Ventured: An Autobiography* (London: Granada, 1982); and Sam Falle, *My Lucky Life: In War, Revolution, Peace and Diplomacy* (Oxford, UK: ISIS, 1996). The UK's handling of publications purportedly containing state secrets is even more confusing than it is in the United States. For one useful analysis, see "Secrets, Spies and Whistleblowers: Freedom of Expression in the UK," by Article 19 and Liberty (printed by the Guardian, November 2000), https://www.article19.org/data/files/pdfs/publications/secrets-spies-and-whistleblowers.pdf.

31 Wilber, *Adventures in the Middle East*, 151. Wilber's interactions with the CIA descended to the level of the absurd when he was ordered to return a personal letter he had received from DCI Allen W. Dulles dated January 1954. Wilber refused, so a PRB legal advisor offered a compromise: that Wilber "physically excise (with some sort of bladed instrument used for cutting paper)" two "items" from the letter. The items consisted of one "two letter prefix" and "two letters, a dash and a number." They were considered sensitive enough to require Wilber's personal intervention. The CIA official next instructed Wilber to write the word "Declassified" on the document and alert the agency when he had done everything as directed. (See PRB letter to Wilber, July 5, 1983, reprinted in Wilber, *Adventures in the Middle East*, 167–8.)

32 Years later, this remained a topic of debate, even inside the CIA, according to an agency representative attending a June 2–3, 2008, meeting of the State Department's Historical Advisory Committee. See meeting minutes at https://history.state.gov/about/hac/june-2008.

33 John Hollister Hedley, "Reviewing the Work of CIA Authors: Secrets, Free Speech, and Fig Leaves," *Studies in Intelligence* 4, 5 (Spring 1998): 75–83.

34 Greg Miller Julie Tate, "CIA probes publication review board over allegations of selective censorship," *The Washington Post*, May 31, 2012. The CIA evidently updated its regulations the same year. See David Kris, "The CIA's New Guidelines Governing Publicly Available Information," *Lawfare*, March 21, 2017. For more recent complaints, see Jack Goldsmith and Oona Hathaway, "More Problems with Prepublication Review," *Lawfare*, December 28, 2015; and Thomas Reed Willemain, "A Personal Tale of Prepublication Review," *Lawfare*, January 10, 2017.

35 See Malcolm Byrne, "CIA Confirms Role in 1953 Iran Coup," National Security Archive Electronic Briefing Book No. 435, August 19, 2013, featuring records from the British National Archives about Precht's presentation and the subsequent scramble to engage American officials over FCO concerns.

36 See the discussion in Chapter 9, "The Erosion of Transparency, 1978–1985" by Joshua Botts in William B. McAllister, Joshua Botts, Peter Cozzens, Aaron W. Marrs, *Toward "Thorough, Accurate, and Reliable": A History of the Foreign Relations of the United States Series*(Washington, DC: Office of the Historian, U.S. Department of State, 2015).

37 McAllister et al, *Toward "Thorough, Accurate, and Reliable,"* based on internal US government documentation about the *FRUS* process, remains the most authoritative account, especially Chapters 9–10 by Joshua Botts. See also Bruce Kuniholm, "Foreign

Relations, Public Relations, Accountability, and Understanding," American Historical Association, *Perspectives on History*, May–June 1990, and Stephen R. Weissman, "Censoring American Diplomatic History," American Historical Association, *Perspectives on History*, September 2011. And see Ervand Abrahamian's chapter in this volume.

38 See George C. Herring, "My Years with the CIA," speech delivered in January 1997 and published in the newsletter of the Organization of American Historians, May 1997.

39 See, most famously, Daniel Patrick Moynihan, *Secrecy: The American Experience* (New Haven, CT: Yale University Press, 1998), Chapter 6. Other examples include: Dr. Rob Johnston, "Analytic Culture in the U.S. Intelligence Community: An Ethnographic Study," CIA, Center for the Study of Intelligence, 2005, xvi; and Dusko Doder, "Culture of Secrecy," *National Security and the Future* 3–4, 1 (2000): 94.

40 Herring, "My Years with the CIA." An ardent case for the DO's views on disclosure is N. Richard Kinsman, "Protecting the CIA's Interests: Openness and the Future of the Clandestine Service," *Studies in Intelligence* 10 (Winter–Spring 2001): 55–61.

41 HAC minutes, September 8–9, 2014, https://history.state.gov/about/hac/september-2014.

42 Richard Immerman, "Report of the Advisory Committee on Historical Diplomatic Documentation, January 1–December 31, 2016," published April 14, 2017, accessed through H-Net: https://networks.h-net.org/node/175694/pdf.

43 Unnamed official, interview with author, June 13, 2018.

44 See the British records from 1978, cited above. As of this writing, a second edition of the volume is "In Production." It will reportedly incorporate two additional American memoranda of conversation with British officials who came to Washington in late 1952 to propose the idea of a coup to the Truman administration. The documents were first posted online by the National Security Archive in August 2017. (See Malcolm Byrne and Mark Gasiorowski, "1953 Iran Coup: New U.S. Documents Confirm British Approached U.S. in Late 1952 About Ousting Mosaddeq," National Security Archive Electronic Briefing Book No. 601, August 8, 2017.) The decision to add these two items to *FRUS* is a modestly positive development, but still leaves an undetermined quantity of American documentation about the British role unjustifiably beyond public reach. Furthermore, indications are that US sensitivity to allied "equities" will continue to be a significant hold-up for future *FRUS* volumes on other topics.

45 The most detailed and authoritative account is in James C. Van Hook, *Foreign Relations of the United States*, "Iran, 1951–1954" (retrospective volume) (Washington, DC: US Government Printing Office, June 2017), "Sources" section, especially pp. XV–XVI.

46 Donald N. Wilber, Clandestine Services History, "Overthrow of Premier Mossadeq of Iran: November 1952–August 1953" (Central Intelligence Agency, March 1954).

47 "Declaration of William H. McNair, Information Review Officer, Directorate of Operations, Central Intelligence Agency," National Security Archive v. Central Intelligence Agency, Civil No. 99–1160 (CKK), August 13, 1999.

48 Scott A. Koch, *"Zendebad, Shah!": The Central Intelligence Agency and the Fall of Iranian Prime Minister Mohammed Mossadeq, August 1953*, CIA History Staff, June 1998.

49 The reason the CIA released that sentence was that it had previously appeared in Wilber's memoirs, which the author described as a "shambles" after the agency had finished with it (see *Adventures in the Middle East*, 157).

50 See National Security Archive v. CIA, "Plaintiff's Motion for Revised *Vaughn* Index," Civil No. 99–1160 (CKK), August 2, 2000. The Archive was represented by Thomas Sussman and Todd Richman of the law firm Ropes and Gray.

51 See "Secret Writing: CIA's Oldest Classified Documents," CIA website, https://www. cia.gov/news-information/blog/2016/cias-oldest-classified-docs.html. Archivist of the United States David S. Ferriero presented copies of these documents from 1917 to 1918 to the National Security Archive during a visit to our offices in July 2011, shortly after they had been declassified.

52 This particular instance was related to an intelligence agency effort beginning in 1999 (with the approval of the National Archives and Records Administration) to reclassify certain government archival records. See Harold C. Relyea, "Security Classified and Controlled Information: History, Status, and Emerging Management Issues," Congressional Research Service, updated February 11, 2008, 29.

53 See Nicholas Cullather, *Operation PBSUCCESS, The United States and Guatemala, 1952–54*, Center for the Study of Intelligence, 1994; and "Inspector General's Survey of the Cuban Operation and Associated Documents," October 1961. On the Archive's success in getting the Bay of Pigs fifth volume declassified, see Lauren Harper and Thomas Blanton, "CIA Releases Controversial Bay of Pigs History," National Security Archive Electronic Briefing Book No. 564, October 31, 2016.

54 See James Risen, "Secrets of History: The C.I.A. in Iran—A Special Report; How a Plot Convulsed Iran in '53 (and '79)," *The New York Times*, April 16, 2000. Some speculate that Wilber was the leaker. He died two years earlier, in 1998, but his memoir claims that he retained all of the text from his unsanitized original manuscript: "Shall I place them in an envelope and write on it: OPEN ONLY in the year 2000?" (*Adventures in the Middle East*, 158).

55 Laingen interview with the author, July 25, 2005. Also cited in Stephen Kinzer, "Inside Iran's Fury," *Smithsonian Magazine*, October 2008. It should be noted that perceptions of the coup have varied across Iran and among émigré Iranians over the years. The postrevolutionary leadership generally considered Mossadeq's followers as political rivals although that has not prevented hard-liners from holding up 1953 as a prime example of American interference.

56 Ray S. Cline, *Secrets, Spies and Scholars: Blueprint of the Essential CIA* (Washington, DC: Acropolis Books, 1976), 132–3.

57 See Danielle Siegel, "CIA Caught between Operational Security and Analytical Quality in 1953 Iran Coup Planning," *Unredacted* blog, March 19, 2018, https:// unredacted.com/2018/03/19/cia-caught-between-operational-security-and-analytical-quality-in-1953-iran-coup-planning/.

58 As one example, the CIA's 2005 and 2015 "decennial reviews" of operational file designations, the two latest iterations required under the 1984 CIA Information Act, retreated from the first review that occurred in the more transparency friendly atmosphere of the mid-1990s.

9

An Event So Inevitable Yet Unforeseen: The United States and the Iranian Revolution

David Collier

Attempts to explain the 1979 Iranian Revolution have been frequent and varied. Some have pointed to the sudden dashing of Iranian expectations as severe economic downturns in the mid-1970s prevented the realization of Mohammad Reza Shah Pahlavi's much hyped plans for development.[1] Others argue the revolutionary period formed in response to rapid modernization that clashed with more traditional religious and social beliefs.[2] Political factors, such as the breakdown of the state and the formation of effective opposition groups, or social factors stemming from the brutal and repressive policies of the shah's regime, have also been blamed.[3] Some have stressed the importance of Shi'ism, growing fears of Westoxification, and a shah increasingly seen as nothing more than an American puppet by his people.[4] Focusing on American involvement, the catalyst has been placed on American presidents from Eisenhower,[5] Kennedy,[6] Johnson,[7] Nixon and Ford,[8] and Carter.[9]

All of these factors played a role and help explain why the revolution happened when it did, but this chapter frames the revolution as the continuation of a movement that had existed for almost a century. The desire of the Iranian people to be free of arbitrary and autocratic rule began in the late nineteenth century and, for a short while, succeeded in placing constitutional limits on the monarchy. The return of the crown and the rise of the Pahlavi dynasty temporarily silenced these voices but not their fundamental desire. At intervals, the movement resurfaced—briefly in the 1940s, at the beginning and end of the 1950s, and into the early 1960s—causing much anxiety in Washington. American intelligence officials and numerous administrations up until around 1963 understood that revolution was inevitable in Iran unless the shah instituted meaningful political reform to give people greater rights and protections. Pushing such reforms onto an unwilling shah had been a key plank of American policy toward Iran since the shah came to power in 1941.[10] Starting in the early 1960s, however, this knowledge began to fade away as Washington took less of an interest in Iran's internal situation. By the time the revolution began in 1977, Americans had little knowledge of events inside Iran and were therefore unable to adequately respond. Examples of American ignorance during the revolution are legion, such as the basic questions asked by National Security Advisor Zbigniew Brzezinski after almost two years of revolutionary activity:

a. Who are the various opposition groups?
b. What does each of them represent?
c. What would each of their programs be if they were able to come to power?
d. Who is financing each of them?
e. Are there any connections between any of these groups and the Iranian military?[11]

This chapter places the revolution in context and explains why an event that had been predicted as early as the 1950s came as such a shock by the late 1970s. At the center of this explanation will be an examination of American linkage with Iran. The United States quickly established political, social, and economic relations with Iranian life and the knowledge gained was used to craft effective policy and monitor Iran's opposition movements. The steady dismantling of this web during the 1960s and the 1970s explains why American policymakers reacted so slowly when the inevitable revolution finally arrived.

The first manifestation of Iran's popular movement against autocracy arose in the early 1890s. The Qajar shah, Nasir al-Din, faced increasing pressure from foreign intervention and needed urgent financial assistance. In response, he granted a fifty-year monopoly over the production, sale, and export of tobacco to the British citizen, Major Gerald F. Talbot. The loss of control over a major export badly impacted Iranian merchants and protests began immediately once news of the concession became public. They were joined by anti-imperialist religious leaders who rejected the sale of Iranian resources to Europeans. As the protests spread, a religious edict was issued against all use of tobacco and a national boycott began that was observed by Muslims and non-Muslims alike. It was reported that even the shah's wives ended use of tobacco and his personal butler would no longer prepare the shah's water pipe.[12] Tobacco use was so ubiquitous in Iran that it was said that as soon as a worker "received his daily salary, he would first go buy tobacco and use the remainder of the money for bread and fruit," and that the "first things Iranians would do at the breaking of the fast during the month of Ramadan was light their pipes."[13] The protests by a coalition of religious leaders, merchants, and secularists, alongside strict adherence to the ban on tobacco use, forced the shah to cancel the concession in what was the first successful mass protest movement in Iranian history.

This served as prelude to the more wide-ranging protests against ineffective authoritarian rule that became known as the Constitutional Revolution (1905–11). A similar alliance of business interests, clerics, and secular or modernist reformers came together to protest Qajar rule and, drawing inspiration from Western ideas of liberalism and democracy, sought to place the monarchy under constitutional control. The victory of newly constitutional Japan over Russia in 1905, and the resulting Russian revolution, heightened the popular desire for change.[14] The overarching aims of this movement were to assert Iranian national sovereignty, establish a decent socioeconomic order, and to create a law-abiding government that would be responsive to the demands and expectations of the Iranian people.[15]

And initially it was successful. By 1907, with the formation of a constitution and a national consultative assembly (*Majles*), Iran looked to be a modern constitutional monarchy. But, authoritarianism is persistent. The coronation of a new shah opposed to constitutionalism and support from Russia and Great Britain ultimately undermined the revolution. Although the Qajar regime soon fell, it was replaced not by a popular government but by the new authoritarianism of Reza Khan, who swept to power in 1921 and established the Pahlavi dynasty four years later. In just two decades of rule he transformed and modernized Iran at a rate unprecedented in the country's history but, instead of allowing space for political reform, he maintained strict authoritarian rule. As Ali Ansari concludes, to his followers, Reza Shah "personified the charismatic savior they yearned for. But to the growing throng of critics he was little more than a traditional patrimonial ruler with the additional benefit of modern institutions of government to support him."[16]

The desire for political reform that kick-started the Constitutional Revolution remained unfulfilled throughout his reign. Victor Hugo once observed that "you can resist an invading army, but you cannot resist an idea whose time has come."[17] Reza Shah's effective and strong rule did succeed in stifling demand for political reform, but he was less able to resist invading armies. Citing wartime exigencies, the British and Soviet armies invaded in 1941 and forced the shah to abdicate. Whether Iran could continue to resist demands for political reform would rest with his young son, Mohammad Reza Pahlavi.

In their seminal study on regime change, Steven Levitsky and Lucan A. Way argue that the West can encourage countries to democratize if they have high levels of linkage and leverage.[18] With leverage, the West has bargaining power over the regime or the regime is dependent upon outside assistance for survival. Linkage refers to the density of ties between countries, which can be social, political, or economic and include both country-to-country relations as well as the myriad of nonstate actors.[19] Strong linkage allows one country to more intimately understand the pressures and movements within another and enables the crafting of effective policy. For example, high levels of linkage give insight into how vulnerable a government is to various kinds of pressure, how viable certain opposition movements are, and what sources of instability exist within that country.

American linkage with Iran developed quickly once the United States became an active participant in the Second World War. As Iran occupied an important supply route between the eastern and western fronts, President Franklin D. Roosevelt declared the country vital to American national interests.[20] Numerous American missions were therefore established to help stabilize Iran which meant that by 1943, the United States had insight into almost all aspects of Iranian life.[21] At the center of this nascent web of linkages was the US diplomatic legation, which was soon upgraded to the status of embassy in recognition of Iran's importance to the United States.

The first few years of US-Iranian relations also happened to be some of the best years for advocates of political reform in Iran. The removal of the strong, autocratic Reza Shah and his replacement by his young and more timid son gave space for Iranians to once again express themselves. Political prisoners were released, the ban on public debates lifted, and dozens of newspapers were established, creating a sense of social and political vibrancy in Iran.[22] According to Habib Ladjevardi, these years were the closest Iran came to a functional constitutional monarchy.[23] The desires of freedom from arbitrary and autocratic rule clearly remained vibrant despite years of subjugation.

However, the instability inherent in transitions away from authoritarian rule caused concern among Western powers that needed Iran to remain steady as the world war gave way to the Cold War. The rise of Muhammad Mossadeq, a populist leader who advocated constitutionalism, concerned the West as he also championed Iranian sovereignty and neutrality rather than continued Iranian cooperation in this new conflict. As the chapters by Ervand Abrahamian and Malcolm Byrne in this volume demonstrate, in response to Mossadeq's refusal to submit, the British and the Americans made full use of their linkages within Iranian society to organize a coup that removed him from power in August 1953.[24] With Western support, Mohammad Reza Shah Pahlavi returned to the center of the government and was encouraged to crack down on opposition and reestablish strong and stable royal rule.

In early November 1978, Ambassador William H. Sullivan wrote a famous memo that asked the Carter administration to think the unthinkable by considering the possibility that the shah might not survive the revolution.[25] The memo stunned Washington as the prevailing notion was that the shah's position was untouchable. However, a very similar memo warned of the precarious nature of his rule just a few years after the 1953 coup as the reemergence of protests caused consternation over the longevity of his rule. The concerned US ambassador to Iran, Selden Chapin, asked Washington whether "the United States [should] rely entirely on the shah's government, if danger signs are already appearing that it might not last?"[26] Contingency plans were drawn up but without a suitable alternative, the Eisenhower administration chose instead to convince the shah of the importance of reform, especially political reform, to satisfy internal demands.[27]

In response, the shah lifted certain restrictions, allowed a limited freedom of the press, and established a political party system to give his people a greater say over the government. As always, when given space, Iranian society responded. By 1957, Ambassador Chapin witnessed greater civic action and the emergence of newspaper articles that "no editor would have dared to run two months ago."[28] However, the shah did not share the belief that his position was in jeopardy and most of the reforms turned out to be mere window dressing designed to satisfy American demands rather than the demands of his people. A November 1958 National Security Council report recommended that the United States do more to modify the shah's "present dictatorial role to allow some scope for the expression of opposition sentiment," whereas another warned that unless "meaningful steps towards reform" were taken, "the regime is in danger of an early overthrow."[29] The embassy even reported that it "is now not uncommon to hear casual mention [of the] possible assassination [of the] shah among otherwise sober middle-class civilians."[30]

This was not just idle gossip. The shah had already survived one assassination attempt in 1949 and would escape another in 1965. Moreover, the deep levels of linkage that the United States had with Iran meant they received detailed and frequent accounts from various forces in opposition to the shah's rule. So involved were they that conspiracies against the shah were uncovered that even his own intelligence services missed. In 1958 for instance, senior State Department officials held meetings with conspirators from the Iranian army who wished to overthrow the shah citing the lack of freedom in Iran.[31] Links were also maintained with powerful tribal leaders in case they saw an opportunity to stake a claim to power.[32]

Nearby countries showed what could happen in Iran. In 1952, an anti-imperialist revolution in Egypt toppled its king while six years later, a coup d'état overthrew the Hashemite monarchy in Iraq. The deposed Egyptian king ominously warned that "soon there will be only five kings left—the King of England, the King of Spades, the King of Clubs, the King of Hearts, and the King of Diamonds."[33] Allen Dulles, head of the CIA, concluded from the evidence that unless the shah seriously considered political reforms, his "days will be numbered." By March 1959, a National Intelligence Estimate put the shah's chances of remaining in power at "little more than fifty-fifty."[34]

Nevertheless, the shah resisted change and tempered American pressure by moving closer to the Soviets who offered financial assistance without demands for reform. Moscow also predicted a revolution from the masses but was less concerned by its outcome than the Americans.[35] A breakdown in relations with the Soviet Union in the run-up to the 1960 parliamentary elections, however, made the shah once more amenable to American wishes. To satisfy the growing desire for political representation, the Eisenhower administration pressed the shah to allow the elections to be run in a free and honest manner to which the shah grudgingly consented.[36] Restrictions were again relaxed on public dissent and expectations were raised once more that Iran might return to a period of constitutionalism where the shah reigned but did not rule. Again, the shah's promise of reform was not followed up with action and instead the royalist forces resorted to the usual tactics of ballot stuffing and other electoral chicanery to ensure victory for their candidates.[37] Protests swept the country. The resignation of the shah's prime minister and an announcement that new elections would be held temporarily calmed the situation, but when these too were rigged, the CIA described the ensuing protests as "better organized and longer sustained ... than we have seen in Iran since the ousting of Mossadegh in 1953."[38]

It is possible this could have spelled the end of the Pahlavi regime. Indeed, a National Intelligence Report published on the eve of Kennedy's inauguration in January 1961, predicted that "a political upheaval could take place in Iran at any time."[39] But the well-timed appointment of the reformist Ali Amini as prime minister and a hastily organized reform plan dissipated much of the anger, and order was somewhat returned. The shah agreed to step back from personal rule and the new government tackled corruption, land reform, inflation, and income inequality, while speaking of establishing a platform upon which lasting democracy could be built.[40]

Iranians had repeatedly demonstrated their desire for political reform and the Americans were sure that without it, the shah would eventually be overthrown. But they were also aware that without the shah, Iran would likely fall out of the American orbit as Iranians increasingly called for a more neutral foreign policy in the Cold War. With a choice between two bad options, the Kennedy administration was split between those calling for more support to the shah to ensure stability, and those advocating greater political reform to avoid a future uncontrollable revolution.

Initially those who advocated reform were more influential, and the United States supported the government of Amini despite the shah's anger at being pushed away from personal rule. By mid-1962, however, the reformist government had made little progress and unrest began to resurface. Unable to see a viable alternative, the Kennedy administration returned their support to the shah in the hope that he could at least restore order in the short term. Once back in control however, the shah was determined not to let the Americans dictate to him anymore. He had been in power for over two decades and relied upon American backing in lieu of having any popular base of support within Iran. Now approaching his mid-forties, he finally felt ready to chart his own course.[41]

Anticipating the return of American pressure for reform the shah acted quickly and unveiled his own reform package in January 1963. Called the White Revolution, it included many of the extensive social and economic reforms that the United States had been calling for but ignored the issue of political reform. Rather than reforms laying the groundwork for future democracy, the shah envisioned the White Revolution as modernizing Iran while also strengthening his own personal rule. For instance, his land reform program proved hugely popular among Iran's peasantry and with their support, the shah's internal position became much stronger.

The Americans had tried to convince the shah for years to take the need for change seriously and now finally it seemed that he understood. Although the absence of political reform meant the White Revolution was fundamentally flawed, the Americans signaled their approval that some progress to modernize Iran was better than none. According to Robert Komer, a senior staff member of the National Security Council and one of the lead advocates calling for Washington to intervene more forcefully to promote reform in Iran, it may not be perfect, but the Americans were just "going to have to ride this tiger" due a to lack of viable alternatives.[42] Any remaining concerns were dispelled when the shah finally showed himself able to deal more effectively against internal dissent. Major protests against his rule broke out in June 1963 but were dispersed so violently that no similarly sized protests were held again until the time of the revolution. Estimates place the number of casualties as high as five thousand although it is likely the figure was closer to two hundred as reported by the US embassy—a still significant number.[43] Hundreds of opposition figures were arrested, including the increasingly influential cleric, Ayatollah Ruhollah Khomeini, and it finally seemed the shah could guarantee both stability and modernization.

By coopting the mantle of reform, the shah negated the need for the United States to intervene in Iran. So long as he maintained order and continued modernization, the United States was satisfied and could focus on other pressing domestic and foreign crises. Iran was no longer a concern and, as a result, it became less important to maintain the deep levels of linkage that had built up. So long as relations remained strong at the top, Washington cared little about what went on elsewhere within Iranian society. Warning signs remained of course. In 1965, the academic William Polk, worried about the lack of actual political reform in Iran, warning that "a similar situation existed before each of the major revolutions in the last two centuries ... if [the moderate opposition in Iran] fail through peaceful means to bring about a sharing of political power ... they will be thrust aside and others will use more violent means."[44] A more dramatic sign that all was not well within Iranian society came as bombs were detonated around Tehran during the state visit by President Nixon in 1972, yet still the United States felt unconcerned about Iran's internal situation.[45] Successive administrations felt certain that the shah would continue to deal effectively with all signs of opposition and chose not to intervene.

The dismantling of American linkage with Iran was swift. By the late 1960s, one US embassy official recalled that the White House "didn't want to know that the shah had any problems domestically. They didn't encourage the embassy to inquire if the country was stable before making a military commitment. They assumed it was stable and didn't want to look further into such questions."[46] Another State Department official explained that standard practice became not to "report on an ally once he's become 'The Chosen Instrument' [of stability in the region]. It's bad manners."[47]

Instead of being the center of American internal monitoring efforts, the embassy was repurposed to focus externally on the Soviet Union. This was most clearly illustrated by the selection of former director of Central Intelligence Richard Helms as US ambassador in 1973. Despite being a close personal friend of the shah, he knew little about Iran's internal situation but was an expert in the art of spycraft and surveillance of the USSR. Charles McCaskill, who worked in the embassy in the early 1970s, doubts that anyone there even knew a mullah and recalls how embassy officials relied upon information fed to them by the royal court.[48] Any criticism of the shah's rule by any member of the embassy was met with censure and often a quick return to the United States.

By 1977, the embassy had only two staffers tasked with internal political reportage and neither was encouraged to establish sources outside of the shah's inner circle or his intelligence services. In the early 1960s there had been seventeen such personnel, each with extensive and independent contacts that kept Washington informed of the daily changes within Iranian society. Similarly, intelligence officers working on Iran had been stripped of resources by the time of the revolution and were disorganized, inefficient, and their reports largely ignored in Washington.[49] Therefore, the revolution came as a complete shock to the Americans who had gradually allowed themselves to become blind to the need for political reform in Iran.

Recent scholarship has refocused attention on the mistakes of the Carter administration, which failed to either predict or adequately respond to the revolution in Iran.[50] This is accurate, but it does not tell the whole story. To explain the revolution in isolation neglects decades of protest and revolutionary activity in Iran. Moreover, as linkage had all but disappeared by the time Carter assumed the presidency, the blame is misplaced. The Carter administration was blind to events in Iran. Rather than see the revolution coming, misinformed American intelligence reports repeatedly predicted the shah would remain in power through the 1980s, with the CIA infamously stating in August 1978 that "Iran was not in a revolutionary or even pre-revolutionary state."[51] This explains Brzezinski's questions in October 1978 as well as President Carter's numerous public statements about the shah's stability despite ongoing protests. So ignorant was the Carter administration that when religious and secular opposition leaders approached the US embassy with offers of cooperation and compromise, they were rejected by confused officials who often did not even know who they were.[52] The shah's fragility was only made clear to the Americans late in 1978 but without linkage, the administration was unable to formulate a sensible or coherent response.

Revolutions are easy to predict in hindsight but in Iran, the events that took place had been predicted by Washington decades earlier and were the natural continuation of a movement that dated back to the nineteenth century. The arbitrary and ineffective autocratic rule of kings was considered outmoded by influential clerics and secularists by the beginning of the twentieth century. That rule by shahs continued for another seventy years says much about the skill and persistence of authoritarian regimes as well as the influence of foreign powers in Iran that helped maintain royal rule. Russia and Britain conspired to halt the Constitutional Revolution, the United States and Britain helped restore the shah in 1953, and from 1963 on, the United States furnished the shah with almost unlimited financial and military aid to further strengthen his regime. At times when it seemed Iran was on the verge of upheaval, such as in the late 1950s and early 1960s, timely American pressure on the shah to institute minimal political reforms helped avert disaster.

President Kennedy once said that "those who make peaceful revolution impossible will make violent revolution inevitable."[53] But starting during his presidency, the United States did exactly that. Supporting the shah's personal rule over peaceful calls for political reform made the revolution inevitable. But Iran's journey is not over. The Islamic regime that formed after the shah's departure faces similar calls for reform and demands for greater representation, as demonstrated by large protests in 1999, 2009, and 2018. The ability of the regime to resolve these issues will be a major challenge for Iranian leaders and not one that can be ignored or silenced through repression. If they look to history they will realize that while you may be able to delay its arrival, you cannot resist an idea whose time has come.

Notes

1　Mark Downes, *Iran's Unresolved Revolution* (Burlington: Ashgate, 2002), 66–7; John Stempel, *Inside the Iranian Revolution* (Bloomington: Indiana University Press, 1981), 9; Nikki R. Keddie, "Iranian Revolutions in Comparative Perspective," *American Historical Review* 88, 3 (1983): 579–98.

2　Barry Rubin, *Paved with Good Intentions: the American Experience and Iran* (New York: Penguin Books, 1980), 195; Cyrus Vance, *Hard Choice: Four Critical Years in Managing America's Foreign Policy* (New York: Simon and Schuster, 1983), 345; Jack C. Miklos, *The Iranian Revolution and Modernization: Way Stations to Anarchy* (Washington, DC: National Defense University Press, 1983).

3　Mehran Kamrava, *Revolution in Iran: The Roots of Turmoil* (New York: Routledge, 1990); Ervand Abrahamian, *Iran between Two Revolutions* (Princeton, NJ: Princeton University Press), 1983.

4　Theda Skocpol, "Rentier State and Shi'a Islam in the Iranian Revolution," *Theory and Society* 11, 3 (1982): 265–83; Michael Axworthy, *Revolutionary Iran: A History of the Islamic Republic* (New York: Oxford University Press, 2013), 131–2.

5　James A. Bill and Wm. Roger Louis, eds., *Musaddiq, Iranian Nationalism, and Oil* (London: Tauris, 1988); Mark J. Gasiorowski, *US Foreign Policy and the Shah: Building a Client State in Iran* (Ithaca: Cornell University Press, 1991); Mary Ann Heiss, *Empire and Nationhood: the United States, Great Britain, and Iranian Oil, 1950–1954* (New York: Columbia University Press, 1998); Mark J. Gasiorowski and Malcolm Byrne, eds., *Mohammad Mosaddeq and the 1953 Coup in Iran* (Syracuse: Syracuse University Press, 2004); Stephen Kinzer, *All the Shah's Men: an American Coup and the Roots of Middle East Terror* (Hoboken, NJ: John Wiley & Sons, 2011).

6 James Goode, "Reforming Iran During the Kennedy Years," *Diplomatic History* 15, 1 (1991); April R. Summitt, "For a White Revolution: John F. Kennedy and the Shah of Iran," *Middle East Journal* 58, 4 (2004): 560–75; Victor V. Nemchenok, "In Search of Stability Amid Chaos: US Policy Toward Iran, 1961–63," *Cold War History* 10 (2010): 341–69; David R. Collier, "To Prevent a Revolution: John F. Kennedy and the Promotion of Democracy in Iran," *Diplomacy & Statecraft* 24, 3 (2013), 456–75; Andrew Warne, Psychoanalyzing Iran: Kennedy's Iran Task Force and the Modernization of Orientalism, 1961–3," *International History Review* 35, 2 (2013): 396–422.

7 Castiglioni, "No Longer a Client, Not Yet a Partner: the US–Iranian Alliance in the Johnson Years," *Cold War History* 15 (2015): 491–509; Andrew Johns, "The Johnson Administration, the Shah of Iran, and the Changing Pattern of US-Iranian Relations, 1965–1967: 'Tired of Being Treated like a Schoolboy'," *Journal of Cold War Studies* 9, 2 (2007): 64–94; Stephen McGlinchey, "Lyndon B Johnson and Arms Credit Sales to Iran, 1964–1968," *Middle East Journal* 67, 2 (2013): 229–47.

8 Andrew Scott Cooper, The *Oil Kings: How the US, Iran, and Saudi Arabia Changed the Balance of Power in the Middle East* (New York: Simon and Schuster, 2011).

9 Ofira Seliktar, *Failing the Crystal Ball Test: The Carter Administration and the Fundamental Revolution in Iran* (Westport, CT: Praeger, 2011); Javier Gil Guerrero, *The Carter Administration and the Fall of Iran's Pahlavi Dynasty: US–Iran Relations on the Brink of the 1979 Revolution* (New York: Palgrave MacMillan, 2016).

10 For more on this see David R. Collier, *Democracy and the Nature of American Influence in Iran* (Syracuse: Syracuse University Press, 2017).

11 Memorandum, Director of Central Intelligence to Deputy Director for National Foreign Assessment, "Meeting with Dr. Brzezinski, 27 October 1978," October 30, 1978, CIA-RDP81B00401R002000120002-8, CREST, NARA.

12 Nikki R. Keddie, *Modern Iran: Roots and Results of Revolution* (New Haven, CT: Yale University Press, 2003), 61; Mateo Mohammad Farzaneh, *The Iranian Constitutional Revolution and the Clerical Leadership of Khurasani* (Syracuse, NY: Syracuse University Press, 2015), 48.

13 Rudi Matthee, *The Pursuit of Pleasure: Drugs and Stimulants in Iranian History, 1500– 1900* (Princeton, NJ: Princeton University Press, 2005), 128.

14 Fakhreddin Azimi, *The Quest for Democracy in Iran: A Century of Struggle against Authoritarian Rule* (Cambridge, MA: Harvard University Press, 2008), 28.

15 Ibid., 29.

16 Ali M. Ansari, *Modern Iran Since 1921: The Pahlavis and After* (New York: Longman, 2003).

17 Victor Hugo, *The History of a Crime: The Testimony of an Eye-Witness* (New York: Mondial, 2005), 409.

18 Steven Levitsky and Lucan A. Way, *Competitive Authoritarianism: Hybrid Regimes after the Cold War* (New York: Cambridge University Press, 2010).

19 Ibid., 43.

20 Roosevelt to Edward R. Stettinius, memo, March 10, 1942, Official File 134, NARA.

21　James A. Bill, *The Eagle and the Lion* (New Haven, CT: Yale University Press, 1988), 19.

22　"Iranian Political Parties and the Forthcoming Elections for the XIVth Parliament," July 22, 1943, 891.00/2037, Box 5819, NARA.

23　Habib Ladjevardi, "The Origins of US Support for an Autocratic Iran," *International Journal of Middle Eastern Studies* 15, 2 (1983): 225.

24　For more on the coup see Ervand Abrahamian, *The Coup: 1953, the CIA, and the Roots of Modern US-Iranian Relations* (New York: New Press, 2015).

25　William H. Sullivan, *Mission to Iran* (New York: W.W. Norton, 1981), 201–2.

26　Dispatch from US Embassy to State Department, March 26, 1956. 788.00/4-2156, Box 3809, NARA.

27　Supplementary Courses of Action for the Outline Plan of Operations for Iran, OCB, August 22, 1956. WHO, NSC Staff papers, 1948–61, OCB Central File Series, Box 44, DDEL.

28　Dispatch from US Embassy to State Department, April 27, 1957. 788.00/6-357, Box 3881, NARA.

29　National Security Council Report, NSC 5821/1, November 15, 1958. White House Office, NSC Staff: Papers, 1948–61, Disaster File, Box 66, DDEL; Briefing Note for NSC, November 13, 1958. White House Office, NSC Staff: Papers, 1948–61, Special Staff File, Box 4, DDEL.

30　Telegram from Wailes to Department of State, August 14, 1958. *FRUS*, 1958–60, XII, 583–4.

31　See "Memo for the Record," February 6, 1958. "FRUS, 1958–1960," 539; Mark J. Gasiorowski, "The Qarani Affair and Iranian Politics," *International Journal of Middle East Studies* 25, 4 (1993), 625–44.

32　See memo of conversation between Douglas, Mohammad Hosein Qashqai, and John Bowling, February 8, 1955. 788.00/2-855, CSTH, Box 3808, NARA.

33　Stanton Griffis, *Lying in State* (New York: Doubleday, 1953), 220.

34　Allen Dulles at the 376th Meeting of the NSC, August 15, 1958. FRUS, 1958–60, XII, 585; National Intelligence Estimate 34–59, March 3, 1959. *FRUS* 1958–60, XII, document 70.

35　Walter Lippmann, "Lippmann Believes Khrushchev Feels Red Triumph is Inevitable," *Washington Post*, April 18, 1961.

36　Memorandum of Discussion at the 449th meeting of the NSC, June 30, 1960; Abrahamian, *Iran between Two Revolutions*, 422.

37　See Andrew F. Westwood, "Elections and Politics in Iran," *Middle East Journal* 15, 2 (1961): 153–64.

38　CIA Position Paper, attached to Memo from Sam Belk to McGeorge Bundy, February 24, 1961, NSF Box 115a, JFKL; H. E. Chehabi, *Iranian Politics and Religious Modernism: The Liberation Movement Under the Shah and Khomeini* (Ithaca: Cornell University Press, 1990), 148–52.

39　National Intelligence Estimate, NIE 34–61, February 28, 1961, *FRUS*, 1961–3, 37.

40　For more on this see Collier, *Democracy*, 201–7.

41　"Back of the Boom in Iran," *US News & World Report* January 27, 1963, 50.

42　Memo from Komer to McGeorge Bundy, January 29, 1963. NSF Box 116a, JFKL.

43　See Keddie, *Modern Iran*, 147; Marvin Zonis, *The Political Elite of Iran* (Princeton, NJ: Princeton University Press, 1971), 63; Richard W. Cottam, *Nationalism in Iran* (Pittsburgh: University of Pittsburgh Press, 1979), 306–9; Ansari, *Modern Iran*, 160; Abbas Milani, *The Shah* (New York: St. Martin's Press, 2014), 299; Andrew

Scott Cooper, *Fall of Heaven: The Pahlavis and the Final Days of Imperial Iran* (New York: Picador, 2018), 116.

44 Polk quoted in Roland Popp, "An Application of Modernization Theory during the Cold War? The Case of Pahlavi Iran," *The International History Review* 30, 1 (2008): 93–4.

45 Cooper, *The Oil Kings*, 64.

46 Kennedy, Charles Stuart, and Henry Precht. Interview with Henry Precht. March 8, 2000. Manuscript/Mixed Material. Retrieved from the Library of Congress, https://www.loc.gov/item/mfdipbib000947/.

47 Richard Sale, "Carter and Iran: From Idealism to Disaster," *Washington Quarterly* 3, 4 (1980): 86.

48 Interview with Charles W. McCaskill, Foreign Affairs Oral History Collection of the Association for Diplomatic Studies and Training, Library of Congress.

49 Robert Jervis, *Why Intelligence Fails: Lessons from the Iranian Revolution and the Iraq War* (Ithaca: Cornell University Press, 2011), 24.

50 See Luca Trenta, "The Champion of Human Rights Meets the King of Kings: Jimmy Carter, the Shah, and Iranian Illusions and Rage," *Diplomacy & Statecraft* 24, 3 (2013): 476–98; Christian Emery, *US Foreign Policy and the Iranian Revolution: the Cold War Dynamics of Engagement with Strategic Alliance* (Basingstoke: Palgrave Macmillan, 2013); Guerrero, *The Carter Administration*.

51 Jimmy Carter, *Keeping the Faith: Memoirs of a President* (Fayetteville: University of Arkansas Press, 1982), 438.

52 These entreaties were made by significant figures such as Mehdi Bazargan and Grand Ayatollah Kazem Shariatmadari. See Trenta, "The Champion of Human Rights," 488.

53 John F. Kennedy, "Address on the First Anniversary of the Alliance for Progress," March 13, 1962, The American Presidency Project http://www.presidency.ucsb.edu/ws/?pid=91006trr6t.

10

Confronting the Arc of Crisis: The Carter Administration's Approach to Security Building in the "Greater Gulf" Region, 1977–80

Adam M. Howard and Alexander R. Wieland[1]

Over the past four decades, scholars examining the US military, economic, and political engagement in the Middle East have pointed to 1979 as the defining transformative moment. Some argue that the 1979 Iranian Revolution[2] and the Soviet invasion of Afghanistan catalyzed a US strategic response that "at long last" assumed the "lonely burden of protecting Western interests in the Persian Gulf," and, in doing so, enshrined the region's importance in Washington's larger Cold War foreign policy calculations.[3] Others take the argument further, identifying the response of Jimmy Carter's administration to these events as the start of a long commitment that became a quagmire, engulfing successive Republican and Democratic administrations alike.[4] However, recently declassified documents featured in the *Foreign Relations of the United States* (*FRUS*) series confirm the events of 1979 as an "extension of growing concerns," as inflection points, rather than starting points, in the creation of a new strategic posture in the "greater Gulf"[5] region.[6] The Carter administration's development of a strong Gulf security infrastructure was well underway before the fall of the shah; the acceleration of this drive in 1979–80 built on foundations that had already been laid in response to other contemporary foreign policy challenges in the region.

Scholars covering the Carter administration have typically viewed its foreign policy as a split personality, both figuratively and literally.[7] Carter entered office with many Americans perceiving the United States as mired in material and moral decline, as a superpower in winter, lacking direction and purpose in an increasingly complex and insecure world. As a candidate, Carter posited that the United States needed a new approach to foreign policy, one that placed a greater emphasis on respect for human rights and on finding solutions to global problems of resource and income inequality as bases for international stability. He cautioned that "our influence and respect should go beyond our military might, our political power, and our economic wealth—and be based on the fact that we are right, and fair, and decent, and honest, and truthful."[8]

Once elected, however, Carter, and his foreign policy team grappled with the complexities of translating this vision into actionable policy. In doing so, Carter's advisors, most notably Secretary of State Cyrus Vance and National Security Advisor Zbigniew Brzezinski, clashed as each sought to assert their own balance between the president's desire to re-center US policy (favored by Vance) and more familiar strategic considerations of the Cold War conflict (Brzezinski). The resulting "whirlpool of disagreement over the fundamental nature of national and world security," as historian Gaddis Smith described Carter's foreign policy, was sharpened further by "a combination of world events, political developments within the United States, and decisions by the Administration [which] brought multiple currents more visibly into conflict than at any time since the United States became a world power."[9] By late 1979, this argument goes, these developments had helped Brzezinski win the policy fight, pushed Carter into reappraising his earlier views, and resulted in a more muscular US foreign policy.[10]

At first glance, the story of the Carter administration's policy development toward the greater Gulf region seems to fit neatly into this narrative. Indeed, the January 1980 articulation of the Carter Doctrine, the effort to create an overall Persian Gulf Security Framework, and the creation of the Rapid Deployment Joint Task Force (RDJTF), the forerunner of US Central Command, represented a visible embrace of classic Cold War strategic thinking. Brzezinski later described it in dramatic terms with far-reaching consequences. The "events and decisions of 1979–80," he wrote, were not merely a watershed for the administration, but represented instead a "strategic revolution in America's global position."[11]

But this shift had already been underway at the start of the administration. By examining the newly declassified documentation in the *FRUS* series, it is apparent that, when it comes to the Gulf, continuity was more prevalent than change. Much like their predecessors in the Nixon and Ford administrations, Carter-era officials' thinking about the region from the beginning focused on traditional Cold War concerns over alliance building, basing rights, and military aid—and, to a lesser extent, East–West détente—all with the goal of minimizing Soviet political, strategic, and economic penetration and other threats to Western interests, particularly oil flows. Moreover, these concerns shaped policymakers' views regardless of which part of the policymaking community they represented. At the same time, while there is little doubt that the tempo of US regional defense planning increased dramatically after the fall of the shah of Iran, Mohammad Reza Pahlavi, and accelerated further after the December 1979 invasion of Afghanistan, these later efforts built on a dialogue that was already occurring in response to earlier security challenges in the greater Gulf. Moreover, the *FRUS* documents reveal a more complex bureaucratic competition for the ear of the president, one that went beyond the standard Vance–Brzezinski dichotomy. On Gulf defense, Secretary of Defense Harold Brown and the Joint Chiefs of Staff (JCS) emerged as significant voices shaping US policy, particularly in the last two years of the administration.

When the Carter administration looked at the Middle East at the start of 1977, the Gulf was not a particular worry. In a February 2, 1977, memorandum prepared for Brzezinski, entitled "Four Year Goals in the Middle East," National Security Council (NSC) staff members William Quandt and Gary Sick identified the Arab-Israeli dispute as the preeminent regional issue, one "which will affect virtually all the others in some fashion." Economic development was listed as the next area of concern, in line with Carter's stated priorities, but expectations of major new initiatives were muted. The Arabian Peninsula and the Persian Gulf were discussed last. Here, Carter's team had inherited a Gulf security policy that rested on the twin pillars of Iran and Saudi Arabia, Washington's designated pro-Western bulwarks since Britain's withdrawal in 1971; little in the memorandum seemed to indicate an inclination to revise this. "US interests in this area," Quandt and Sick noted, "revolve almost entirely around questions of oil production, price and supply, together with protection and encouragement of the considerable US commercial investments in the region. From these interests, we derive an immediate stake in the security and stability of the Persian Gulf region, both in terms of the regional balance and in terms of our strategic relationship with the USSR."

Nevertheless, the authors foresaw possible challenges to this stable status quo, nearly all of which came down to traditional Cold War considerations: the Soviet need for resources and ability to project military power would continue to grow into the 1980s and its regional clients, especially Iraq, would continue to rise in political and economic importance. To address these challenges, Quandt and Sick recommended improving relations with the Iraqis, which hinged upon progress on Arab-Israeli peace encouraging "the development of closer cooperation and coordination among the nations of the Gulf on political, economic, and security matters," and exploring with the USSR "the possibility of establishing mutually acceptable limitations on military presence in the Indian Ocean" to forestall an "upward spiral of Soviet military presence."[12]

As a guide to policy during the first year of the administration, the Quandt and Sick memorandum provides a fairly reliable outline. Although early aspirations to normalize diplomatic relations with Iraq did not amount to much (relations would not be reestablished until 1984), the last two policy recommendations saw early action. To forestall Soviet encroachment and gain regional support for the peace process, efforts to strengthen bilateral security relationships in the Arabian Peninsula began almost immediately.

One of the first issues for the new administration to address was the Saudi request to purchase F-15 fighter aircraft, one of the most advanced models then in production. Up to that point, Israel was the only approved foreign customer for the model; indeed, the aircraft had only entered the US inventory the previous year. The Saudi request, first submitted in 1974, was an early test of the Carter team's commitment to the kingdom. Domestic opponents of the sale feared that the jets' sophisticated technology could be compromised and/or utilized to target Israel. The Saudis, for their part, wasted little time reiterating their interest, emphasizing shared security objectives.

Saudi defense minister Prince Sultan raised the issue with the US ambassador two days after Carter's inauguration and submitted a formal letter shortly thereafter.[13] Although they disagreed on how much should be promised to the Saudis (numbers, timetable, etc.), as well as a potential deal's ability to withstand its critics, both Brzezinski and Vance supported Carter's submission of the F-15 proposal to Congress in May 1977.[14] Shortly thereafter, Secretary of Defense Brown met with Saudi crown prince Fahd, who expressed appreciation for Washington's "new thinking" toward his country's defense needs. Secretary of Defense Brown responded by recognizing that

Saudi Arabia had "very faithfully lived up to" assurances that its weapons requests were "for their own use and security." Brown added gently that, while the Royal Saudi Air Force might also find the (lower-tech and, therefore, less politically fraught) F-14 or F-16 just as adequate for its needs as the F-15, "we are prepared to seek agreement from Congress for whatever aircraft Saudi Arabia elects to purchase."[15] At the same time, the Department of State reopened discussions with the government of Bahrain regarding the provision of logistical support facilities for the United States Navy's Middle East Force (MIDEASTFOR), the only permanent US military presence in the Gulf region at the time, substantially revising the Bahrainis' 1975 decision to terminate completely the Navy's long-standing basing rights in the country.[16] As an adjunct of this arrangement, Under Secretary of State for Political Affairs Philip C. Habib authorized approaches to other "friendly" Persian Gulf and Indian Ocean governments, including Iran, Saudi Arabia, Kenya, and Pakistan, in order to secure increased port access for MIDEASTFOR's ship-based "afloat" command structure and its constituent vessels.[17]

While modest in themselves, these early moves helped forge working arrangements that would prove essential in coming years. But it was events in the Horn of Africa that proved critical in elevating the strategic importance of the region in the eyes of US officials. In July 1977, Somalia invaded the contested Ogaden desert region of eastern Ethiopia, home to large numbers of ethnic Somalis. In the years leading up to the conflict, both states moved closer to the Soviet Union, but by the outbreak of hostilities, the trajectories of their respective relationships with Moscow were moving in opposite directions. Somalia, under the leadership of General Mohamed Siad Barre, had developed a client–state relationship with the Soviet Union beginning in the late 1960s, exchanging access to port facilities in Berbera for arms and technical assistance. Ethiopia, a staunch US regional ally until the 1974 overthrow of longtime ruler Emperor Haile Selassie by a military junta known as the Derg, had similarly developed a military supply relationship with the Soviets and other Eastern Bloc states to fight a growing insurgency in Eritrea. On March 17, 1977, the Carter administration ordered a review of US policy in the Horn in Presidential Review Memorandum/NSC 21.[18] In response, the NSC's Policy Review Committee decided to accelerate the closure of Kagnew Station, a United States naval communications unit in Asmara, and reduce the scope of the Military Assistance Advisory Group in Addis Ababa to the provision of "non-lethal" aid only, citing the danger to US troops and mounting unease with the Derg's "brutal" counterinsurgency.[19] Shortly thereafter, the Derg abruptly expelled all US personnel from Ethiopia.[20]

At the same time, the Somalis, somewhat paradoxically, looked askance at Soviet aid to the Ethiopian military and chafed at the growing impression that Moscow favored Addis Ababa's view of the Ogaden sovereignty dispute. In early May, Somalia's ambassador in Washington, Abdullah Addou, met with Secretary Vance, who took a dim view of the Somali regime's human rights record. Addou conveyed a request from Siad Barre for US economic and military aid, since "Siad does not believe that Somalia and Ethiopia can be in the same camp at the same time."[21] Expanding further on this point in a follow-up meeting with Vice President Walter Mondale, Ambassador Addou stated that the "Soviets have as their objective the creation of a cluster of states, including Ethiopia, Somalia, Aden [i.e., the People's Democratic Republic of Yemen or "South Yemen"], and Djibouti, under Moscow's influence." When Mondale tried to deflect the request for arms and affirm the administration's willingness to provide economic aid, as Vance had done earlier, Addou went further by playing a Cold War card. The ambassador stated that "military assistance from the U.S. definitely would lead Somalia to reduce the Soviet presence." He asserted, "Somalia would end its military arrangements with the Soviet Union," adding that the Soviet use of the installations in Berbera "might be reconsidered."[22] Mondale demurred, but played a card of his own, telling Addou that "unlike the Soviets, we have no designs on Somalia" and promised to take his message to President Carter.[23] Meeting with Addou a month later, Carter similarly equivocated on military aid, but left little doubt as to the US view of a Somali tilt, acknowledging the "strategic importance" of Somalia and noting "the steady but very gratifying trend toward the removal of past doubts and misunderstandings and difficulties."[24]

With this backdrop, the outbreak of hostilities set in motion the development of a new strategic landscape in the Indian Ocean littoral. Early victories allowed Somali forces to capture nearly two-thirds of the Ogaden by August and, combined with a renewed offensive by the Eritrean insurgents, threatened the collapse of the Ethiopian military. This forced both Washington and Moscow to evaluate their priorities in the Horn and their commitment to the region. Uncomfortable as they were over increased Soviet involvement with the Ethiopians, Carter and his foreign policy team were equally reluctant to get too close to Siad Barre's regime, described by the NSC staff member assigned to the region as "essentially a police state."[25] Temporizing, they sought to bolster friendly regimes in Sudan and Kenya and encouraged African leaders to call for a general arms embargo to the belligerents, while continuing to resist repeated Somali entreaties for military assistance.[26] The Soviets, on the other hand, escalated their support for Ethiopia. In a November 12 memo to Carter, Vance reported that the USSR had increased arms shipments to the Ethiopians that "coupled with the increasing number of Cuban military advisers (now estimated at 400) seemed likely to tip the scales against Somalia in the coming months."[27] On November 28, following Somalia's decision to abrogate their 1974 Treaty of Friendship that provided Moscow access to Berbera, the Soviet air force initiated an airlift to prop up the Derg's beleaguered forces.

To address the mounting crisis, Brzezinski, Vance, and Brown, along with other representatives of the Departments of State, Defense, Justice, and the Central Intelligence Agency (CIA), met on December 21 to discuss US policy in the Horn and "cause developments to move in directions more favorable to our basic interests." Brzezinski sought consideration of "means of denying the Soviets an opportunity to consolidate their position in Ethiopia."[28] As US officials grappled with the escalation of events in the Horn, the crisis began to assume a broader regional character.

The growing Soviet and Cuban presence in Ethiopia alarmed European allies and pro-US governments in the Middle East alike. Meeting with Carter, French president Valery Giscard d'Estaing, whose military continued to maintain troops in recently decolonized Djibouti, encouraged the president to look at the regional impact of the Horn, noting that "we must find a way to restrain the Soviets, and to give aid, not just military aid, but economic and political support" to African states.[29] Likewise, the shah of Iran, Mohammad Reza Pahlavi, when summarizing recent discussions for the embassy in Tehran, stated that he found the Egyptians and Saudis "gravely concerned" by Soviet activities in Ethiopia and that he "considered the Saudis 'petrified' by [the] prospect of Soviets across the Red Sea."[30] These concerns, along with US alarm that the Soviets would cultivate further ties with the Marxist regime in South Yemen in order to support the Ethiopian airlift, prompted the administration to look at new ways to reassure their allies. Although policymakers disagreed on the tactics to be employed, the US response nevertheless had a gradual effect on the way the Carter team approached the region strategically. Over the course of 1978, these moves would not only increase Washington's direct military engagement in the region, but they would also form the foundation for the development of permanent security architecture in the years that followed.

By the spring of 1978, US tactical thinking about the Horn and strategic thinking about the wider region, as well as its importance for the administration's worldwide security policy, began to converge. This convergence was reflected in a March 17 memorandum from Secretary of Defense Brown to the Joint Chiefs, entitled "Review of US Strategy to Safeguard Availability of Oil from the Middle East and Persian Gulf." In it, Brown wrote: "The President and I have stated that the Middle East and Persian Gulf cannot be separated from our security and that of NATO and our allies in Asia; and that the United States intends to safeguard the production of oil and its transportation to consumer nations without interference by hostile powers." However, Soviet moves in the Horn signaled Moscow's intent to expand its influence to the Gulf as well and thus posed a risk to this important objective. As a result, Brown concluded, "I believe it appropriate for us to review Soviet and U.S. strategy, plans, force structure, and deployments as they relate to these important U.S. and allied interests."[31]

The results of the review, sent by new JCS chairman, General David Jones, to Secretary Brown on September 7, were emphatic in their assessments and conclusions. The timing of the report is significant. Undoubtedly, its tone was shaped by the evolving situation in the Horn, where deepening Soviet and Cuban involvement in Ethiopia eroded the administration's resistance to supporting Siad Barre, as well as developments in the Arabian Peninsula. In the latter, Washington offered additional military assistance to the Yemen Arab Republic (North Yemen) following the June assassination of that country's president by forces backed by Moscow-supported South Yemen.[32] In the summary memorandum that accompanied the complete 48-page report, Jones identified four main conclusions. First, the USSR stood poised to move in the region. "The Soviet Union," the review asserted, "has well-defined interests and specific objectives, an opportunistic and congruent strategy, and the capability to pursue that strategy. Additionally, it is increasing its military capability and, given the opportunity, may opt for more overt military measures to further its interests." Second, three main US interests were at stake: ensuring "continuous access to petroleum resources," preserving the "survival of Israel as an independent state in a stable relationship with contiguous Arab states," and "preventing an inimical power or combination of powers from establishing hegemony." Third, "Existing US strategy should be expanded to provide adequate guidelines to ensure that national interests are protected and advanced." Last, the review concluded that there were "two main obstacles to the realization of US objectives in the area: the turmoil produced by the Arab-Israeli conflict and the diametrically opposed strategic aims of the Soviet Union."[33]

To address this situation, Jones stated that the "Joint Chiefs of Staff consider *the development and implementation of a comprehensive US strategy for the region a matter of utmost urgency* [emphasis added]." The JCS's immediate recommended objectives were not particularly novel, as they took as its bases objectives that had underpinned US thinking about the region since the 1950s—a "full or partial Middle East settlement enhanced by guarantees (which, if necessary, could include the presence of US military forces)," a "revitalized" Central Treaty Organization "with a more active planning and leadership role by the United States," and a "firm and public commitment" to Iran and Saudi Arabia—but its proposed strategy clearly foreshadowed later developments. Jones wrote that a "public declaration of policy" that "embraced" the US objectives "could serve to counter or deter Soviet military presence in the region and enhance regional stability." Militarily, the United States should bolster the declaration by "countering" the Soviet presence in the region, "assisting" the "development of local base infrastructures" that would be "adequate to support the introduction of significant US military forces to the region," "maintaining" a "limited" US military presence that is "sufficient to provide evidence of US interest in the region, enhance stability, and facilitate the introduction of surge forces," and seek to prevent "any major conquests by a regional power or powers." In conclusion, the JCS recommended that this be "used as the basis for a strategy for the next decade, the implementation of which conveys to the USSR as well as US friends and allies the importance the US attaches to stability and security of the region."[34]

Although events in Iran would soon reveal the limitations of many of the JCS's specific recommendations, the growing appreciation for a concerted military strategy and support architecture that the review expressed meant that the Carter administration had some much-needed foundations it could build upon once the shah fell in January 1979. To a significant degree, the JCS memorandum envisioned a strategic posture requiring greater direct US regional involvement and a more diverse constellation of partnerships. Indeed, even as the Iranian monarchy was in its last hours, General Jones sent a follow-up memorandum to Secretary Brown on January 11, 1979, that suggested looking at possible alternative basing arrangements with Saudi Arabia, Oman, and other states in the "Lower Gulf."[35] With the shah's ouster, the groundwork laid in 1977–8 became vital for developing US responses to the crisis, the perceived power vacuum in the region, and the Cold War implications of both.

For all the benefit this advance work would have for organizing a new US regional posture in time, the collapse of the shah's regime was nevertheless a deep blow to Washington, one that would thereafter haunt the Carter administration and its legacy. When it came to Iran, Justin Vaïsse writes, "advanced policy planning was not at issue," instead, events "called for crisis management."[36] In this, the administration found itself continually wrong-footed. As the Iranian political situation deteriorated throughout 1978, it was repeatedly forced to catch up to rapidly accelerating events on the ground, a task made even more challenging by a (sometimes self-inflicted) litany of missed signs, bureaucratic divisions, inadequate or underappreciated intelligence, and indecision at critical junctures. Even as the shah's position deteriorated, Carter, like his predecessors, found himself unable to envision an Iran without the shah. A feature of US Middle East policy since the 1950s, Washington's strategic, political, and economic investment in his regime had ramped up dramatically over the past decade. This process, as David Collier discusses in this volume and other scholars have suggested, was driven as much by the shah himself as by his counterparts in the White House.[37] Reflecting years later in his memoirs, Carter recalled that "there was no question in my mind that he deserved our unequivocal support." "Not only had the shah been a staunch and dependable ally of the United States for many years, but he remained the leader around whom we hoped to see a stable and reformed government organized and maintained in Iran."[38]

For all of the administration's struggles in its attempts to manage the Iranian crisis on the ground, US officials saw the Cold War implications of it much more clearly. "Aware of the 1,500-mile border shared by Iran and the Soviet Union," Carter wrote, "I was concerned that the Soviet leaders might be tempted to move in, a repetition of what they had already done three times in this century."[39] Alarmed at indications that Moscow was mounting a propaganda campaign to exploit the unrest in Iran, the president warned Soviet general secretary Leonid Brezhnev in a November 21, 1978 message that the "United States remains fully committed to the independence and integrity of Iran" and that any Soviet "interference would be a matter of the utmost gravity to us."[40]

Stepping back from the fray, Brzezinski tried to place the Iranian situation in a broader regional context and divined an interrelated pattern tying it together with events along the entirety of the northern Indian Ocean littoral. He articulated this in a December 2, 1978 memorandum to Carter, in which he described the formation of an "Arc of Crisis," stretching "from Chittagong (Bangladesh) through Islamabad to Aden"; in it would be found "the area of currently our greatest vulnerability." "There is no question in my mind that we are confronting the beginning of a major crisis, in some ways similar to the one in Europe in the late 40's," he continued, the "resulting political vacuum might well be filled by elements more sympathetic to the Soviet Union. This is especially likely since there is a pervasive feeling in the area that the U.S. is no longer in a position to offer effective political and military protection." If his analysis was correct, he noted, "the West as a whole might be faced with a challenge of historic proportions." "Before too long, we may have to consult also with our primary allies regarding the need for a collective response, lest the kind of instability that we are seeing in Pakistan and Iran becomes also manifest in the Persian Gulf."[41]

With the shah's departure from Iran on January 16, 1979, the administration had to grapple with the diverse array of political forces—left and right, bourgeois and proletarian, military and civilian, secular and religious—seeking to fill his place. "Having not prepared itself for the shah's fall," Scott Kaufman writes, "the Carter administration had no certainty as to what it could expect from the new Iranian government."[42] Although Ayatollah Ruhollah Khomeini and the Revolutionary Council emerged as the dominant players, other components of the opposition that brought down the Peacock Throne, particularly on the left, were viewed as poised to exploit the situation. A January 12 CIA assessment noted that "religious leaders," who "have dominated the [opposition] movement," appeared unable to hold "radicals" in check and "are worried by a leftward trend among the rank and file." Spurred by an active "pro-Soviet Communist Tudeh Party," leftist elements, it noted "could become more influential in the future."[43] The same day, Brzezinski observed in a memorandum to Carter that further uncertainty invited the emergence of leadership that resembled other recent experiences, a "[Libyan leader Mu'ammar] Qadafi or even worse a Mengistu who might invite Soviet intervention."[44]

Given the uncertainty in Iran, the need for "collective response" to the regional situation took on new urgency. Brzezinski observed in a March 1979 memorandum, the situation in Iran "has added a new and dangerous dimension to the crisis in the Middle East." Regionally, he perceived things approaching a breaking point. "The stakes at the moment are extremely high. Another major setback to U.S. policy in the area," he warned, "could put the region dangerously out of control."[45] Assessing the situation weeks later, the CIA described the fall of the shah as a "windfall for the Soviets because of the setback to strategic U.S. interests." Moscow, it believed, would continue to seek "instability" on the ground in Iran without openly antagonizing the new government in the hope of achieving a pro-Soviet regime in the future; elsewhere, it would "court" more "traditional" Arab states in the Gulf, "particularly Saudi Arabia," in order to "take advantage of the current absence of a restraining power to undermine the same states."[46] The State Department shared Brzezinski's assessment, but expressed it in far less dramatic terms, emphasizing the continuity of shared strengths rather than new vulnerabilities. In February, Foggy Bottom completed a review of the US regional posture in the Gulf in the wake of events in Iran and elsewhere in the region by concluding that "U.S. policy of encouraging regional cooperation and orderly development" remained "a fundamentally sound policy." Nevertheless, in "our presentation and implementation of it," it recommended, "we need to reflect recognition of changed circumstances, which include not just the weakening of Iranian contribution to stability in the region, but also the significant progress the Arabian Peninsula Gulf States have made in developing strong societies and strengthening the trend toward regional cooperation."[47]

Faced with this new strategic landscape, the Carter administration's drive for a robust security footprint in the greater Gulf drew on the intellectual spadework already done the year before in response to events in the Horn of Africa and the Arabian Peninsula. While Brzezinski would remain a driving force behind this process, he was joined by Secretary of Defense Brown and General Jones. Over the remainder of Carter's time in office, Brown and Jones became increasingly important voices in shaping the development of the Persian Gulf Security Framework and the expansion of the US military footprint in the region, culminating in the creation of the RDJTF in March 1980.

For some in Carter's foreign policy team, Harold Brown's position on how far the United States should go in the wake of Iran's revolution was unclear. In his memoirs, Brzezinski described Brown's position as one of "ambiguity until late 1979," adding that the secretary needed to be pushed by his colleagues at the Pentagon, particularly his deputy Graham Claytor and Under Secretary for Policy Robert Komer, to embrace the security framework.⁴⁸ During the crisis over the Horn, Brzezinski noted that Brown, along with General Jones and the Department of State, seemed to "be badly bitten by the Vietnam bug and as a consequence are fearful of taking the kind of action which is necessary to convey our determination and to reassure the concerned countries in the region."⁴⁹

To some extent, Brzezinski's assessment appears accurate. His March 1978 memorandum notwithstanding, Brown, along with Vance and the Department of State, had earlier opposed the deployment of a US aircraft carrier to the region and were reluctant to authorize the movement of naval forces to Diego Garcia in response to events in the Horn. Jones and the JCS, however, had been proponents of the deployment proposals and, as demonstrated in the September 1978 memorandum, were actively advocating moves to counter the Soviets. Concurrently, Brzezinski's assessment of Brown's thinking also falls somewhat short. Brown's reluctance to commit a carrier was, at least in part, predicated upon his belief that the United States would not actually use it in the event Ethiopian troops invaded Somalia, thereby undercutting the impact of the move, rather than a deeper strategic aversion.⁵⁰

As a recent study of Brown's Pentagon tenure suggests, the secretary was willing to look expansively at US options in the region; tellingly, Brown reacted to the September 1978 JCS paper by noting that while it provided "good background" for policy formulation, it was also "not very imaginative."⁵¹ Moreover, Brown supported the idea of a deepening US commitment to the region much earlier than Brzezinski indicated, even if he had some reservations about how this should best be achieved. Returning from a February 1979 trip to Israel, Egypt, Jordan, and Saudi Arabia, undertaken to reassure the leaders of those countries unnerved by the events in Iran, Brown argued in a memorandum to Carter that "[o]ur assurances of greater US interest and involvement are perishable. *We must follow through.* [emphasis in the original]." Aware of Egyptian, Jordanian, and Saudi reluctance to host US forces in their own countries Brown recommended the United States "further explore forms of US presence—short of permanent bases" that would underline the administration's commitment. Moreover, he suggested that the United States should lay "the basis for multinational security cooperation. We should concentrate on situations where stability is threatened by Soviet surrogates, in particular North Yemen and possibly Oman."⁵²

Throughout 1979, Brown and Department of Defense (DOD) officials advocated for greater US military involvement in the greater Gulf region.⁵³ In a June 19 memorandum to Brzezinski, NSC staff members Gary Sick and Fritz Ermarth noted that their DOD colleagues were driven "by a sense of acute anxiety based upon a perception of vulnerability: US interests in the area are extremely vital; the potential threats to them are immediate and powerful; US capabilities in the area, under stress, are very weak."⁵⁴ At the same time, Brown also noted that the strategic environment was a complicated one and required a sensitive approach. Arab governments "fear" the Soviet threat, he argued in a Policy Review Committee meeting days later, but "intervention by the Cubans" and, especially, "internal subversion" were more likely threats. Emphasizing the unease that potential partners in the region expressed at the prospect of a large-scale deployment of US forces, in particular ground forces, Brown highlighted the value of naval deployments. He noted that since the Iranian Revolution, the United States had increased its naval presence to a "very high level" and that the results appeared "positive, not negative, in terms of regional reaction." Furthermore, there was ample space to develop security ties with Arab allies through pre-positioning agreements and other measures that enhanced US capabilities in a crisis. Brown added that, in his meetings with regional officials, there was a reservoir of goodwill for the United States to draw upon: "all of them were delighted regarding the security actions which we were taking with regard to the Soviets. Moreover, our actions during the Yemen crisis have them believing we are able to produce on the security side."[55] What remained was finding a way to strengthen US capabilities without endangering these relationships.

On July 11, 1979, Brown spelled out for President Carter specific moves his department intended to take. First, the DOD would continue ongoing efforts to bolster its relationships with "moderate Persian Gulf States," by remaining responsive to arms and equipment requests, and pursuing opportunities for joint military exercises. Second, he proposed the expansion of the permanent surface fleet assigned to the US Middle East Force from three vessels to five or six; increasing the frequency of routine rotational naval deployments that included both aircraft carrier battle groups as well as a Marine Corps air–ground task force; and creating a provision for the regular annual deployment of a tactical air (TACAIR) squadron to the region. Added to this would be continuing study of "near-continuous or continuous naval presence" in the Indian Ocean. Third, Brown suggested upgrades to US "surge" potential, to include: negotiations with regional allies to facilitate overflight and basing rights to be used in crisis contingencies and in peacetime; "refining" contingency planning; "considering expansion" of US facilities on Diego Garcia; "exploring the need and opportunities for pre-positioning equipment and supplies in the region;" and "improving operational capabilities through increased liaison and exercises with local states." No doubt anticipating lingering Middle Eastern anxieties, Brown cautioned that these moves needed to be conducted in a "low-key" manner, especially with regard to US deployment plans.[56]

Although President Carter was receptive, implementation of these proposals presented challenges that would consume the remainder of the administration's time in office. The twin desires to bolster (or even create) partnerships with regional powers on the one hand, while building up a credible US military presence on the other, required more than a little diplomatic maneuvering and organizational restructuring. The results, however, were significant. In approximately eighteen months, the Carter team developed a concrete security architecture that began to confront concerns about Soviet penetration that had plagued it since the outbreak of the Horn crisis. Along the way, this push to create a new Cold War bulwark in the greater Gulf region started a process that would ultimately come to define the terms of US involvement there for the next four decades.

In the "low-key" drive for improved security relationships in the region, and with them the types of access, overflight, and basing rights that Brown discussed in his July 1979 memorandum, US policymakers were taken in new directions. With the overthrow of the shah's regime in Iran, Israel and Saudi Arabia were the two Middle Eastern countries with which Washington had the deepest ties. Yet, the Carter administration quickly determined that neither would be central to the stationing of new forces in the region. The need to keep Gulf policy separate from the entanglements of the Arab-Israeli dispute meant, as William Odom of the NSC noted, that "bases in Israel and the Sinai are not appropriate for increasing our military presence in the region."[57] Saudi Arabia was thought to be more promising, and indeed a "Saudi-centric" approach was thought to be workable. Yet, Saudi Arabia, like its neighbor Oman, suffered from two critical weaknesses: the lack of "domestic institutions for an effective military establishment" and the absence of "institutions for coordinating a peninsula-wide interstate security system."[58] Although the Saudis pledged to support US negotiations with other regional partners and would offer financial assistance to Washington's efforts, agreements for more permanent physical arrangements were not forthcoming. "Our position, if we are to build one," Odom wrote, "must rest primarily on the perimeter of the Arabian Peninsula."[59]

Egypt, which had moved closer to the United States under President Anwar Sadat after years as a Soviet client and which had forged good working relations with the Carter administration over the Arab-Israeli peace process, was also problematic. In 1979, Sadat floated the idea of redeveloping an existing base on the Red Sea for the United States. Analyzing the offer in a memorandum to President Carter, Secretary Brown noted that the proposal had a number of major drawbacks, but in July 1980, Carter approved reapproaching Egypt about securing a rear base for US forces at Ras Banas on the Red Sea coast. However, while this became an important goal for the administration in its remaining months, spiraling costs ultimately precluded a final agreement before Carter left office.[60]

Far more promising were the positive reactions to the administration's overtures expressed by the leaders of Oman, Kenya, and, Somalia, three countries with which hitherto the United States had peripheral (if not worse) relations. In the case of Somalia, this ironic twist required some compartmentalization. During a meeting of the Special Coordination Committee in late January 1980, Brzezinski observed that a US presence there might provoke the sort of Ethiopian-Soviet-Cuban response it sought to contain, a scenario that would force the administration to follow through on any security assurances. "We would have to be prepared to take action on Somalia's behalf," he noted, adding that the administration was already providing the Siad Barre regime defensive weaponry. Nevertheless, Brzezinski continued, "[w]e should make clear" to him that we "oppose the Ogaden war, that an increase in the violence or his use of regular forces would jeopardize our security ties, and that we would not respond to an attack he provokes."[61] By the end of the summer in 1980, a series of agreements were struck with all three countries, allowing US forces access to military facilities.[62]

Negotiations were also initiated with the UK to secure expanded facilities in Diego Garcia, as required under the terms of the 1976 agreement with London that governed US military use of the British-administered outpost. This Indian Ocean atoll, located approximately 1,800 miles from southern India and 2,000 miles west of the African coast, was remote from the places Washington was most concerned about. However, Brown noted, the distance was advantageous as it offered a "visible" sign of US commitment to the "Indian Ocean/Persian Gulf region," while still "far enough from the Gulf for such an upgrade not to cause embarrassment for our friends there."[63] Its value as a possible operational staging area was highlighted in November 1979 when, in the midst of the emerging hostage crisis in Tehran, an attack on the Grand Mosque in Mecca by militants opposed to the Saudi government, and the burning of the US embassy in Pakistan, Carter ordered the increase of US refueling capacity and the stationing of additional helicopters on Diego Garcia.[64] To augment the island's 12,000-foot runway, storage facilities, naval communications station, and deep water harbor able to accommodate an aircraft carrier battle group, the administration sought additional basing rights to add to crisis-response capabilities. In July 1980, Carter approved the stationing of seven additional pre-positioning ships and the development of support facilities that could accommodate a 12,000-strong Marine Corps amphibious force.

The result of this mind-set led to the prioritization of the Gulf region for US policymakers. The March 1980 creation of the RDJTF and the elevation of the Gulf region to a level equal to that of Western Europe and East Asia proved the Carter administration's lasting legacies for US strategic policy in the Middle East. The idea for a multidivisional Rapid Deployment Force (RDF), which could respond quickly to crises in places like the Gulf, was conceived as early as 1977, in Presidential Directive 18 covering the global military force structure, though little had been done since.[65] Although Carter administration officials frequently debated the means by which the United States could enhance its military presence, it was not until 1979 that the RDF concept was explored as a vehicle for this. On January 25, 1980, Brown recommended deploying an Amphibious Task Force to supplement two carrier task forces already operating in the Arabian Sea. The following day, Brown informed Carter that he had directed the JCS to develop RDFs for missions in the region and the establishment of a controlling task force headquarters to be placed at MacDill Air Force Base in Florida.

Brzezinski, as noted earlier, saw these actions as so significant that he described them in tectonic terms, situating them firmly within a broader Cold War narrative. Following Carter's 1980 State of the Union address, Brzezinski noted in his memoirs that the administration had made the Middle East and Gulf a vital strategic theater in the struggle against Moscow. Days before leaving office, a year after the speech, the Carter administration issued a document that summarized what it believed it had accomplished. In Presidential Directive/NSC-63, one of the final policy documents the administration produced, signed on January 15, 1981, the president outlined the "considerable progress" in its efforts to "develop a broad range of military and related response options in and outside the region against the Soviet Union." These included building up US force projection capabilities, enhancing the security of regional allies, "diminishing radical influences," "improving access to facilities in the region while remaining sensitive to the special historical experience of the region," and taking a "regional approach to securing our economic and political interests rather than basing their defense wholly on drawing a line to protect specific countries in the region." "To ensure this trend continues," Carter offered his vision for the Persian Gulf Security Framework's future, outlining an integrated diplomatic, economic, and strategic approach, combining expanded US and allied military capabilities with deepened collaboration with states ranging from Western Europe to the Horn of Africa and from the Arabian Peninsula to South Asia.[66]

In short, Carter presented a blueprint for the continued waging of the Cold War in the greater Gulf region. The importance of the Carter administration's moves, diminished by its contemporary critics, has become clearer over time. In terms of influencing the end of the Cold War on terms favorable to US interests, one study has noted the administration's impact was deeper than may have been apparent in 1981 and helped poise the United States "surprisingly well for a geopolitical comeback" in the 1980s.[67] Yet, given the interest shown by the administration in waging the Cold War in the greater Gulf throughout its tenure, this should seem less surprising. From at least the winter of 1977–8, the Carter administration was pushed to consider its strategic options in confronting what seemed to be a renewed Soviet political offensive in the Horn of Africa and the southwest Arabian Peninsula. The events of 1979 proved to be further confirmation of the region's vulnerability and drove the Carter team to increase the tempo of its efforts in pursuit of a broader Persian Gulf Security Framework and a US military presence to bolster it. Therefore, beyond the question of whether its efforts impacted the Cold War's outcome, it is clear that the administration's moves helped ensure that the Gulf would be an area of acute US interest in the decades that followed. For better or worse, since the strategic elevation of the greater Gulf region in 1980, the US presence has become a fixture in Washington's foreign and security policies.

Notes

1 *Disclaimer: The views expressed in this chapter are those of the authors and are not necessarily those of the US government. This chapter is based on publicly available archival and published sources.*

2 This chapter seeks to focus on the Carter administration's responses to the Iranian Revolution in the context of the Gulf region rather than the individual developments of events that occurred on the ground in Iran. For more on political developments within Iran during this time, see Chapters 9 and 11.

3 Douglas Little, *American Orientalism: The United States and the Middle East since 1945* (Chapel Hill: University of North Carolina Press, 2002), 147; also see H. W. Brands, *Into the Labyrinth: The United States and the Middle East, 1945–1993* (New York: McGraw-Hill, 1994), 169.

4 For an example of this argument, see Andrew J. Bacevich, *America's War for the Greater Middle East: A Military History* (New York: Random House, 2016).

5 The Carter administration's use of "Persian Gulf" as a loose geographic shorthand, often liberally applied to the entire Gulf/Southwest Asia/Indian Ocean region, presents a definitional challenge. This study will try to reconcile this usage, recognizing that the Gulf and the countries that surround it were central to US officials' strategic concerns and the geographic diversity of territories connected to its policies by using the term "greater Gulf."

6 Raymond L. Garthoff, *Détente and Confrontation: US-Soviet Relations from Nixon to Reagan*, rev. ed. (Washington: Brookings, 1994), 729. *FRUS* volumes cited here are: Kelly M. McFarland, ed., *FRUS*, 1977–80, Vol. XVIII, Middle East Region; Arabian Peninsula (Washington: Government Printing Office, 2015); Louise Woodroofe, ed., *FRUS*, 1977–80, Vol. XVII, Part I, Horn of Africa (Washington: Government Printing Office, 2016); Alexander R. Wieland, ed., *FRUS*, 1977–80, Vol. IX, Arab-Israeli Dispute, August 1978–December 1980, 2nd rev. ed. (Washington: Government Printing Office, 2018); Kristin A. Ahlberg, ed., *FRUS*, 1977–80, Vol. I, Foundations of Foreign Policy

(Washington, Government Printing Office, 2014); Melissa Jane Taylor, ed., *FRUS*, 1977–80, Vol. VI, Soviet Union (Washington: Government Printing Office, 2013).

7 See Gaddis Smith, *Morality, Reason, and Power: American Diplomacy in the Carter Years* (New York: Hill and Wang, 1986); Betty Glad, *An Outsider in the White House: Jimmy Carter, His Advisors, and the Making of American Foreign Policy* (Ithaca, NY: Cornell University Press, 2009); and Scott Kaufman, *Plans Unraveled: The Foreign Policy of the Carter Administration* (DeKalb: Northern Illinois University Press, 2008). Aspects of this critique are also developed in Louise P. Woodroofe, *Buried in the Sands of the Ogaden: The United States, the Horn of Africa, and the Demise of Détente* (Kent, OH: Kent State University Press, 2013); Nancy Mitchell, *Jimmy Carter in Africa: Race and the Cold War* (Palo Alto, CA: Stanford University Press, 2016); and Brian Auten, *Carter's Conversion: The Hardening of American Defense Policy* (Columbia: University of Missouri Press, 2009).

8 Address by Jimmy Carter, May 28, 1975; *FRUS*, 1977–80, vol. I, Foundations of Foreign Policy, Document 2.

9 Smith, *Morality, Reason, and Power*, 12.

10 See Auten, *Carter's Conversion*; David Skidmore, *Reversing Course: Carter's Foreign Policy, Domestic Politics, and the Failure of Reform* (Nashville, TN: Vanderbilt University Press, 1996); and Justin Vaïsse, *Zbigniew Brzezinski: America's Grand Strategist* (Cambridge, MA: Harvard University Press, 2018).

11 Zbigniew Brzezinski, *Power and Principle: Memoirs of a National Security Adviser, 1977–1981* (New York: Farrar, Straus, Giroux, 1983), 454.

12 Memo: Quandt and Sick to Brzezinski, February 2, 1977; *FRUS*, 1977–80, vol. XVIII, Document 1.

13 Telegram From Embassy in Saudi Arabia to Departments of State and Defense, January 23, 1977; and Telegram From Embassy in Saudi Arabia to Department of State, February 9, 1977; *FRUS*, 1977–80, Vol. XVIII, Documents 145 and 147.

14 Memo: Brzezinski to Carter, May 21, 1977; *FRUS*, 1977–80, Vol. XVIII, Document 149.

15 Memorandum of Conversation, May 24, 1977; *FRUS*, 1977–80, Vol. XVIII, Document 151.

16 Covered in *FRUS*, 1977–80, Vol. XVIII, Documents 2–5.

17 Action Memo: Bartholomew/Atherton to Vance, May 2, 1977; *FRUS*, 1977–80, Vol. XVIII, Document 5.

18 PRM/NSC 21, March 17, 1977; *FRUS*, 1977–80, Vol. XVII, Part I, Document 4.

19 Summary of Conclusions of PRC Meeting, April 11, 1977; *FRUS*, 1977–80, Vol. XVII, Part I, Document 11.

20 Report Prepared by the Interagency Ethiopia Working Group, undated (c. April 24, 1977); *FRUS*, 1977–80, Vol. XVII, Part I, Document 15.

21 Telegram DOS to Embassy in Somalia, May 4, 1977; *FRUS*, 1977–80, Vol. XVII, Part I, Document 17.

22 Memo: Mondale to Carter, May 12, 1977; *FRUS*, 1977–80, Vol. XVII, Part I, Document 18.

23 Ibid.

24 Memcon, June 16, 1977; *FRUS*, 1977–80, Vol. XVII, Part I, Document 20.

25 Memo: Henze to Brzezinski, August 24, 1977; *FRUS*, 1977–80, Vol. XVII, Part I, Document 26.

26 Summary of Conclusions of PRC Meeting, August 25, 1977; *FRUS*, 1977–80, Vol. XVII, Part I, Document 27.

27 Memo: Vance to Carter, November 12, 1977; *FRUS*, 1977–80, Vol. XVII, Part I, Document 34.

28 Memorandum for the Record, December 21, 1977; *FRUS*, 1977–80, Vol. XVII, Part I, Document 37.

29 Memorandum of Conversation, January 5, 1978; *FRUS*, 1977–80, Vol. XVII, Part I, Document 39.

30 Telegram from Embassy in Iran to DOS, January 11, 1978; *FRUS*, 1977–80, Vol. XVII, Part I, Document 40.

31 Memo: Brown to Joint Chiefs, March 17, 1978; *FRUS*, 1977–80, Vol. XVIII, Document 9, footnote 2.

32 Memo: Aaron to Carter, July 26, 1978; Briefing Memo: Veliotes to Newsom, August 8, 1978; Telegram: Embassy YAR to DOS, DOD, and Embassy Saudi Arabia, August 11, 1978; and Memo: Hoskinson to Brzezinski, August 16, 1978; *FRUS*, 1977–80, Vol. XVIII, Documents 249–52. The June 24, 1978, assassination of YAR president Ghashmi also resulted in the overthrow and execution of South Yemeni president Salim Rubayi Ali shortly thereafter. For discussion of this episode, see Memo: Vance to Carter, June 24, 1978; Telegram Embassy YAR to DOS, June 27, 1978; and Memo: Sick to Brzezinski, June 28, 1978; *FRUS*, 1977–80, Vol. XVIII, Documents 243–5.

33 Memo: Jones to Brown, September 7, 1978; *FRUS*, 1977–80, Vol. XVIII, Document 9.

34 Ibid.

35 Memo: Jones to Brown, January 11, 1979; *FRUS*, 1977–80, Vol. XVIII, Document 11.

36 Vaïsse, *Zbigniew Brzezinski*, 332.

37 See also Roham Alvandi, *Nixon, Kissinger, and the Shah: The United States and Iran in the Cold War* (New York: Oxford University Press, 2014).

38 Jimmy Carter, *Keeping Faith: Memoirs of a President* (New York: Bantam, 1982), 440.

39 Ibid., 440.

40 Backchannel Message: Brzezinski to Toon, November 21, 1978; *FRUS*, 1977–80, Vol. VI, Document 160.

41 Memo: Brzezinski to Carter, December 2, 1978; *FRUS*, 1977–80, Vol. I, Document 100.

42 Kaufman, *Plans Unraveled*, 161.

43 CIA Intelligence Memorandum: "Iran: The Radicals in the Opposition," January 12, 1979, as found in Cold War International History Project Document Collection, "The Carter Administration and the 'Arc of Crisis': Iran, Afghanistan, and the Cold War in Southern Asia, 1977–1981," ed. Malcom Byrne, July 25, 2005, accessed July 13, 2018, https://www.wilsoncenter.org/publication/the-carter-administration-and-the-arc-crisis-iran-afghanistan-and-the-cold-war-southern.

44 Memo: Brzezinski to Carter, "Information Items," January 12, 1979, as quoted in Mattin Biglari, "'Captive to the Demonology of the Iranian Mobs': U.S. Foreign Policy and the Perceptions of Shi'a Islam During the Iranian Revolution, 1978–79," *Diplomatic History* 40, 4 (2016): 598.

45 Memo from Brzezinski, "Consultative Security Framework for the Middle East," March 3, 1979, as found in Cold War International History Project Document Collection, "The Carter Administration and the 'Arc of Crisis': Iran, Afghanistan, and the Cold War in Southern Asia, 1977–1981," ed. Malcom Byrne, July 25, 2005, accessed July 13, 2018, https://www.wilsoncenter.org/publication/the-carter-administration-and-the-arc-crisis-iran-afghanistan-and-the-cold-war-southern.

46 Intelligence Assessment, CIA, "Changes in the Middle East: Moscow's Perceptions and Options," (excerpts), June 1979, as found in the Cold War International History Project Document Collection, "The Carter Administration and the 'Arc of Crisis': Iran, Afghanistan, and the Cold War in Southern Asia, 1977–1981," ed. Malcom Byrne, July 25, 2005, accessed July 13, 2018, https://www.wilsoncenter.org/publication/the-carter-administration-and-the-arc-crisis-iran-afghanistan-and-the-cold-war-southern.

47 Telegram from the Department of State to Multiple Diplomatic Posts, February 8, 1979; *FRUS*, 1977–80, Vol. XVIII, Document 18.

48 Brzezinski, *Power and Principle*, 444.

49 Ibid., 183–4.

50 Record of an SCC Meeting, March 2, 1978; *FRUS*, 1977–80, Vol. XVII, Part I, Document 65.

51 Edward C. Keefer, *Harold Brown: Offsetting the Soviet Military Challenge, 1977–1981* (Washington, DC: Office of the Secretary of Defense Historical Office, 2017), 334.

52 Memo: Brown to Carter, February 19, 1979; *FRUS*, 1977–80, Vol. XVIII, Document 20.

53 Keefer, *Harold Brown*, 334.

54 Memo: Sick and Ermarth to Brzezinski, June 19, 1979; *FRUS*, 1977–80, Vol. XVIII, Document 24.

55 Minutes of PRC Meetings, June 21, 1979–June 22, 1979; *FRUS*, 1977–80, Vol. XVIII, Document 26.

56 Memo: Brown to Carter, July 11, 1979; *FRUS*, 1977–80, Vol. XVIII, Document 27.

57 Memo: Odom to Brzezinski, November 28, 1979; *FRUS*, 1977–80, Vol. XVIII, Document 34.

58 Ibid.

59 Ibid.

60 Memo: Brown to Carter, December 10, 1979; *FRUS*, 1977–80, Vol. IX, Document 311. Memo: Brzezinski to Muskie, Brown, Jones, and Turner, July 22, 1980, *FRUS*, 1977–80, Vol. XVIII, Document 87; and Memo: Brown to Muskie, July 31, 1980; *FRUS*, 1977–80, Vol. IX, Document 395. Keefer, *Harold Brown*, 341.

61 Summary of an SCC Meeting, January 30, 1980; *FRUS*, 1977–80, Vol. XVIII, Document 50.

62 As an adjunct to this, joint economic agreements were also struck to facilitate the upgrade of existing facilities and the generation of political goodwill.

63 Memo: Brown to Vance and Brzezinski, November 3, 1979; *FRUS*, 1977–80, Vol. XVIII, Document 126.

64 Jimmy Carter, *White House Diary* (New York: Farrar, Straus, and Giroux, 2010), 371; Brzezinski, *Power and Principle*, 483.

65 Keefer, *Harold Brown*, 342.

66 Presidential Directive/NSC-63, January 15, 1981; *FRUS*, 1977–80, Vol. XVIII, Document 98.

67 Hal Brands, *Making the Unipolar Moment: U.S. Foreign Policy and the Rise of the Post – Cold War Order* (Ithaca, NY: Cornell University Press, 2016), 39.

11

The Rise of the Iranian Leviathan: US-Iranian Relations and the Evolution of the Postrevolutionary State

Pedram Maghsoud-Nia

Since the 1979 Iranian Revolution, US-Iranian relations have been marked by intense hostility.[1] For the past forty years, Washington has predominantly portrayed Iran as a source of threat to the United States' interests and a disruptive force that undermines the security of US allies in the Middle East.[2] To curb the perceived Iranian threat, American officials have contemplated an array of options, ranging from diplomatic isolation to military action and regime change.[3]

For the Iranian leadership, the existence of such scenarios and the possibility of a collision with the sole remaining global superpower have been alarming and evocative of the fate of other regimes ousted from power by the United States.[4] Even during President Barack Obama's tenure, when rapprochement seemed to be replacing acrimony in the relations between the two countries, repeated reminders by US officials that "all options," including military attacks were on the table, stoked anxiety among the Iranian leadership.[5] Facing such an ominous prospect, the Iranian regime has strived to ensure its survival. To this end, Tehran has taken a wide range of actions to enhance its defensive capabilities and deter US threats.[6]

From a theoretical standpoint, external threats are deemed to positively influence the development of states' capacities, a process that is captured by Charles Tilly's aphorism, "War made the state and state made the war."[7] Nevertheless, the relationship between external threats and state-building is far from preordained. History is fraught with examples of interstate rivalries and wars that have adversely affected states' control over power.[8] Cognizant of the anomalous cases, in recent years, scholars have tried to identify the conditions under which external threats transform states and lead to the expansion of state power versus those that weaken the impact of threats and hamper state-building.[9]

The evolution of the postrevolutionary Iranian state provides an opportunity to examine the relationship between external threats and state-building. While Iran's actions to withstand US threats have been widely scrutinized,[10] however, there has been little discussion about the broader impact of Tehran's reactions on the institutional structure of the postrevolutionary Leviathan.[11] This chapter seeks to address this issue by comparing the impact of US threats on the evolution of state capacities at two different stages of the postrevolutionary regime's trajectory: from the early 1980s to 2002, and from early 2002 to the present. I contend that US threats have had qualitatively different effects on the development of the state's capacities during these two episodes. For the first two decades of the postrevolutionary regime's rule, Washington's hostile foreign policy toward Tehran induced limited change in the Iranian state's capacities. However, during the second phase, US threats resulted in major enhancement of the state's coercive and extractive capacities.

Foreign Threats and Their Impact on the State's Capacities

Interstate relations influence domestic politics.[12] Facing external threats, rulers must improve their military power, a costly venture that is often defrayed through taxation.[13] To collect taxes and ensure the continuity of large-scale mobilization, states must create civilian bureaucracies.[14] Therefore, external threats enhance military and administrative capacities, the two pillars of the modern state.[15]

In an international system defined by power imbalance, weaker states are more susceptible to challenges and threats emanating from outside their borders than the superpowers. Czechoslovakia in 1968, Chile in 1973, and Vietnam after the Second World War all attest to the vulnerability of weaker states against aggression by the superpowers.[16] Suffering from systemic vulnerabilities, ruling elites in weaker and peripheral states are expected to take systematic steps to forestall foreign threats, a process that leads to the strengthening of the state. Nevertheless, the relationship between external threats and state-building has not always followed this straightforward path.[17] In fact, among developing and non-European countries warfare and interstate rivalries have frequently impeded state-building and in some cases have led to state failure.[18] The discrepancy between theoretical expectations and empirical realities implies that other variables must intervene with political elites' strategic calculations and their response to external threats. By augmenting or mitigating the perception of threats, the intervening factors influence the strategies that elites adopt to tackle external threats. Therefore, to better understand the micro-level processes and the incentive structures that define elites' strategies, a closer attention to the context and the background against which threats unfold is advantageous.[19]

One form of contextual change is a shift in the enemy's discourse. Perception of threats by a group of ruling elites might alter because of the changes in their enemy's discourse. Threats are often perceived as multidimensional phenomena that are irreducible to any single aspect, including hard power.[20] In fact, discursive and hard power dimensions of threats shape the perceptions of targeted groups in tandem.[21] Political elites might become even more alarmed by changes in their enemy's discourse than by the sheer size of its military power or the change in its military posture.[22]

Another intervening factor with the potential to impact elites' response to external threats is the nature of resources that are utilized to cover the cost of military buildup. To become "revenue maximizers," political elites need to face a condition of resource scarcity.[23] Otherwise, the ease of access to natural resources might hinder the development of the state's extractive capacity as the rent wealth reduces the need to tax.[24]

Based on these two points, the next section explains why the US threats had a qualitatively different impact on the Iranian elites' strategies and subsequently on the evolution of the postrevolutionary state. I argue that this was not simply the product of the change in US military posture toward Iran and the increase in its military presence in the Middle East. Instead, the shift in Iran's defensive strategy and its efforts to enhance its extractive capacity occurred because of the alteration in the discourse of Washington's foreign policy toward Tehran that implied an intent to weaken the Iranian regime and ultimately subvert it through hostile economic and military actions.

The US Threats and the Evolution of the Postrevolutionary State in Iran

Prior to the 1979 Revolution, Iran and the United States were close allies. The roots of friendship went back to the early 1940s, when the young Mohammad Reza Shah Pahlavi sought Washington's involvement to compensate for his own inexperience, an involvement that deepened further after the 1953 Coup.[25] The alliance between the two countries reached its zenith in the early 1970s when Washington viewed the shah's regime as the main pillar of US regional strategy against the Soviet Union.[26] Nevertheless, the 1979 Revolution and its ensuing events upended the close alliance between Iran and the United States.

Relations between the two countries came to a head soon after the revolution when a group of students, affiliated with the radical factions of the new regime, invaded the US embassy and took fifty-three American diplomats hostage.[27] The occupation of the US embassy was the harbinger of the enmity that overshadowed relations between the two countries for subsequent decades. Soon after the incident, the United States sided with Saddam's regime in the war against Iran.[28]

Defying the predictions of an early defeat, the Iranian regime managed to withstand the initial wave of Iraq's onslaught.[29] During the second phase of the war when Iran was on the offensive, Washington provided vital diplomatic, intelligence, and material support to Iraq. In retaliation to US intervention, the Iranian regime undertook a chain of hostile activities, including bombing and kidnapping American targets in Lebanon.[30] Hostility between the two countries climaxed in 1988. In response to Iran's attacks on vessels and oil tankers in the Persian Gulf, the United States struck Iran's navy ships and oil platforms.[31] Shortly after, the US Navy downed an Iranian commercial aircraft, an incident interpreted by the Iranian regime as a deliberate attempt to pressure Tehran into accepting a ceasefire with Iraq.[32] Nevertheless, extreme hostility and sporadic military confrontation do not accurately represent the essence of US-Iranian relations during the war years.

For almost a decade after the 1979 Iranian Revolution, Washington's perception of the Iranian regime was shaped within the context of the Cold War and based on the necessities of containing the Soviet Union. Undoubtedly, during this period, the Islamic regime was seen as a source of threat, a point corroborated by occasional punitive measures that Washington undertook to tame Tehran's radicalism and revolutionary zeal. However, the Iranian regime was also viewed in Washington as a potential asset in the campaign against communism.[33] In devising its policy toward Tehran, Washington prioritized the latter concern over the former. Therefore, despite its concerns about Tehran's disruptive behavior, during the first decade of the postrevolutionary regime's rule, the United States was reluctant to witness the postrevolutionary regime's downfall. Moreover, Washington's unwillingness to remove the Iranian regime from power was clearly conveyed to Tehran, and the Iranian elite were aware that they were immune to subversive plots concocted by the United States.[34]

The end of the Cold War altered US perception of the Iranian regime. With the collapse of the Soviet Union, the incumbent regime in Iran lost its value, and the image of Iran as a destabilizing force in the region and supporter of terrorism eclipsed its strategic significance. Nefarious steps by Iran's leadership, such as issuing a death sentence for the Nobel laureate author Salman Rushdie and the Khobar Towers bombing, helped to cement this negative perception.[35] Gradually, Iran became the centerpiece of Washington's fight against extremism.[36] American officials not only began to express their readiness to use military options against Iran but also openly discussed the idea of regime change.[37] Nevertheless, in practice, US policy toward Tehran did not undergo a significant change.

In the 1990s, the absence of any diplomatic leverage over Tehran and the risks associated with military action discouraged Washington from adopting a radically novel approach toward Iran. The lack of options became salient when the Clinton administration decided to adhere to the "dual containment" strategy that was initially designed to contain Iran and Iraq through a protracted and mutually destructive war. The absence of any effective strategy for forcing Tehran to change its behavior led the Clinton administration to resort to economic sanctions, the same weapon that has been utilized against Iraq since its invasion of Kuwait. Although in the case of Iran, the imposed sanctions were far more limited in terms of their scope and effects.[38] Meanwhile, the rise of a reformist president, Mohammad Khatami, to power persuaded the Clinton administration to entertain the idea of a rapprochement, a decision that further complicated US foreign policy toward Tehran.[39] However, confusion in Washington's approach toward Tehran did not last long. The arrival of President Bush at the White House and the 9/11 terror attacks eroded the possibility of reconciliation and put US-Iranian relations back on a hostile track.

In Washington, the dominance of neoconservatives in the Department of Defense deepened animosity toward Iran and heightened tensions between the two countries.[40] Relying on its swift victories in Iraq and Afghanistan, Washington seemed determined to use the momentum to increase the pressure on the Iranian regime. Perhaps the most ominous existential threat to the Islamic Republic since its rise to power was delivered when President George W. Bush designated Iran, next to Iraq and North Korea, as a member of "Axis of Evil," a trio of rogue states placed in the crosshairs of US aggressive foreign policy.[41]

The revelation of Iran's clandestine nuclear program heightened the hostilities between Washington and Tehran. After the disclosure of Iran's nuclear activities, the United States spearheaded an international diplomatic front against Iran and in partnership with Europe, Russia, and China imposed stringent sanctions on Tehran.[42] The pressure on Iran intensified after Barack Obama entered office. Despite President Obama's early campaign promises to reset relations with Iran, his administration adopted even more extensive punitive measures compared to his predecessors. The Comprehensive Iran Sanctions, Accountability and Divestment Act, passed in July 2010 by the UN's Security Council, was the "most restrictive economic sanctions on the Iranian regime to date."[43] New sanctions cut the country's access to the global financial markets, hampered its maritime transportation, and most importantly curtailed the export of oil, the country's economic lifeline. As a result of sanctions, Iran's oil exports in 2012 dropped to the lowest level since 1986, generating only $69 billion in revenues, $26 billion lower than the previous year.[44] The decline in oil production also resulted in a 1.9 percent contraction of Iran's Real GDP from 2011 to 2012.[45]

The collapse of the Cold War modus vivendi and the post-9/11 shift in Washington's strategy toward Iran presented Iran's leadership with a grim prospect. The rhetorical change in US policy toward Iran and the emphasis on "regime change"—a policy that was in full swing in Iran's two neighboring countries—were worrisome developments for Tehran and forced Iranian elites to adapt themselves to the rapidly changing environment.[46] Adaptation primarily manifested itself in Tehran's efforts to enhance its defensive capabilities. In the period between 2002 and 2006, Iran was the only country in the region that saw an increase (from 2.2 percent to 3.3 percent) in the share of military expenditure as a percentage of GDP (Table 11.1).[47]

The Iranian regime's efforts to enhance its coercive capacity in the post-9/11 era—especially after President George W. Bush's "Axis of Evil" speech—are also reflected by longitudinal and temporal changes. After the Iran–Iraq War, the share of military expenditure from Iran's GDP declined sharply.[48] Although the number began to increase during the first half of the 1990s, the rise of reformist president Mohammad Khatami and the prospect of reconciliation with the United States as well as other

Table 11.1 Military Expenditures (Percentage of GDP)

Country	Military Expenditure as Percentage of the GDP (2002)	Military Expenditure as Percentage of the GDP (2006)
Egypt	3.4	2.7
Iran	**2.2**	**3.3**
Israel	8.3	7.4
Saudi Arabia	9.4	7.8
Turkey	3.8	2.4
United Arab Emirates	4.9	3.2

Source: Stockholm International Peace Research Institute (SIPRI), *Yearbook: Armaments, Disarmament, and International Security*. Data available at the World Bank website.

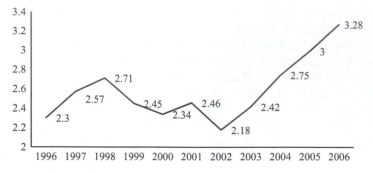

Figure 11.1 Military Expenditures (Percentage of GDP)

Source: Stockholm International Peace Research Institute (SIPRI), *Yearbook: Armaments, Disarmament, and International Security*. Data available at the World Bank website.

regional rivals resulted in a decrease in the share of military expenditure from the GDP. However, rhetorical changes in US policy toward Tehran seemingly forced the Iranian regime to revise its defensive strategy and increase its military expenditures (Figure 11.1).[49]

While sanctions restricted Iran's access to the global arms market, the lion's share of military expenditure went into building an indigenous arms industry.[50] Nothing captures the advancement of Iran's indigenous military industry better than the expansion of its ballistic missile program, a program that was initially established with the assistance of North Korea, Russia, and China, but gradually moved toward self-reliance.[51] In addition to its sprawling missile program, Iran also took major steps toward obtaining nuclear enrichment technology. Although Iran's surrounding environment and regional rivalries did not justify the high cost of developing a nuclear program, Tehran strived to indigenize nuclear knowledge and technology as a preemptive measure.[52]

The Bush administration's "regime change" rhetoric also galvanized Iran's ruling elite to enhance their coercive capacity against homegrown threats. From the mid-1980s until the late 1990s, the Iranian regime did not face an organized opposition. During this period, major oppositions groups—including the leftists and the *Mujahideen-e Khalq* (MeK)—were brutally supressed by the regime.[53] However, the youth bulge and the expansion of the middle class inspired a strong demand for democratic ideals and unleashed a prodemocracy movement in Iran.[54] Washington's endorsement of "velvet revolutions" was one of the key factors that made the Iranian elite wary of the nascent prodemocracy movement and its potential to disrupt the regime's rule.[55] To suppress students and prodemocracy activists, the regime took a wide range of steps including adding a new layer to the state's intelligence apparatus through establishing the Islamic Revolutionary Guard Corps' (IRGC's) intelligence arm (*Sazman Etelaat Sepah*). Moreover, the regime revamped its most effective tool for containing street protests and mass demonstrations, the militia force known as the *Basij*. By reorganizing its militia forces into a more centralized structure with stronger connections to the IRGC, the Iranian regime managed to contain two waves of prodemocracy movements that engulfed Tehran and other major cities in 1999 and 2009.[56]

Perhaps the most important transformation, and one that is directly attributable to US threats, has been the expansion of the Iranian state's extractive capacity. Crippling sanctions imposed on Iran's oil industry and declining oil revenues forced the Iranian elite to reconsider their overdependence on oil exports and urged them to extract more from society. Therefore, tax revenues gradually acquired a larger share in making up the state's budget. According to the International Monetary Fund, the strengthening of tax administration in Iran resulted in an increase in the number of registered taxpayers and improvements in tax collection. Because of these changes, in 2016, for the first time since the early 1970s, the government's tax receipts exceeded its revenues from the export of oil.[57]

The increase in tax revenues was a major accomplishment for the Iranian government. Before the 1979 Revolution, Iran's ruling monarchy relied heavily on oil revenues to pay for its ambitious modernization projects. The Pahlavi regime's uninterrupted ability to exploit and sell oil made it almost independent from collecting taxes and adversely affected the evolution of the state's extractive capacity. Data from the World Bank indicate that from 1974 to 1979 the average share of taxes from the state's revenues was only around 7 percent.[58] After the 1979 revolution, at three points the share of tax revenues from the government's budget rose to around 20 percent. The first was at the height of Iran–Iraq War, when Iran's export of oil was interrupted by skirmishes in the Persian Gulf. The second occasion was in 1998, when oil prices reached their lowest level since 1973. Finally, in 2009, tax revenues accounted for 19.34 percent of Iran's budget after the price of oil dropped significantly because of the 2008 global financial crisis.[59] However, since 1972, the share of taxes of the government's revenue never went beyond twenty-five percent, which indicates the significance of the recent increase in Iran's tax revenues (Figure 11.2).

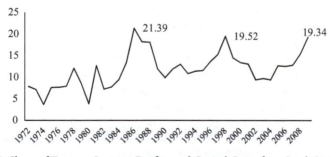

Figure 11.2 Share of Taxes on Income, Profits, and Capital Gains from Iran's State Revenues (1972–2009)

Source: International Monetary Fund, *Government Finance Statistics Yearbook*, and data files. Data available at the World Bank website.

Conclusion

Since the rise of the incumbent Iranian regime to power, it has continuously faced threats from the United States. Nevertheless, the Iranian elite engaged in systematic state-building only from the early 2000s when a rhetorical shift in Washington, compounded by sanctions on Iran's oil industry, posed serious threats to the survival of the regime in Tehran.[60] Prior to these developments and during the first two decades of the regime's rule, the Iranian elite failed to engage in expansive state-building even after the United States threatened or used military force. In other words, the shift in Washington's language and the crippling sanctions imposed on Iran's oil industry seem to have had the unintended consequence of increasing the Iranian state's core capacities.

From a theoretical standpoint, Iran's example illustrates some of the key contextual variables that influence how besieged states respond to external threats. The change in an enemy's discourse and restrictions in access to nontax-based revenues are two of those factors. The former change prompts elites in targeted states to increase their coercive capacity and defensive power whereas the latter leads them to improve the state's taxation and extractive capacity. The history of European state-building demonstrates the linkage between taxation and representation. In exchange for taxing society, rulers had to concede and allow the establishment of representative institutions.[61] Therefore, the expansion of the state's extractive capacity resulted in the formation of democratic institutions and indirectly boosted the state's legitimacy. This important step toward legitimizing political rule has yet to be taken in Iran. The Iranian elites have so far managed to increase the state's coercive and extractive capacities without making the concessions that led to gradual democratization in other societies. However, the shortage of legitimacy may prove costly and threaten the survival of the regime, especially if its coercive power is directed toward deterring foreign threats.

The argument presented in this chapter will likely face a key test during Donald Trump's presidency due to the simultaneous increase in bottom-up pressure from Iranian society and escalating tensions between Tehran and Washington. While the 2015 Joint Comprehensive Plan of Action agreement with the P5+1 countries, comprising the United States, China, France, Russia, the UK, and Germany, paved the way for thawing US-Iranian relations, the Trump presidency has cast serious doubts on the prospect of reconciliation and appears to have put Iran and the United States on a collision course once again. Whether Washington's belligerence and its efforts to undermine the Iranian regime will urge Tehran to continue fortifying itself or will endanger the survival of the postrevolutionary state, is a question that remains to be answered.

Notes

1   Zbigniew Brzezinski, Robert M. Gates, and Suzanne Maloney, *Iran: Time for a New Approach* (New York: Council on Foreign Relations, 2004), 9.

2 Iran is accused of sponsoring terrorism, trying to subvert American allies, overturning regional status quo, and inflicting harm on the United States. On the top of all these accusations, Iran is chastised for its efforts to acquire nuclear weapons. Kenneth Pollack, *Unthinkable: Iran, the Bomb, and American Strategy* (New York: Simon and Schuster, 2013), 63–4. Although Washington "has experimented with a variety of different tactics to persuade Tehran to alter its policies," nevertheless, since the seizure of the US embassy in 1979, "the contours of bilateral relationship has demonstrated considerable consistency." Suzanne Maloney, "Tehran and Washington: A Motionless Relationship?" The Brookings Institute, 2011, 2.

3 For example, on March 5, 2009, at a hearing session before the Committee of Foreign Relations of the Senate, former national security advisor Zbigniew Brzezinski pointed at different strategic objectives that the United States can seek while dealing with Iran. According to Brzezinski, at the one extreme was regime change, a goal that can be achieved through threatening Tehran with sanctions and exercise of military force (US strategy regarding Iran: hearing before the Committee on Foreign Relations, United States Senate, One Hundred Eleventh Congress, first session, March 5, 2009, 5).

4 The most notable example of regimes toppled by the United States was the former Iraqi regime. According to Roy Takeyh, from the perspective of Iranian leaders, especially the hard-liners, "[t]he United States was seen as a formidable threat … with the capacity to subvert Iran's character and turning the masses against the republic." Ray Takeyh, *Guardians of the Revolution: Iran and the World in the Age of the Ayatollahs* (New York: Oxford University Press, 2009), 163. The Iranian leadership's words corroborate Takeyh's observation. For example, in a speech in 2015, the supreme leader of Iran, Ayatollah Khamenei, iterating his accusation against the United States, claimed that since the 1979 revolution, Americans have been incessantly conspiring against Iran. They tried to orchestrate a coup, supported opposition groups, provoked ethnic minorities, encouraged Saddam to invade Iran, all with the single objective of overthrowing the revolutionary regime of Iran (The Office for Preserving and Publishing Grand Ayatollah Khamenei's Works, http://farsi. khamenei.ir/newspart-index?tid=4077#57113).

5 Mehran Kamrava, *Troubled Waters: Insecurity in the Persian Gulf* (Ithaca: Cornell University Press, 2018), 73. According to a secret cable released by Wikileaks, in a 2009 meeting with Israeli prime minister, Benjamin Netanyahu, President Obama mentioned that to stop Iran's nuclear program "all options remain on the table, a point confirmed by Secretaries Clinton and Gates." See "Codels Ackerman and Casey Meetings with Prime Minister Netanyahu," https://wikileaks.org/plusd/cables/09TELAVIV1184_a.html.

6 Part of Iran's deterrence strategy was focused on sabotaging US presence in the region and increasing its own influence across the Middle East. According to an unclassified 2012 Department of Defense report, "Iran's grand strategy remains challenging U.S. influence while developing its domestic capabilities to become the dominant power in the Middle East. Iran's security strategy remains focused on deterring an attack, and it continues to support governments and groups that oppose U.S. interests" (Annual Report on Military Power of Iran, April 2012, 2).

7 Charles Tilly, "Reflections on the History of European State-making," in *The Formation of National States in Western Europe*, ed. Charles Tilly (Princeton, NJ: Princeton University Press, 1975), 42.

8 For example, the Falkland Islands/Malvinas war in 1982 "led directly to the exit of the Argentina military dictatorship the following year." Dankwart A. Rustow,

"Democracy: A Global Revolution." *Foreign Affairs* 69 (1989): 77. Another example is the war between Israel and Egypt that had divergent effects on the evolution of each state; positive in the former case and negative in the latter. See Michael N. Barnett, *Confronting the Costs of War: Military Power, State, and Society in Egypt and Israel* (Princeton, NJ: Princeton University Press, 1992).

9   One of the latest attempts to reassess the relation between warfare and state transformation is the following: Lars Bo Kaspersen and Jeppe Strandsbjerg , eds., *Does War Make States? Investigations of Charles Tilly's Historical Sociology* (Cambridge, UK: Cambridge University Press, 2017).

10   An investigation of Iran's asymmetrical strategy to confront US threats is conducted in Gawdat Bahgat and Anoushiravan Ehteshami, "Iran's Defense Strategy: The Navy, Ballistic Missiles and Cyberspace," *Middle East Policy* 24, 3 (2017): 89–103.

11   Thomas Hobbes, the seventeenth-century political philosopher envisaged the state as the worldly incarnation of the biblical figure, Leviathan. Resembling the state or the earthly Leviathan to its biblical image, Hobbes contended, "There is nothing on earth, to be compared with him. He is made so as not be afraid. He sees every high thing below him; and is King of all the children of pride." Quoted in Thomas Hobbes, *Leviathan: Or, the Matter, Forme and Power of a Commonwealth, Ecclesiasticall and Civil* (New York: Collier Books, 1962), 452. On the ascent and transformation of the modern state from the Hobbesian Leviathan to "a regime of discursive expertise," see Charles S Maier, *Leviathan 2.0* (Cambridge, MA: Harvard University Press, 2014).

12   Peter Gourevitch, "The Second Image Reversed: The International Sources of Domestic Politics," *International Organization* 32, 4 (1978): 881–912.

13   Even the prospect of embroilment in interstate wars urges leaders to mobilize resources. The experience of Latin American states demonstrates that "interstate rivals, whether operationalized as 'enduring' or 'strategic' rivals, have a positive effect on the state's extractive capacity." Cameron G. Thies, "War, Rivalry, and State Building in Latin America," *American Journal of Political Science* 49, 3 (2005): 451.

14   Francis Fukuyama, *The Origins of Political Order: From Prehuman Times to the French Revolution* (New York: Farrar, Straus and Giroux, 2011), 114. Also see Richard Bean, "War and the Birth of the Nation State," *The Journal of Economic History* 33, 1 (1973): 203–21. Bean argued that around AD 1500 the "dramatic rise in the size of armies" led to a "large increase in the ability to raise revenue."

15   Fukuyama, *The Origins of Political Order*, 424. State, according to Max Weber, is a "human community that (successfully) claims the monopoly of the legitimate use of physical force within a given territory." Max Weber, C. Wright Mills, and Hans Gerth, *From Max Weber: Essays in Sociology* (New York: Oxford University Press, 1958), 78. The core of each state consists of administrative, coercive, and extractive organizations. Theda Skocpol, "Bringing the State Back In: Strategies of Analysis in Current Research," in *Bringing the State Back In*, eds. Peter B. Evans, Dietrich Rueschemeyer, and Theda Skocpol (Cambridge, UK: Cambridge University Press, 1985), 7.

16   Gourevitch, "The Second Image Reversed," 883.

17   According to Hillel Soifer, a "creeping functionalism" mires the extant literature on state-building. By overemphasizing the relations between systemic vulnerabilities and the increase in state power, the literature overlooks negative cases that do not substantiate the sequential relations between threats and state-building. Hillel David. Soifer, "The Development of State Capacity," in *The Oxford Handbook of*

Historical Institutionalism, eds. Orfeo Fioretos, Tulia G. Falleti, and Adam Sheingate (Oxford: Oxford University Press, 2016), 186.

18 See Hendrik Spruyt, "War and State Formation, Amending the Bellicist Theory of State Makin," in *Does War Make States? Investigations of Charles Tilly's Historical Sociology*, eds. Lars Bo Kaspersen, and Jeppe Strandsbjerg (Cambridge, UK: Cambridge University Press, 2017), 74. Theda Skocpol's observation that political crises emerge when states are caught in "intensified military competition or intrusions from abroad" also supports this point. Theda Skocpol, *States and Social Revolutions: A Comparative Analysis of France, Russia and China* (Cambridge, UK: Cambridge University Press, 1979), 285. Although the extraction–coercion cycle, developed by scholars like Finer and Tilly, offered a useful heuristic model to explain the rise of European nation-states, nevertheless, readers are often cautioned by the same scholars against overstretching the theory that was built based on the unique experience of Europe. For example, Charles Tilly emphasized that "[i]n no simple sense can we read the future of the Third World countries from the past of European countries." For extraction–coercion cycle, see Samuel E. Finer, "State and Nation Building in Europe: The Role of the Military," in *The Formation of National States in Western Europe*, ed. Charles Tilly (Princeton, NJ: Princeton University Press, 1975), 96, and Charles Tilly, "War Making and State Making as Organized Crime," in *Bringing the State Back In*, eds. Peter B. Evans, Dietrich Rueschemeyer, and Theda Skocpol (Cambridge, UK: Cambridge University Press, 1985), 96.

19 Spruyt, "War and State Formation," 74.

20 According to Joseph Nye, hard power includes economic and military might that "rest on inducements ('carrots') or threats ('sticks') and can "get others to change their positions." Joseph S. Nye, *Soft Power: The Means to Success in World Politics* (New York: Public Affairs, 2004), 5.

21 According to Stuart Hall, discourse is a group of statements that provide a language for talking about and representing a topic. Therefore, the discourse makes it possible to construct the topic in a certain way. More importantly, discourse influences social practices. See Stuart Hall, "The West and the Rest: Discourse and Power," in *Race and Racialization: Essential Readings*, ed. Tania DasGupta (Toronto: Canadian Scholars' Press, 2007), 86.

22 Previous research has shown that threat perception by political elites at the domestic level is shaped by various factors such as opposition groups' deviation from accepted cultural norms and the change in their strategy. In fact, these factors often play a more important role in strategic calculations of elites than the opposition's usage of violence. See Christian Davenport, "Multi-Dimensional Threat Perception and State Repression: An Inquiry into Why States Apply Negative Sanctions," *American Journal of Political Science* 39, 3 (1995): 683–713. Extending this argument to interstate relations, the change in an enemy's discourse might seem more alarming than objective changes in its military power or posture.

23 Richard F. Doner, Bryan K. Ritchie, and Dan Slater, "Systemic Vulnerability and the Origins of Developmental States: Northeast and Southeast Asia in Comparative Perspective," *International Organization* 59, 2 (2005): 340.

24 Michael Herb, "No Representation without Taxation? Rents, Development, and Democracy," *Comparative Politics* 37, 3 (2005): 310.

25 Rouhollah K. Ramazani, *Independence without Freedom: Iran's Foreign Policy* (Charlottesville: University of Virginia Press, 2013), 52.

26 In the early 1970s, Washington's Middle East strategy, unofficially known as the "twin pillars" strategy, was based on the view that the security of the region rests on the collaboration and empowerment of two "staunchly anti-communist powers in the region: Iran and Saudi Arabia." The latter's oil wealth and the former's military power were supposed to help the United States in containing the Soviet threat. See David Crist, *The Twilight War: The Secret History of America's Thirty-Year Conflict with Iran* (New York: Penguin Books, 2012), 28. In his study of the US and Iran relations under President Nixon, Roham Alvandi presents a slightly modified version of the above view and contends that in 1970 "a consensus had emerged in the administration that Iran—and Iran alone—could be relied upon to contain the Soviet influence in the Gulf." Roham Alvandi, *Nixon, Kissinger, and the Shah: The United States and Iran in the Cold War* (New York: Oxford University Press, 2014), 49.

27 To expedite the release of the hostages, the Carter administration tried a "two-track strategy" of maximizing communication with and pressure on Iran. The official communication channels were established through the Swiss government, the Palestine Liberation Organization (PLO) and the United Nations. In the meantime, the United States tapped into secret intermediaries including the Hashemi brothers who had promised the release of the hostages through establishing indirect contacts with Ayatollah Khomeini, and if those contacts failed through a military operation, perhaps a coup, carried out by Admiral Ahmad Madani, a high-ranking member of Iranian armed forces. Other individuals— Professor Richard Cottam, Sadegh Ghotbzadeh, and Sadegh Tabatabai—also tried to mediate and secure the release of hostages. The Carter administration even resorted to military option. But the rescue mission was aborted when one of the helicopters involved in the operation collided with a refueling aircraft, killing eight military servicemen. Finally, the hostages were released with the help of Algerian negotiators and only after Iran received $8.1 billion dollars in addition to the payoff of $4.8 billion-dollar outstanding bank loans. See Joint Report of the "October Surprise Task Force" (1993): 29–60.

28 Gary Hart, *The Fourth Power: A Grand Strategy for the United States in the Twenty-First Century* (Oxford: Oxford University Press, 2004), 93.

29 Pierre Razoux, *The Iran-Iraq War* (Cambridge, MA: Harvard University Press, 2015), 146–7.

30 On September 24, 1984, an explosion at American embassy in Beirut killed twenty-four people. The incident happened while several Americans including William Buckley, the CIA chief in Beirut had been kidnapped by Iran's proxies in Lebanon, the Shia militant group—the Islamic Jihad, which later evolved into Hizbollah. Ibid., 279–80.

31 After an American frigate was struck and damaged by a mine allegedly planted by Iran, the US Navy orchestrated "Operation Praying Mantis." It was the largest battle in which the US Navy had taken part since the end of the Second World War, and led to the destruction of two Iranian frigates, one gunboat, two fighter jets, and two oil platforms. Joseph J. Marie and Shahdad Naghshpour, *Revolutionary Iran and the United States: Low-Intensity Conflict in the Persian Gulf* (London: Routledge, 2016), 168–72.

32 Patrick Clawson, "What to Do about Iran," *Middle East Quarterly* 2, 4 (1995): 46.

33 The two countries' interest also converged on the critical front: Afghanistan that was under the occupation of the Soviet forces. In Afghanistan, Iran was assisting Mujahedin in their fight against Soviets and at the same time hosting over two million

refugees. Donette Murray, *US Foreign Policy and Iran: American-Iranian Relations since the Islamic Revolution* (London: Routledge, 2010), 47.

34 For example, the essence of US policy during the Iran and Iraq war was to prevent either of the two parties from achieving a decisive victory. Sasan Fayazmanesh, *The United States and Iran: Sanctions, Wars and the Policy of Dual Containment* (London: Routledge, 2008), 45. Toward this goal, the Reagan administration decided to supply Iran with desperately needed arms to continue its war with Iraq. In 1985, in exchange for the release of seven American hostages in Lebanon, the Israeli government offered to sell US-manufactured missiles to Iran. President Reagan approved Israel's offer as well as the proposal by National Security Council staffer Lt. Col. Oliver North to use the profits to fund the *Contras*, the opposition group to the Nicaraguan socialist regime. The first installment was sent to Tehran through a mission headed by the former national security advisor Robert McFarlane (Iran-Contra Investigation Report 1989: 3–25). However, the Lebanese magazine, *Al-Shiraa*, reported on McFarlane's secret trip to Tehran and the deal between Iran and the United States. The disclosure brought President Reagan under vehement criticism for dealing with a terrorist regime and unleashed an investigation of the affairs by the Congress, an episode known as Iran-Contra (ibid., 285).

35 Salman Rushdie was the author of *The Satanic Verses*, the novel the evoked the wrath of many Muslims for insulting the prophet Muhammad. In reaction to the novel, Ayatollah Khomeini, the supreme leader of Iran, issued a death sentence for Rushdie. The Khobar Towers bombing happened in 1996 and killed 19 US Air Force servicemen stationed in Saudi Arabia. Washington suspected that the attack was masterminded by Tehran and implemented by Shia groups close to the Iranian regime. The 2015 arrest of Ahmed al-Mughassil, a Saudi born Shiite, in Lebanon further supported this assumption. Ali Soufan, "Did Iran Give Up the Khobar Towers Terrorist?," *Foreign Policy*, 2015.

36 Murray, *US Foreign Policy and Iran*, 87–8.

37 Newt Gingrich, then Speaker of the House of Representatives and a key leader in the Republican Party, was an advocate of regime change and the main supporter of the CIA's covert operations against the Islamic regime. Also, military plans were developed in the United States to punish Iran for the Khobar explosion in Saudi Arabia (ibid., 100).

38 Fayazmanesh, *The United States and Iran*, 65. Under President Clinton, for the first time, the United States banned "involvement with Petroleum development in Iran." According to Iran-Libya Sanctions Act, non-US firms investing more than $40 million in Iran's oil and gas industry were penalized by the US government. See Murray, *US Foreign Policy and Iran*, 102. The sanctions were specially aimed at a contract awarded to Conoco to develop the Sirri field in the Persian Gulf. Patrick Clawson, "Iran," in *Economic Sanctions and American Diplomacy*, ed. Richard N. Haass (New York: Council on Foreign Relations, 1998), 87.

39 In Iran's highly factionalized political system, the hard-liners were anxious about the effect of reconciliation with the United States on intricate interfactional balance of power in the country. Therefore, Washington's symbolic gambits—such as expressing regret for involvement in the 1953 coup—were rebuffed by the hard-liners. David E. Sanger, "U.S. Ending a Few of the Sanctions Imposed on Iran," *New York Times*, March 18, 2000.

40 The "neocons" consisted of a group of commentators, former government officials, and foreign policy analysts hailing from magazines such as *The Weekly Standard*

and think tanks such as the American Enterprise Institute who were decisive in controlling all "aspects of policy surrounding the [Iraq] war and the subsequent occupation." The most prominent names among them were Deputy Secretary of Defense Paul Wolfowitz, Pentagon advisor Richard Perle, and Undersecretary of Defense Douglas Feith. See Joshua Micah Marshall, "Remaking the World: Bush and the Neoconservatives," *Foreign Affairs* 82, 6 (November/December 2003): 142–6. The group also adopted a hawkish stance toward Iran.

41 Greg Ryan, *US Foreign Policy towards China, Cuba and Iran: The Politics of Recognition* (London: Routledge, 2017), 110–11. Iran's inclusion in the "Axis of Evil" dismayed the Iranian leadership. They were under the impression that their cooperation with the United States in the war against al-Qaeda and the Taliban would urge Washington to reconsider its policies toward Tehran.

42 In August 2002, Iran's main opposition group, the organization of *Mujahideen-e Khalq*, revealed Iran's enrichment activities in Natanz and Arak (Arms Control Association).

43 Alex Mintz and Carly Wayne, *The Polythink Syndrome: US Foreign Policy Decisions on 9/11, Afghanistan, Iraq, Iran, Syria, and ISIS* (Stanford, CA: Stanford University Press, 2016), 113.

44 US Energy Information Administration.

45 International Monetary Fund, "World Economic Outlook Transitions and Tensions," 2013, 75.

46 For example, the Congress promoted the Iran Liberation Act, a move that was supported by hard-liners within the administration. Alex Miles, *US Foreign Policy and the Rogue State Doctrine* (London: Routledge, 2012), 138.

47 According to the Stockholm International Peace Research Institute's (SIPRI) trend indicator values, from 2002 to 2006 on average, Iran spent $260 million per year to transfer military capability from abroad. However, the number was lower when compared to what its regional rivals spent. For example, within the same period Saudi Arabia on average spent $450 million to transfer military capability from abroad (SIPRI trend indicator value measures "transfers of military capability rather than the financial value of arms transfers" (SIPRI Fact Sheet 2012, 1)). In terms of total military spending, there is also a gap between Iran's expenditure and those of other regional powers. While Iran spent roughly $16,000 million on its military in 2016, Saudi Arabia spent around $57,000 million. See Gawdat Baghta and Anoushiravan Ehteshami, "Iran's Defense Strategy: The Navy, Ballistic Missiles and Cyberspace," *Middle East Policy* 24, 3 (2017): 90.

48 According to the World Bank data (provided by SIPRI), military expenditure as a percentage of GDP was at 5.9 percent in 1988, the final year of the Iran–Iraq War. After gradually declining to 1.73 percent in 1993, it began to rise again.

49 A comparison with the First Gulf War is illuminative. Despite strong US military presence in the region and rapid victory over Iraq, Tehran did not appear to be perturbed by these developments as Washington had not indicated any intention to use its military presence against the Iranian regime. Therefore, after the First Gulf War the share of military expenditure from Iran's GDP not only did not increase but also fell for three consecutive years (1991, 2.20 percent; 1992, 1.80 percent; 1993, 1.73 percent).

50 According to independent investigations, Iran is now a major exporter of arms to several countries including some in Africa. Although Iran closely guards its annual military export figures and customer identities, ten separate and independent

investigations have traced Iranian weapons and ammunition used by a variety of nonstate entities in Cote d'Ivoire, the Democratic Republic of the Congo, Guinea, Kenya, Niger, Nigeria, South Sudan, Sudan, and Uganda, not to mention primary beneficiaries such as Hizbollah in Lebanon and Iraqi Shia militias. Farzin Nadimi, "How Iran's Revived Weapons Exports Could Boost Its Proxies," *The Washington Institute*, 2015.

51 According to the CSIS Missile Defense Project, the number of missile launches and exercises by Iran significantly increased from the early 2000s onward, especially during the presidency of Mahmoud Ahmadinejad (2005–13). The pace of missile activities by Iran remained "roughly steady" for the past decade, with the only exception of a "brief hiatus in 2013–2014 during negotiations over Iran's nuclear program" (https://missilethreat.csis.org/iranian-missile-launches-1988-present/). Also see Gawdat Baghta and Anoushiravan Ehteshami, "Iran's Defense Strategy: The Navy, Ballistic Missiles and Cyberspace," *Middle East Policy* 24, 3 (2017): 95.

52 Despite Iranian leaders' claims that the nuclear technology was pursued for civilian purposes, the International Atomic Energy Agency's (IAEA) findings of Iran's research on nuclear explosive devices cast doubt on Iran's assertion of peaceful usage. See Kenneth Katzman, *Iran's Foreign and Defense Policies*, Congressional Research Service, 2018, 8. Although, Washington's threats do not account for the origin of Iran's nuclear program, threats of regime change since 2002 urged Tehran to insist on continuing its nuclear program despite international opposition. Shahram Chubin, *Iran's Nuclear Ambitions* (Washington, DC: Carnegie Endowment for International Peace, 2006), 16.

53 Ervand Abrahamian, *Tortured Confessions: Prisons and Public Recantations in Modern Iran* (Berkeley: University of California Press, 1999), chapter 5.

54 Kevan Harris, *A Social Revolution: Politics and the Welfare State in Iran* (Berkeley: University of California Press, 2017), 147.

55 For example, the supreme leader of Iran, Ayatollah Khamenei, called the 2009 uprisings in Iran a plot orchestrated by the United States and based on the model of "color revolutions" (Farsnews, Janury 9, 2015, www.farsnews.com/news /13941019000712/). See also Afshon Ostovar, *Vanguard of the Imam: Religion, Politics, and Iran's Revolutionary Guards* (New York: Oxford University Press, 2016): 188.

56 Ibid., 188–90.

57 International Monetary Fund, Selected Issues: Islamic Republic of Iran, 2017, 19. The rise of tax receipts above oil revenues took place for the first time in fifty years. See Saeed Kamali Dehghan, "Iran earns more from tax than oil for first time in almost 50 years," *The Guardian*, September 27, 2015.

58 https://data.worldbank.org/indicator/GC.TAX.YPKG.RV.ZS?end=2009&locations =IR&start=1974, https://data.worldbank.org/indicator/NY.GDP.PETR.RT.ZS?end= 2016&locations=IR&start=1974. In 1979, the last year of the Pahlavi monarchy, oil rents formed more than 30 percent of the country's GDP. But the share of oil in the government's budget went down to only 13 percent in 2016, the first year after the removal of sanctions, when Iran was once again allowed to sell its oil on the global markets.

59 Data on oil prices from: Elena Holodny, "Timeline: The Tumultuous 155-Year History of Oil Prices," *Business Insider*, December 20, 2016 (http://www.businessinsider.com/ timeline-155-year-history-of-oil-prices-2016-12).

60 Despite its factionalized character, an ideological consistency characterizes the top echelons of power in Iran. Moreover, decision making in the realms of security and

foreign policy has remained the prerogative of an exclusive circle of elite with close ties to the supreme leader. Therefore, ideological diversity among the regime's factions can hardly account for strategies that the regime adopted to tackle US threats during the first and second halves of the regime's lifespan.

61 According to Charles Tilly, representative institutions "were the price and outcome of bargaining with different members of the subject population for the wherewithal of state activity, especially the means of war." Charles Tilly, *Coercion, Capital, and European States, AD 990 – 1990* (Cambridge, MA: Basil Blackwell, 1990), 64.

12

The American Factor: US Diplomacy and the Trajectory of Iran's Nuclear Issue, 2003–15

Abolghasem Bayyenat

In July 2015, the five permanent members of the United Nations Security Council (UNSC) plus Germany, known as the P5+1, reached a historic agreement with Iran over its nuclear program. Known as the Joint Comprehensive Plan of Action (JCPOA), the agreement was signed almost thirteen years after Iran's nuclear program came into the international spotlight. Understanding why a long-term solution to the international dispute eluded negotiations and how it was finally achieved requires examining US policy toward Iran. Whether directly or indirectly involved in the negotiations, Washington was a key stakeholder and its positions influenced the chances of a resolution.

Given the dominant US position in the international system, many scholars and policy analysts have explained Iran's decisions to accept limitations on its nuclear program as products of US pressure and coercive diplomacy. From 2003 to 2005, Iranian president Mohammad Khatami faced a mounting American military presence on Iran's borders following the US invasions of Afghanistan and Iraq coupled with the threats of referral to the UNSC. Analysts assert that the combination of diplomatic and military pressure forced the Iranian leadership to temporarily cease its uranium enrichment program in arrangements negotiated with major European powers.[1] Ten years later, the rigorous US-led economic sanctions regime was credited with persuading Tehran to roll back the sensitive elements of its nuclear program with the JCPOA under president Rouhani after eight years of resistance.[2]

This chapter does not deny that pressure from Washington played an important role in persuading Iran to accept limitations on its nuclear program. After all, Tehran would have had little incentive to take any confidence-building measures with respect to its nuclear program in the absence of international demands and pressures. However, this chapter demonstrates that pressure alone was not sufficient to produce a long-term solution to Iran's nuclear issue. To date, little systematic attention has been paid to how America's diplomatic position prolonged and eventually contributed to the resolution of the dispute. To this end, this chapter argues that the United States' maximalist position prolonged the dispute over Iran's nuclear program. Rather, it was

Washington's pragmatic approach and recognition of Tehran's core nuclear rights that facilitated a resolution.

The Nature of the Nuclear Dispute

Washington's preoccupation with Iran's nuclear activities dates to the early 1980s. The International Atomic Energy Agency (IAEA) and US officials were not only aware of Iran's interest and efforts in obtaining nuclear fuel cycle technologies and materials, but the United States was also vigorously involved in thwarting Iran's lawful nuclear procurements both within and without the IAEA. Throughout the 1980s and 1990s, the US government effectively blocked the transfer of technologies and materials associated with uranium conversion and enrichment as well as fuel fabrication and plutonium processing by Russia, China, Argentina, and other countries to Iran.[3] By the early 1990s, US intelligence officials believed that Iran's nuclear program was geared toward developing nuclear weapons capability. They publicly accused Iran of pursuing a covert nuclear weapons program.[4] These concerns were echoed by the US media outlets. In addition, leading think tanks debated the implications of a nuclear-armed Iran for US interests in the region. Israeli prime ministers Yitzhak Rabin and Benjamin Netanyahu also warned the United States and other Western countries during this period that Iran was only a few years away from building a nuclear weapon. Israel was also advocating the use of military force against Iranian nuclear installations.[5]

Yet what transformed Iran's nuclear program into a matter of critical importance and concern for the United States and other Western powers since early 2003 was the extent of Iran's success in developing its nuclear fuel cycle infrastructure despite draconian technical and political measures blocking its access to any sensitive, though lawful, nuclear technologies throughout the 1980s and 1990s.[6] In November 2004, the IAEA concluded "Iran has conducted experiments to acquire the know-how for almost every aspect of the fuel cycle. Iran's current nuclear program, as the Agency understands it, is aimed, upon completion, at an independent front end of the nuclear fuel cycle, including uranium mining and milling, conversion, enrichment, fuel fabrication, a light water reactor, heavy water production, a heavy water research reactor and associated R&D facilities."[7] These revelations prompted Washington to revise its previous intelligence assessments about Iran's uranium enrichment program as well as its plutonium path to nuclear energy.[8]

Although the IAEA found no evidence of the diversion of Iran's nuclear program for military purposes, Tehran's failure to report the import of nuclear materials and its subsequent microscale experiments with them, or what the IAEA characterized as the "practice of concealment,"[9] documented in various agency reports since June 2003, turned Iran's nuclear program into a matter of international concern. These developments were sufficient cause for world powers to demand indefinite suspension of Iran's nascent uranium enrichment program as well as ongoing work on its heavy-water nuclear research reactor. They also called on Tehran to adopt the optional Additional Protocol to the Nuclear Non-Proliferation Treaty (NPT). From 2003 to

2012, twelve resolutions by the IAEA Board of Governors and six UNSC resolutions on Iran's nuclear program gave legal weight to these political demands.

Since 2002, the international dispute over Iran's nuclear program reflected the efforts and demands spearheaded by the United States and its European allies to put an end to Iran's nascent nuclear fuel cycle program and Tehran's insistence on its rights under the NPT to develop peaceful nuclear technologies. The US and European powers maintained that an indigenous nuclear fuel cycle capability would bring Iran closer to the nuclear weapons threshold and increase the proliferation risks in the region. The vast majority of American officials of all partisan affiliations as well as nonpartisan policy experts viewed a nuclear-armed Iran as a grave challenge to US interests in the Middle East, the nuclear nonproliferation regime, and the security of Israel.[10] Preventing this scenario was considered the highest priority for US policy toward Iran.[11]

Although Iranian political elites rejected the pursuit of nuclear weapons on both strategic and religious grounds, they regarded an indigenous nuclear fuel cycle capability as essential for the country's energy independence and scientific and technological development. Some of them also believed that it would serve as a virtual nuclear deterrence since it would give Iran the option to produce fissile materials for a nuclear weapon relatively quickly, if circumstances so required.[12] Furthermore, Iranian political elites argued that relinquishing their national right to peaceful nuclear technology was contrary to the principles of justice and political independence as the main pillars of the collective identity of postrevolutionary Iran.[13] The outcome of this conflict was determined in large parts by how these two opposing perspectives interacted and shaped international and domestic political realities over Iran's nuclear issue.

US Maximalist Demands and Iran's Minimalist Cooperation, 2003–5

After the revelations of Iran's plans for the development of a commercial-scale uranium enrichment program in 2003, US officials accused Iran of pursuing a covert nuclear weapons program. Much of the initial US efforts, spearheaded by John Bolton, the undersecretary of state for Arms Control and International Security, during this period was aimed at persuading the international community that Iran's nuclear program was a cover for developing nuclear arms by linking its past nuclear activities to weaponization. Despite the IAEA's testimony to the absence of any evidence pointing to the diversion of Iran's nuclear activities to military purposes, the George W. Bush administration interpreted Iran's past secrecy in conducting some of its nuclear procurements and research and development activities on nuclear fuel cycle technology as indicative of its military intent. Also, to make the case that the only rationale for Iran's extensive uranium enrichment program was to provide the foundations for a nuclear weapons program, US officials tried to debunk Iran's case for energy independence and its economic justifications for the development of a nuclear fuel cycle program. Notwithstanding the wholehearted US support for the shah's ambitious nuclear program on economic grounds from the 1950s through the 1970s,[14] American policymakers argued that Iran's miniscule known domestic natural uranium reserves could not support a single nuclear power plant for its lifetime much less save substantial amounts of oil and gas for export or make Iran independent in its nuclear energy needs.[15]

Washington's efforts to delegitimize Iran's nuclear activities were intended to build international support for demanding an end to Iran's nascent uranium enrichment program and imposing a more intrusive and rigorous inspection regime on its nuclear program. In dealing with Iran, US officials explicitly sought to replicate the Libyan model, whereby Iran would accept to dismantle its nuclear fuel cycle program and relinquish all its sensitive nuclear activities for good. Washington justified these demands by arguing that Iran's past failures in reporting its nuclear activities to the IAEA, or what they claimed to be its noncompliance with its safeguards obligations, stripped it of its rights under the NPT.[16] The US strategy of mounting international pressure on Iran to give up the sensitive elements of its nuclear program and accept a more intrusive inspection regime appeared to be founded on two main pillars: building the legal case within the IAEA for referral of Iran to the UNSC; and developing international consensus and a broad coalition against Iran's nuclear program.

From the outset, the United States advocated for the IAEA to determine that Iran was not compliant with its obligations and trigger a referral to the UNSC. In addition, American officials repeatedly raised the specter of referring Iran to the UNSC whenever new evidence of Iran's past failures was released in the IAEA's periodic reports or when Tehran dragged its feet in maintaining a comprehensive suspension of its nuclear fuel cycle activities as part of its arrangements with the foreign ministers of Britain, France, and Germany (known as the EU3).[17]

On September 12, 2003, the IAEA Board denounced Iran's past failures and called on Tehran to "suspend all further uranium enrichment-related activities" until the peaceful nature of its nuclear program was established and for Iran to adopt and implement the NPT's Additional Protocol. The IAEA's deadline for Tehran's compliance was the end of October 2003.[18] On October 21, 2003, Iran opted to defuse the international crisis by promising to provide full transparency on its past nuclear activities, apply the Additional Protocol, and temporarily suspend its pilot-scale uranium enrichment activities at Natanz in an agreement with the EU3.[19] Iran's decision to cooperate reflected in large part its deteriorated regional security environment in the aftermath of the September 11, 2001 attacks and Washington's Global War on Terror.[20] Although it was cooperative with the United States in the toppling of the Taliban regime in Afghanistan and played a pivotal role in the country's postconflict political transition, Iran was included in President Bush's "Axis of Evil" and came under mounting political pressures by Washington for allegedly supporting terrorism and pursuing weapons of mass destruction.

Despite pressure from Washington, Tehran was not willing to commit to a permanent cessation or even a long-term suspension, much less dismantling, of its nuclear fuel cycle program. Hassan Rouhani, the secretary of Iran's Supreme National Security Council under the reformist president Mohammad Khatami, who led Iran's nuclear negotiations with the EU3 from early 2003 to August 2005, emphasized in numerous encounters with his European interlocutors that Iran considered uranium enrichment its inalienable right under the NPT and that any suspension would be of a "voluntary" and "temporary" nature.[21]

Contrary to the expectations of the United States and the EU3, Iran also adhered to a minimalist definition of the scope of its voluntary uranium enrichment suspension. This became a matter of contention with its European interlocutors, and the cause for multiple resolutions against Iran by the IAEA Board. The EU3 asserted that suspension covered a ban on all activities related to uranium enrichment at its various stages, including the very act of introducing nuclear materials into centrifuges, production of feedstock for enrichment, and even the manufacture and assembly of centrifuge components. However, Tehran subscribed to a conventional understanding of suspension, which was limited only to the first type of restraint. Thus, Iran continued the manufacture and assembly of centrifuges for several months after the Tehran declaration and briefly operated its uranium conversion factory at Esfahan to produce feed material for enrichment. Tehran eventually adopted a comprehensive suspension in new arrangements agreed with the EU3 in February 2004 and more notably under the Paris Agreement in November 2004.[22]

From November 2004 to August 2005, Iran maintained an expansive suspension while engaging in negotiations with the EU3 for a comprehensive nuclear deal. Although it was initially wary of Iran's intention to live up to its promises, Washington did not oppose the EU's involvement as long as Iran upheld its suspension promise and implemented the Additional Protocol. The United States became more supportive of the EU3's nuclear negotiations with Iran after the Paris Agreement. As part of its support for the European diplomatic engagement with Iran, the United States lifted its opposition to the consideration of Iran's application for accession to the World Trade Organization and relaxed its ban on the sale of spare parts for civilian aircraft to Iran in May 2005.[23]

However, the US maximalist position left no room for the EU3 to strike a long-term deal with Iran. Tehran's ability to sustain a comprehensive suspension was compromised by both the EU3's inflexibility and growing domestic opposition to continuing the suspension in light of the control of Iran's parliament by conservative political forces. Iran tabled multiple negotiating offers from March 2005 through July 2005, proposing to phase out the resumption of its uranium enrichment activities and provide technical assurances that its nuclear program would not be diverted to military purposes.[24] Tehran was willing to continue the suspension for six more months and thereafter maintain a small pilot-scale uranium enrichment program for a prolonged duration before embarking upon a commercial-scale program. However, the European powers were unwilling to accept a nuclear fuel cycle program of any scale.[25] Instead, the EU3's August 2005 proposal provided for an indefinite cessation of Iran's enrichment activities in return for the promise of a secured nuclear fuel supply and the prospect of economic cooperation with Tehran. As Peter Jenkins, the British ambassador to the IAEA during this period noted, the EU3 failed to fully realize in 2005 "that Iran was not prepared to give up enrichment as the price of a settlement." "We believed that if we could come up with sufficient incentives and scare Iran with the threat of referral to the Security Council, they would give in," Jenkins recalled.[26]

The EU3's insistence on an indefinite suspension marked the collapse of the nuclear talks. On August 8, 2005, Iran resumed the operation of the Uranium Conversion Facility at Esfahan. In response, the EU3 halted their negotiations with Tehran. With President Mahmoud Ahmadinejad in office and Washington's maximalist negotiating strategy, Iran and the United States entered a new phase of confrontation on the nuclear issue that lasted for eight years.

US Maximalist Demands Meet Iran's Maximalist Resistance, 2005–8

With negotiations at an impasse, the pressing issue for the United States and its European allies was to convince Tehran to reestablish comprehensive suspension of all its uranium enrichment-related activities. In its September 24, 2005, resolution, the IAEA Board declared that Iran was not complying with its commitments under the NPT and raised the prospect of a referral to the UNSC.[27] The United States and the EU3 were hoping that the threat of imminent referral to the UNSC would be sufficient to compel Tehran's cooperation. However, Iran upped the ante and resumed its uranium enrichment research and development activities at its Natanz pilot plant in January 2006. This action prompted the EU3 to call for an extraordinary meeting of the IAEA Board. Less than a month later, the United States was successful in convincing other members of the IAEA Board, including Russia, to refer Iran's nuclear case to the UNSC.[28]

As in the previous period, the United States defined the goal as preventing Iran from developing not only nuclear weapons but also any technologies and knowledge that would give it the option to build nuclear arms. On April 10, 2006, President Bush declared, "We do not want the Iranians to have a nuclear weapon, the capacity to make a nuclear weapon, or the knowledge as to how to make a nuclear weapon."[29] Thus, a uranium enrichment program of any scale (including a pilot-scale research and development program) and any enrichment-related and reprocessing activities were to be opposed as they could potentially allow Iran to master the process of producing fissile materials for a nuclear weapon.

For American policymakers, diplomacy had entered a new phase. Despite frequently emphasizing that all options, including, if necessary, the use of military force, were on the table, Bush administration officials insisted that there was time, and a high probability, that diplomacy would solve Iran's nuclear issue. The administration offered to directly participate with the EU3, Russia, and China, in the newly constituted P5+1 group, in nuclear negotiations with Iran, if Tehran agreed to resume the suspension of uranium enrichment.[30] This tactical shift in US policy was aimed to boost the credibility of the incentives and commitments in the eyes of Iranians by making Washington a party to the talks.[31] Indeed, some Iranian political elites blamed the failure of the talks with the EU3 on Washington's absence from the negotiations. In June 2006, the P5+1 led by Washington, offered Tehran a package of incentives, embodied in a proposed framework for a comprehensive nuclear agreement. The proposed package envisaged the prospects of technical assistance in the civil nuclear field as well as cooperation in various economic and technological fields if Iran reestablished and maintained its suspension of uranium enrichment and reprocessing activities and resumed implementation of the Additional Protocol during the course of negotiations for a comprehensive nuclear deal.[32]

The proposed packages failed to convince Tehran to repeat its earlier experience of voluntary confidence building with the EU3, but strengthened Washington's efforts to mobilize international support for imposing economic sanctions on Iran. Led by the United States, the UNSC passed five resolutions against Iran, three of which imposed targeted sanctions against its nuclear activities, ballistic missile development, and other arms procurements and exports. These resolutions also included provisions authorizing financial measures against Iranian trade that were of a nonbinding nature.[33] Although these multilateral economic sanctions were not mandatory, they paved the way for more coercive unilateral economic measures against Iran by the United States and other Western powers. Washington used this newly gained international legitimacy to ratchet up painful economic pressure on Iran.

The Bush administration closed off the access of several major Iranian banks to the US financial system due to their alleged "support for terrorism and Iran's proliferation activities."[34] Moreover, US officials also vigorously lobbied Iran's major trade partners, international financial agencies, and private firms to apply similar financial restrictions against the Iranian government and financial institutions and to curtail their businesses in Iran. In addition, Washington convinced major European countries and Japan to reduce their loans and export credits to Iran[35] while also pressuring the leading European banks, including HSBC, Commerzbank, and Credit Suisse, to cut their financial transactions with Iranian banks.[36] In October 2007, the Financial Action Task Force, the world's standard-setting body for anti–money laundering and counterterrorism financing, declared Iran a country of risk for financial business, further deterring private financial firms from doing business with Iran.[37] Less than a year later, the EU also sanctioned a number of Iranian entities and imposed an asset freeze on Iran's largest state-owned bank, Bank Melli.[38]

In parallel with these economic and financial measures, Washington also pursued other avenues of pressure against Iran. Two aircraft carrier battle groups were stationed in the Persian Gulf while augmenting US security assurances to Arab states in the Persian Gulf region.[39] The Bush administration also augmented its efforts for regime change in Iran. While declaring that "freedom is on the march in the broader Middle East," Bush announced in February 2006 that he had requested $75 million in emergency funds from the US Congress to help the Iranian people to "win their own freedom" and "organize and challenge the repressive policies of the clerical regime."[40] The Bush administration used these funds to strengthen Iranian opposition groups and dissident civil society organizations in collaboration with international nongovernmental organizations and to support opposition radio and television broadcastings into Iran.[41]

Furthermore, US policymakers thought that even if the referral of Iran to the UNSC was not effective enough to bring a change in its course on the nuclear path, the rising pains of the economic sanctions would force it to do so. Unlike North Korea, the Bush administration asserted that Iran does not want and cannot afford to be isolated from the international community, since its economy is heavily integrated into the international economy and its people are connected with the world.[42] With foreign investment in Iran's oil and gas sector coming to a near halt, the country's public revenues would gradually decline, thus putting the Iranian government on the brink of a budget crisis.[43] American officials maintained that, sooner or later, some Iranian elites would conclude that their current path was too costly and would push for a change in Iran's nuclear policy.[44]

However, these hopes were not realized during Bush's term. Instead, Iran minimized its cooperation with the IAEA by immediately suspending its voluntary application of the Additional Protocol and other nonbinding IAEA inspection procedures. By the time Bush left office in January 2009, Iran had installed 5,537 centrifuges at the Fuel Enrichment Plant at Natanz, had mastered enrichment with a 3,000-centrifuge unit, and had produced 1,010 kg of low-enriched uranium, while also conducting research and development activities on a more advanced generation of centrifuges.[45]

Why wasn't the Bush administration's strategy successful? The first main political constraint the Bush administration encountered was the reluctance of other members of the UNSC, namely Russia and China, to join it in adopting crippling economic and financial sanctions on Iran. While Moscow and Beijing supported US efforts in imposing forceful targeted sanctions against Iran's nuclear and ballistic missile programs, they only consented to nonbinding economic and financial sanctions. In the absence of mandatory multilateral economic and financial sanctions, not all of Iran's trade partners were willing to sever relations with Tehran and follow the United States' unilateral sanctions. For example, Chinese-Iranian trade experienced a significant boost over this period.[46]

International energy market realities were another constraint on Washington's policy. Crude oil prices remained elevated throughout this period and reached their record peak of over $161 per barrel in June 2008. Any drastic cut in the world's petroleum supply by shutting off Iran's oil exports would have led to an even more dramatic increase in oil prices with serious implications for the world economy. This largely explains why the United States did not seriously consider sanctioning Iran's oil exports and contented itself with curtailing foreign investment in Iran's energy sector as it would have a more gradual and incremental impact on the world oil supply.

Finally, the US maximalist position did not serve Washington's goal of denying Iran the option to build nuclear weapons. Iran was willing to accept limitations on the scale of its uranium enrichment program and not embark upon a commercial-scale nuclear fuel cycle program for a long transition period but in the absence of such an agreement it felt free to expand its program within two and a half years.[47] As Scott Sagan has noted, "Allowing Tehran to maintain its experimental 164-centrifuge cascade, which poses no immediate danger and yet is an important status symbol for the Iranian regime, could help Tehran save face and sell a deal with Washington to its domestic constituencies by allowing it to claim that the arrangement protects Iran's 'sovereign right' to have a full nuclear fuel cycle."[48] It would take another four years and a new American as well as Iranian president before Sagan's advice was realized.

US Maximalist Pressures Meet Iran's Maximalist Resistance, 2009–13

Many observers expected that US policy toward the Iranian nuclear issue would undergo a significant shift under Obama. During the 2008 presidential campaign as well as his early months in office, Obama had advocated serious engagement with Iran on the nuclear issue without self-defeating preconditions attached. Upon taking office, he sent two private letters to Iran's supreme leader proposing direct negotiations between the two countries on the nuclear issue. The United States also became a full participant in the P5+1 nuclear talks with Iran as a notable shift from the Bush administration's insistence on suspension of uranium enrichment activities by Iran as a precondition for American participation in the negotiations. However, it did not take long for Obama's Iran policy to mirror that of the Bush administration: pressure coupled with a veneer of engagement.

The Obama administration initially sought partial confidence-building agreements with Tehran, thinking that such arrangements would create momentum and time for reaching a long-lasting solution to the nuclear issue.[49] However, such efforts proved short-lived and half-hearted. Popular protests in Iran after the disputed June 2009 presidential elections and Iran's disclosure of its backup uranium enrichment facility near Qom in September 2009 exacerbated the already negative political climate for engagement with Iran in the United States and its European allies. This predisposed American policymakers, who were already more invested in the pressure track, to prematurely abandon efforts to reach a partial confidence-building arrangement with Iran over a nuclear fuel swap deal in 2009 and early 2010.[50]

While partial confidence-building initiatives faced unfavorable chances for success during Obama's first term, there were even far more daunting challenges to reaching a long-term comprehensive solution to the nuclear issue. Obama's foreign policy team essentially adhered to the Bush administration's negotiating mantra that the endgame of any nuclear engagement must be an indefinite suspension of Iran's nuclear fuel cycle activities as demanded by the UNSC and the IAEA. There were no indications that Washington would be willing to accept a limited uranium enrichment program in Iran during Obama's first term. Instead, the dominant conviction among Obama's foreign policy team was that with unprecedented pressure, it was only a matter of time before Tehran returned to the negotiating table and acceded to US demands. Like Bush, Obama believed that all that was required was time for the increased pressure on Iran to sink in.[51]

The Obama administration initiated its pressure campaign by proposing a UNSC resolution that would impose tough sanctions against Iran. Iran's initial wavering in acceding to a confidence-building arrangement with the United States, coupled with the disclosure of its backup under-construction enrichment facility in September 2009 and its decision to enrich uranium to 20 percent level in February 2010, though all permissible under the NPT, helped the United States immensely to garner international support for a sanctions resolution. Adopted in June 2009, UNSC Resolution 1929 imposed a set of binding and nonbinding sanctions targeting

Iran's arms procurements, ballistic missile development, shipping services, and its international financial relations. Although the resolution fell short of imposing the "biting" sanctions desired by Washington, due to Chinese and Russian objections, it paved the way for more rigorous unilateral sanctions by the United States and its allies against Tehran.[52]

From 2010 to early 2013, Washington broadened and deepened its preexisting unilateral sanctions against Iran while also adopting new measures. The US sanctions regime, developed and rigorously enforced over this period, targeted Iran's energy, financial, and shipping sectors. These measures were primarily intended to crack down on Iran's export revenues by hindering much-needed foreign investment in the country's energy sector, disrupting the sale and delivery of Iran's energy products, and financial transactions. Also, US officials hoped that by reigning in Tehran's major sources of revenues and cutting Iran off from the global economy, Iranian officials "would have no choice but to come back to the negotiating table with a serious offer" that would meet US demands.[53] The Obama administration also launched a "worldwide diplomatic campaign" aimed at encouraging and warning foreign governments, private energy companies, and financial institutions to sever their business ties with Iran.[54] This led a number of major foreign energy companies, shipping agencies, and banks to end their business ties with Tehran.[55]

The most dramatic and unprecedented measure came in December 2011 when Obama signed legislation requiring Iran's oil customers to significantly reduce their oil imports from Iran in six-month intervals, with the goal of bringing their oil purchases ultimately to nil. The US government embarked on a global diplomatic offensive urging Iran's trade partners to find alternative sources for their oil imports, while encouraging other leading oil exporters to increase production to stabilize the world petroleum market.[56] The Obama administration was assisted in this campaign by a surge in the United States' own domestic oil production. Former secretary of state Hillary Clinton explained, "As American domestic oil and gas production increased dramatically, thanks to new technologies and exploration, our energy imports plummeted. This took pressure off the global market and made it easier to exclude Iran, as other nations could rely on the supply America no longer required."[57]

As a result of these measures, eleven European countries and nine Asian nations importing Iranian oil significantly cut their oil purchases in 2012.[58] In January 2012, the EU imposed a total ban on the import of oil and petrochemical products from Iran while also ordering a freeze on the Iranian central bank's assets within the jurisdiction of all its twenty-seven member states.[59] The sanctions cut Iran's crude oil exports by 1.5 million barrels per day leading to a nearly $52 billion downfall in Iran's export revenues within a year.[60] The drastic cut in Iran's export revenues not only affected Iran's oil-dependent public budget, including the government's development expenditures, and pushed Iran's economic growth rate in the negative, but also had a destabilizing effect on Iran's national currency by substantially reducing the supply of foreign exchange into the Iranian market. Iranian currency experienced a sharp depreciation in 2012 and early 2013, losing nearly 60 percent of its value over this period. The weaker currency in turn exacerbated the already high inflation in Iran bringing it up to 35 percent in 2013.[61] While the rigorous US-led sanctions were not the only cause of Iran's dismal economic performance, they visibly had a major role in intensifying Iran's economic troubles over this period.

Despite its success in inflicting indiscriminate economic pain on both the government and civilian population of Iran, the sweeping US economic sanctions failed to produce any tangible political gains during this period. Iran not only refused to suspend its uranium enrichment program and other sensitive nuclear activities, but it completed the construction of its backup enrichment facility near Qom and upgraded its uranium enrichment to 20-percent level, all while substantially expanding its nuclear fuel cycle infrastructure. Iran augmented the number of its installed centrifuges from 5,537 in early 2009 to over 19,000 in late summer of 2013 before Rouhani took office. Similarly, Iran's stockpile of low-enriched uranium (LEU) dramatically increased from 1,010 kg to 10,357 kg over the same period while also producing 410 kg of 20-percent enriched uranium.[62]

Iran also stood its ground in the nuclear negotiations with the P5+1 and refused to suspend its uranium enrichment activities through the last round of talks in April 2013.[63] The back-channel bilateral talks between Washington and Tehran in Muscat, Oman, launched by Omani sultan Qaboos in July 2012, were also unsuccessful.[64] American diplomacy in Obama's first term, like the Bush era, lacked a willingness to accept a limited nuclear fuel cycle program in Iran. With the coming to power of a moderate president in August 2013 in Iran, the stage was set for pragmatic leniency by the United States and "heroic flexibility" by Iran.

US Pragmatism Meets Iran's "Heroic Flexibility," 2013–15

With Rouhani in office, American officials realized that the chances of achieving a comprehensive long-term nuclear deal with Iran were favorable. Rouhani ran on the platform of removing economic sanctions on Iran and improving the economic conditions of all Iranians while questioning the nuclear diplomacy of his predecessor for being imprudent and inflexible. Obama's foreign policy team thought that this was perhaps the best time when the formidable economic sanctions architecture, painstakingly erected over many years by two American administrations, could be translated more effectively into political leverage at the negotiating table. Furthermore, ten years of maximalist nuclear demands from Iran backed up by unprecedentedly rigorous economic sanctions, military threats, covert sabotage operations against Iranian nuclear facilities, and even assassination of key Iranian nuclear scientists, allegedly sponsored by Israeli intelligence, had failed to stem the tide of Iran's nuclear progress.

Convinced that implementing even more stringent sanctions on Tehran would not compel it to give up its nuclear fuel cycle program, American officials opted for a more realistic negotiating outcome that would constrain rather than dismantle Iran's nuclear program. To prepare the grounds for a nuclear compromise at home that would substantially roll back Iran's nuclear program, the Obama administration's foreign policy discourse shifted from denying Iran "nuclear weapons capability" to expanding the "breakout time" on Iran's nuclear program.[65] The goal was no longer eliminating Iran's capacity and knowledge to produce fissile materials for potential nuclear weapons, but to create a safe distance between a possible decision to dash toward nuclear weapons and actual weaponization by Iran. This was in recognition of the fact that it was neither technically nor politically feasible to eliminate Iran's nuclear fuel cycle expertise and technology.[66]

Because reaching a comprehensive nuclear deal would require sustained and intensive negotiations, Obama's foreign policy team sought to freeze the expansion of Iran's nuclear program while negotiations for a long-term deal were underway by exploring a confidence-building agreement with Iran.[67] This was achieved with the Joint Plan of Action (JPA) or the interim nuclear deal, reached in November 2013.[68] The JPA defined the contours of a final nuclear deal and assigned specific confidence-building tasks for the parties for an initial duration of six months. Most important, Iran agreed to freeze the expansion of the most sensitive elements of its nuclear program while the United States and other parties undertook not to impose any new nuclear-related sanctions on Iran and allow Iran's oil exports to continue at their current level.[69] More notably for Iran, the JPA also recognized that the final nuclear deal "would involve a mutually defined enrichment programme with practical limits and transparency measures" for Iran.[70]

Agreement over a comprehensive nuclear deal proved far more elusive than anticipated by nuclear negotiators. It took the Iranian and the P5+1 nuclear negotiators approximately sixteen months after the JPA was adopted to reach consensus on the outline or key parameters of the final nuclear deal in April 2015 and another several months to finally cement the historic JCPOA. The JCPOA[71] imposed major long-term restrictions on Iran's nuclear program including, reducing its uranium enrichment capacity by two-thirds to around six thousand centrifuges, removing its existing stockpile of nearly ten metric tons of LEU, and prohibiting it from accumulating any significant amount of LEU for fifteen years.

In return for these concessions, Iran ostensibly gained relief from nearly all multilateral and national "nuclear-related" economic sanctions, including international restrictions on foreign investment in its oil and gas sectors, limitations on its oil exports, and most banking and financial restrictions. As a result of this agreement, Iran's nuclear issue was also virtually removed from the agenda of the UNSC as a threat to international peace and security and Iran was authorized to maintain a limited uranium enrichment program, subject to various restrictions, for a transitional period of ten to fifteen years before entering a state of normalcy under the NPT.

Following intensive domestic political debates and deliberations, Iranian authorities officially adopted the JCPOA in September 2015 and the IAEA has since regularly verified Iran's compliance by its commitments. Several factors facilitated the adoption of the JCPOA by Iranian authorities and helped build the necessary political support for the nuclear deal and contain domestic opposition to it among the elites and the public. The leading factor was the face-saving nature of the agreement, which was enabled by a pragmatic shift in US policy toward the nuclear issue during Obama's second term. The Obama administration's departure from Bush's zero-enrichment policy toward Iran's nuclear program or its willingness to accept a limited uranium enrichment program in Iran enabled Iranian leaders to sell the nuclear deal as a win to their constituencies.

Iranian leaders were able, at least temporarily, to frame the nuclear deal as a diplomatic success for Iran. They juxtaposed the negotiating gains under the JCPOA against Western powers' refusal to accept even a single operating centrifuge in Iran during the EU3 talks from 2003 to 2005 as well as their insistence on zero enrichment in Iran throughout the following decade. In several of his speeches following the adoption of the JCPOA, Khamenei used the 2003–5 negotiations with the European powers as a historical reference point against which he evaluated Iran's negotiating gains and justified its concessions under the JCPOA.[72] In a speech on January 20, 2016, Khamenei stated that "once, the enemies were not willing to tolerate even a single nuclear centrifuge in Iran and now they have been forced, due to the realities on the ground, to accept several thousand operating centrifuges in Iran. This is not their favor to us but the result of our own struggle and the efforts of our scientists."[73]

Conclusion

As a major party and stakeholder to the international dispute over Iran's nuclear program, US diplomacy had a disproportional influence on the direction of this international dispute. Viewing Iran's nuclear program as a cover for the pursuit of nuclear weapons and overlooking other important motives behind Iran's quest for nuclear technology put Washington on the path of coercive diplomacy toward Tehran. Relying on coercive policies including mainly the threat of, and eventually the actual referral of, Iran to the UNSC, raising the option of military force, and economic strangulation through crippling sanctions, the United States sought to raise the costs of Iran's nuclear policy and change its "strategic calculus" to realize its maximalist demands on the nuclear issue. Not fully anticipating Iran's higher tolerance threshold for economic and security costs, in the absence of other necessary conditions, US coercive diplomacy failed to significantly impede the progress of Iran's nuclear program or persuade Tehran to accept long-term restrictions on its nuclear activities.

Therefore, while US economic pressure created the necessary incentives for a nuclear compromise by Tehran, Washington's maximalist position played a major part in squandering earlier opportunities for the resolution of the nuclear issue and unnecessarily prolonging the dispute. Obama's pragmatic flexibility ultimately paved the way for the settlement of this long-running international standoff. Granted that the empowerment of moderate political forces in Iran led by Rouhani, and Iran's dismal economic conditions exacerbated by the US-led sanctions, among other variables, all contributed to the settlement of Iran's nuclear issue, but in the absence of the US pragmatism in accepting a limited nuclear fuel cycle program in Iran this international conflict would have most likely lingered on now and for the foreseeable future. Indeed, under the Donald Trump administration it has returned.

With the successful conclusion and implementation of the JCPOA, a long-running international dispute, which had the potential to lead to another catastrophic military conflict in the Middle East, was peacefully resolved. With the return of the United States to its time-tested maximalist position on Iran's nuclear issue under the Trump administration and its controversial withdrawal from the JCPOA in May 2018, the future of the agreement is at serious risk. It remains to be seen whether the remaining parties will be able to salvage the nuclear deal. Yet the significance of this exercise in international diplomacy cannot be overstated for the nuclear nonproliferation regime and regional and international peace and stability.

Notes

1 For example, see Shahram Chubin, *Iran's Nuclear Ambitions* (Washington, DC: Carnegie Endowment for International Peace, 2006), 22; and Elliot Abrams and Robert Wexler, "Attacking Iran's Nuclear Project: Two Views," *World Affairs* 175, 1 (May–June 2012): 34.

2 For example, see Richard Nephew, *The Art of Sanctions: A View from the Field* (New York: Columbia University Press, 2018); and Farhad Rezaei, "Sanctions and Nuclear Rollback: The Case of Iran," *Middle East Policy*, 24, 4 (Winter 2017).

3 Gareth Porter, *Manufactured Crisis: The Untold Story of the Iran Nuclear Scare* (Charlottesville, VA: Just World Books, 2014), 26–57; Kori Schake and Judith Yaphe, "The Strategic Implications of a Nuclear-armed Iran," *Institute for National Strategic Studies*, National Defense University, May 2001, 11–21; Michael Eisenstadt, "Living with a Nuclear-Armed Iran," *Survival* 41, 3 (1999): 14; Colin Dueck and Ray Takeyh, "Iran's Nuclear Challenge," *Political Science Quarterly* 122, 2 (2007): 190.

4 Porter, *Manufactured Crisis*, 91, 106.

5 Ibid., 113–14, 132–3.

6 Ray Takeyh, "Iran's Nuclear Calculations," *World Policy Journal* 20, 2 (Summer 2003): 21.

7 IAEA, "Implementation of the NPT Safeguards Agreement in the Islamic Republic of Iran: Report by the Director General," (GOV/2004/83), November 15, 2004.

8 Dueck and Takeyh, "Iran's Nuclear Challenge," 191.

9 Iranian officials maintained that they had no choice but to pursue some of their nuclear procurements in secret since publicizing them would have allowed the United States and other Western powers to disrupt their purchases and peaceful nuclear cooperation with other countries, given the past record of the US government in contravening the provisions of the NPT by blocking Iran's lawful and peaceful nuclear procurements from various countries as well as its request for technical assistance from the IAEA itself. See Mohamed Elbaradei, *The Age of Deception: Nuclear Diplomacy in Treacherous Times* (New York: Metropolitan Books, 2011), 119; Porter, *Manufactured Crisis*, 41.

10 For a representative official American view of the risks of a nuclear-armed Iran and an Iran with the capacity to produce fissile materials for a potential nuclear bomb, see Robert G. Joseph, "Iran's Nuclear Program," Statement Before the House International Relations Committee, *U.S. Department of State*, March 8, 2006, https://2001-2009.state.gov/t/us/rm/63121.htm; Nicholas Burns, "Interview with CNN Moscow Correspondent Matthew Chance," *U.S. Department of State*, February 21, 2006, https://2001-2009.state.gov/p/us/rm/2006/61847.htm; and Barack Obama, "Remarks by the President at AIPAC Policy Conference," *The White House*,

March 4, 2012, https://obamawhitehouse.archives.gov/the-press-office/2012/03/04/remarks-president-aipac-policy-conference-0.

11 For a sample of American policy think tanks' perceptions of a nuclear-armed Iran, see Eric Edelman, Andrew Krepinevich and Evan Montgomery, "The Dangers of a Nuclear Iran: The Limits of Containment," *Foreign Affairs* 90, 1 (2011); Eisenstadt, "Living with a Nuclear-Armed Iran"; and Schake and Yaphe, "The Strategic Implications of a Nuclear-armed Iran."

12 Seyed Hossein Mousavian, *The Iranian Nuclear Crisis: A Memoir* (Washington, DC: Carnegie Endowment for International Peace, 2012), 14.

13 Homeira Moshirzadeh, "Discursive Foundations of Iran's Nuclear Policy," *Security Dialogue* 38, 4 (2007).

14 For an analysis of the historical role of the United States and other Western powers in the development of Iran's nuclear program from the 1950s to the late 1970s see Mustafa Kibaroğlu, "Iran's Nuclear Ambitions from a Historical Perspective and the Attitude of the West," *Middle Eastern Studies* 43, 2 (March 2007).

15 John R. Bolton, "U.S. Efforts to Stop the Spread of Weapons of Mass Destruction," Testimony before the House International Relations Committee, *U.S. Department of State*, June 4, 2003, https://2001-2009.state.gov/t/us/rm/21247.htm; John R. Bolton, "The Bush Administration's Nonproliferation Policy: Successes and Future Challenges," Testimony Before the House International Relations Committee, *U.S. Department of State*, March 30, 2004, https://2001-2009.state.gov/t/us/rm/31029.htm.

16 Nicholas Burns, "Interview with Voice of America Persian Service," June 6, 2005, *U.S. Department of State*, https://2001-2009.state.gov/p/us/rm/2005/47894.htm; Bolton, "U.S. Efforts."

17 For example see Paula A. DeSutter, "Iranian WMD and Support of Terrorism," Testimony Before the US-Israeli Joint Parliamentary Committee, *U.S. Department of State*, September 17, 2003, https://2001-2009.state.gov/t/vci/rls/rm/24494.htm; Colin L. Powell, "Interview by The Washington Post," *U.S. Department of State*, October 3, 2003, https://2001-2009.state.gov/secretary/former/powell/remarks/2003/25139.htm; John R. Bolton, "The New World After Iraq: The Continuing Threat of Weapons of Mass Destruction," Remarks to the Bruges Group; London, UK, *U.S. Department of State*, October 30, 2003, https://2001-2009.state.gov/t/us/rm/25752.htm; Bolton, "Bush Administration"; John R. Bolton, "Iran's Continuing Pursuit of Weapons of Mass Destruction," Testimony Before the House International Relations Committee Subcommittee on the Middle East and Central Asia, *U.S. Department of State*, June 24, 2004; and Nicholas Burns, "United States' Policy toward Iran," Statement before the Senate Foreign Relations Committee, *U.S. Department of State*, May 19, 2005, https://2001-2009.state.gov/p/us/rm/2005/46528.htm.

18 IAEA, "Implementation of the NPT Safeguards Agreement in the Islamic Republic of Iran: IAEA Board of Governors Resolution Adopted on September 12, 2003," (GOV/2003/69), September 12, 2003.

19 Full text of the Tehran Declaration is accessible at BBC News, "Full Text: Iran Declaration," October 21, 2003, http://news.bbc.co.uk/2/hi/middle_east/3211036.stm.

20 Chubin, *Iran's Nuclear Ambitions*, 22; Saira Khan, *Iran and Nuclear Weapons: Protracted Conflict and Proliferation* (New York: Routledge, 2010), 2, 18–19.

21 The Tehran Declaration.

22 IAEA, "Implementation of the NPT Safeguards Agreement in the Islamic Republic of Iran," (GOV/2004/11), February 24, 2004; IAEA, "Implementation of the NPT Safeguards Agreement in the Islamic Republic of Iran: Report by the Director

General," (GOV/2004/34), June 1, 2004; IAEA, "Communication dated 26 November 2004 Received from the Permanent Representatives of France, Germany, the Islamic Republic of Iran and the United Kingdom Concerning the Agreement Signed in Paris on 15 November 2004," (INFCIRC/637), November 26, 2004.

23 Burns, "United States' Policy"; Burns, "Interview."

24 Kelsey Davenport, "History of Official Proposals on the Iranian Nuclear Issue," *Arms Control Association*, January 21, 2014, https://www.armscontrol.org/factsheets/Iran_Nuclear_Proposals.

25 Mousavian, *The Iranian Nuclear Crisis*, 161–75.

26 Porter, *Manufactured Crisis*, 156.

27 IAEA, "Implementation of the NPT Safeguards Agreement in the Islamic Republic of Iran: Resolution adopted on 24 September 2005," (GOV/2005/77), September 24, 2005.

28 Condoleezza Rice; "On-the-Record Briefing by Secretary of State Condoleezza Rice," *U.S. Department of State*, January 12, 2006, https://2001-2009.state.gov/secretary/rm/2006/59083.htm; Nicholas Burns and Robert Joseph, "Briefing by Under Secretary for Political Affairs R. Nicholas Burns and Under Secretary for Arms Control and International Security Robert Joseph," *U.S. Department of State*, February 5, 2006, https://2001-2009.state.gov/r/pa/prs/ps/2006/60437.htm; Secretary Condoleezza Rice, "Interview with Bob Schieffer of CBS's Face the Nation," *U.S. Department of State*, February 12, 2006 https://2001-2009.state.gov/secretary/rm/2006/60969.htm.

29 George W. Bush, "Helping Iraqis Build a Democracy," Remarks at the Paul H. Nitze School of Advanced International Studies, Johns Hopkins University, *U.S. Department of State*, April 10, 2006, https://2001-2009.state.gov/p/nea/rls/rm/2006/64290.htm.

30 In early 2007, the US secretary of state Condoleezza Rice also offered to personally meet with Iranian officials "at any place and at any time" to discuss the nuclear issue provided that Iran suspends its sensitive nuclear activities. See Nicholas Burns, "United States Policy toward Iran," Testimony Before the House Committee on Foreign Affairs, *U.S. Department of State*, March 6, 2007, https://2001-2009.state.gov/p/us/rm/2007/81470.htm; Rice, "Interview with Bob Schieffer." In July 2008, the US undersecretary of state for Political Affairs William Burns actually participated in the P5+1 nuclear talks with Iran in Geneva, Switzerland. Rice stressed that the participation of the US delegation in these talks did not represent any shift in US position on the necessity of uranium enrichment suspension by Iran as a precondition for U.S. involvement in any nuclear talks with Iran. See Condoleezza Rice, "Interview with CNN's Wolf Blitzer," *U.S. Department of State*, July 18, 2008, https://2001-2009.state.gov/secretary/rm/2008/07/107253.htm.

31 Condoleezza Rice, "Interview on NBC Nightly News with David Gregory," *U.S. Department of State*, May 31, 2006, https://2001-2009.state.gov/secretary/rm/2006/67207.htm.

32 "Text of June 2006 Proposal to Iran by P5+EU Rep," UN Security Council Resolution 1747 (2007) (S/RES/1747 (2007), March 24, 2007.

33 The UNSC resolutions passed were Resolution 1696 (2006), S/RES/1696 (2006), July 31, 2006; Resolution 1737 (2006), S/RES/1737 (2006), December 27, 2006; Resolution 1747 (2007), S/RES/1747 (2007), March 24, 2007; Resolution 1803 (2008), (S/RES/1803 (2008) March 3, 2008; and Resolution 1835 (2008), S/RES/1835 (2008), September 27, 2008.

34 Burns, "United States Policy"; Condoleezza Rice, "Remarks with Secretary of the Treasury Henry M. Paulson," *U.S. Department of State*, October 25, 2007, https://2001-2009.state.gov/secretary/rm/2007/10/94133.htm.

35 Nicholas Burns, "United States Policy toward Iran," Testimony Before the Senate Foreign Relations Committee, *U.S. Department of State,* March 29, 2007, https://2001-2009.state.gov/p/us/rm/2007/82374.htm.

36 Patricia McNerney, "North Korea and Iran: An Administration Perspective," Remarks at National Defense University Symposium, *U.S. Department of State,* May 8, 2008, https://2001-2009.state.gov/t/isn/rls/rm/104548.htm.

37 Condoleezza Rice, "Remarks with Secretary of the Treasury Henry M. Paulson," *U.S. Department of State,* October 25, 2007, https://2001-2009.state.gov/secretary/rm/2007/10/94133.htm.

38 William J. Burns, "U.S. Policy toward Iran," Opening Statement before the House Foreign Affairs Committee and the Senate Foreign Relations Committee, *U.S. Department of State,* July 9, 2008, https://2001-2009.state.gov/p/us/rm/2008/106817.htm.

39 Burns, "United States Policy," March 29, 2007.

40 George W. Bush, "President Addresses American Legion, Discusses Global War on Terror," *The White House,* February 24, 2006, https://georgewbush-whitehouse.archives.gov/news/releases/2006/02/print/20060224.html.

41 Condoleezza Rice, "Realizing the Goals of Transformational Diplomacy," Testimony Before the Senate Foreign Relations Committee, *U.S. Department of State,* February 15, 2006, https://2001-2009.state.gov/secretary/rm/2006/61209.htm; George W. Bush, "President Delivers Commencement Address at the United States Merchant Marine Academy," *The White House,* June 19, 2006, https://georgewbush-whitehouse.archives.gov/news/releases/2006/06/text/20060619-1.html; "Two Senior Administration Officials On U.S. Support for Democracy in Iran," Background Briefing; Office of the Spokesman, *U.S. Department of State,* February 15, 2006, https://2001-2009.state.gov/r/pa/prs/ps/2006/61313.htm.

42 Condoleezza Rice, "Interview with the Associated Press Editorial Board," *U.S. Department of State,* May 8, 2006, https://2001-2009.state.gov/secretary/rm/2006/65975.htm; Nicholas Burns, "Deadlines Loom in Iran Nuclear Standoff," Excerpt from NPR's Talk of the Nation with Neil Conan, *U.S. Department of State,* August 21, 2006, https://2001-2009.state.gov/p/us/rm/2006/70984.htm.

43 Gregory L. Schulte, "Iran's Nuclear Ambitions: Confronting a Common Security Challenge," Remarks to the German United National Association, Bavarian Chapter, *U.S. Department of State,* February 7, 2007, https://2001-2009.state.gov/p/io/rls/rm/80203.htm.

44 Condoleezza Rice, "Interview with Mike Allen of The Politico and Yahoo! News," *U.S. Department of State,* August 6, 2008, https://2001-2009.state.gov/secretary/rm/2008/08/107992.htm.

45 IAEA, "Implementation of the NPT Safeguards Agreement and Relevant Provisions of Security Council Resolutions 1737 (2006), 1747 (2007), 1803 (2008), and 1835 (2008) in the Islamic Republic of Iran: Report by the Director General," (GOV/2009/8), February 19, 2009.

46 For example, see Nicholas Burns and Stuart A. Levey, "Briefing on Iran," *U.S. Department of State,* October 25, 2007, https://2001-2009.state.gov/p/us/rm/2007/94178.htm; and McNerney, "North Korea and Iran."

47 At some point Iran was content with operating only a 20-centrifuge cascade but the EU3, constrained by the US maximalist position, did not accommodate Tehran's request. See IAEA, "IAEA Director General's Press briefing," November 25, 2004, https://www.iaea.org/newscenter/mediaadvisories/iaea-director-general-press-briefing-25-november-2004.

48   Scott Sagan, "How to Keep the Bomb from Iran," *Foreign Affairs* 85, 5 (2006): 58–9.

49   Hillary Clinton, *Hard Choices* (London & New York: Simon & Schuster, 2014), 465–8.

50   Iran's request for 20-percent enriched nuclear fuel for its Tehran Research Reactor from the IAEA in June 2009 provided an opportunity for a confidence-building arrangement under which Iran would trade the great bulk of its LEU stockpile for nuclear fuel. Lack of trust and domestic political pressures prevented the parties from reaching a speedy agreement over the details of the exchange desired by Washington. For details of this interaction, see Trita Parsi, *A Single Roll of the Dice: Obama's Diplomacy with Iran* (New Haven and London: Yale University Press, 2012), 212–13; and Sverre Lodgaard, *Nuclear Disarmament and Non-Proliferation: Towards a Nuclear-Weapon-Free World?* (New York: Routledge, 2011).

51   Obama, "Remarks at AIPAC"; Barack Obama, "Remarks by the President to the UN General Assembly," *The White House*, September 25, 2012.

52   Clinton, *Hard Choices*, 470–1, 476–7.

53   Ibid., 482–3.

54   Ibid., 482–4; Hillary Clinton and Tim Geithner, "Remarks: Measures to Increase Pressure on Iran," *U.S. Department of State*, November 21, 2011, https://2009-2017. state.gov/secretary/20092013clinton/rm/2011/11/177610.htm.

55   Wendy Sherman, "Administration Perspectives on Implementing New Economic Sanctions One Year Later," Statement Before the Senate Banking Committee Hearing, *U.S. Department of State*, October 13, 2011, https://2009-2017.state.gov/p/us/ rm/2011/175436.htm.

56   Clinton, *Hard Choices*, 484.

57   Ibid., 484–5.

58   "Implementation of Section 1245 of the 2012 National Defense Authorization Act (NDAA)," Special Briefing, Senior State Department Official, *U.S. Department of State*, March 20, 2012, https://2009-2017.state.gov/r/pa/prs/ps/2012/03/186122. htm; Hillary Clinton, "Regarding Significant Reductions of Iranian Crude Oil Purchases," Press statement, *U.S. Department of State*, June 11, 2012, https://2009-2017.state.gov/secretary/20092013clinton/rm/2012/06/192078.htm; Hillary Clinton, "Regarding Significant Reductions of Iranian Crude Oil Purchases," Press Statement, *U.S. Department of State*, June 28, 2012, https://2009-2017.state.gov/ secretary/20092013clinton/rm/2012/06/194200.htm.

59   "Implementation of Section"; "United States Welcomes Additional European Union Sanctions on Iran," Media Note, Office of the Spokesperson, *U.S. Department of State*, January 23, 2012, https://2009-2017.state.gov/r/pa/prs/ps/2012/01/182350.htm.

60   Central Bank of Iran, Annual Review, 2012.

61   Central Bank of Iran, Annual Reviews, 2011–15.

62   IAEA, "Implementation of the NPT Safeguards Agreement and Relevant Provisions of Security Council Resolutions in the Islamic Republic of Iran: Report by the Director General," (GOV/2013/40), August 28, 2013.

63   Wendy Sherman, "U.S. Policy Toward Iran," Written Statement before the Senate Foreign Relations Committee, *U.S. Department of State*, May 15, 2013, https://2009-2017.state.gov/p/us/rm/2013/202684.htm; Matt Williams, "Iran Nuclear Talks End with Two Sides Far Apart on Substance," *The Guardian*, April 6, 2013. https://www. theguardian.com/world/2013/apr/06/iran-nuclear-talks-almaty-kazakhstan; David Herszenhorn, "Nuclear Talks with Iran End without Accord or Plans for Another Round," *The New York Times*, April 6, 2013, http://www.nytimes.com/2013/04/07/ world/middleeast/talks-on-irans-nuclear-program-remain-far-apart.htm.

64 For details of the back-channel talks, see Clinton, *Hard Choices*, 477–80, 484–7; Jay Solomon, "Iran Wish List Led Nuclear Deal Talks with U.S.," *The Wall Street Journal*, June 28, 2015, http://www.wsj.com/articles/iran-wish-list-led-to-u-s-talks-1435537004; "Joziat-e chand sal mozakereh va siasat khareji dar goftegu ba salehi,"{Conversation with Salehi on the Details of Several Years of Negotiation and Foreign Policy Making} *Tabnak News Website*, December 11, 2015, http://www.tabnak.ir/fa/print/553356.

65 For example see John Kerry, "Interview with MSNBC's 'Morning Joe,'" *U.S. Department of State*, November 14, 2013, https://2009-2017.state.gov/secretary/remarks/2013/11/217575.htm; Barack Obama, "Remarks by the President in a Conversation with the Saban Forum," December 7, 2013, https://obamawhitehouse.archives.gov/the-press-office/2013/12/07/remarks-president-conversation-saban-forum.

66 Obama, "Conversation with Saban Forum."

67 "Background Briefing on P5+1 Negotiations," Special Briefing, Senior Administration Official, *U.S. Department of State*, October 14, 2013, https://2009-2017.state.gov/r/pa/prs/ps/2013/10/215369.htm; John Kerry, "Press Availability," Remarks, Geneva, Switzerland, *U.S. Department of State*, November 10, 2013, https://2009-2017.state.gov/secretary/remarks/2013/11/217409.htm.

68 The text of the JPA is accessible at the following URL: http://www.nytimes.com/interactive/2013/11/25/world/middleeast/iran-nuclear-deal-document.html.

69 For details of the parties' specific commitments under the JPA see Barack Obama, "Fact Sheet: First Step Understandings Regarding the Islamic Republic of Iran's Nuclear Program," *The White House*, November 23, 2013, https://obamawhitehouse.archives.gov/the-press-office/2013/11/23/fact-sheet-first-step-understandings-regarding-islamic-republic-iran-s-n.

70 Text of the JPA.

71 Texts of the Joint Comprehensive Plan of Action (JCPOA) and the UN Security Council Resolution 2231 adopting it are accessible at the following URL: http://www.securitycouncilreport.org/atf/cf/%7B65BFCF9B-6D27-4E9C-8CD3-CF6E4FF96FF9%7D/s_res_2231.pdf.

72 For example, see Seyed Ali Khamenei, "Khotbehha-ye eid-e fetr 1 shavval-e 1436," *Office of the Supreme Leader*, July 18, 2015.

73 Seyed Ali Khamenei, "Bayanat dar didar-e dastandarkaran-e bargozari-ye entekhabat,' *Office of the Supreme Leader*, January 20, 2016.

13

Toward Confrontation: A Roundtable Discussion on the Present and Future of US-Iranian Relations

This roundtable discussion with Abrahamian, Byrne, Collier, Howard, Maghsoud-Nia, and Bayyenat explores relations between Tehran and Washington over six decades.[1] They discuss how the 1953 Coup is perceived in Iran and the United States and the implications of the recently declassified documents on US-Iranian relations. The participants assess how the Iranian Revolution shaped US foreign policy toward Iran and the Persian Gulf region as well as the intended and unintended consequences of Washington's policies. They discuss the factors threatening the Iranian nuclear deal as well as relations between Beijing and Tehran.

Osamah F. Khalil

The release of the *Foreign Relations* series related to the 1953 Coup after numerous delays and controversy surrounding the previous version raises the questions: Does the 1953 Coup still matter in Iran? And why? And does it still matter here in the United States? Or in the UK? And why? Malcolm, let's begin with you.

Malcolm Byrne

There has been a long-standing strain of thought that the 1953 Coup really doesn't matter. It's ancient history, and the Iranian regime is basically using it as a prod to the United States and to its own population to say, look at what's been going on. I think that it's true that it's been a political weapon, and that's one of the reasons why I point to the need to have reconciled ourselves to declassifying this stuff a long time ago, take that weapon out of anyone's hands. But I think that point of view also ignores a genuine and much more broadly based idea among Iranians, both within the country and outside the country.

I just spoke to a couple of students the other day who are angry at what the United States and Britain did 60 something years ago. Their parents were barely alive at that point. But they still see it as an issue. And I think it's important to see

---

[1] This chapter is based on a moderated roundtable discussion hosted at Syracuse University's Maxwell School of Citizenship and Public Affairs in September 2017. The discussion drew on papers presented by the participants, which were early versions of the chapters in this volume.

it not just as an act of a few days in August 1953 but as a representation of what the United States has done since then. In the country itself, not just restoring the shah and getting rid of this complicated personality in Mossadeq. There is still a lot of disagreement about Mossadeq, but that's because the United States allowed the shah to pursue a set of policies and follow a trajectory that made things increasingly worse in the country. So you can't just look at the event itself. You have to look at what followed.

And if you talk to former CIA officials, as I did before some of them passed away, you get a different sense of what happened. John Waller[1] said, we used to cry in our beer about what had happened in Iran and that they, in the CIA, thought that this coup was a good idea, but it was the fault of the presidents that followed for not holding the shah's feet to the fire.

Ervand Abrahamian

Anything about 1953 has a lot of interest in Iran. I wouldn't say it's a serious historical interest because there are very few, I would say, professional historians left in Iran doing modern history. There weren't during the time of the shah, and there aren't now either. So it's usually the press that's interested. And invariably, for journalists there is an agenda. They're not actually interested in what happened. It's how they can use it in contemporary politics so it's very much presentism, you can say.

So some use 1953 to criticize the clergy. It's easy to latch onto Ayatollah Kashani or which individuals were in the pay of the CIA or another intelligence service. So it's not really an interest in the historical event, but how they can use it. And sometimes, it's used in strange ways. For instance, when [Mahmoud] Ahmedinejad was president, the reformers felt that he was dangerous and would lead to a confrontation with the United States.

And the way they used 1953 was to say, Mossadeq refused to compromise, and now you're refusing. What will happen now? There will be a crisis. This was said without knowing that Mossadeq wasn't actually offered a compromise. And Ahmedinejad's situation was very different. But he also used the 1953 example to argue that Mossadeq was right to nationalize oil and that Iran is right to have nuclear energy. He claimed, we are doing the same thing, and the West is trying to do the same thing it did in 1953 with an embargo, sanctions, etc. He was using history without really looking at the history itself.

David Collier

When Jimmy Carter was president, he was asked about the coup. He dismissed it saying, "that's ancient history." But during the revolution and again in 2009, people carried Mossadeq's picture. Iranian Foreign Minister Javad Zarif has repeatedly referenced Mossadeq and the coup when talking about the nuclear issue and American threats of regime change. So it's still a living history that's important and Mossadeq is still a powerful symbol that's used by both the regime and the people to express national pride and the desire for change.

Adam Howard[2]

One of the things our office does is to teach Foreign Service officers before they go abroad. We try to convey as historians to those Foreign Service officers that there's a historical amnesia that most Americans have and that Foreign Service officers need to be sensitive to this episode no matter whether they think it was a good thing or a bad thing. The fact that it happened and it is remembered and used by others is the important part. For example, one can look at how the Islamic State used the Sykes-Picot Agreement as a weapon against the West. So this is something that Foreign Service officers need to have more sensitivity to so that they understand what's coming toward them when engaging with those who have a perception of historical episodes far different or unfamiliar to many Americans.

Khalil

On this issue of historical amnesia, do Americans really understand how much Washington has intervened abroad? After the 2016 election, is there an opportunity to educate Americans on this issue?

Abrahamian

There are scattered but perceptive statements in the correspondence back and forth from the Tehran embassy to the State Department that too deep an involvement in Iranian politics, especially in parliamentary elections, could undermine American prestige in Iran.[3] They were being self-conscious about how much the United States had been meddling. And the irony is, of course, this was the deep imprint. But as David Collier shows in his chapter, by the end of the shah's rule, the United States had no influence.

This is where paranoia comes in with the Islamic Republic that the United States could have either prevented the revolution or attempted a counterrevolution. This is completely off the wall, because by then, there was really no institution inside the country that the CIA could have mobilized for a counterrevolution and its presence inside Iran was limited. There's a story that the CIA agent who was sent to Tehran after the revolution, he walked out of the embassy and got quickly lost. He was in no position to carry out a coup.

But this type of framework was not there among the new elites. They felt that the United States had all this omnipotent power. They did it in 1953 and they could do it again.

Pedram Maghshoud-Nia

Building on that point about the momentous impact of the 1953 Coup, if you ask many Iranians from older generations: "How did the revolution happen?" They would say: "Foreign powers gathered at the 1979 Guadeloupe Conference and decided to topple the shah's regime." There was a common view among Iranians that after 1953, the shah owed his throne to the Americans and the British. He remained submissive until the mid-1970s, but then the oil bonanza gave him an elusive and self-aggrandizing perception of power. Suddenly, the shah started bragging about his achievements and rebuking the Westerners, the "blue eyed people," for their complacency and dependency on cheap oil.

So, according to many Iranians, the West decided to put the shah in his place and therefore let the revolution happen. They also draw on some facts to bolster this view. For example, many Iranians think that General Robert Huyser was sent by President Carter to prevent an imminent coup by the Iranian army.[4] The way it is interpreted is that Washington instructed the army to betray the shah and allow the revolutionaries to take power. What the advocates of these views sometimes ignore is that the West was dumbfounded that Iran, the country that was seen as the "island of stability," was unexpectedly grappling with unrest and turmoil.

Conspiracy theories fail to explain how in a period of only a few months millions of Iranians rose against a government that had successfully improved the economy and had delivered unprecedented levels of welfare especially to urban populations. What mechanisms were at work to bring about such a massive mobilization? I doubt that Westerners were involved in that process or even knew what was happening. This is why the uprising in 1979 led to sharp disagreements between the top officials in the Carter administration like National Security Advisor Zbigniew Brzezinski and Secretary of State Cyrus Vance. The United States was reacting to domestic developments in Iran rather than dictating them. But conspiracy theories ignore this reality. And these notions were popular because the 1953 Coup was such a momentous event that overshadowed the collective psyche of Iranians for several generations.

Byrne

I just wanted to say that it's extraordinary how many times we hear our leaders talk about how we don't intervene in other countries' affairs. Are they fooling themselves? Are they completely ignorant of what's been going on? It's an extraordinary thing. And there's a quote from one of these documents. It's actually, I think it's an earlier version of a March 1953 National Security Council (NSC) meeting, which is just before Eisenhower makes up his mind that he's going to authorize the coup.

According to the notes of the meeting, the president said it was a matter of distress to him that we seemed unable to get some of the people in these "downtrodden" countries, meaning in the Middle East, to like us instead of hating us. And that is what we see today in some of the circles of power. And it's not limited to the United States. I think it's other countries as well.

Abrahamian

Then it continues, actually, somewhere in the meeting it says, "if you give us enough money, we can raise enough other people to shout long live America."

Byrne

Right. Fill the crowds.

Khalil

David, your chapter counters many of the prevailing myths and conspiracy theories that Pedram mentioned and that are still so vibrant. How were the indications about the brewing revolution missed? Or were they actively ignored because the alternatives to the shah were unpalatable from Washington's perspective?

Collier

I think signals were both missed and ignored. When Richard Helms went to Iran [as US ambassador], his embassy really didn't allow any of the officials there to critique the shah in any way even though they knew that there were disturbances. Nixon went to Iran in 1972, and was almost caught up in a series of bombings there. He was forced to wait in his car for an hour until the "all clear" was given and he could continue his ceremonial duties. But they didn't want to really question the shah's rule. When officials at the embassy made offhand remarks to one another about how the shah should stop spending so much money on the military or should spend more money on infrastructure, they were sent home. So by the time of the Nixon administration, Washington was really not interested in hearing any criticism about the shah and embassy officials were tasked with spying on the Soviet Union rather than building contacts with the Iranian opposition. So that was a purposeful reaction to seeing that the shah was really their chosen instrument for regional stability.

By the time of the Carter administration then, Washington had little information about opposition in Iran or the fragility of the shah's rule even though when you go back to the 1950s and early 1960s, the Americans were intently concerned by his lack of progress on political reform.

And going back to the story of conspiracies, I mention in my book,[5] there's a moment when Gary Sick, a member of the NSC under Carter, was surprised when some Iranians asked him why the United States wanted to bring Khomeini to power and Sick called such questions absurd. But going back, the United States had brought numerous prime ministers to power, some even against the shah's wishes. The shah so despised Ali Amini that he once said he'd make him take his dream of becoming prime minister to the grave. Yet after pressure from Washington, the shah consented to his appointment in 1961. Ali Razmara was also foisted upon an unwilling shah and his government's reform program was largely written by Americans.

The United States had wielded amazing influence in Iran during the 1940s, the 1950s, and into the 1960s so it may be not a massive leap for some to assume the United States must have assented to the shah's removal. So I don't think the United States should have been too surprised that these conspiracy theories came about but because they had disengaged from Iran, they didn't understand their previous history had been so influential.

Abrahamian

We can talk about conspiracy theories indefinitely, but it long predates this. It's just that America fits neatly into a tradition that existed with the British. If you go to the 1890s, Lord Curzon, in his book, actually has long extracts about how in Persia there were all these conspiracy theories about how Britain was behind everything.[6] He claimed that Persians tended to detect a British "cloven hoof behind the skirt of every robe." So conspiracy theories had a long narrative in Iran.

Collier

Yes, but there's also much more truth behind some of these conspiracies than I think has been given credence. If the United States maintained the same level of linkage with Iran as they had up until the early 1960s, I'm sure Washington would have influenced events to a different outcome. The difference was that whereas the Americans had once been capable and informed, they had disengaged and could no longer influence Iran as they once had. Conspiratorial minds may be common but after seeing what the United States was able to achieve in 1953, how they had bossed the shah around in the early Kennedy years, it's not unreasonable to assume they were involved behind the scenes during the revolution. But by the time Carter became president, those days were gone.

Khalil

Building on David's discussion of the Carter administration, Adam, what lessons do you think we can learn from the "arc of crisis" discussions and planning in Washington after the revolution? Especially, since we can trace the foundations of America's military presence in the Persian Gulf back to that period?

Howard

I think it reveals the limits of viewing events through a singular lens and the dangers that come with it; it just limits the ability of policymakers to see the importance of other factors. It's not unique to this situation. For example, the Sino-Soviet split occurred much earlier than US policymakers picked up on because they had this singular lens of the Chinese and Soviet Union being joined at the hip when maybe they could have exploited that divide earlier.

Now, I'm sure there are other factors. Maybe the fact that President Johnson couldn't go to China; only Nixon could go to China for the political reasons that allowed a renowned anti-Communist to take the political risks that came with initiating a diplomatic opening to a communist country. But it seems to me there's nuances lost when you have the singular lens. If I was going to do a presentist approach, I think that's the lesson for most policymakers.

Khalil

How much does personality play a role versus institutions? As Adam discussed, there was an alignment that overcame personal preferences.

Collier

I think there was a great deal of continuity among the administrations. The institutional argument is very informative. There were a few people who would argue against the status quo but generally were ignored. Major General Patrick Hurley, President Franklin Delano Roosevelt's envoy to Iran, argued for the United States to play a greater role to encourage democracy in Iran during the mid-1940s, but was defeated by the more realist State Department, which focused on the stability offered by the shah as leader. Similarly, Robert Komer, a member of the NSC's Iran bureau, and Kenneth Hansen, assistant director of the Bureau of the Budget, during the Kennedy years argued for American influence to back the office of prime minister rather than the shah's personal rule. Supreme Court justice William O. Douglas was active for decades calling for a move away from American support for the shah, but all were unsuccessful. Each administration concluded the shah was America's best bet for stability. Personalities were important, but overall there was that compulsion to maintain the status quo in US relations with Iran and the broader Middle East as well. So I think the institutional argument is probably more compelling.

Khalil

Pedram, this idea that the United States sees Iran as the implacable enemy, how much do you think that view has been accepted in Tehran? And from their perspective that there is no way to bridge this divide?

Maghsoud-Nia

The key point is that political institutions don't emerge out of thin air. They are the products of the actions and decisions of individuals, especially political elites. Foreign threats are powerful motives for political elites to build strong armies and mobilize resources. The tools that political elites utilize to accomplish these objectives gradually morph into a set of institutionalized mechanisms and practices that increase the control of the state over its citizens. When a state starts taxing its citizens it necessarily keeps a better record of what they do and where they are. It also needs to create new branches to collect taxes and go after tax evaders. Consequently, taxation leads to more effective control over citizens. So, the unintended consequences of the desire of political elites to remain in power, especially in the face of external threats, is the expansion of a state's authority and capacities.

Postrevolutionary elites saw Washington's policies toward Iran as a serious threat to their survival. Therefore, they were galvanized to take a series of defensive steps that inadvertently strengthened the Iranian state. It wasn't that the ruling elite planned to build a stronger state, but the moment they realized that they were losing oil revenues, they had to make the painful switch to taxation. Taxation is something that regimes like the one in Iran are generally averse to undertake because in return they need to be more accountable to their citizens. So, they prefer not to take that step. But, facing the United States' sanctions, the Iranian state had to cut its dependence on oil and rely more on tax revenues. Threat perception contributed to certain institutional outcomes, and in the case of the postrevolutionary Iranian state, an enhancement of its capacities.

Khalil

Abolghasem, how does this align with your assessment of the competing discourses in Iranian politics? Do both radicals and moderates see the United States as an eternal enemy? Or do the moderates believe that a rapprochement with Washington is possible?

Abolghasem Bayyenat

There are at least two competing state identity discourses which have been able to capture institutional power and become influential over Iran's foreign policy. There are of course marginalized discourses, such as secular nationalist and liberal democratic discourses which have been present in Iran's public sphere, but have never captured institutional power.

There is considerable divergence between these two official competing discourses. The revolutionary Islamists view the United States as the "other" because of its "imperialist and hegemonic" character and think opposition to the United States is a source of international prestige for Iran. They believe that the United States and the Islamic Republic are antithetical and naturally opposed to each other and thus cannot develop a normal relationship with each other as long as either of them is true to itself. Tactical engagements with the United States over topical issues, such as negotiating the nuclear deal, are permissible based on state expediency, but such exceptional instances of cooperation do not and must not transform the antagonistic relationship between the two countries.

In contrast, the moderates and the reformists do not construct Iran's national identity in opposition to the United States. To them, the United States is another great power much like Russia, China, the UK, and other great powers. All great powers pursue their own national interests and follow the same policies toward Iran in identical circumstances. Thus, they believe that Iran should establish normal relations with the United States and avoid creating unnecessary costs for its national interests through ideological opposition to the United States.

Given the fractured nature of Iran's political system and the nature of its political institutions, the moderate Islamists can never gain a monopoly of influence over Iran's foreign policy decision-making and can only become influential over Iran's foreign policy by gaining control of the executive branch and the parliament through elections. When there is a balance of political forces between moderates and conservatives, Iran's foreign policy reflects a compromise between these contending perspectives.

Abrahamian

Iran's foreign policy exists on two levels. One is the polemical level for the public, where the United States is an inherently evil threat and so on. There's also a pragmatic side. And even in Khomeini's time, America was described not just as an imperial power, but as an arrogant power. The presumption is, if it ceases being arrogant, then it's fine and we can have a normal relationship. There's always an opening.

After the revolution, there was the perceived threat of the United States, but then the complication came that it was Iraq that invaded Iran. So the regime's argument was that Iraq was doing it for the United States. And that still allowed them to focus on the United States. The Iran–Contra scandal was an added problem. If the United States is really evil, then how come the regime went to the evil power to get aid?

The individual that revealed the information [about the scandal], was later executed. And if you look at his public confession and the trial, he's not charged with leaking this information. Instead, he was charged with a host of crimes, including sorcery, and attempting to use black magic to kill the supreme leader. So, obviously, the regime didn't want to discuss the question of Iran's links with United States over that. So you can call it cynical or pragmatic.

I often like to point out that if Iran is such an Islamic state, how come it has for the last two decades had better relations with Armenia, a Christian state, then with Azerbaijan, a Shi`a Muslim one. Clearly national interests trump religion here.

Khalil

How does China's Belt and Road Initiative provide moderate reformers in Iran with the opportunity to say our future is toward the East rather than Europe and the West?

Collier

I think that's been happening for a while. Even before the United States withdrew from the Iran deal, Iran was looking for more trade with China and Russia. Although Europe is trying to salvage something from the Joint Comprehensive Plan of Action (JCPOA) and strengthen relations with Iran, American threats to reimpose sanctions scared many European businesses away from deepening ties with Iran as they are so tied in with the American economy.

Now that the United States has withdrawn from the JCPOA that has become all the more clear. But India appears to be moving forward with its plans to develop the port of Chabahar so there are alternatives for Iran. The economies of places like Russia and China are far less vulnerable to pressure from Washington so it's only natural that Iran will now look more in that direction. There are less issues for Iran in trading with the East compared to trading with Europe, the West, and the weight of history that remains there.

Maghsoud-Nia

There's no doubt that after the revolution, the shift toward the East happened. But the Iranian leadership seems to be aware that neither Russia nor China is going to damage their already strained relations with the West for Iran. The main example underlining this attitude is China and Russia's approval of sanctions imposed on Iran for its nuclear program. Both countries agreed with the UN sanctions against Iran.

Moreover, Russia delayed the sale of arms (S-300 missiles) as well as the completion of the Bushehr nuclear reactor for a long time. Russia has close ties with Iran's regional rivals such as Israel and Saudi Arabia and it is hard to believe that they will allow Iran to dominate the region at the cost of Russia's close friends.

Bayyenat

Close ties with China and Russia as an alternative to the West is the preferred foreign policy strategy of conservative political groups in Iran. Moderates and reformists would like to maintain close ties with Europe while also broadening their options by developing Iran's relations with China and Russia. They didn't expect much economic benefits from the nuclear deal with the United States because Washington's primary sanctions are still in place and only the secondary sanctions have been lifted. The bulk of economic benefits from the nuclear deal were to emanate from closer economic ties with Europe and increased European investment in Iran's oil and gas sectors as China and Russia had not terminated their economic ties with Iran under the sanctions. This was realized to a meager extent, especially through the presence of French and German companies in Iran, but not to the extent that Iran had expected and wished for. However, even these meager economic benefits have mostly evaporated following the withdrawal of the United States from the JCPOA and reimposition of its sanctions on Iran.

The moderates and reformists favor close economic ties with Europe in part because they think Europe can offer Iran more advanced technologies than Russia and China. They also want to expand their options as they think that Iran should not antagonize both Europe and the United States simultaneously. And you can't solely rely on China and Russia because, understandably, they would not be willing to sacrifice their own ties with the United States over Iran. And Beijing and Moscow have proved that they are prone to major shifts in their policies toward Iran when faced with American pressure or incentives.

Abrahamian

At the present time, Iran looks like it is in a good position. But in reality, they know that they can have economic trade with Europe, with Russia, and with China. But if it comes to a real political crisis, they can't really depend on them. Those countries are more interested in economic benefits. And Europe, Russia, and China are not going to actually jeopardize their relations with America over Iran. So even with Trump in power, they don't want to jeopardize their trade with the United States just to protect Iran. So I think that actually puts Iran in a weak position.

Collier

I think that the United States as a superpower has been fading for some time now and can no longer dictate to other countries in ways it once did. As the United States becomes weaker, countries like China can have a greater individual say regarding who they want to deal with and will receive much less pressure from Washington.

Khalil

Are the tensions between the United States and Iran merely rhetorical or is the animosity real and entrenched?

Maghsoud-Nia

It is a combination of both. Undoubtedly, the animosity between Iran and the United States is real. The two countries constantly exchange threats and try to undermine the interests of each other through different means. But part of it, especially in Iran's case, is also rhetorical and for domestic purposes. Inside the Iranian regime, hard-liners have used the anti-American discourse to cast doubt on the loyalty of their rivals, the reformists, to the core values of the 1979 Revolution. For hard-liners, it is convenient to label their rivals as pro-American and eliminate them from the political process. Hostility to the United States also helps the regime to mobilize supporters and showcase their power and support to their domestic opposition and foreign enemies. The key point to remember is that certain factions within the Iranian regime benefit from perpetuating the animosity with the United States.

Howard

I think it just generally speaks to the power of history that there is a narrative. And even if the leaders are tapping into that and they're cynical about it, there's clearly a base of people who sincerely believe in it. And that's one of the great takeaways of how historical narratives are so critical to geopolitical power.

Collier

Since the revolution there have been many instances of Iran trying to appeal to the United States and find a grand compromise so they have at times shown an interest in putting aside the rhetoric and improving relations. The same goes for the United States, which has also put aside the rhetoric at times. But harsh rhetoric appeals to significant portions of the electorate in each country and within the main political camps. President George W. Bush's inclusion of Iran in the "Axis of Evil" is an example of how sensitive both sides are to the history of relations between the two countries. Now with a number of Iran hawks within the Trump administration it seems the harsh rhetoric will not be disappearing anytime soon.

Bayyenat

I think that the hostility and tensions between the United States and Iran are both genuine and contrived to varying degrees. This is of course does not mean that when these tensions are not genuine they do not serve any purpose. Even when not justified by strategic national interests, fueling these hostilities may serve diversionary purposes or advance the interests of domestic or foreign interest groups. The role of pro-Israel lobbies in fueling and perpetuating US hostilities toward Iran even when Tehran pursues a cooperative posture toward the United States on major issues of contention between the two countries is a case in point. The need to appease pro-Israel lobbies who wield significant influence over both the US Congress and the executive branch sometimes pushes US politicians to rhetorically mount tensions with Iran. A similar mechanism is also at work in Iran. Hyping rhetorical tensions with the United States diverts public attention from domestic economic challenges and shields the government from public criticisms over its economic performance. However, one should not underestimate the major conflict of interests between the two governments.

Khalil

How does that political rhetoric limit the ability to conduct historical research? Even for topics that are decades old? Which takes us back to the beginning of this conversation.

Byrne

Yes. I think there is a real parallel. I've made eight or nine trips to Iran since 1998, and I see this clear parallel between what I'm doing on my low track two or scholarly level with what the high policy has been and is. The issues that you confront, the arguments that you find on all sides often seem to be one and the same. I spent a lot of time looking at the Iran-Contra affair, for example, and joining in the fun that everybody made of [former national security advisor Robert] McFarlane and all these guys going to Tehran, until I went to Tehran and found some of the same kinds of issues.[7]

"I don't understand what these guys mean! They never say no. But does that mean they really are agreeable to everything? And why can't one person just make a decision? Why does it have to be clouded in all this [ambiguity]?" I mean, these are very anecdotal and individual kinds of experiences, but it is something that strikes you when you try to figure out what is going on, what are the internal dynamics that you experience at different levels.

And the work that the National Security Archive is trying to do—if we're going to a place like Iran or Moscow or Beijing or somewhere like that, or Havana, some place where we have a history of hostility with that particular government—you get a lot of insights into what the overall historical relationship has been like when you're trying to push for similar kinds of interactions but on a much more modest level.

Notes

1 John Waller served as the CIA's chief of the Near East Division from 1972 to 1975 and as inspector general from 1976 to 1980. A partially declassified interview for the CIA's *Studies in Intelligence* newsletter is available through the CIA's electronic Reading Room, https://www.cia.gov/library/readingroom/docs/DOC_0006122540.pdf.
2 All views expressed here by Adam Howard are his own and do not necessarily represent those of the US government.
3 See "Letter From the Officer in Charge of Iranian Affairs, Office of Greek, Turkish, and Iranian Affairs, Bureau of Near Eastern, South Asian, and African Affairs, Department of State to the First Secretary of Embassy in Iran," November 6, 1953, Document 345; "Despatch from the Station in Iran to the Chief of the Near East and Africa Division, Directorate of Plans, Central Intelligence Agency," November 13, 1953, Document 346; "Letter from the First Secretary of the Embassy in Iran to the Bureau of Near Eastern,

South Asian and African Affairs," November 30, 1953, Document 350; "Iran December 1953 – Monthly Report Prepared in the Directorate of Plans, Central Intelligence Agency," undated, Document 354, *Foreign Relations of the United States, 1952–1954, Iran* (2017), https://history.state.gov/historicaldocuments/frus1951-54Iran/d350.

4 Robert Huyser was an air force general who was sent by President Carter to Tehran in the days leading to the 1979 Revolution. Many Iranians believed that Huyser's mission was to neutralize the Iranian Revolution. However, recently declassified cables show that the main objective of Huyser's trip was to persuade the military to support the civilian government of Bakhtiar (Andrew Scott Cooper, "Declassified Diplomacy: Washington's Hesitant Plans for a Military Coup in Pre-Revolution Iran," *The Guardian*, February 11, 2015).

5 David Collier, *Democracy and the Nature of American Influence in Iran, 1941–1979* (Syracuse, NY: Syracuse University Press, 2017).

6 Lord Curzon's book was originally published in 1892 and was recently republished, George Nathanial Curzon, *Persia and the Persian Question*, vol. 2 (Cambridge, UK: Cambridge University Press, 2018).

7 Robert McFarlane led a secret delegation to Tehran in May 1986 as part of the ill-fated Iran arms-for-hostages deals approved by President Ronald Reagan." See Malcolm Byrne, *Iran-Contra: Reagan's Scandal and the Unchecked Abuse of Presidential Power* (Syracuse, NY: Syracuse University Press, 2014).

Afterword

Making Sense of the History of US Foreign Relations: Policy, Practice, Presentism, and the Profession

Richard H. Immerman

Historians are comfortable writing and teaching about the past. That's what we're trained to do; exploring the influence of change over time is the core of our discipline. Many of us, however, and I'd posit almost all of us who specialize in the history of US foreign relations and/or international history, entertain frequent requests to hold forth on the present. We do not receive training for such undertakings, and for historians they are inherently problematic. Yet we almost always accept. We do so in part because that's the expectation, particularly if we are on the faculty of a college or a university. But in larger part we seize opportunities to provide commentary on the present because it's fun, it's challenging, it's stimulating, and it allows us to show off that we are not irrelevant necrophiliacs. We can add value to almost any discussion by drawing upon our skill sets in order to contextualize the present by historicizing it. Our historical sensibility is the coin of our realm.

Nevertheless, as historians we must tread carefully when addressing current events, or even when drawing connections between current events and past ones, and vice versa. A personal anecdote can serve as an illustration. Midway through my graduate program I decided to ignore my advisors' warnings and roll the dice that I could declassify a sufficient number of documents to write my dissertation about the American-orchestrated project in 1954 to effect regime change in Guatemala. I followed that decision with another: to end my story by linking the events of the 1950s to the horrific bloodshed produced by the decades-long civil war that followed and was still raging at the time when I was writing. The choices I made unquestionably gave my professional trajectory a shot in the arm. Examining what then was a little known CIA operation attracted attention, and I had more success with the Freedom of Information Act (FOIA) than I had reason to expect. Further my arguments were generally well regarded—albeit not by everyone. The reviewer in the *American Historical Review* (*AHR*) characterized my account as "the most complete to date" and expressed his doubt that the release of additional material in the future would change the story "too much." Still, he alleged, my story was wrong because I was "presentist."[1]

Ouch. One can make the case that there can be no more damning critique of a work of history than to apply to it, and its author, the adjective "presentist." As Harvard's Bancroft (and other) Prize winner Jill Lepore remarked in a widely circulated quote, "The American historical profession defines itself by its dedication to the proposition that looking to the past to explain the present falls outside the realm of serious historical study."[2] By charging me with—and indeed catching me—violating that proposition even before I'd received tenure, the *AHR* reviewer could have stopped my career in its tracks. My selection of a covert operation as a subject exacerbated my recklessness. Regardless of what success I experienced with my FOIA requests, I was painfully aware that my access to the documentary record was incomplete. As a substitute for still-classified archives, therefore, I conducted oral interviews with participants. Or more accurately, I supplemented those archives that I could access with oral histories. Today that is accepted practice. Back then it was not.

If for historians "looking to the past to explain the present" is a perilous enterprise, seeking to identify patterns that might be applicable to the future, which in addition to providing grist for international relations mills is integral to producing intelligence estimates, can prove to be disciplinary suicide. To engage questions about the future direction of the history of US foreign relations as a subfield of American foreign relations, international, or transnational history has become all but a cottage industry. Indeed, at least since Charles Maier chastised "diplomatic historians" decades ago for "marking time," we've turned assessments of and prescriptions for our future into an art form, and with positive results. The farther we push the envelope, the better.[3]

But for a historian to opine about the future of Sino-American relations, for example, or US-Iranian relations, or the path ahead for North and South Korea is to walk out onto very thin ice. Not only is the future incompatible with examining change over time, but also that change for historians is driven by contingencies that are impossible to forecast. We reject parsimony, assume complexity, and possess an irresistible urge to "to complicate." Consequently, we are content to cede to our colleagues in political science and cognate disciplines the task of identifying norms, or to cite one distinguished theorist of international relations, "lawlike statements" of behavior.[4]

This chapter recognizes that this dynamic—historians' aversion to presentism and reluctance to apply their historical sensibilities to estimate the likelihood of future scenarios—is eroding. This development, I argue, is salutary for the discipline, the profession, and the public. To begin with, if the subfield of the history of US foreign relations is to remain viable and vibrant, we must engage the past, the present, and the future, and we must engage all three systematically and institutionally. In today's political and economic environment, if one of us accepts an appointment elsewhere or retires, the norm has become for our line to evaporate or either the department or administration to redefine it. Hence, if only for the wrong reasons—self-defense and survival—we are forced to propose and teach more and more courses on contemporary history.

That we must reflects a sea change in higher education that most notably affects and in fact threatens to cripple the liberal arts. When I was an undergraduate in the late 1960s, hundreds and hundreds of students flocked each semester to my university's survey course on the history of US foreign policy, which essentially ended with the Korean War. That was in no small part because the gifted Walt LaFeber was teaching that course during a time of intense intellectual ferment.[5] LaFeber is one of a kind. Nevertheless, in the 1980s and the 1990s many of us mortals were able to bolster our enrollments by offering lecture courses that resonated with contemporary students. Most prominent among these were courses on the Vietnam War, which many students had at least heard about. But the policies of the Reagan administration also prompted us to teach about the United States and Central America, the United States and the Middle East, and other more regionally oriented offerings that enveloped contemporary flashpoints.

Those courses remain popular. Still, with the end of the Cold War coinciding with the arrival of first generation X and then millennials on campuses, they are not as popular as they once were. Perversely, however, we have benefited from the tragedy of 9/11 and the misguided invasion of Iraq by offering more courses with a contemporary flair. While many of these remain regional, an increasing number are topical, examining the CIA, globalization, terrorism, neoliberalism, immigration, human rights, and the like. We recognize that with history majors occupying fewer and fewer seats in our classes, we are more likely to attract a student in the business school by offering a course on international sports than on international relations, conventionally defined. Whenever possible we include the word "empire" in our course titles, and we exclude from our course descriptions sure-to-be-unfamiliar terms such as Yalta and Tet let alone the Farewell Address and Open Door. Even as I write this chapter I can imagine a young historian designing a course with the title "How Easy Is It to Win a Trade War, and What Would Victory Look Like?" And courses on arms control may make a comeback. If we build it they will come, we tell our colleagues and chairs during debates over hiring priorities. And maybe that will persuade administrators to allot the department another faculty position or two.

No historian of US foreign relations should have qualms about this trend toward teaching presentist-oriented courses as a strategy for self-preservation. The courses raise the level of student awareness about contemporary concerns, they provoke students to reflect and question, and they provide opportunities to introduce students to the value of historical thinking so that they can develop their own historical sensibility. But I am confident that more than self-interest is driving historians to focus more on the present, or put it differently, to strive toward more "policy relevance." Surely an equally salient variable is our increased recognition that historians have a responsibility beyond the academy, that we can and must contribute to national conversations and debates about current policy and the future direction of policy.

Of course historians have frequently crossed that boundary between past and present previously. We spoke at teach-ins during the Vietnam War and reprised that role during the Reagan years, especially with regard to Central America. And on occasion we wrote an article with policy implications, although more times than not we submitted it to a scholarly journal that was unlikely to be read outside of a small circle that included few policymakers and fewer general readers. Indeed, I have often thought it revealing—and depressing—that probably the "historian" most publicly identified as intervening in national debates over US foreign policy from the 1960s through the end of the century was Noam Chomsky. I don't intend to minimize Chomsky's contributions.[6] But I do have a problem with a linguist seizing the historian's pulpit largely by default. Our training should count for something.

For this reason the extent to which historians have recently stepped up to the public plate represents welcome and much-needed progress. That this progress is doubtless a function of the inchoate global environment that followed the end of the Cold War and the concomitant amnesia that consumed the American consciousness makes it that much more welcome and needed. Historians en masse found it unconscionable that not only young students but also large swatches of the adult public were oblivious to the historical forces that made somewhat intelligible the seemingly endless challenges the globe confronted. The tragedy of the attacks on 9/11 and the George W. Bush administration's response, particularly the campaign against al-Qaeda and the Taliban in Afghanistan, the invasion of Iraq, and the declaration of a global war on terrorism added both momentum and a sense of urgency to what seemed like an obligation to inform.[7]

Frankly, some of these efforts were disappointing. Too often they reflected, or represented, the kind of "lessons of history" approach that Ernest May taught us but also warned us about.[8] Among the most popular were the many analogies drawn between the war in Iraq and the war in Vietnam. The merit of these analogies increased once the focus of the military effort turned more toward counterinsurgency. Nevertheless, because the war in Iraq, its origins, conduct, and goals diverged from more than it paralleled the war in Vietnam, unless expertly crafted, this framework frequently obscured more than it clarified. What is more, as the historian Mark Lawrence expresses so well, the divergent lessons drawn from the Vietnam War allowed for their wildly conflicting and even contradictory application to Iraq.[9]

More successful albeit more narrow were the efforts of historians to identify the conditions that contributed to the achievements of the occupations of Japan and West Germany after the Second World War and distinguish them from conditions in Iraq following Bush's "Mission Accomplished" declaration. In these instances respected scholars provided the public with informed and sophisticated insights by exploiting their substantive expertise and sensitivity to complexity and contingency.[10] They were thus able to explain how the past informs the present without drawing a straight line to the future. Increasingly, moreover, historians are applying similar insights from post-Tet Vietnam to assess the prospects of the Trump administration's "strategy" for "winning" and/or exiting the war in Afghanistan.[11] But while such interventions illustrate the added value that historical sensibility can bring to the table, their effect on policy, or on US international behavior, remains by and large the equivalent of a backseat driver in a car with the radio volume turned high.

Whether historians' voices end up resonating more during the age of Trump than they have up to now remains to be determined. On the one hand, President Trump's disregard for past norms, precedents, and conventions, his embrace of alternative facts, his boast about his not needing information or advice, and the conflict that inheres between his mercurial impulses and the requisites of strategic thinking don't suggest reasons for optimism. All too often the president relies on the input of individuals with whom he is comfortable but who betray both ignorance and contempt for history.

The exemplar is son-in-law Jared Kushner, who in discussing the way forward in the Middle East, one of the many issues assigned to his portfolio, stated publicly that "We don't want a history lesson. We've read enough books."[12]

But on the other hand, Kushner's comment was widely quoted and roundly criticized, including by American Historical Association executive director James Grossman. Consequently, it served as something of a call to arms throughout the profession. Historians also took some solace in the reported clash between Kushner and H. R. McMaster, who Trump appointed national security advisor in the aftermath of the Michael Flynn travesty. McMaster, of course, earned a PhD in history and wrote a well-received book criticizing the Joint Chiefs of Staff for their collective "dereliction of duty" during the Vietnam War. But McMaster displayed little historical sensibility during his tenure, never gained the president's confidence, and after thirteen months Trump replaced him with John Bolton. Bolton filters his understanding of history through the lens of ideology and was replaced as well. [13]

The ahistoricism that pervades the current administration and the president's endless fabrications (when showing the Oval Office off to French president Emmanuel Macron, Trump distorted the history of a desk even though it had a visible plaque affixed to it[14]) have provided historians with more incentives than ever to intervene more aggressively in the public sphere. There is precedent, and for historians of American foreign relations, Melvyn Leffler is probably the most well-known and respected. Although he earned his reputation by studying the interwar period and the Cold War, Leffler's scholarship at least since the prize-winning *A Preponderance of Power* came out in 1992, I'd argue, has had a "presentist" dimension to it. I make that claim because the history he writes illuminates the dynamics and the phenomenon of policymaking that are not temporarily bounded.[15]

Nevertheless, Leffler's efforts to create a usable past, to draw on history to better understand the present and perhaps inform policy, current and future, became more explicit when in *Soul of Mankind* he addressed the questions of why the Cold War ended when it did and not earlier. And that effort became more explicit still after the election of George W. Bush, the attacks of 9/11, the launch of the Global War on Terror, and perhaps most significantly, the formulation of the 2002 national security strategy. As Leffler wrote in the introduction to his recently published collection of essays, *Safeguarding Democratic Capitalism*, he reached the conclusion that, following in the path of Ernest May, "if memory—personal memory and collective memory—shaped policy, historians had an obligation to clarify the past and inform 'memory,' based on their research."[16]

Leffler took that obligation personally. In the course of his ongoing project on George W. Bush's policies, itself a dramatic departure from the norm for historians, he edited books and wrote historical articles on national security, defense spending, grand strategy, the consequences of fear and hubris, and other topics that are unequivocally policy-relevant. He published these articles in such traditional academic outlets such as *Diplomatic History* and *International Affairs*. But he also published them in venues that historians have long considered off-limits or out of reach, like *Foreign Policy* and *Foreign Affairs*. As a consequence, he attracted attention far beyond the academy. For example, for his 2013 article in *Foreign Affairs* he drew on an invited talk he gave at the Aspen Institute, aptly titled the Ernest May Memorial Lecture, which he subsequently presented in Washington to a gathering of the Joint Chiefs of Staff and combatant commanders. What better sign can there be that historians of US foreign policy are coming in out of the cold, and without compromising our methodology, that we can be policy relevant? [17]

There are other signs as well, robust signs. "All over the academy," wrote Stanford University's Priya Satia in a 2018 article for the *Chronicle of Higher Education*, "historians are producing work relevant to policy and easily accessible to policy makers. Many work hard to share their work with the public." The *Washington Post* can serve as an illustration, although it is but one among many. Halfway through Trump's "jarring" first year in office, the *Post* launched the "Made by History" blog edited by historians Brian Rosenwald, Nicole Hemmer, and Kathryn Cramer Brownell. The intention is "to situate the events making headlines in their larger historical context." [18]

Historians of American foreign relations have been prominent contributors to the "Made by History" blog, which covers an impressive range of topics and events. Such other blogs as *War on the Rocks* have concentrated almost exclusively on international relations. Originating as a critical response to the George W. Bush administration's "war of choice" in Iraq, *War on the Rocks* explicitly identifies itself as a "platform for analysis, commentary, debate and multimedia content on foreign policy and national security issues." Predictably in light of its origins, it gives pride of place to a realistic perspective, and consequently many of its contributors come from the field of political science. Historians, however, are well represented. Many of these represent a generation greatly influenced by the scholarship and public persona of Melvyn Leffler—and I must add John Lewis Gaddis. Gaddis has also written a great deal of not just policy-relevant but also "prescriptive history.[19] Several of the most notable historians in this cohort in fact were students of Gaddis, who prior to moving to Yale founded what many at the time considered the oxymoronically named Institute for Contemporary History at Ohio University. And once at Yale, Gaddis teamed up with Paul Kennedy and Charles Hill to teach a year-long grand strategy seminar to which students needed to apply to enroll. That course evolved into the well-endowed Brady-Johnson Program in Grand Strategy. Its aim is "to develop students' capacities not only to analyze the past and present, but to act as responsible, thoughtful leaders and citizens of the future."[20]

Appropriately, in 2015 two of Gaddis's former graduate students, Hal Brands and Jeremi Suri, published a powerful cri de coeur entitled *The Power of the Past*. Building on a foundation laid by May's *Lessons of the Past*, May's and Richard Neustadt's *Thinking in Time*, and Alexander George's less known yet arguably more instructive to historians *Bridging the Gap*, *The Power of the Past* addresses the relationship between history and policy, what the editors call the history–policy nexus for explicitly prescriptive— and presentist—purposes. Historians "as a whole have not done *enough* to cultivate sustained dialogue with the policymaking community," lament coeditors Brands and Suri. While the essays themselves focus on diverse "case studies" that surface themes and questions that are relevant to today's challenges, their introduction surveys the dos and don'ts of applying history to inform policymaking and thereby improve decision-making—and maybe policy itself. With think pieces bookending chapters on Vietnam, the Gulf War, the Balkans, Iraq, and humanitarian intervention, to identify only a few of the cases, the volume is informative and provocative. But perhaps what is most significant about its publication is its broad acceptance by the historical community, and I'll wager its broad adoption in history classes.[21]

Even more noteworthy for the aims of this chapter are the appointments of Brands and Francis J. Gavin to chaired professorships in the newly established Henry Kissinger Center for Global Affairs at Johns Hopkins University's School of Advanced International Studies. For many years May held an appointment at Harvard's John F. Kennedy School of Government. As a historian, however, he was an outlier in a school of public policy. Princeton's Woodrow Wilson School of Public and International Affairs never hired a historian to replace Cyril Black after he retired in 1986.[22] This norm for public policy schools and programs has been slowly worn down over the past years. More than a decade after May's death Harvard's Kennedy School finally did hire a replacement (actually it hired both Frederik Logevall and Odd Arne Westad), and while a minority, historians are now represented on the faculty of most if not yet all schools of public policy and/or international affairs.

But Brands and Gavin, both of whom have been at the forefront of those urging historians more deeply and directly to engage policymakers and have committed much of their scholarly agendas to demonstrating the potential rewards of that engagement, were the Kissinger Center's first two hires.[23] Directed by Gavin and with the subsequent appointment of Mary Sarotte to another chair, for a center for global affairs to revolve around historians to this extent is unprecedented.[24] So is its mission: "to generate and apply rigorous historical thinking to the most vexing global challenges."[25] The Kissinger Center is just getting off the ground. But having already received a rich endowment and recruited a critical mass of accomplished young scholars, its prospects for success are excellent. What is more, while the odds are remote that the Kissinger Center will spark the establishment of similar programs, the likelihood is greater that it will influence the integration of more, and a larger percentage, of historians into existing schools, centers, and programs.

Gavin also chairs the editorial board of the newly established *Texas National Security Review*, of which another historian, William Inboden, is the editor-in-chief. A joint project of *War on the Rocks* and the Texas National Security Network, an initiative of retired admiral and former head of the US Special Operations Command William McRaven when he was chancellor of the University of Texas system, its goal is likewise to bridge "the gap between academia and the world of practice and policy."[26] Ironically, Gavin is less optimistic than I am that historians of foreign relations will embrace, and encourage their students to embrace, what he clearly sees as a personal crusade.[27] Perhaps what explains the differences in our outlooks are our experiences. Gavin has been far more central than I have to the cross-fertilization between historians and policymakers. He far more frequently participates in workshops, research projects, and other scholarly undertakings where historians are underrepresented if represented at all. But less by design than circumstance, I literally found myself at the intersection of the "history-policy nexus." There were costs, but the benefits far outweighed them.

I'll interject for context some personal anecdotes. Before I learned better, I considered the relationship between history and policy, and the relationship between history and the contemporary world, quite natural. As was not unusual for my contemporaries, the Vietnam War was pivotal to my decision to pursue a PhD in the history of foreign policy. My ambition at the time was certainly not directly to influence policy. Still, it was for me a truism that if historians wrote good histories and policymakers read them, the result would increase the likelihood that the world would be a better place. Therefore, while predictably I objected to much of the criticism that suffused the *AHR* review of my CIA and Guatemala book, the reviewer was not altogether wrong. I was in fact guilty of presentist concerns. Moreover, partly because I later coauthored a book on Eisenhower's national security strategy with Robert Bowie, who directed the State Department's Policy Planning Staff for most of John Foster Dulles's tenure at Foggy Bottom and then founded and directed Harvard's Center for International Affairs (now the Weatherhead Center for International Affairs), *Waging Peace* was sufficiently grounded in political science to meet the criteria for prescriptive history.[28]

It took another decade, however, for me to take the plunge openly, and what now seems irrevocably, into the history–policy nexus. Confronted with the challenge of speaking to a diverse audience of historians of American foreign relations, many of whom were experiencing the effects of a large noontime meal, I gave a talk that was intentionally presentist and provocative. The talk surveyed the history of successive modern presidents' use of intelligence to formulate policies and strategies, devoting the final portion to an assessment of the Intelligence Community's contribution to the George W. Bush administration's judgments about Iraq's Weapons of Mass Destruction program and their service as a casus belli. I concluded that Bush and his advisors' use, or abuse, of intelligence was particularly egregious. Nevertheless, in the final analysis it was not inconsistent with that of his predecessors. In each of the post–Second World War administrations, I argued, intelligence was less salient to decisionmaking than the president's preconceptions and predispositions.[29]

Broadcast only on C-Span, delivered at an academic conference, and published in a scholarly journal, I expected the talk to receive the kind of attention beyond colleagues in my field that virtually all of my scholarship had received—little or none. But for two, interrelated reasons, the audience and reception confounded my expectations. The first reason is that because it was so "presentist," the article was picked up in the press, particularly by conservatives and neoconservative pundits in the *Weekly Standard*, the *Wall Street Journal*, and like-minded publications. And not surprisingly, those journalists who picked it up all but ignored my "history" and my evidence and focused only on my critique of the Bush administration. According to their consensus, and to illustrate I'll string together representative quotes, my piece "echo[ed] the liberal academic criticism of the administration" and revealed that I was a "declared partisan in the intelligence wars," a "rabid ideologue," and, most venomous of all, guilty of "Michael Moore-type thinking." The polarized politics about global affairs of that year, which played out so demonstrably in the unscripted release of the National Intelligence Estimate (NIE) on Iran's nuclear program shortly before my article's publication, drew what in my experience was unimaginable notice to it—and to me.[30]

I refer to the attention paid to me personally because there's no question that the article's resonance was due to more than my representation of liberal academics. A second and more powerful explanation for the public interest it received was the position in government I held at the time of my article's publication. Weeks before

I gave the talk, but months after I had drafted its text, I had accepted an offer to serve as assistant deputy director of national intelligence for analytic integrity and standards and analytic ombudsman for the Office of the Director of National Intelligence (ODNI). My critics in the press, their writings make unequivocally evident, had no idea what my mouthful of titles signaled were my responsibilities. Yet manifesting their presentism, they had a field day inflating my contribution to what they judged as a fatally flawed NIE on Iran's nuclear program by mocking the juxtaposition of my name and the word "integrity."[31]

I, along with my colleagues at ODNI, initially found my fifteen minutes of fame amusing. Not only was I identified as integral to an immense conspiracy to undermine the Bush administration's determination to eliminate Iran's nuclear program, but also these journalists, had they done a minimum of homework, would have learned that I and my office were explicitly prohibited from contributing to the production of finished intelligence. Our responsibilities were limited to education and evaluation. But the laughter ended when several of the IC's most senior officials sought to have me fired.

Here's where the story takes an interesting twist that connects it to history's contributions to policy. In line with the premises of Suri, Brands, Gavin, and other advocates of greater intercourse between the historical and policymaking communities, I had been offered this position precisely because my direct boss, Deputy Director of National Intelligence Tom Fingar, appreciated how the skill sets of a historian could benefit the production of intelligence analysis. That was my mission: to improve the quality of the intelligence products that served policymakers, war fighters, and even those local law-enforcement officers entrusted with homeland security. And in this instance, Fingar responded to those seeking to rid the IC of me by schooling them on that skill set by directing them to my scholarship. He underscored in particular the priority I, as a historian, placed on sources and methods. That defense proved successful, that much more so because, it turned out, one of my most severe critics in the IC had apparently read in the press about my article but not the article itself—the kind of serious lapse in tradecraft that I was recruited to eliminate. Conversely, the brouhaha over the article generated a greater readership within the IC, which may well have gained more support for my efforts and that of my office. I was in fact told as much by several National Intelligence officers and analysts in both the CIA and the State Department's Bureau of Intelligence and Research.

That last sentence provides a segue to a final "lesson" of this episode. To reiterate, the deputy director of national intelligence for analysis offered me a senior position with responsibilities for improving the quality of the workforce he supervised because I was a historian. As expected, therefore, the analytic tradecraft standards my office developed (my predecessor, the late Nancy Tucker, was also a historian), which an IC directive required that all analysts adhere to, derived from the historical methods we learn during our first year in graduate school. Chief among them are making transparent the sources on which the analysis is based, assessing the reliability of those sources, distinguishing between evidence, assumptions, and interpretation, and highlighting contingency and change over time.[32] My interactions with elite policymakers are limited. But my experience with the full range of intelligence analysts is extensive. And on that basis I can attest that they uniformly possess a healthy respect for historians; they recognize the value historical methods add to their products; and the improvement in their intelligence products provided policymakers with better information on which to make decisions. There is also a flipside to this relationship. The opportunities presented to me by my time in government enhanced my own scholarship on the history of intelligence, foreign relations, and national security policy. The history–policy nexus is mutually beneficial.

Before I conclude let me highlight another sphere in which historians interact with government officials that is well known among historians of US foreign relations but rarely commented upon in this context. I refer here to the State Department's Historical Office (HO), historians from which are so conspicuous in this volume. The HO is rightly celebrated for its responsibility for producing the *Foreign Relations of the United States* (*FRUS*) series. Yet it does a great deal more for scholars and policymakers, much of which is underappreciated.

For historians of US foreign relations, the HO's value is inestimable. We have long recognized *FRUS* as an inimitable source. But perhaps because we have become so accustomed to filing our own Freedom of Information and Mandatory Declassification Review requests, we sometimes forget, or take for granted, how vital a role the HO is in the declassification process. And, as attested to the recent publication of the retrospective volume on Iran 1953, how dogged and relentless.[33] The *FRUS* volumes are never perfect. The number of documents that can be sensibly included in any single volume is limited, and the HO's requests for declassification are denied just like the rest of ours' are. But because the HO has means that none of the rest of us do, and because its historians are so determined, their successes facilitate subsequent successes by individual researchers. Following the footnotes in *FRUS* is a methodological best practice.

The HO contributes to the history–policy nexus through multiple other avenues as well. One, inseparable from its publication of *FRUS*, is its digitization of the volumes, including the backlog that ultimately will extend back to the first one in 1861. The digitized volumes, of course, greatly facilitate research. But because they are fully searchable and allow for easy cross-referencing, they in addition reveal the competing demands on policymakers, how the interconnectiveness of multiple actors and issues forces the policymaker to make tradeoffs. Such insights can lead to better histories. And these histories will not only better inform the public's understanding of policy, but also appeal to policymakers by generating more empathy for and sensitivity to their dilemmas.

The historians in the HO provide a more direct service to policymakers through their briefings and position papers. In 2016 it prepared essential briefings to the Barack Obama administration and then to Donald Trump's during the transition. More regularly, it writes briefings and papers for diplomats and State Department offices, for congressional committees, and for other government officials who can profit from learning about the antecedents to and context of contemporary issues. The topics range from previous negotiations to achieve peace, trade, and arms agreements to development and reorganization efforts. The HO also provides critical documentation for adjudicating matters of international law and promoting human rights. For example, the HO played an important role in the recent success of the presidential project to document human rights abuses during Argentina's "dirty war" between 1975 and 1984.[34] The HO historians, in short, make available to policymakers a usable past.

We conventionally think of appointments to the Policy Planning Staff, the National Security Council, the Office of the Secretary of Defense, the staff of a Senate or House Committee, or a similar position in a department, the White House, or Congress as the only ways to effect policy. My argument is that those who work in the State Department HO—reviewers, compilers, editors, division chiefs, whatever—also contribute valuably. And although perhaps not as directly, so do almost all federal historians. But even those of us far removed from government can influence policy through our teaching and our scholarship. But to do so we must reject the false dichotomy between historicism and presentism and recognize that to historicize the present is not to compromise the integrity of our craft. Likewise, we must assume greater risks in selecting our subjects and strive to be more rigorous and aggressive in collecting evidence to support our arguments. To plagiarize from *FRUS*'s guiding statute, our histories must be "thorough, accurate, and reliable."[35]

Never have the hurdles to achieving that goal been greater. We live in an era when too often secrecy trumps transparency, when policymaking is as opaque as it is convoluted, and when the continual growth of the national security state coupled with the proliferation of electronic records makes both record keeping and declassification more difficult and more byzantine. Historians are uniquely equipped to take on this challenge, and for reasons of self-interest and the public interest we must. No matter how great the challenges, the rewards are greater. And the international environment in which we live leaves us no choice. When we read in newspapers about the US national security advisor applying the "Libyan model" to North Korea or the president of the European Union assessing the US withdrawal from the Joint Comprehensive Plan of Action regarding Iran's nuclear program as a grave threat to the Atlantic Alliance, can we dare question that policy relevance is anathema to good history?[36]

Notes

1 Robert Freeman Smith, "Review of Richard H. Immerman, *The CIA in Guatemala: The Foreign Policy of Intervention* (Austin: University of Texas Press, 1982)," *American Historical Review* 88, 3 (1983): 781–2.

2 Jill Lepore, "Tea and Sympathy: Who Owns the American Revolution?," *The New Yorker*, May 3, 2010, https://www.newyorker.com/magazine/2010/05/03/tea-and-sympathy-2.

3 Charles Maier, "Marking Time: The Historiography of International Relations," in *The Past Before Us: Contemporary Historical Writing in the United States*, ed. Michael Kamen (Ithaca, NY: Cornell University Press, 1980), 355–87. See also *Explaining the History of US Foreign Relations*, 3rd ed., ed. Frank Costigliola and Michael J. Hogan (New York: Cambridge University Press, 2016). The first edition, published in 1991, included essays published in the *Journal of American History* 77, 1 roundtable in 1990 largely in response to Maier's critique. Also included in the initial volume were some of the essays, also responding to Maier, published as a 1990 symposium in *Diplomatic History* 14, 4.

4 Jack S. Levy, "Too Important to Leave to the Other: History and Political Science in the Study of International Relations," *International Security* 22, 1 (1997): 22–33.

5 Andrew J. Rotter and Frank Costigliola, "Walter LaFeber: Scholar, Teacher, Intellectual," *Diplomatic History* 28, 5(2004): 625–35.

6 Beginning during the Vietnam War era with his publication of *American Power and the New Mandarins* (New York: Random House, 1969) and extending through the Trump era with *Who Rules the World* (New York: Metropolitan Books, 2016), Noam Chomsky has published virtually a book a year, almost certainly establishing himself in the mind of the public as the leading critic of US foreign policy.

7 For example see *Understanding the U.S. Wars in Iraq and Afghanistan*, ed. Beth Bailey and Richard H. Immerman (New York: New York University Press, 2015).

8 Ernest R. May, *"Lessons" of the Past: The Use and Misuse of History in American Foreign Policy* (New York: Oxford University Press, 1973). See also Richard Neustadt and Ernest R. May, *Thinking in Time: The Uses of History for Decision Makers* (New York: Free Press, 1986); Yuen Khong, *Analogies at War: Korea, Munich, Dien Bien Phu, and the Vietnam Decisions of 1965* (Princeton, NJ: Princeton University Press, 1992); and Margaret McMillan, *Dangerous Games: The Uses and Abuses of History* (New York: Modern Library, 2009).

9 Mark Atwood Lawrence, "The Lessons of History? Debating the Vietnam and Iraq Wars," NOT EVEN PAST [blog], January 20, 2014, https://notevenpast.org/the-lessons-of-history-debating-the-vietnam-and-iraq-wars/. Exceptions include Jeffrey Record and W. Andrew Terrill, *Iraq and Vietnam: Differences, Similarities, and Insights* (Carlisle, PA: U.S. Army War College Strategic Studies Institute, 2004); and Robert K, Brigham, *Iraq, Vietnam, and the Limits of American Power* (New York: Public Affairs, 2008).

10 John Dower, "Lessons from Japan about War's Aftermath," *New York Times*, October 27, 2002; Ken Gewertz, "Looking at Germany, Japan, Iraq: A Tale of Three Occupations, *The Harvard Gazette,* March 8, 2004, https://news.harvard.edu/gazette/story/2004/03/harvard-gazette-looking-at-germany-japan-iraq-a-tale-of-three-occupations/.

11 Gregory A. Daddis, "Thoughts on General McMaster and on Withdrawing from Afghanistan and Vietnam," *FP*, August 18, 2017, http://foreignpolicy.com/2017/08/18/thoughts-on-general-mcmaster-and-on-withdrawing-from-afghanistan-and-vietnam/.

12 Ashley Feinberg, "Kushner on the Middle East: 'What Do We Offer on the Middle East That's Unique? I Don't Know,'" *Wired*, August 1, 2017, https://www.wired.com/story/jared-kushner-middle-east/.

13 James Grossman, "Historians: 'Defending History' is Complicated in the US," *CNN Opinion*, August 19, 2017, https://www.cnn.com/2017/08/19/opinions/historians-confederate-statues-opinion-roundup/index.html; Patrick Radden Keefe, "McMaster and Commander: Can a National-Security Advisor Retain his Integrity if the President has None," *The New Yorker*, April 30, 2018, https://www.newyorker.com/magazine/2018/04/30/mcmaster-and-commander; Peter Baker, "Fiery National Security Adviser For a Powder-Keg Presidency," *New York Times*, April 9, 2018. McMaster published his dissertation as *Dereliction of Duty: Johnson, McNamara, the Joint Chiefs of Staff, and the Lies that Led to Vietnam* (New York: Harper, 1997).

14 Sarah Poulis, "Trump Told the French President That the Resolute Desk Was from 1814. Try Again," *Washington Post*, April 26, 2018, https://www.washingtonpost.com/news/reliable-source/wp/2018/04/26/trump-told-the-french-president-that-the-resolute-desk-was-from-1814-try-again/?utm_term=.117222e15353&wpisrc=nl_source&wpmm=1.

15 Melvyn P. Leffler, *A Preponderance of Power: National Security, The Truman Administration, and the Cold War* (Stanford, CA: Stanford University Press, 1992). Attesting that his concerns extended beyond the academy, as a Council on Foreign Relations fellow during the last year of Jimmy Carter's presidency, he worked on arms control and contingency planning in the Office of the Secretary of Defense.

16 Melvyn P. Leffler, *For the Soul of Mankind: The United States, the Soviet Union, and the Cold War* (New York: Hill & Wang, 2007); Leffler, *Safeguarding Democratic Capitalism: US Foreign Policy and National Security, 1920–2015* (Princeton, NJ: Princeton University Press, 2017), 23.

17 Melvyn Leffler, "9/11 and American Foreign Policy," *Diplomatic History*, 29, 3 (2005): 395–413; Leffler, "9/11 and the Past and Future of American Foreign Relations, *International Affairs* 79, 5 (2003): 1045–63; Leffler, "Is Bush a Radical?" *Foreign Policy* 144 (September/October, 2004): 22–30; Leffler, "Defense on a Diet: How Budget Crises Have Improved U.S. Strategy," *Foreign Affairs* 92, 6 (2013): 65–76.

18 Priya Satia. "The Whitesplaining of History is Over," *The Chronicle of Education*, March 28, 2018, https://www.chronicle.com/article/The-Whitesplaining-of-History/242952; "The *Washington Post* launches 'Made by History,'" *Washington Post*, June 26, 2017, https://www.washingtonpost.com/pr/wp/2017/06/26/the-washington-post-launches-made-by-history/?utm_term=.cd4914e5e3bc; Brian Rosenwald and Nicole Hemmer, "Welcome to Made by History," *Washington Post*, June 26, 2017, https://www.washingtonpost.com/news/made-by-history/wp/2017/06/26/welcome-to-made-by-history/?utm_term=.86e41284696b.

19 Probably still most notable is John Lewis Gaddis, *Strategies of Containment: A Critical Appraisal of Postwar American National Security* (New York: Oxford University Press, 1982). But other examples include *The Long Peace: Inquiries into the History of the Cold War* (New York: Oxford University Press, 1987); *Surprise, Security, and the American Experience* (Cambridge, MA: Harvard University Press, 2004); and immediately following the publication of George W. Bush's National Security Strategy in 2002, "A Grand Strategy of Transformation," *Foreign Policy* 133 (November–December): 50–57.

20 War on the Rocks website (About), https://warontherocks.com/about/; Yale University Brady-Johnson Program in Grand Strategy website, https://grandstrategy.yale.edu/. See also John Lewis Gaddis, *On Grand Strategy* (New York: Penguin, 2018).

21 *The Power of the Past: History and Statecraft* , ed. Hal Brands and Jeremi Suri (Washington, DC: Brookings, 2015). Th e quotes can be found on p. 4. While the coeditors include the previously cited May, *Lessons of History* and Neustadt and May *Thinking in Time* in an endnote that includes about two-dozen sources, revealingly they do not cite Alexander George , *Bridging the Gap: Theory and Practice in Foreign Policy* (Washington, DC : US Institute of Peace , 1992), notwithstanding its relevance for historians. Brands and Suri, *The Power of the Past* , 21–22n6.

22 The Woodrow Wilson School did conduct an unsuccessful search for a senior joint appointment with the History Department.

23 In addition to coediting *The Power of the Past*, Brands's scholarship that historicizes presentist concerns includes *What Good Is Grand Strategy? Power and Purpose in American Statecraft from Harry S. Truman to George W. Bush* (Ithaca, NY: Cornell University Press, 2014); *Making the Unipolar Moment: U.S. Foreign Policy and the Rise of the Post-Cold War Order* (Ithaca, NY: Cornell University Press, 2016); and *American Grand Strategy in the Age of Trump* (Washington, DC: Brookings, 2018).

Francis J. Gavin has been an even more explicit and aggressive advocate of applying historical knowledge and methodology to the benefit of policymaking. While his best known work is *Nuclear Statecraft: History and Strategy in America's Atomic Age* (Ithaca, NY: Cornell University Press, 2012), representative of his writings are "History and Policy," *International Journal* 63, 1 (2007/8): 162–77; With James B. Steinberg, "Mind the Gap: Why Scholars and Policymakers Ignore Each Other, and What Should Be Done about It," *Carnegie Report* 6, 4 (2012), http://teaching-national-security-law.insct.org/wp-content/uploads/2012/07/Carnegie-Corporation-of-New-York%C2%A0Mind-the-Gap.pdf; "Policy and the Public Minded Professor," *The Journal of Strategic Studies* 40, 1–2 (2017): 269–74; "Thinking Historically: A Guide for Strategy and Statecraft," *War on the Rocks*, November 17, 2017, https://warontherocks.com/2016/11/thinking-historically-a-guide-for-strategy-and-statecraft/.

24 In 1992 I founded along with my colleagues in Temple University's History Department the Center for the Study of Force and Diplomacy (CENFAD). It is much less policy-oriented, however. Although founded some two decades after CENFAD and with a writ much broader than the Kissinger Center, under the guidance of its director, the historian Jeffrey A. Engel, Southern Methodist University's Center for Presidential History is perhaps more comparable.

25 Francis J. Gavin, Welcome Letter to the Henry A. Kissinger Center for Global Affairs, https://kissinger.sais-jhu.edu/letter.html.

26 Texas National History Review website, https://tnsr.org/.

27 Francis J. Gavin, "The Last Word: Goodbye to All That," *Passport* 49, 1 (2018): 77–8. See also Gavin's more recent broadside, co-authored with Brands, "The Historical Profession is Committing Slow-Motion Suicide," *War on the Rocks*, December 10, 2018, https://warontherocks.com/2018/12/the-historical-profession-is-committing-slow-motion-suicide/.

28 Robert R. Bowie and Richard H. Immerman, *Waging Peace: How Eisenhower Shaped an Enduring National Security Strategy* (New York: Oxford University Press, 1998).

29 The talk was later published. Richard H. Immerman, "Intelligence and Strategy: Historicizing Psychology, Politics, and Policy," *Diplomatic History* 32, 1 (2008): 1–23.

30 Bill Gertz, "Inside the Ring," *Washington Times*, March 14, 2009; Gabriel Schoenfeld, "The Real Bush Intelligence Failure," *Wall Street Journal*, April 1, 2008; Schoenfeld, "If Michael Moore Had a Security Clearance: How Did the Rabid Ideologue Richard Immerman Get Put in Charge of the 'Standards and Integrity of the Intelligence Community,'" *Weekly Standard*, March 3, 2008. The press uniformly used what Schoenfeld in his Michael Moore op-ed labeled the "bizarre National Intelligence Estimate (NIE) on Iran."

31 Enacted on December 17, 2008, Public Law 108–458, The Intelligence Reform and Terrorism Prevention Act (IRTPA), specifies my responsibilities in sections 1019 and 1020. Section 1019, subsection (b), paragraph (A) reads, "may be responsible for general oversight and management of analysis and production, but may not be directly responsible for, or involved in, the specific production of any finished intelligence product." Public Law 108–458, S.2845, 108th Congress, Intelligence Reform and Terrorism Reform Act, December 17, 2004, https://www.gpo.gov/fdsys/pkg/PLAW-108publ458/pdf/PLAW-108publ458.pdf.

32 Intelligence Community Directive (ICD 203), "Analytic Standards," January 2, 2015, https://www.dni.gov/files/documents/ICD/ICD%20203%20Analytic%20Standards.pdf; ICD 206, "Sourcing Requirements for Disseminated Analytic Products," https://

www.dni.gov/files/documents/ICD/ICD%20206.pdf. These current ICDs are revisions of the original ones approved on June 21 and October 17, 2007, respectively.

33 *Foreign Relations of the United States, 1952–1954, Iran, 1951–1953*, ed. James C. Hook and Adam Howard (Washington, DC: Government Printing Office, 2017), https://history.state.gov/historicaldocuments/frus1951-54Iran. More than twenty-five years passed since the publication of the flawed original *FRUS* volume on Iran, 1952–4, which precipitated this retrospective one. *Foreign Relations of the United States, 1952–1954*, X: *Iran, 1951–1954*, ed. Carl N. Raether and Charles S. Sampson (Washington, DC: Government Printing Office, 1989).

34 Richard H. Immerman et al., "Report of the Advisory Committee on Historical Diplomatic Documentation to the Department of State," January 1–December 31, 2016, *Passport* 48, 2 (2017): 61–2.

35 "The Foreign Relations Authorization Act Fiscal Years, Fiscal Years 1992 and 1993," October 28, 1991 (Public Law 102–138 [105 Stat. 647, codified in relevant part at 22 U.S.C. § 4351 *et seq.*]), https://www.gpo.gov/fdsys/pkg/STATUTE-105/pdf/STATUTE-105-Pg647.pdf. See also William B. McAllister, Joshua Botts, Peter Cozzens, and Aaron W. Marrs, *Toward "Thorough, Accurate, and Reliable": A History of the Foreign Relations of the United States Series* (Washington, DC: US Department of State Office of the Historian, 2015).

36 Megan Specia and David E. Sanger, "For U.S., Libya Is a Model. For Kim, It's a Bad Omen, *New York Times*, May 17, 2018; David M. Herszenhorn and Maïa de La Baume, "EU's Tusk slams 'capricious' Trump," *Politico*, May 16, 2018, https://www.politico.eu/article/eu-summit-bulgaria-sofia-donald-tusk-slams-capricious-donald-trump-iran-deal-rebuke/.

Index